DISTURBANCE

Philippe Lançon

DISTURBANCE

*Translated from the French
by Steven Rendall*

Europa
editions

Europa Editions
214 West 29th Street
New York, N.Y. 10001
www.europaeditions.com
info@europaeditions.com

Translation by Steven Rendall
Original title: *Le Lambeau*
Translation copyright © 2019 by Europa Editions

Library of Congress Cataloging in Publication Data is available
ISBN 978-1-60945-556-9

Lançon, Philippe
Disturbance

Book design by Emanuele Ragnisco
www.mekkanografici.com

Prepress by Grafica Punto Print – Rome

Printed in the USA

CONTENTS

Some given names have been changed, as few as possible.

DISTURBANCE

Chapter 1
Twelfth Night

The evening before the attack, I went to the theater with Nina. We were going to the Quartiers d'Ivry theater on the outskirts of Paris to see *Twelfth Night*, a play by Shakespeare I hadn't seen or couldn't remember. The director was a friend of Nina's. I didn't know him and was completely unfamiliar with his work. Nina had insisted that I accompany her. She was happy to bring together two people she liked, a director and a journalist. I went along, relaxed and carefree. No article was foreseen—which is always the best way to end up writing one, out of enthusiasm and, in a way, by surprise. In such cases, the young man who used to go to the theater meets the journalist he has become. After a moment, more or less prolonged, of hesitation, timidity, and feeling each other out, the young man communicates to the journalist his spontaneity, uncertainty, and virginity, then leaves the room so that the other, pen in hand, can go back to doing his job and, unfortunately, to being serious.

I don't specialize in theater, though I've always liked it. I haven't ever spent five or six evenings a week going to plays, and I don't think I'm a genuine critic. I started out as a reporter. I became a critic by accident; I remained one by habit and perhaps by carelessness. Criticism has allowed me to comprehend—or try to comprehend—what I saw and to give it an ephemeral form by writing about it. It's the result of an experience that is at once superficial (I don't have the credentials necessary to arrive at a sound judgment of the works concerned) and internal (I can't read or see anything without filtering it through a set of images and associations of ideas that nothing outside me justifies). The day I understood that, I think I felt freer.

Does criticism allow me to combat forgetting? Of course not. I've seen many plays and read many books that I don't remember, even after writing an article about them, probably because they didn't elicit any image, any genuine emotion. Worse yet: I often forget what I wrote about them. When one of these spectral articles happens to resurface, I'm always a bit scared, as if it had been written by another person who bears my name, a usurper. Then I wonder whether I didn't write it to forget, as soon as possible, what I had seen or read, like people who keep a diary to empty their memory daily of what they have experienced. At least I did until January 7, 2015.

During the performance, I took out my notebook. The last words I scrawled that evening, in the dark, were by Shakespeare: "Nothing that is so, is so." The following words are in Spanish, scribbled in much larger letters but just as badly. They were written three days later, in a different kind of obscurity, at the hospital. They are addressed to Gabriela, my Chilean friend, the woman I was in love with: "Hablé con el médico. Un año para recuperar. ¡Paciencia!" *A year to recuperate?* Nothing you are told is so when you enter the world where what is so can no longer be truly expressed.

I had known Nina for a little less than two years. We'd met at a party, during the summer, in the garden of a château in the Lubéron. It took me some time to understand the source of the affinity that she immediately inspired in me. She was a born go-between, sensitive and unaffected. She had the simplicity, the tenderness, the warmth that lead us to mix our friends, as if their qualities, by rubbing against one another, might grow greater. She took pleasure in the sparks, but was too modest to boast about them. She was almost self-effacing, like a discreet, sarcastic, and benevolent mother. When I saw her, I always felt like a fledgling she had hatched who was returning to the nest from which, by imprudence or carelessness, I had fallen. The sadness or concern that floated in her dark, lively eyes disappeared as soon as one began to talk with her. I had not always behaved well toward her. She had resented it, then ceased to resent it. She had less rancor than generosity.

She and I spent an evening together from time to time, including this one. As she is the last person with whom I shared a moment of pleasure and insouciance, she has become as precious to me as if I had spent a whole life with her—an uninterrupted life, henceforth almost fantasized, and that stopped on that evening, in a theater, with old Shakespeare. Since then, I haven't seen Nina often, but I don't need to see her to know what she reminds me of or to feel that she is continuing to protect me. She has the strange privilege of being both a friend and a memory—a distant friend, a living recollection. There is no chance that I will forget her, but although she will not be very present in the rest of this book, that is because I find it hard to bring her to life outside that evening and everything it reminds me of. I think about her, everything springs back to life and dies away, sometimes successively, sometimes in parallel. Everything is a dream and a passage, perhaps an illusion, as in *Twelfth Night*. Nina remains the last point on the opposite bank, at the entrance to the bridge that the attacks blew up. Sketching her portrait allows me to remain there a little while longer, balanced on the ruins of the bridge.

Nina is a small, plump, auburn-haired woman with soft skin, an aquiline nose, and dark, bright, amused eyes, who softens with humor emotions that are always strong and that her kindness seems to surrender to the whims of others. She's a lawyer. She's a good cook. She forgets nothing. She's a socialist, but of the left—there still are some of those. She looks like a blackbird, tenderhearted, severe, and well-fed. She lives

alone with her daughter, Marianne, to whom I gave my trans-
verse flute, an instrument I no longer played and will probably
never be able to play again. Her experience with men has disappointed her, I believe, without making her bitter. Maybe she
thinks she doesn't deserve more pleasure and love than she has
received from them; but she gives so much in friendship, and
to her daughter, that the state of love, the fiction people try to
write by means of the body, is no longer an absolute necessity.
And maybe also because, as in politics, she always senses a
looming disappointment that her good nature is preparing to
overcome. She does not give up her feelings any more than she
gives up her convictions. The fact that the left constantly
betrays the people does not mean that Nina, like so many others, will end up on the right. The fact that so many men are
selfish, vain nullities does not mean that Nina will stop loving.
Tenderness resists principles. One detail that makes me admire
her is that she never comes empty-handed, and what she brings
with her always corresponds to the expectations or needs of
those whom she is going to see. In short, she pays attention to
others as they are, and where they are. That's not so common.

I add that she's Jewish, don't forget that, and that being
Jewish subtly, discreetly, reminds her that no one is ever sure
to escape disaster. I sense this in her smile, in her eyes, when I
see her, when we talk; it's something that simplifies life and
exists so naturally only in a very small number of persons, and
I'm grateful to her for it. A Jewish joke is always floating in the
air, between the wine and the pasta, like a fragrance that there
is no need to mention. I don't think I could have finished my
earlier life with anyone better adapted to the situation.

Her father, a professor of American literature, had been
an excellent translator of Philip Roth, a writer I liked, though
I had never been able to finish any of his books—with the
exception of *Patrimony*, in which he recounted the illness
and death of his father, and the ones I'd been asked to review,

a task I never managed to do very well, probably because I wasn't really sure what to think about them. I couldn't see Nina without imagining this father, whom I did not know, translating this or that book of Roth's over there, in the United States, in the snow of winter or under a warm summer sun, in front of a coffee pot and a full ashtray. This image, undoubtedly false, reassured me. It superimposed itself on that of Nina, and I always tried to imagine the resemblances between father and daughter. Later on, she showed me a photo of him, in the late 1970s, I think. He had a big black beard, long hair, and glasses with tinted lenses. He exuded the militant energy and libertarian ease of those years. I was a child then, and this world that still seemed to promise something different, another life, disappeared so quickly that I didn't have time to experience it or even to give it up. It was a period that I neither lived nor forgot.

The evening that we went to the theater, Nina was no longer alone. For some time she'd had a new companion, a farmer who lived in the Ardennes. I 'd never seen him. I no longer know whether she talked to me about him that evening. She was meeting him that weekend. She talked to me about harvests, about picking strawberries. I called him "the wild boar." I asked Nina: "How's the wild boar doing?" She replied with a small, mute, embarrassed smile; she was too sensitive to tell me that, nonetheless, she was hurt. "A wild boar is clumsy and crude. He's not like that." "Hey," I said to her once, "it's just a manner of speaking, because of the Ardennes. I could just as well have called him Verlaine or Rimbaud." "But you didn't." No, I hadn't.

It was cold and a bit damp on the evening of January 6, 2015. I left my bike at the Jussieu station and took Metro line 7 as far as the Mairie-d'Ivry station. Nina sent me a text message at 8:53 P.M. to tell me that she was waiting for me in a bistro near the Metro exit. She has kept the text messages, that's why the time is so precise; mine disappeared along with my phone. Since I was late, she'd gone to the theater, and I found her there with a friend, in the bar, where they were drinking a glass of red wine and eating cold cuts and cheese, seated at a little round table. I ordered a glass of white wine and ate some cold cuts with them. "You were ecstatic," she wrote me months later, "you'd just learned that you were going to teach literature at Princeton for a semester. All that remained was to work out the details." I don't recall that joy, or even that I talked to them about it.

However, e-mails from those days confirm that I had just learned that in a few days I would be in Princeton and that my life was going to change, at least for a time. Nina's father had taught, I wrongly thought, at Princeton. The university is one hour away from New York, where Gabriela lived; over there, she was struggling with endless problems: family, paperwork, her job. Thus I could go back to her, and life, through action guided by a project, would begin to find a new unity. Did I want the history that the attack had destroyed? Or did I dream it until it woke me up? I really don't know.

For me, Princeton was the university of Einstein and Oppenheimer—and also of Faulkner's great first translator, Maurice-Edgar Coindreau. I was going there almost by chance, with a feeling of complete illegitimacy, to teach a few novels about Latin-American dictators. The relation between literature and violence is a mystery that Latin American soil had made particularly fertile and that had flourished over there, both in History and on the page, and that had fascinated me like a child. Studying it was the only way to see whether I could think about it as an adult. Even if an adult's ideas rarely rise to the level of a child's visions—or of his fear.

Before I got to the theater, the director had answered questions raised by a class of middle-school students about the play by Shakespeare that the troupe was to perform, and about his work. He had told them that he had become a director even though he had no particular aptitude for it.

Nina remembers my arrival: "You were warmly dressed, with a hat, a sweater, and a warm jacket." It was the first time I had ever left my bike at the Jussieu metro station. She reminded me of my childhood, of the time when my mother was teaching biochemistry at the Jussieu campus —the time of the photo of Nina's father. Along Rue Cuvier, there were sometimes pungent odors. In my mother's laboratory there were chemical odors. I liked them all. I liked the smells of my childhood, even and especially the strongest ones, because they were the most intense, and often the only, traces of that bygone time.

A year later, in the winter of 2016, every Friday morning I passed in front of the yellowish building on Rue Cuvier and smelled once again the bad odors as I walked along the walls of the Jardin des Plantes and the quays on my way to the Pitié-Salpêtrière hospital. The slow process of mending was like that of childhood without ever merging with it. Sometimes I was going to see one of my surgeons, sometimes to see my psychologist, and sometimes one of them after the other, in accord with one of those hospital rituals that henceforth punctuated my life. They had become my unknown friends. The psychologist had a brisk walk, an upright carriage, and an elegant, austere charm that reminded me of my mother at her age, when she was working in her laboratory. When she appeared, for a few seconds I no longer knew what time I was living in or what my age was. Perhaps psychologists who know how to listen to us inhabit an ideal time, because they make us return to the age when we were heroes surrounded by heroes, and because by helping us see that age again and understand it, they help us leave it behind.

To reach her office in the oral medicine department I walked through pale underground corridors where I regularly got lost among busts and photographs of dead surgeons, imagining that behind every door there was a laboratory in which I would find my mother and her friends preparing a magic formula that would restore peace or afford oblivion. I always got there ten minutes early, knowing that I would need the extra time to find my way through this labyrinth. I finally came upon the waiting room, where I sat alone next to a couple of weary green plants. From time to time, an African cleaning woman passed through the room, from which I could see the slightly inclined pine tree that for months had occupied my field of vision from the second floor of the hospital. I took a book out of my old black knapsack stained with blood, but hardly had the time to read three lines before my psychologist arrived. She was never late, and neither was I. It was the sound of her steps that first awakened the memory of my mother. My psychologist was vintage, in short, and that was about all it took to obtain a slight relaxation of the jaw, an incipient confession, and a vague feeling of eternity.

The bicycle that I had attached to a railing at the Jussieu metro station had initially belonged to my mother: it was a sea-green Luis Ocaña from the late 1970s, bought when this Spanish champion, then at his peak, had just won the Tour de France. She had never used it much, she hated sports, and gave it to me when I decided to pedal around Paris the way I had become accustomed to do since spending a little time in Havana and various Asian countries to which my work as a reporter had taken me. That was twenty years earlier.

I'd begun to use this bicycle a little more at the point when Luis Ocaña, retired among his vineyards in the south of France, shot himself in the head. He had supported the National Front, but that was not, so far as I know, why he committed suicide, even if supporting that party could already be seen as the sign of a stupid form of despair. I will never forget the date of his death: it was the day I went to meet, in Madrid, the woman who was coming from Cuba and whom I was soon to marry: Marilyn. When the attack took place, we had been divorced for almost eight years. She was living in eastern France, in a village near Vesoul, with her new husband and their son. She did not know Nina, but they were alike in many ways, physically, morally, and, as subsequent events showed, they were soon to become friends, in part as a result of the attack. The first time she stayed at Nina's place, Marilyn had the feeling that she was at home, with the same kinds of clothes, the same décor, and the same atmosphere revealing the same habits. The extent to which they were twin-like dawned on me the day when I saw them, at my apartment, one alongside the other. Then I understood why Nina had imme- diately attracted me during the late-night party at the château in the Lubéron. She was the reassuring, comfortable echo of a past life. I believed that after a divorce and a bout of depres- sion, phenomena that have become almost ordinary in Western life, I would never feel comfortable again. I was wrong.

Although I've forgotten almost everything about the per- formance we saw that night, apart from a few details that are not without importance, I have continued to read and reread *Twelfth Night*. No doubt I have read it in the worst possible way, as a puzzle, seeking in it signs or explanations of what was going to happen. I knew that this was stupid, or at least rather pointless, but that never prevented me from doing it, or from thinking, or rather feeling, despite everything, that a greater truth was to be found in this combination of circumstances than in the observation that they were unconnected. Shakespeare is always an excellent guide when one has to move forward in an ambiguous, bloody fog. It gives shape to what has no meaning and in so doing gives meaning to what has been undergone, experienced.

A boat carrying twins, Viola and Sebastian, sinks, and they wash up separately on an unfamiliar shore. Each believes the other dead. They are solitary orphans, survivors. Viola disguises herself as a man named Cesario. She becomes a page and a go-between for the love affairs of the local duke, Orsino, with whom she quickly becomes infatuated. However, she has to plead Orsino's case with Olivia, who takes her to be a man and falls in love with her. Meanwhile, Sebastian arrives at the court after various adventures. Olivia confuses him with his sister Viola, and falls in love with him as well. Love is the toy of appearances and genders, as we now say, seen against a Machiavellian and Puritanical background embodied by Olivia's steward, Malvolio. Machiavellianism and Puritanism go hand in hand: anyone who wants to punish people for their pleasures and feelings in the name of a good of which he believes himself the representative, believes that he has the right to do anything, no matter how evil, to achieve his ends. Malvolio wants everything, takes everything, and in the end is duped by everything. The happy ending Shakespeare offers us is only a dream; all that precedes it testifies to that. It's all magic, absurdity, feelings and surprising reversals. At the end, the moral of the tale is sung by a clown.

I would never have given this rough summary of the play in an article, for fear of losing my readers along the way. Besides, what article would I have written? What would I have emphasized? I might have explained that, like Olivia, during the play I confused Viola with Sebastian, no longer knowing who was who, and consequently what I was witnessing. Was that due to the direction? To the text? To its translation? To myself? To the wine, the cold cuts, the winter weather? As often happened, I didn't know, and I wrote in part to find out. Circumstances prevented me from carrying out this ordinary operation, and as frivolous as it may seem in comparison with what was to follow, I still regret not having had time to try to understand *Twelfth Night*. Understanding it now seems out of the question. The characters and situations have returned to a magical world that events have made too vague for me to be able to clarify.

If I remember correctly, at certain times the little stage in Ivry represented an old-fashioned hospital: the white beds were separated by light-colored curtains. Nina was sitting between her friend and me. Here, my memory is playing an initial trick on me. Above, I wrote that I had taken out my notebook during the play, as if I'd been gripped by it and was gradually becoming aware that I was going to write an article. In the retrospective e-mail Nina sent me, she rectifies:

> You immediately took out your four-colored ballpoint and your notebook.

The journalist was there from the outset, along with the carefree friend.

Next, Nina describes the set: there really were white hospital beds; then she lists the actors, including, she says, a young woman who caught my eye and whom I do not remember. She adds:

> You liked the play, I think, and you said there would be room in the newspaper to publish a review of it. I was delighted for Clément and his troupe. I was also pleased to have been able to serve as an intermediary. I told myself that Clément would finally have an article about his play, the preceding one having received few reviews. After the play, we went to have a drink. You in fact bought us a glass of wine, perhaps to celebrate your departure for Princeton. You must also have eaten something. Clément stopped by to see us, and some of the actors did, too. Clément told you that the translation was his, that is, it was by Jude Lucas, his official pseudonym. Moreover, when he got home that evening he sent it to you. You asked him to remind you

who spoke a certain line in the play. He went to check, the line had been uttered by Orsino, you wrote it down in your notebook. You talked with Clément about the play and in particular about the confusion of genders. We went home by metro with Loïc, Clément, and some of the actors, including the one who played Malvolio. We took line no. 7 and you got off at Jussieu to pick up your bike.

What was the line spoken by Orsino that had struck me? My notebook had disappeared. It was in my backpack at the time of the attack, however, and it followed me to the hospital; during my first days there I'd used it to communicate, since I couldn't talk.

A year and a half later, I e-mailed the director to ask if he remembered it. This is his reply:

Dear Philippe,

I recall our discussion very well and the fact that you wanted to check one of Orsino's lines. I remember my difficulty, because despite the fact that I had translated and rehearsed the play, and seen it many times, I couldn't locate the line in question, and that's why I had to go check the text. Unfortunately, I don't remember the line. I know that I was a little surprised. I think I can identify the scene. I can offer a hypothesis.

Approche, mon garçon, si tu aimes un jour,
Dans les affres de l'amour souviens-toi de moi.
Car tous les amoureux sont tels que tu me vois,
Indécis et capricieux en toutes choses
Excepté dans la constante contemplation
De l'être aimé.

[Come hither, boy: if ever thou shalt love,
In the sweet pangs of it remember me;
For such as I am all true lovers are,
Unstaid and skittish in all motions else,
Save in the constant image of the creature
That is beloved.]

Or, more likely:

Cette fois encore, Césario,
Rends-toi auprès de ma cruelle souveraine
Dis-lui que mon amour, plus noble que le monde,
Ne s'intéresse pas à ses terrains fangeux
Et parcelles que la fortune lui a légués.
Dis que je n'en fais pas plus cas que du hasard.
Et que c'est bien la miraculeuse beauté
Dont nature l'a ornée qui attire mon âme.

[Once more, Cesario,
Get thee to yond same sovereign cruelty:
Tell her, my love, more noble than the world,
Prizes not quantity of dirty lands;
The parts that fortune hath bestow'd upon her,
Tell her, I hold as giddily as fortune;
But 'tis that miracle and queen of gems
That nature pranks her in attracts my soul.]

Of course, I will make the complete text of our translation available to you if you would find that helpful.

None of the passages he sent me corresponded to the one I was thinking of. Organizing my belongings not long afterward, I came across the notebook that I had that day, and whose existence I mentioned above. It didn't take long to find the page where the lines from Shakespeare were written down. It took longer to decipher them. None of them produced the revelation I was expecting. In any case, none of them was the one that I'd asked Clément to identify, and that in any event I no longer recognize. It was not the remark made by the clown Feste that I quoted above: *"Rien de ce qui est, n'est"* ["Nothing that is so, is so"]. I read and re-read *Twelfth Night* to compare my notes with the text. Perhaps, in the dark and under pressure, I had written it wrongly? No. I didn't find the line that I was looking for. It was like one of those sentences that are so clear in a dream but that awakening erases, if it does not make them banal, idiotic, or incomprehensible. Orsino's speech that ran through my mind for months, that had lulled me during my days and nights in the hospital, the sentence that I had on the tip of my tongue and whose truth had struck, even staggered me, did not exist.

Nina's e-mail ended with these words:

> The next day, the actors had to perform the play and Clément dedicated the performance to you.
>
> The final song was modified and the actors, brandishing pencils, sang: *"Je me mets en route et quoi qu'il m'en coûte, je te retrouverai comme un guignol armé d'une épée* (d'un crayon) *de bois"* ["I'm on my way, and whatever it costs me, I'll find you again like a clown armed with a wooden sword (i.e., with a pencil)"].
>
> This evening remains, for me, suspended between two worlds. The next day, the fall was dizzying. Seeing you so close the night before and knowing the next day that you were so far from humanity itself is unbearable.
>
> I have remained on the good side of life and you have slipped into horror even though we were seated side by side a few hours earlier. These two worlds now seem to be

parallel, and I don't know if they will be able to meet again someday.

They won't, neither in life nor in this book. On the one hand, words, on the other, our meetings, tend to reconstruct the bridge between us that has been destroyed. But there is a hole in the middle. Small enough to allow us to see each other, speak to each other, almost touch each other. But big enough that neither of us can rejoin the other in the zone constituted by habits, improvisations, and friendship, but above all by continuity.

Nina went to see the play when it was revived in 2016. She invited me to accompany her. I didn't have the strength to go. I would have felt that I was visiting the antechamber of a mausoleum or even seeing my own coffin lying open, like Tintin finding his and that of his dog Snowy in *Les Cigares du pharaon* (*The Cigars of the Pharaoh*). I'll go see *Twelfth Night* again when I've forgotten it.

I'm always annoyed by writers who say that they compose every sentence as if it were the last they would ever write. That accords too much importance to writing, or too little to life. What I didn't know is that the attack was going to make me relive each moment as if it were the last line: forgetting as little as possible becomes essential when you suddenly become estranged from what you've experienced, when you feel yourself leaking away on all sides. I've therefore come to think more or less the same about the people who annoyed me, even if for different reasons and under different circumstances: you have to notice the smallest details of what you experience, the tiniest of tiny things, as if you were going to die in the following minute or change planets—the next one being no more hospitable than the one you've left. That would be useful for the journey, and as a memory for survivors; still more useful for ghosts, those who, not being dead any more than the others, went somewhere so far away that they are no longer completely at home here in the world where people continue to go about their occupations as if the repetition of days and acts had a linear, established meaning, as if theater were a mission. The ghosts would read their notes, watch the others live, rub against their memories and their lives. They would compare all that in the light of the spark produced, and warming themselves at it, might recall that they were once alive.

For the future victim, a little thought that comes to mind in the toilet would be more important than a declaration of war, a meeting at work, or a minister's resignation. Writing would suspend time, whose framework it restitutes, and then, once the page was written, the play would continue until it was suddenly interrupted. It would not be exactly *Les Choses de la vie (The Things of Life)*, Claude Sautet's film in which the hero, the victim of an automobile accident, reviews the most important moments in his life just when he is about to lose it. No, it would not be a question of noting the essential things, the main stages; that is the perspective of someone who is alive and healthy. At first, there would be only the very little things, those of the last minutes, the tiny ashes of the condemned man's last cigarette, the man who does not yet know that sentence has been passed and that the executioner is on the way, with everything he owns in the trunk of a stolen car.

Obviously, I didn't do all that. I didn't take these notes on the hours that preceded the appearance of the killers, since it was a morning like any other, but I have the feeling that someone else did it for me, a practical joker who decamped and whom I am trying, by writing, to catch.

I slept alone at home, between sheets it was time to change. I am fanatical about fresh sheets, they enchant my sleeping and my waking, and one of the things that make me regret leaving the hospital is that they were changed every morning. So I woke up in a bad mood, wearied by an indefinable dissatisfaction. This indefinable something was no doubt exaggerated by the weather, gray and cold and lightless. Watching, after I returned from the theater, an interview with Michel Houellebecq on France 2 regarding his new novel, *Soumission (Submission)*, didn't help. One should never watch television before going to bed, I said to myself, it weighs on one's consciousness and stomach as much as dirty sheets do. I remember that. The impression of having been trapped by a lazy, late-evening curiosity, my own, that ends the day with a program on current events rather than with silence, and if possible, a flourish.

I had published a review of Houellebecq's book in *Libération* the preceding weekend, and for the occasion, the newspaper had organized a discussion that was to be announced on the front page. I will return to this subject, dear reader, and I fear at some length, since the figure of Houellebecq is now mixed with the memory of the attack: for others, it is a coincidence, comical or tragic; for those who survived the killers, it is an intimate experience. *Soumission* was in fact published on January 7.

In the world of blowhards with instantaneous opinions, everyone, or almost, was necessarily going to express his view, since Houellebecq was involved. In the program I watched before going to sleep, he looked like an old, not very nice mutt, abandoned near a fast-food restaurant at a highway rest stop, which made me like him, but he also looked like Droopy and Gai-Luron, the dog imagined by Gotlib, which made me find him funny. "I feel a kind a heavy torpor descending on me." The torpor arising from any foreseeable interview and the storm that it was going to provoke.

People would talk all the more because this time Houellebecq was evoking a particularly explosive fantasy, that of a repetition of the medieval Battle of Poitiers: the fear of Muslims and of Islamists coming to power in France. I laughed a lot as I read *Soumission*, with its scenes, its portraits, its coyly downplayed provocations, its *fin de siècle* melancholy about the end of civilization. Seeing an important Islamist minister put in the apartment of the former head of the *NRF* publishing house, Jean Paulhan, that implacable Jesuit grammarian, gave me special pleasure—even if it was a pleasure for the *happy few*. If the novel deserved to exist, the reason was that it enabled the reader to imagine anything, anyone, in any situation whatever, as if it were about this world and one's own life.

I had discovered Houellebecq back when he was writing columns full of malevolent wit in a fashionable cultural weekly, columns that I almost never missed. There are very few good columnists: some limit themselves to important topics of the moment and the ambient morality; others try to show how clever they are by opposing currently accepted ideas. The former are slaves to society, the latter slaves to their mask. In both cases they seek to create a distinctive style and quickly fade. Houellebecq's pessimism and laconic sarcasm had a naturalness that did not fade. At that time, I imagine that he was thought to be left-wing. It's true that people still didn't know that the left was continuing to run around like a chicken with its head cut off. Later on, I enjoyed reading his books. When I had turned the last page, a certain threat and a taste of plaster hung in the air like a cloud of dust over a field of ruins, but inside the cloud there was a smile. His misogyny, his reactionary irony, all that didn't bother me: a novel is not a place of virtue. At first, I found Houellebecq sometimes lazy about facts, never about form, until I understood, a little tardily, that the stereotype (touristic, sexual, artistic) was one of his raw materials, and for him it was essential not to avoid it. I don't know whether, as has been said, he was the great novelist, or one of the great novelists of the Western middle classes. I don't do sociology when I'm reading a novel and not much more after I've finished it. I believe wholly and exclusively in the destinies and natures of the characters, just as I did when I was ten years old. I followed Houellebecq's characters as I would have followed losers who, in a supermarket, fill their baskets with sale items and transform their loot, once they are out in the parking lot, into coldly prophetic signs of human poverty.

Like every time I'd written about a book, I'd been determined to avoid reading or listening to anything about *Soumission*, whose sole effect would have been to cause me a slight nausea: sitting through the TV program after

Shakespeare had been enough for me. I wanted to avoid it even more because I was supposed to talk with the writer the following Saturday. Having written the review and organized the discussion that *Libération* was devoting to it, I hadn't the foggiest idea what questions I was going to ask him. I'd have to talk about something else, about everything and anything but *Soumission*. He wasn't going to tell me what I should have read and I wasn't going to tell him what I thought I'd read. Most interviews with writers or artists are useless. They merely paraphrase the work that has elicited them. They feed advertising and social buzz. As an interviewer, I contribute to this buzz. By nature, it disgusted me. I saw in it an assault on privacy, on the autonomy of readers, who were not sufficiently compensated by the information they were given. What they needed was silence, and what I needed was to move on to something else, but I already knew, like everyone who had read it before it was published, that *Soumission* would not be granted any silence. Maybe that was what it was to be a famous moralist: a man who writes books that are judged only as proofs of his genius or of his guilt. This was not a new phenomenon. With Houellebecq it took on proportions disturbing enough to justify his pessimism and his success.

At the moment, on that morning of January 7, the prospect of this national debate and of this interview in particular simply put me in a bad mood. I'd gone to bed under the sign of Shakespeare and Houellebecq. I got up under the sign of Houellebecq and I was going to have to write about Shakespeare. Strange day.

It was about eight o'clock. I watched the gnats flying around the curtains in the living room—too many books, too much disorder, too many old tissues. I went downstairs to get the copy of *Libération* from my mailbox. When I returned to my apartment, I killed a few gnats with it. They made little stains like ink spots on the ceiling. Killing was a way of warming up. Next, I flipped through the paper as I drank my coffee, then I opened my computer to read the e-mail that had come in overnight.

From New York, the friend and professor to whom I owed the position at Princeton congratulated me. He took advantage of the opportunity to speak to me about the article on Houellebecq. I wrote a brief reply. Another e-mail, this one from Clément, the director of *Twelfth Night*. He was sending me his translation of the play, adding:

> So here's the text of *Twelfth Night* as you heard it last night—the exact night of the play. *Twelfth Night* is the twelfth night after Christmas: January 6.

I read the beginning of the translation, at the same time comparing it with those that were in my library. I felt incapable of judging their respective values. But why would I have wanted to?

I bought a plane ticket for New York, where I was to supposed meet Gabriela a week later. Then I closed my computer and, as I did every morning, looked at my old apartment—or, more precisely, my landlord's apartment—wondering where to begin.

I'd been living there for twenty-five years. The carpet was worn out; the wallpaper had yellowed. Books, newspapers, records, notebooks, objects, and trinkets had invaded everything. Twenty-five years of life! And nothing, probably, that would deserve to survive. Unless it was a rather fine sleigh bed that was in poor condition. It had been given to me, the year I moved in, by a friend of my parents. Her husband used to stretch out on it to read, write, or take a nap. He was an excellent journalist; alcohol had both kept him going and destroyed him. His personality changed when he drank. When I started out, I worked for the same newspaper he did. He liked trains, and one day he threw himself under one of them at the

Villeneuve-Saint-Georges switchyard. He was stocky, with metallic gray-blue eyes squeezed into a red, square face. He spoke little and articulated still less. Although he wasn't sober, his writing was. For several of us, I think, his death marked the end of an era. A professional era that I hardly knew except, precisely, through people like him. It was going out, like the tide, when I had just dipped my toes in the water for the first time. The day after the event, his wife suggested that I come get the sleigh bed. She no longer wanted it, but she preferred that it not end up with someone she didn't know. When I lie down on it to read or take a nap in my turn, it seems to me that the dead man's spirit is watching over me.

The big carpet that occupied the living room came from Iraq. I had bought it in Baghdad, in a souk, in January 1991, two days before the first American bombardment. I was one of three journalists there, as I recall, and we drank tea, talking and joking with the old merchant in an atmosphere that seemed unreal to us, since war was coming. Most of the Westerners had left town during the preceding days. The embassies were closed. Nothing is more flattering or more exciting than finding oneself in a place that others have deserted, in the eye that waiting hollows out at the center of the hurricane. We were young, uneasy, and hungry. History seemed to be our adventure and our property. We had the enthusiasm and the weakness of special envoys, those privileged adventurers: when they die on assignment, their obituaries are all alike, praising the courage that their readers lack.

The carpet was about five meters long and two meters wide. It was long and heavy. The old merchant in Baghdad rolled it up, tied it with twine, and put it in a sack, which I carried away. Twenty-five years later, it had traveled a lot. Holes had gradually destroyed its beauty, its tones of mainly brick-red. It tended to develop folds, like an old man's skin, and seemed to have digested dirt which, as it was deposited, had taken on a sort of patina. Fabric and dirt were irreversibly bound together by the odor, an odor that was difficult to define, mixing those of morning coffee, vacuum cleaner powders scented with pine needles, shoe soles, spilled liquids, rug shampoos, and Tibetan incense.

Two days after buying the carpet, I took the last plane for Amman with it. That was an error, which the newspaper I was then working for allowed me to commit, the management having decided that I alone could make the decision to stay or not. I was twenty-seven years old. That was already no longer an excuse for making a mistake. I should have remained in Baghdad to cover the bombardments, along with a handful of other individuals who were strange, crazy, self-interested, exalted, such as always exist on this kind of raft, a whole crew that made me feel I was witnessing less an epic than a farce: I had not yet understood to what extent the two are compatible. The hotel where guests and journalists had been brought together by the Iraqi authorities resembled by turns a theater or an asylum: everyone there was a thespian or a neurotic, and it was never boring, either in the rooms or at mealtime.

What all of Saddam Hussein's last "guests" had in common, in any case more than their support for him, was their hatred of the American government. They came there to testify to the misdeeds of the Evil Empire. The most burlesque of them were the North-American pacifists, who were delighted to play their role as useful idiots and human shields. The journalists present—if I except most of the Arab journalists, who were incapable of taking any distance—had hardly any compassion for these imbeciles who were putting a clown's grin on the event. They did it by supporting a dictator of the worst kind, a former best friend of the West, whose cellars reeked of beatings and torture. If the crusade pursued by Bush Sr. worried and disgusted almost all of us journalists, it did not prevent us from recognizing the nature of the regime it was directed against. In this case, there were not only idiots but also cynics, and evildoers.

Among the "guests" was Daniel Ortega, who was no longer a Marxist guerilla and not yet a Christian caudillo. With his cowboy boots, he looked like a small-time hooligan from the suburbs of History. I was stupefied: I had believed (half-heart-edly, it is true) in the Sandinistas' struggle. The man I saw reminded me of reporting on the housing projects back in the days when you could still go there casually and without worry-ing. When I talked with him I wondered if, like some "young people" he was going to ask Saddam for a "meeting room" or subsidies so that he could feel that he existed. Was this really the former leader of Nicaragua? Every time he appeared in the dining room he seemed smaller, more pathetic. It was the man who was shrinking. As he shrank, he shrank History, that old, greedy bawd. He had not yet become a Christian demagogue.

Louis Farrakhan, the black head of the Nation of Islam, was completely chic and scornful. Surrounded by his bodyguards and wearing a black, flawlessly pressed suit, he strode through the room full of white people as if they did not exist. He occa-sionally spoke to them, because some of them were journalists; but he replied to their questions without looking at them. I felt like a Jew interviewing a Nazi in a world in which the former had not yet been liquidated by the latter. This was the place for that sort of thing: *Mein Kampf* could be found in the display windows of Baghdad's bookstores. The Arab world didn't need the Internet, which did not yet exist, in order to spread conspiracy theories on which it had no monopoly. There were all sorts of them, blue, green, red, all equally idiotic and adding to the general atmosphere of unreality. None of them failed to refer to the Jews.

Jean-Edern Hallier was already no longer a writer that peo-ple read: a wretched clown of the same name had replaced him in the minds of most of his former readers. He was accompanied by a little secretary, silent, well-dressed, and carrying a small black briefcase; his name was Omar. Those who had associated with this strange pair in the framework of *L'Idiot international*, the newspaper that Hallier directed and financed, liked to describe Omar as his henchman. At the dining table, the writer bellowed about his anti-Americanism and his heroic life to anyone who would listen. Omar silently opened the briefcase and handed around photos that corresponded to the heroic episodes his master was recounting. Hallier was there out of a taste for paradox and spectacle, to make people talk about him and to claim the despicable for himself, no matter on which side it was to be found. He made the event his personal possession. When he spoke, he turned his blind eye toward one person, then another, like a cyclops or an animal, drawing attention to the madness of the world by displaying his own. He had even more candor than egocentrism or cunning, which is saying something; and for once, the context had neutralized his malevolence. Perhaps he was right, and all this was just a comedy in which the clown-puppet and the scribe had to be improvised. Hallier was so full of his own image and the traveling circus he carried with him that he had absolutely no fear of what might have happened to him. He was a fairground caricature of Chateaubriand, whom we listened to and looked at, a caricature that transformed the hotel and the city into a pasteboard stage setting. The day of the bombardment, he left with Omar and a driver to visit the ruins of Babylon. Reconstituted with all the local bad taste, they were a fine place from which to witness the Apocalypse that we were promised—while not seeing it. I left before the great little man returned and have never seen him again.

The closer the time set by the ultimatum came, the more the hotel resembled the animal fable it incarnated. Was this the event? Was it really serious? I could have read Malraux or

Lawrence out loud without changing anything: my sense of History was limited by what I saw and my respect for those who were making it was close to zero—in this male and mustachioed part of the world, in any case. The French ambassador had left, like most of the others. The man who replaced him had closed the embassy two days before the ultimatum. The journalists were all there. He had been ordered to leave. With a half-smile, he hinted that we should stay. We felt that he did not even understand that we might hesitate. He was firm, reassuring, calm. We emptied the bottles in the cellar and everyone telephoned his family at the embassy's expense, sitting on the floor in a room full of electronic devices whose black cords looked like squid's ink spaghetti. It was one of those moments that remind me that I knew a time when cell phones did not exist. Then the diplomat and his little team locked up the building and the cars took them across the desert into the night, toward the Jordanian border. We watched them leave. The novices, of which I was one, suddenly felt all alone, as if abandoned to the jaws of the uncertain event. The veterans had knowing looks on their faces. The eyes of some of them began to light up: at last, this adventure was becoming interesting.

One of the veterans had already collected a considerable supply of water and canned food. He told me, with a smile simultaneously calm, excited, and provocative: "If there's gas, I'll go to a cellar in the hotel and wait there. A month, if I have to. I'm ready for anything." He was expecting disaster, pressure, something new. He had been living on it ever since the age when Rimbaud left Charleroi. He came from a tribe in which journalism was the narrative of an experience lived by the person who was recounting it. Blond, short, and stocky, he resembled Tintin. He died three years later, at the age of thirty-five, of an illness he caught during an assignment in Asia. When I read this in a newspaper, I was overwhelmed. He was so young and had already taken so many risks that I thought he would survive everything, because he already seemed so old, so lucid. I must have believed that an intelligent and informed insouciance would make him eternal, but I no longer remember what I thought. I had a tendency to admire those who succeeded in what I was incapable of undertaking. Him, dead? So, it was possible to die on a reporting assignment? To fall off the flying carpet on which we soared over the world? Yes, it was possible. I was naïve, optimistic, afraid, almost innocent. I think that at that time almost all of us were. The world that was ending still allowed us to remain young as long as possible.

In Baghdad, ISIS's future killers were still secular killers working for Saddam, a rather corpulent figure whose badly painted portraits were displayed everywhere. In the Arab world, they were distributed in the form of pins, just as brooches were made in the form of Scuds—the Scuds with which Iraq was trying to hit Israel. The Gulf War was a tasteless, deadly boring story, and the only reading material I had taken to Baghdad was *The Thousand and One Nights*. The great danger filled the marbled void of the hotel from which we sent reports by fax.

Ben Bella smiled, like Tintin soon to be dead, when journalists asked him if he was going to leave before the American bombardment. He said: "Don't you think I've seen worse in the cellars of Algiers?" He knew the value of his public figure, no matter how out of date he might be. Die in Baghdad? Not everyone has an opportunity to die of stomach cancer on Saint Helena, or the genius to live what preceded. Perhaps Ben Bella also felt that if the Iraqi people was paying the price for several decades of chaos, the international witnesses of the origin of this chaos were in no danger. He had experience, points of comparison. He was tall, powerful, rather heavy, which surprised me: I had imagined, I don't know why, that the FLN's former combatants were all small, skinny, and nervous, as if

they were still living in the scrubland of some wilayah or operating clandestinely in the shantytown of Nanterre. Among so
many charlatans, politicians gone astray, and international
scoundrels, he alone impressed me; or more exactly, he alone
made me feel that we were witnessing the end of a history—
that of decolonization—and the beginning of something disturbing. We were experiencing it without knowing it: the air of
history was still quite lighthearted, the reporters seemed carefree. It is often said that the current disaster began with the
Iranian Revolution. In my case, everything began in Baghdad.
Everything that was going to lead to, among other things, the
events of January 7. I was there, but I left too early. On
January 7 I was there, too, but I got up to leave too late.

When you're a reporter, you have to stay where the event is
taking place, and do so, if possible, on the side of those who
are weak and unknown, ordinary people caught up in an
extraordinary situation, in order to give them a name and as
much life as possible at a time when a power, no matter which
one, is seeking to take it away from them. Thus I should have
remained with the Iraqis, even if their leader was a criminal,
even if that luxurious hotel from which it was difficult to
escape was a site of propaganda and theatrics, even if investigation had become almost impossible in that country. I should
have done that because the great powers were against them
and because it was necessary just to testify, as much as possible, to the effects of the bombardment. It's as simple as that,
and I didn't do it. In the end, those who stayed were expelled
the day after the bombardment. They saw almost nothing. But
we couldn't have guessed that. Why did I leave? Because I was
scared? Everyone, or almost, was scared, and yet a few of them
stayed. Because I couldn't control my fear? That's possible: it's
not even certain. In Amman, a few days later, a friend who had
taken the last plane with me, said to me: "You came back
because of the carpet." He wasn't wrong, that's all one can say.

I continue to think that on that day, by taking the plane for Amman with the last European journalists—the Americans had left long before, obeying the orders of their superiors, who were themselves obeying their government's commands—I gave up the career as a reporter that seemed to await me. A possible life died, a life that probably consisted of backpacks and solitude, I don't know, in any case another life, a life that this carpet symbolized.

The evening of the bombardment, I was supposed to go to dinner at the home of a Palestinian diplomat to whom I had been introduced by an old Iraqi painter I'd met in this city a few years before. I hadn't canceled this dinner, because that morning I still believed I would go there. Had I remained, I would have seen from his residence the night sky lit up by the bombardment. We might have ended up in his cellar, drinking wine, champagne; he, too, had seen it all before. That would have created bonds between us. He would have become a friend. He would have introduced me to his friends, some of whom would have become my friends. I might have been, on January 7, 2015, a semi-expert on this part of the world, and not a culture critic for *Libération* and a columnist for *Charlie Hebdo*. And then, from Baghdad, what reports I would have written! Instead of which I had fled and, at the same time, without yet suspecting it, more or less said farewell to the Arab world in which I was beginning to feel at ease, and which, twenty-four years later, in an unforeseeable form and in the heart of Paris, was going to catch up with me. This carpet had spent all those years under my nose, under my feet. It constantly reminded me of Iraq, of that Palestinian diplomat who would still be waiting for me to arrive for dinner, and of the shame and regrets that had followed, the regrets and then the forgetting—a certain kind of forgetting. It had fallen apart little by little, like my memory, like all that was the most bitter and the most anodyne in it.

I looked at the carpet, as I did every morning, thinking, as I did every morning, that it was time to throw it away, and knowing that I wouldn't do it, because it could still carry me aloft, without my knowing exactly how or why. Then I stretched out on it to do my exercises, as I did every morning, with the radio on. The guest on France Inter that day was— think of that!—Michel Houellebecq. I remembered that only after doing some research, a year later, to find out whom I might have been listening to that morning. I'd forgotten all about it. Since then, I have listened to the interview again. So, the killers were getting ready while he was talking in a feigned sleepy voice about the republic and Islam. They were checking their weapons while he was murmuring his provocations in a minor mode. In two hours, his fiction would be overtaken by an outgrowth of the phenomenon it had imagined. We never control the development of the illnesses we diagnose, provoke, or maintain. The world in which Houellebecq lived had even more imagination than the one he was describing.

I stretched my muscles as he described *Soumission* as a "satire," a "political fiction, not necessarily very credible." I did my push-ups while he said that the reelection of François Hollande in 2017 would be "a case of sleight of hand that would produce a disturbance, a strange situation in the country." I did a headstand as he was saying that democracy would be ridiculed by that election, and I must have started working on my abs when he said that the Islam described in *Soumission* appeared to him, all things considered, to be rather moderate. "It seems to me that there are much worse things," he said, laughing imperceptibly, as I was breathing and contracting my muscles. Within two hours, he would be right.

I must not have been completely distracted as I listened to the interview. I am now going to describe it as I might have in the column for the next issue of *Charlie*, the one for January 14, if the attack hadn't rendered null and void what he said that

morning. The anchorman, Patrick Cohen, who has too many listeners not to merge his role, his personality, and his function,
seems surprised, almost scandalized by the oil the writer is
throwing on the fire. He says to him: "I remind you that in
France, Muslims are five percent of the electorate. Five percent!" Houellebecq: "Yes. So what? I'm sorry, but for my part
I find it very disturbing when people cannot be represented."
As is often the case, he is not wrong: Muslims are poorly represented in France, and, as always, he is perverse: he makes this
group a threat, even as he claims to defend its right to representation. Cohen reacts: "You're essentializing Muslims."
"What do you mean by 'essentializing'?" replies the writer,
who always implacably spots what Gérard Genette calls the
"medialect": all the big words that my profession goes on
repeating without thinking and that are merely the signs of an
automatic morality. Cohen flounders a bit and, since he likes to
have the last word, attacks: "Basically, what you recount, what
you imagine, in this novel, is the death of the republic. Is that
what you want, Michel Houellebecq?"

At that point, the interview slipped into the usual misunderstanding—a misunderstanding that Houellebecq's virtuoso
ambiguity nourishes. That was probably the point when I
chose to do my knee bends with the help of a broomstick.
Cohen was no longer questioning his guest as a novelist but as
an ideologue or politician: anything to avoid talking about the
text. Houellebecq understood that long ago, maybe he has
always known it, and if he crosses over and over again the borderline between literature and politics, like a glorious smuggler, he does so primarily to increase the value of his trade. I'm
a bird, see my wings, I'm a mouse, long live rats! "I don't know
what I want," he told Cohen, adding, with his sly irony: "I can
adapt to various systems . . . " In the video, you see him scratch
his ear like an old dog. He seems to be brushing off the lice
with which his interlocutor is infesting him. Cohen: "You don't

have a point of view?" Houellebecq: "No, not really." The journalist persists: "Reading you, one can't help thinking that such a novel can't be written without having a point of view." Houellebecq replies as a novelist: "Well, I disagree; to write such a novel one must precisely *not* have a point of view. There are plenty of characters who have points of view in this novel. It's best not to have a point of view in order to let them speak in turn."

Then they turn to the relation between France and its Muslims, and the writer says: "No, on the whole, after a close reading of the Quran, I'm sure negotiation is possible. The problem is that there's always room for interpretation. By taking a *surah* and exploiting it fully, and by eliminating five other *surahs*, one can end up with a jihadist. It takes a major dose of dishonesty to read the Quran and arrive at that conclusion, but it's possible." What were the killers doing at that moment? Were they reading a *surah* that they were going to exploit fully in two and a half hours? I think I finished my exercises at the moment that Houellebecq was saying that the republic was not one of his absolutes. I turned off the radio and went to take a shower.

Next, I reflected on *Twelfth Night*. When I left, I still didn't know whether I was would go directly to write my article at *Libération* or first attend *Charlie*'s editorial meeting. The offices of the first paper were on the way to those of the second. Since it was the first meeting of the year, I would be glad to meet everyone again, and especially Wolinski, whom I always enjoyed seeing. But Shakespeare was waiting for me . . . I hadn't made up my mind.

I wrote Gabriela that Princeton had confirmed my position and that I had bought a plane ticket. I wrote to an editor that I would like to meet the writer Akhil Sharma in New York. He was publishing a novel, *Family Life*, whose opening pages had pleased me, but which I never finished reading.

Later, between operating rooms and nurses, between morphine and insomnia, I often imagined the story that derived from this interview. I met the writer in his neighborhood in Brooklyn or in Queens, depending on my dream. We drank tea and talked about India, where he was born and where I had not been for a long time. We discussed immigration and literature as ideal female companions, even if they were generally separate. We went to walk in the New York neighborhood of his childhood. Later, I returned there to dine with Gabriela, who was crazy about Indian food. I examined in detail the dishes, the odors, the places, the servers, our discussions. Sometimes I ended up in India with Gabriela, in Bombay or Madras rather than in Delhi. When it was in Madras, we embraced in the little aquarium described by Henri Michaux, which I had visited for that reason. Preferably, we kissed in front of one of those exotic fish called tetraodons, which, according to Michaux, looked "so filled up, swollen, shapeless, ready to burst." You resemble them, she told me, since I was disfigured. And we laughed. Then we imagined the life of each animal, not a fable, but its history: how it had landed there, what it felt, how the sensations of the trap, the light, eyes behind the glass, and death, floated in it. I gave up these reveries a little too late not to feel saddened and exhausted by their faintness, their impossibility, and the nervous pain they provoked.

The mysterious Akhil Sharma was not the only person who occupied bits of life I had not had. I regularly imagined the various encounters I would have had in Cuba had I escaped the attack. A week earlier, my former mother-in-law had returned to Havana, where she had lived before, and she had urged me to accompany her. I was tempted, but the prospect of meeting Gabriela in New York made me refuse: I expected to go to Cuba on assignment for *Libération* the following month. I have never returned there since. The editor sent me

Akhil Sharma's address and phone number three-quarters of an hour after the attack. She did not yet know that it had taken place. I read her e-mail message about ten days later. Like so many other things, it came from another world. I answered it only in February.

I wrote another message, about Houellebecq, to Claire, my friend and department head. Annoyance, which is never very far away in my case, rose up again. I told her that on France 2 and France Inter he seemed to me "a kind of guru-ized figure who says nothing, and other people's chatter and judgments sink into that void—as if he were a sort of prophet. It's very astonishing, this madness of the system people. That leaves room, Saturday, for an interview that I hope will be more reasonable and precise."

I'm not proud of this e-mail message and a few others of the same kind written in its wake, any more than I am of the frivolity from which they arose and which they fed. I would have liked to "finish" my earlier life with sentences that were a little calmer, more amusing, and more interesting, even if not at all definitive. I don't believe I would have liked to write "as if it were the last sentence of my life." In any case, when what follows happens by accident, you don't have time to prepare your clothes, your gestures, and your last words. I wrote those harmless lines, which are rather scornful and not without self-satisfaction, as if life were going to continue. That is why I feel a certain compassion for the person who sent them: they are the last words of an ordinary, thoughtless journalist. Words written before the attack that was being prepared as he was writing them. The last ones, if I except an e-mail informing a colleague that I was thinking about writing that day on a book about jazz entitled *Blue Note*, which I had just received. This book, as we will see, probably saved my life, and I am writing this, as I write every day, a few meters away from it. It is my immobile talisman; it's a little too heavy to carry with me. As for my annotated copy of *Soumission*, it was left lying around at *Libération*, where it disappeared.

An e-mail from Gabriela arrived just as I was about to shut down my computer. She replied with a single word:

Yahoo!

It was 4 A.M. in New York, she was not asleep, and just as I was slipping on my pea coat and my cap to go out, she called me on FaceTime. Her sleepy, smiling face appeared in the dark of her New York apartment. I could make it out, faintly illuminated by the bluish glow of her cell phone. I felt, as I often did, a slight pain arising from the frustration of not being able to pass through the screen to feel her presence, her warmth, her breath, her smell. I would have liked to start my night again over there. We said "te quiero" to each other, we repeated that we would soon be together, and then I murmured that I was running late and that I'd call her after lunch. She kissed me on the screen, which must have misted over on her side. I hung up and went out. I got on my bike and it was then, on the boulevards, near the Monoprix, where I stopped to buy a yogurt drink, that I chose to go first to *Charlie*.

When I got there, the meeting had already begun. I wanted to get a copy of the day's paper, but there were none left, and again I felt annoyed. Grumbling, I went into the room where everyone was sitting. A seat was waiting for me at the back, between Bernard Maris and Honoré. I remember having said, more or less: "Really, it's incredible that there aren't enough copies of the paper for each of us on the day it's published and when we're supposed to talk about it." Charb had an ironic and benevolent smile that meant: "Well, so Lançon is doing his irritable number!" Honoré, with his habitual kindness, took one of his two copies out of his bag and gave it to me. We were a band of pals who were more or less close and who worked for a little paper that was now broke, almost dead. We knew it, but we were free. We were there to have fun, to yell at each other, to refuse to take an appalling world seriously. I was ashamed of my reaction and looked at the front page.

It had been drawn by Luz, who was late that morning. It depicted Houellebecq as a wan, crazy demi-tramp holding a cigarette; he had a drunkard's nose and wore a starred cap on his head that suggested he'd imbibed too much bad wine the night before. Above the image, these words: "The predictions of Houellebecq the magician." And below it, the predictions: "In 2015, I'm going to lose my teeth . . . in 2022, I'm observing Ramadan!" Luz had foreseen everything, truly, except the attack. A few lines and two balloons summed up, better than I could have, my irritation at the looming circus: that is the aggressively elliptical virtue of caricature. At the bottom of the page, there was an ad for a "special number" on the life of baby Jesus. While I was examining the front page in greater detail, the discussion that my entrance had interrupted resumed. I looked up and listened. They were talking about Houellebecq.

CHAPTER 3
THE MEETING

W hy was I always late to this meeting, though I am
almost never late? There was a kind of brioche in
front of Cabu. Wolinski was drawing in his notebook and at the same time looking with amusement at this or
that speaker. In general, he usually drew a woman, mostly
naked, with rather slender curves, and he made her say something funny, unexpected, absurd, which had been inspired in
him by someone who made a remark that was funny, but less.
That is why I liked to sit next to him. I watched his talent transform reality, deforming it to make it not more acceptable, but
more intelligent, more imaginative and more burlesque: to
make it something suitable to be included in life as drawn by
Wolinski. That morning, there was no seat next to him.

Fabrice Nicolino had not yet begun one of his nervous,
melancholic tirades against the ecological destruction of the
world. Fabrice needed to be indignant in order not to be desperate, but he was desperate nonetheless—a desperate *bon
vivant*. Elsa Cayat's booming, shrill voice resounded, followed
by an immense, wild laugh, the laugh of a libertarian witch. I
liked Elsa very much: she always seemed to be laughing at
Macbeth, the minions surrounding him, and his criminal
derangement. Tignous might have been drawing. He sometimes drew during the meeting, and always when it was over. I
liked to watch him work: an old child, stocky and concentrated, applying himself, slow, with heavy shoulders, a crafts-
man. Often, he brought part of a brioche, but it wasn't his that

was in front of Cabu that morning. Sitting behind him, Laurent Léger, whose tall figure and discreet smile masked worry about a new crusade against an abuse of power or a corrupt practice. Franck Brinsolaro, Charb's bodyguard, seemed to be listening distractedly to the words and tirades, and looking at his face I wondered once again what he must think of all the bullshit flying around the table, since that was what we were there for: to bullshit. To say whatever came into our heads, to yell at each other and have fun without worrying about propriety or competence, without being reasonable or knowledgeable, not to mention wise. We talked to wake ourselves up.

I emphasize this, dear reader: on that morning, as on all the others, humor, shouting, and a theatrical form of indignation were the judges and guides, the good and evil geniuses, in a very French tradition that was worth what it was worth, but what was to follow showed that most of the world didn't appreciate it. It had taken me some time to rid my mind of seriousness in order to accept it, and I had, moreover, not entirely succeeded in doing so. I hadn't been programmed to understand it, and then, like most journalists, I was a bourgeois. Around this table, there were artists and militants, but few journalists and even fewer bourgeois. Bernard Maris no doubt remained at *Charlie* these past years for the same reason that I did: because he felt free and at ease there. Talking nonsense about a writer or an event didn't matter so long as it led to something else that transformed it: an idea, a joke, or a drawing. Words ran like hungry dogs from one mouth and body to another. In the best cases, they found a prey. In the worst case, they went nowhere and were forgotten between an empty cup and a bit of greasy wrapping paper. People obsessed by their competence write rigorous articles, to be sure, but they end up lacking imagination. Here we said or shouted lots of vague, false, banal, idiotic, spontaneous things, we said them the way people limber up their bodies, but when it worked, imagination followed. It was tasteless enough not to spare us any of its consequences.

Since I had not yet entered the discussion, I examined the place that served as its theater. It was a very small room in a very small building located in a very small street, a street that looked like nothing other than a cul-de-sac. The street bore a name that I could never remember, that of an industrialist who, at the end of the eighteenth century, had invented a new method of food preservation and opened the world's first cannery. Nicolas Appert was the son of innkeepers. After making a fortune, he had been ruined by Napoleon's continental blockade. He died at the age of ninety-one and was buried in the potter's field. The street is still called Nicolas-Appert, and now I recall his name, but it hasn't been long. It's located between Bastille and République, between Révolution and the Commune, as some of my friends would have said, but that would be to do too much honor to this miserable urban segment where architects seemed to have joined together to win an ugliness contest.

The offices were on the third floor of the building, which had lots of windows, looked like it had been built of Legos, and which one wanted to enter about as much as into a dishwasher or a police station. The shared lavatory was outside *Charlie*'s offices, a few meters down a hallway that was always deserted. Later, at the hospital, this lavatory took on a retrospective importance for me—as a door that I would never cease to open. It dangled before me escape into another destiny, but it opened only onto a brick wall. I imagined that I was taking a piss when the killers came in. No, I didn't imagine it: amid the tubes, I lived it. I was in the lavatory when they arrived and I was pissing while they were killing everyone, without knowing or hearing it.

In one scenario, I emerge just as they are leaving *Charlie*, I meet them in the hallway, and they kill me. In another scenario, they take me hostage and, for some mysterious reason that my condition prevents me from discovering, they spare me. In a third scenario, one of the killers goes into the lavatory to see if they had missed anyone, and I hold my breath, perched precariously on a toilet. How many times had I seen this kind of scene in the movies? Sometimes the killer finds me, sometimes not. In a fourth scenario, I come out of the lavatory after they've left, without having heard anything, and I find the massacre, my dead and wounded companions. The scenario stops there, because, having been wounded, I can't divide myself up to the point of imagining myself racing to help myself. Each scenario provoked, at one point or another, a state of panic and sorrow that I could no longer escape anywhere but in that damned lavatory.

I return to *Charlie*'s offices. They indicated the gradual, shambolic, and cheerful impoverishment of the paper that occupied them. We yelled at each other at close quarters, as if, confronted by the disappearance of readers—those ingrates!—the walls had little by little contracted, like those of a garbage truck, around bodies and words. The cries, laughs, and tirades reminded me of Cuba, an island where people talk loudly and spread extravagant moods, like madmen in an asylum where no one can hear them, and end up being right by saying anything and everything. It was likely that the old satirical weekly would end its days here, soon, we knew that and, being fatalists, laughed about it. We? Was I part of that "we"? And if I was, what did that mean?

During my adolescence and youth in the suburbs south of Paris, I read *L'Express*. It was the newsmagazine my parents subscribed to. At that time, it was a good magazine: it had a project, a style, a unity, great reporting, good columns, major writers. I admired Raymond Aron, who represented for me everything that I seemed to lack: culture associated with reason.

I ended up writing to him, maybe because it was impossible to write to a dead man called Sartre, and he received me at his office. He had pale, parchment-like skin, a large nose, and I would not have been more impressed had I been facing a diplodocus. I think he was happy to receive a young man, even a young man with no particular talent, especially since he had been treated by the Sartrians and the rebels of 1968 as a professor combined with an old fool. We talked about Sartre's *Nausea* and Kafka's *Metamorphosis*. I told him that I had had trouble reading the former in high school. He was annoyed that we had been made to read it so early. He shook his head as he grumbled: "It's much too difficult for you! Much too difficult . . . You have to be a little older to understand the import of that book." And I sensed, as he was talking, all his melancholic admiration for Sartre. Concerning *The Metamorphosis*, he uttered a banality: "It's an enormous nightmare!" I felt guilty for not being able to say anything that would have transformed that banality into gold, but I deserved it. I didn't deserve better. I was the banality.

I also sometimes read *Charlie Hebdo*, at the home of one of my classmates, and laughed at it with him. If one of our heroes was Corto Maltese, the other was Reiser, each of whose cartoon albums we perused with an almost frenetic joy. Since I had no political sense, this went no further. All I remember from *Charlie* at that time is a cover: a big measuring stick that allowed you to measure your dick; beyond a certain limit, the drawing explained, you were in the category of niggers, yids, Arabs, wops. At least, that's how I remember it, and I don't want to verify it. In any case, it summed up the paper's state of mind. Take the most abject or ridiculous point of view and turn it inside out by absurdity, in a great burst of laughter, and with the worst taste possible, that was the spirit of *Charlie* at a time when "common sense" was usually the rug under which flatterers swept their little piles of shit in post–de Gaulle

French society. *Charlie* was a skull-and-bones flag flying over the thirty years of postwar prosperity. For teenagers revolted by everything, often without their knowing it, and who so often drowned their revolt in their silliness, this humor served as a guide, an outlet, and a corrosive.

So far as I recall, however, I was scared by the brutality of the attitudes and words of that period. After a brief episode of revolt and hope, society subsided into grayness again before turning to the trashy flashiness of the 1980s and the uncultured, demagogic, inegalitarian abjection from which we have still not emerged. I wasn't aware of either of these developments. I was too young, too asleep, and too poorly informed for that; but I felt this change and I suffered from it. In my family, we were on the right. At middle school and high school, people were on the left. For my part, I wasn't anything. The militants of all kinds who were still flourishing horrified me by the noise they made. Giscard was president; Barre was prime minister; the geometrical relation between their bodies—one tall and slim, the other short and plump—that was what amused me. Their puppets didn't yet exist. I fabricated them for myself.

However, the leftists had favorite targets that circulated in the high school. They bore the names of ministers who are now dead and who, if I mentioned them, would no longer mean anything to anyone except those who have themselves fallen into complete oblivion. People were beginning to talk again about Mitterrand, whom I found ugly, with his buckteeth and his blinking eyes, while Giscard seemed to me ridiculous with his aristocratic lisp. Was that what politics was? I was fifteen years old, I was reading Céline and Cendrars—and I leave it to the reader to understand how these writers could lead a young boy to want to escape the perspectives of his environment. To participate in demonstrations, a few professors sometimes gave us a ride in a van. I followed, I got in, I marched, I forgot. There was a lot of talk about racism.

In high school, most of the Arabs were at that time relegated to the LEP, the occupational high school. They were a foreign group, of which we met only the most aggressive members in the underground garage, where some of them "stripped" mopeds while others kept watch. They were said to have knives, and we avoided going down to the garage when there were few people there. It was perhaps a fantasy. I didn't go to check. My moped, a Peugeot 104, was stripped several times. I was saddened, but I wasn't really surprised, because being robbed seemed to me part of my condition as a petit-bourgeois. I didn't feel that I belonged to any group, but I was on the left, I imagine, without knowing and without worrying about it. Like many children of the white middle class, I lived in a world without Arabs, without blacks, except at a distance, and during those years I think I never heard the word "Muslim" uttered even once. We called the Ayatollah Khomeini, who was beginning to make himself known, "Ayatollah Grosminet" ("Aytollah Bigpussy"). This bearded old man who looked like a grandfather with a turban on his head and who reminded us of the Grand Vizier Iznogoud ("Isnogood"), was no more serious than a cartoon or a comic strip. Violence was everywhere, but it didn't exist. In the classroom, a Jewish friend called Napoleon little Hitler, and the history teacher, a communist who loved Gracchus Babeuf, didn't tell him he was wrong. I really liked the teacher who taught an optional course on literature. She was a hippie, enthusiastic and eccentric. She introduced me to Richard Wright and Panaït Istrati, among others. I have forgotten neither her smell of incense, her heavy figure untidily wrapped in bits of fabric as if she were returning from a stay in an ashram, nor her long brown hair, which she never combed, fighting with the scarves that surrounded it; but I've forgotten her name.

In my parents' library, there were lots of bestsellers, prize-winners: the middle class bought books, and contrary to what is often thought, it read them. That was how I discovered and liked Cavanna's two books, *Les Ritals* and *Les Russkoffs*. People never cease to be all those they have been: when twenty-five years later I saw at *Charlie* this refined, heavyset man, with his high-pitched voice that didn't carry and his big white mustache, it wasn't the journalist at *Libération* who looked at him first, but the high school student who had read all his books, lying on a bunk bed, by the light of a small hurricane lamp, next to a big map of Indochina.

Right to the end, Cavanna intimidated me. The young reader remained stronger, more present, than the man who had become the novelist's colleague. I didn't miss any of his last columns, which grew shorter and shorter, in which he recounted with anger and humor his struggle with Parkinson's and his decline. One day, Charb said to me, with a happy smile: "Another column that's leaving us. He'll write to the end, he's not going to spare us, and you'll see, he'll continue even when he's in his grave, he'll tell us about the life of maggots." Cavanna was right to go as far as possible, to refuse to let go of anything, and I'd give a great deal to enable the dead who accompany me to write about what they are experiencing or not experiencing, from where they are, as they are. I'd like to know their decomposition manual, their subterranean laughter, probably because there was a time a few weeks ago when I seemed still to be living with them, among them, in them, and when sensing that they were moving away from me caused me more sorrow and solitude than anything else I had to contend with.

There were lots of people at Cavanna's burial in the Père-Lachaise cemetery. Artists drew pictures during the ceremony. If I recall correctly, I was seated next to Tignous, along with other members of the team. As always, I felt out of place and proud to be there, among them and one of them. It was February 6, 2014. It was raining more or less. I appeared for two seconds in a YouTube video, outside, with Charb, Luz, Catherine and Patrick Pelloux. One of them died, the others have left. My head is seen between their heads, in the background, and I'm smiling. A big bald head shines from behind under the gray sky: I don't know who it is. I'm wearing a rust-colored cap, the pea coat, and the face that I will wear for the last time on the day of the attack. Charb is plumper than I remember him. Did the memory of his death make him thinner? His expression is phlegmatic. Catherine looks somber. I'm looking at us living, a few fleeting images, while Cavanna is buried, and I'm thinking about something else. A few days after the fatwa pronounced by Ayatollah Khomeini against Salman Rushdie, the latter attended the funeral of his friend Bruce Chatwin. During the ceremony, another writer, Paul Théroux, turned toward him and said: "Next year, we'll be here again, but for you." At Cavanna's burial, no one showed this kind of British humor toward the people who were to die. Their death was unforeseeable, or premature. The burial of *Charlie*'s founder was the end of an epoch, as people say, as we all said. It was also the last burial of a comrade before the attack. As long as he could, he had attended the editorial meeting. Had he lived a little longer, he might have come on January 7. There are times when the absent are always in the right.

I have a precise memory of the day when I told another person who was absent, Philippe Val, then the paper's manager and a friend of mine, that I would write for *Charlie*. It was a fine Paris day in the late spring. I'd gone to see him at a vernissage to tell him this news, and then I went to the Luxembourg Gardens to marry two Americans I didn't know. A friend, a newspaper correspondent on assignment in the United States, had met a young lawyer who was defending the Indians' cause in Oklahoma. He'd been charmed by Jon's intelligence, tenacity, and effectiveness. They had become friends. Jon had just married a young woman, Pamela, and the couple wanted to take advantage of their honeymoon trip to renew their marriage vows, symbolically, in Paris. Americans sometimes do that. The city represented love—a pleasant and eternal kind of love, heightened by the grace of its bridges and its buildings. My friend asked me to marry them, and I accepted. My wife, Marilyn, was delighted by this idea. We were supposed to meet them at their hotel on the Boulevard Saint-Michel and help them find the right place for the ceremony. I was to give a speech and perform the marriage. To prepare myself, I reread one of my favorite books, Hemingway's *A Moveable Feast*.

Not long before he committed suicide, Hemingway recalled the Paris of his youth, the city where he was poor, in love, and became a writer. All his laconic depression is expressed in it, all his sensitivity, and all his hardness as well, everything that resides and lives in the lost paradise. I often returned to this book. The older I got, the more it seemed to me that Hemingway was sending readers back to the age, which varies depending on the person, when they were least distant from their dreams. He drew every reader into the inescapable labyrinth of nostalgia, into the pitiless mirror of failures. I continued to reread the book because I still had not found, in myself, that magic, abandoned age. I sought it while Hemingway spoke to me about his. I looked for it, waited for it, didn't find it, and now I know that it will never come back. It is buried somewhere before January 7, if it ever existed at all. It doesn't matter. I no longer have either nostalgia or regrets: in that respect, the event took everything from me.

After the attacks on November 13, 2015, *A Moveable Feast* became a bestseller in France, for a reason that was unrelated to its content, and was linked simply to its French title: *Paris est une fête* (*Paris is a Feast*). People wanted Paris to be a feast, a delight, and to remain one, they wanted it desperately: just as

Hemingway had wanted it desperately, and not completely in vain, one last time, and for himself.

Marilyn and I had dressed for the occasion. I wore a black suit with a round neck collar that made me look like a pastor. Marilyn had put on makeup and had her hair done; she was wearing wine-colored slacks, a white smock, and a Chinese vest we'd bought in Hong Kong the preceding winter. Jon and Pamela were waiting for us, sitting near the entrance of the hotel. They were in shorts and tee shirts, and wore baseball caps. Marilyn looked at me: was that how Americans dressed for a wedding, even if it was merely symbolic? After a moment of confusion, Jon understood that we didn't understand. The marriage was to be the next day. Today, we were going to walk around Paris, do some scouting, as for a film, and select the place where the ceremony would take place. They chose the Medici Fountain, in the Luxembourg Gardens.

After leaving them, we walked in front of the gallery where the vernissage to which Philippe Val had invited me was being held. I told him that I'd made up my mind: I would write for *Charlie*. I'd talked about it with Serge July, the manager of *Libération*. He had no objection to my decision. Serge had been my first boss and he had become my boss again: his opinion was essential, but not for the reasons one might think. *Libération* was no more an ordinary enterprise than *Charlie* was. Freedom reigned there, and it was almost impossible to force anything on anyone. In sum, at *Libération,* the old slogan was still alive: it was almost forbidden to forbid. Those who opposed Serge or the people he had appointed emphasized the "almost," sometimes protesting that it implied censorship. They were right, and he wasn't wrong: that was the game. In reality, *Libération* was a site of power without authority. Conflicts were sometimes violently expressed under Serge's shadow, who was sometimes close and sometimes distant, like a wild animal. There were winners and losers. Serge was never on the losing side. Although this was not likely to please ordinary morality, it was a great virtue. He didn't like failure and in his view, those who lost had lacked intelligence, luck, energy, or all three. Everyone else did more or less what they wanted, what they liked: it was an intimidating pleasure to learn one's trade in a place where people were so high-strung and surprising. Thus the paper consumed the troops it strengthened, and this implacable movement made it possible to grasp the movements of society. There were many deaths at *Libération*, many more than elsewhere. Life went on.

At the time when the paper was on Rue Christiani, on the eastern slope of Montmartre, I had often seen Serge dining alone, with his newspapers, in a little Greek restaurant. His stubborn silence and stoniness seemed to me admirable: despite his power and his connections, he remained solitary and, in short, at war. His love of the cinema, his taste for Stendhal, his metallic intelligence, his independence of mind, his cold violence, and his lack of sentimentality—all that had shaped and impressed me enough that the slightest of his opinions was important to me. He would never have forbidden me to write for *Charlie*, but he might have advised me not to do it. He would have done so with a stern look. I would have felt pinned behind glass and I wouldn't have gone there. In the gallery, Philippe Val told me: "Your column, you do what you want with it. Try things out, transgress, experiment, invent forms. That's what you're there for." And whatever talent I might have, that's what I tried to do.

The next day, Marilyn and I met the Americans again in the early afternoon. This time, they were dressed up. Jon wore a black suit and a bow tie; Pamela, a long, cream-colored dress. They were not supposed to see each other again before the wedding. Marilyn took Pamela to her hairdresser's, and I went for a walk with Jon. In the metro, the previous evening, he had talked with a young Siberian guitarist who was begging and played very well. The guitarist was supposed to meet us in the late afternoon at the Medici Fountain. He showed up at the appointed time. He had extraordinarily light-colored, soft eyes and looked like a deer. In the distance, we saw Marilyn and Pamela coming, adorned and smiling. I had bought champagne and goblets—cheap ones, but they were glass. The couple stood in front of me. I had my back to the fountain. Marilyn photographed us. I read my speech in mediocre English. I have lost this speech, and no longer remember it, but I nonetheless recall part of it, a rather emphatic part. After referring to Hemingway's book, I expressed the wish that Jon and Pamela might experience as long as possible all the love whose abandonment the writer seemed to be regretting before he died, at least on the page. He'd given up the best and most intransigent part of himself, he told us, that hard kernel that is evinced and sometimes lives on in literature, in art, and by doing so he had begun, step by step and no matter what the quality of his work, to tread the path to suicide. This path was, in reality, marked out from the day he left Paris and his first wife, Hadley, to become the tiresome, aggressive, and masochistic figure known as Papa Hemingway. Did I use the word suicide? I don't think so. The constraint of happiness hovered over the fountain. The Siberian guitarist began to play. Marilyn shed a few tears. A guard approached to tell us that all unauthorized private events were forbidden in the Gardens. Marilyn convinced him to be a little less stupid. I watched her speak as I finished my sermon. The guard moved away, but kept an eye on us, as if Marilyn might have been lying about the meaning of what he was seeing. Passersby observed us with ostentatious discretion. We filled the goblets with champagne, and then Jon and Pamela put one on the ground and, in accord with the Jewish custom, smashed it underfoot. Marilyn and I were happy. Life and love were before us, before them, it was a fine spring day and it would never end:

this little affair, of which we were the witnesses and improvised actors, was the proof of that. The same evening, Jon and Pamela took us to dinner, along with the Siberian guitarist, at a restaurant near the Panthéon. The cuisine was traditional French. I had *confit de canard*. I never saw them again. Four years later, Marilyn and I divorced.

I would have had a cup of coffee, but *Charlie*'s coffeemaker often didn't work, or I arrived too late to get any. They were talking about Houellebecq. At first, I wasn't listening, because I was thinking about Shakespeare. I generally left *Charlie*'s offices around 11:30 to go over to *Libération*, fifteen minutes on foot or five minutes by bike, where I walked on their blue carpet, which was as stained as an apron. It had not been changed since it was laid down in 1987—hey, I was there. If a democracy is judged by the state of its news media's finances and offices, France was a democracy in bad shape. We pretended not to know how much that was the case, probably because we couldn't do anything about it. With these two newspapers, I experienced the same thing, in accord with different processes, but for similar reasons: the weaker they grew, the more they were trampled on—reflecting people's tendency to curse the defeated, thumbs down, before they forget them.

Charlie was important until the affair of the caricatures of Muhammad in 2006. This was a crucial moment: most newspapers, and even some famous for their graphics, distanced themselves from a satirical weekly that published these caricatures in the name of freedom of expression. Some of them did so out of a declared concern about good taste; others because speaking truth to Muslims might drive them to despair. One seemed sometimes to be in a tearoom, sometimes in a Stalinist cell. This lack of solidarity was not merely a professional and moral disgrace. By isolating and pointing the finger at *Charlie*, it helped make the latter the Islamists' target. The following crisis estranged the paper not only from a large part of its far-left readers, but also from the cultural high priests and trendsetters who, for a few years, had made it fashionable. Thereafter, its decline was punctuated by a series of new locations that were sometimes ugly and sometimes far away, and that seemed intended only to make us long for our old home on the Rue de Turbigo, in the heart of Paris, with its big meeting room and plate-glass windows. The most dismal location was on one of Paris's outer boulevards; it was set afire by a Molotov cocktail thrown one night in November 2011. We met on a cold, gray morning in front of what remained of the building, the firefighters' water having completed the destruction that the fire had begun. Our archives had been transformed into black sludge. Some people wept. We were overwhelmed by a violence that we did not fully understand, and that society, on the whole—except the far right, whose reasons and goals we could not share—refused to acknowledge. The perpetrators were not known, but there was hardly any doubt regarding their motivations.

On January 7, 2015, around 10:30 A.M., few people in France were prepared to say "I am *Charlie*." We had entered a new age and couldn't do anything about it. The paper was no longer important, except for a few loyal readers, for Islamists, and for all kinds of more or less civilized enemies, ranging from boys in the suburbs who didn't read it to the perpetual friends of the wretched of the earth, who liked to call it racist. We had sensed the rise of this narrow-minded rage that transformed social struggle into a spirit of bigotry. Hatred was an intoxication; death threats were common; filthy e-mails were numerous. I sometimes encountered a newspaper seller, generally an Arab, who claimed, with a defiant look that seemed to avow the lie, that he hadn't received the paper. Imperceptibly, the atmosphere was changing. A time came, probably after the arson of 2011, when I stopped, not without shame, reading *Charlie* in the metro. We attracted malign feelings like a lightning rod—which did not make us, I admit, either less aggressive or more intelligent: we were not saints and couldn't hold other people responsible for the fact that *Charlie*'s state of mind was out of date. At least we knew it and continued to laugh about it. One evening, Charb said to me in an Auvergnat restaurant he liked: "If we start respecting people who don't respect us, we might as well close up shop." Then we went on drinking red wine as we ate our beef, saying to hell with religions and conservatives' great fear that we sensed was rising. Since we no longer felt the need to prove anything to anyone, the Wednesday meeting had become once again the free and convivial time it had ceased to be at the end of Val's time as editor and then manager, and during the crisis that followed his departure. Again, I felt, on the occasion of this crisis, what a gift the far left had for scorn, fury, bad faith, a lack of nuances, and degrading invective. In this regard, at least, it was in no way inferior to the far right. I continue to wonder if, in this process of deformation, it is convictions that deform character, or character that deforms convictions.

Bernard Maris began to say how good he found *Soumission*. Houellebecq had become his friend, and Bernard's admiration for him was clearly accompanied by affection. I suddenly wanted to go to the lavatory, but I held myself back; the conversation was getting animated. Cabu grumbled: "Houellebecq is a reactionary." I had not yet read the nasty text Houellebecq had written about him many years earlier, and I still wonder if Cabu had read it, or if he remembered it. But I know he had not read *Soumission*. Bernard and I were the only ones who had, and we were the only ones defending it. Most of the others kept quiet or attacked it.

I got irritated again. Even here, where everything was permitted and even required, I hated discussing books I'd read with people who hadn't read them. I hated even more, be it said incidentally, the lecture on literature I was getting ready to deliver. It was a useless lecture, because the subject under discussion was not the book, but its author's opinions and provocations—his pedigree, so to speak. Now, this pedigree was not really in doubt: what Houellebecq was attacking almost systematically was in fact everything for which *Charlie* had fought during the 1970s: a libertarian, permissive, egalitarian, feminist, anti-racist society. His novel was clear on that point: Islamism without violence was ultimately not so bad. It put men and women back in their places and if that did not deliver us from evil, it at least rid us of the fear of being free. Of course, as he had said on France Inter, it was a novel: all points of view were expressed in it without it being possible to assimilate any one of them to that of the author. However, an aroma emerged from it, an aroma that corresponded to the period. It was he, Houellebecq, that pop icon, who was radiating that aroma with his talent as a narrator and his effectual ambiguity. He had been able to give form to contemporary panics. *Charlie* is one of my two newspapers, I thought, but a good novelist is always right, because he's the one we read or will read. So I think I did indeed deliver, with Bernard Maris, that *explication de texte*, that defense and praise of Houellebecq, performed before the clear, tender eyes of Sigolène Vinson, whose good will reassured me. Had she come that morning, she who was as delicate as a fawn, on her big Harley-Davidson? I hadn't seen it in the street when I was locking up my bike. Bernard talked, I talked, Cabu grumbled, Wolinski smiled as he drew. I wondered whether I wasn't going to end up in his notebook, across from a naked woman who would be saying to me, more or less: "Shut up!" in a form that I was incapable of inventing. Instead, he was probably drawing another nude inspired by Sigolène, whose charm and figure delighted him. He invented creatures that were beautiful enough, sexy enough, to tell him freely, insolently, everything he would have liked to say or hear. Beauty has that kind of privilege.

I no longer know either how or by whom the discussion was turned from Houellebecq's novel to the state of the suburbs, but I imagine that the Muslims provided us with a natural transition. "How did we get here?" someone asked. "How were we able to allow whole population groups to go off the rails like that?" It was Tignous, I think, who attacked the left and the policies conducted for the past thirty years. Bernard Maris reacted immediately: "No! It's not the state's fault! It has dumped tons of money on the suburbs. It tried everything, and nothing worked!" Tignous raised his voice. He talked about the suburb from which he came, Montreuil, and about his childhood friends. Several of them were dead, in prison, or broken: "I managed to get out," he bellowed, "but what about them? What has been done for them, so that they have a chance? Nothing! Nothing has been done. And nothing is being done for their successors, all those guys who have neither a job nor anything else, who hang around in the housing projects and are doomed to become what is made out of them, Islamists, madmen, and don't try to tell me that the state has done everything for them. The state hasn't done anything at all. It's letting them die. It hasn't given a shit about them for a long time!" I'm summarizing a tirade that was far more cutting, angry, and sharp, came from the heart, was delivered holding a pencil in the air, and was transformed by the cartoonist's popular accent into a furious scream on behalf of the forgotten people of the disadvantaged suburbs, the unemployed, the robbers, the North Africans, the Muslims, the terrorists. Bernard kept silent and I thought it was time to leave.

CHAPTER 4
THE ATTACK

It was 11:25 in the morning, perhaps 11:28. Time disappears just when I would like to recall it down to the second, like a tapestry woven by a Fate named Penelope, the whole of which depends on the slightest point. Everything is connected, but everything falls apart.

I got up and put on my pea coat. It was time to go back to *Libération* to write about *Twelfth Night*, but first about *Blue Note*, the big book on jazz that I'd put in the knapsack that I'd brought back from Medellin, in Colombia, five years earlier. It was a little bag in black fabric, very light, on which caricatures of national celebrities were reproduced. I was seldom without it. It has disappeared.

This bag had been given me by the writer Héctor Abad, the author of a book on the life and death of his father and the tragic history of his country, *El Olvido que seremos* (*Oblivion: A Memoir*). We were in the used bookstore that he had founded over there along with a few friends. I have learned that since then it has moved, for lack of money. I've always loved little bookstores where used books invade everything, to the point of seeming to take the place of air. They are cabins in the depth of cities, in the depth of the woods. It seems to me that nothing bad could happen there: a labyrinth without fear or danger. This was a small one called Palinurus.

Palinurus was Aeneas's helmsman. Apollo makes him fall asleep as he is guiding the ship through the night. Falling into the sea along with part of his steering oar, he washes up on land and is killed by savages. His shade wanders through the underworld, where Aeneas meets him again. He had believed that his helmsman simply drowned. Palinurus's shade tells him how he really died. One has to rejoin the dead to learn how far they have gone, but on that day, at 11:25, perhaps 11:28, with my bag in black fabric on my shoulder, I still didn't know that. Neptune had promised Venus that Aeneas and his men would arrive unharmed at the port of Avernus, but this immunity came at a price: "One shall be lost, / but only one to look for, lost at sea: / One life given for many."

Héctor Abad's father, a militant democrat, was assassinated by paramilitary killers on a sidewalk in Medellin in 1987. His son got there almost immediately. In a pocket of his father's suit, he found a poem attributed to Borges, which begins with this verse, from which his book takes its title: "We are already the oblivion we shall be." That is the talisman and last trace, the last mystery of the dead man. Since it is not to be found among Borges's works, its authenticity has been contested. Hector seeks, from one end of the world to the other, its uncertain origin. His quest is the subject of a second book, *Traiciones de la memoria* (*Treasons of Memory*). Determining whether it is a counterfeit becomes an essential question. That is the message that his father has left him, in spite of himself. The investigation into the traces of a life suddenly interrupted is what remains when death has carried off those whom we miss and what leaves us, in a way, alone in the world. An investigator of this kind is often criticized for his obsession, because one cannot, after all, criticize him for his sadness and distress—at least, not immediately. Those who are not obsessed, those who move on to other things, the elegant and the indifferent people, do not belong to the world in which he has to live. There are, of course, many ways of revising, over and over, the account of one's own sorrows. But just as at school, once the composition has been turned in, not everyone has an eraser to efface what has taken place.

This little bag always reminded me of Hector, his book, his father's death, the life and death of the drug trafficker Pablo Escobar, Borges's poems, and the beauty of Medellin's valley. With him, I always felt here and elsewhere, open to all humanity, and I had the feeling that I could return at any time to Colombia, that country where the worst things had been done amid the most extreme beauty. I was about to leave when, seeing Cabu, I took out the book on jazz to show it to him, to show him above all a photo of the drummer Elvin Jones.

In 2004, after I learned of Jones's death, I wrote a column about him in *Charlie*. Cabu remembered the circumstances under which he saw the drummer, outside, at the Châteauvallon Festival. He told me about it and I put his memory in my column: "Suddenly, the thunderstorm breaks out. It is violent. The musicians and most of the audience, everybody gradually disappears, as everyone disappears in *La Symphony des Adieux*; everybody, except Jones. Wild, excessive, beating the time from beyond the tomb, this giant with steel hands gives life to the drumheads and cymbals amid the lightning bolts, alone like a forgotten god, an Asian god with countless arms. The storm seems to have been created by him, for him. He merges with it. He's fifty years old, the thunder remains." That was in 1977. Twenty-seven years later, Cabu made a drawing of it that, juxtaposed with my column, gave the latter a value it does not have, or at least would not have without the drawing. Being "illustrated" by Cabu, particularly regarding jazz, or rather accompanying one of his drawings in writing, took me back to a happy adolescence, the one I discovered along with Céline, Cavanna, Coltrane, and Cabu. It was rather as if, writing in 1905 a novel that took place in the world of dancers, the book's illustrations were by Degas.

If Elvin Jones had not died, I wouldn't have written that

column. If I hadn't written the column, Cabu wouldn't have made that drawing. If Cabu hadn't made that drawing, I wouldn't have stopped that morning to show him the book on jazz that had reminded me of it. If I hadn't stopped to show it to him, I would have left two minutes earlier and I would have run into the two killers in the entrance or on the stairway, I've recalculated that over and over. They would no doubt have put one or several bullets in my head and I would have joined the other Palinuruses, my companions, on the shore with the savages and in the only hell that exists: the one where one is no longer alive.

I put the jazz book on the conference table and said to Cabu: "Here, I wanted to show you something . . . " It took me a little time to find the photo I was looking for. Since I was in a hurry, I thought that I should have marked the page; but how could I have done that, since I didn't know, one minute earlier, that I was going to show it to him? I didn't know if he would be there that day—even though he rarely missed the Wednesday meeting: Cabu had drawn countless dunces, but he was no truant.

The photo of Elvin Jones dates from 1964 and covers pages 152–153. He's lighting a cigarette with his right hand, which is simultaneously enormous and delicate, and holds two crossed drumsticks. It's a close-up. He's wearing an elegant, finely checked shirt, slightly open at the neck. The sleeves are not rolled up. His eyes closed, he draws on the cigarette. Half of his face, powerful and angular, is framed in the upper triangle of the two drumsticks, as in the forms of a cubist painting. The photo was taken during a recording session for Wayne Shorter's disc, *Night Dreamer*. Cabu found it as beautiful as I did. I was happy to show it to him. Jazz was, ultimately, what brought me closest to him. As for the book, he knew it already.

We leafed through it and I closed it when Bernard, coming up to me, said, "Don't you want to write your column on

Houellebecq?" I was responsive to his enthusiasm, which was always announced by a broad, benevolent smile, to the peculiar candor, not without cunning, that arose from his bursts of fellow feeling and perpetual curiosity, but I replied, more or less, "Definitely not! I've just written in *Libération* what I thought of him, and I've no desire to suck that tit again." From the other end of the table, Charb said: "Oh, please, suck that tit again for us . . . " There were a few smiles, and it was at that moment that a sharp sound like a firecracker and the first screams in the hallway interrupted the flow of our jokes and our lives. I didn't have time to put the jazz book in my little black bag. I didn't even have time to think about it, and then everything ordinary disappeared.

When one doesn't expect it, how long does it take to sense that death is coming? It's not only the imagination that is overwhelmed; it's sensations themselves. I heard other little sharp sounds, not at all the noisy detonations in movies, no, dull firecrackers without reverberations, and for a moment I thought . . . but what did I think, exactly? If I wrote something like: for a moment I thought we had unexpected visitors, perhaps undesirable ones, even absolutely undesirable, I would immediately want to correct it in accord with a grammar that no longer exists. I would bring together all these clauses and, at the same time, distance them enough so that they no longer belonged either to the same sentence, the same page, the same book, or the same world. Like the others, I had probably already slipped into a universe in which everything happens in a form so violent that it is thereby attenuated, slowed down, as it were, consciousness no longer having any way of perceiving the instant that destroys it. I also thought, I don't know why, that it might be kids, but "thought" isn't the right word, it was merely a succession of little visions that immediately evaporated. I heard a woman cry, "But what . . . ," another woman's voice scream, "Ah!," and still another voice shout in rage, more stridently, more aggressively, a kind of "Aaaaah," but I can identify that voice, it was Elsa Cayat's. For me her cry meant simply: "Who the hell are these asshooooles?" The last syllable stretched from one room to the other. In it there was as much rage as fear, but there was still a great deal of freedom. Perhaps that was the only moment in my life when that word, freedom, was more than a word: it was a sensation.

I still thought that what had taken place was a practical joke, though I already sensed that it wasn't one, but without knowing what it was. Like lines on tracing paper inexactly superimposed on a drawing that has already been copied, the lines of ordinary life (of what in ordinary life would represent a farce or, because this was the place for it, a caricature) no longer corresponded to the unknown lines that came to replace them. We were suddenly little figures imprisoned within the drawing. But who was doing the drawing?

The irruption of naked violence isolates a person from the world and it isolates others from the person who is subjected to it. In any case, it isolated me. At the same moment, Sigolène's eyes met Charb's and she saw that he had understood. That is not surprising: Charb had few illusions regarding what people are capable of, he was never dramatic, never pompous, and that is also why he was often so amusing. He undoubtedly did not need the few seconds of life that remained to him to comprehend what kind of pathetic comic strip these two empty, hooded heads bearing bigotry and death came from, to see them as they were before they disfigured him.

Already, I no long saw anything or anybody except, across from me, with his back to the entrance at the other end of the little room, the silent Franck, Charb's bodyguard. He was there because it was his job and, it seemed, his habit. Threats destroy the ordinary perception of life only when they have been fixed by acts. Similarly, bodyguards seem useless, except as ghostly, benevolent escorts, until the day when one would have preferred to see them be good for something, indeed for everything. I saw Franck stand up, turn his head and then his body toward the door on the right, and it was then, observing his actions, seeing him in profile drawing his gun and looking toward that door opening on something unknown, that I understood that this was not a joke, or kids, or even an aggression, but something entirely different.

I was still unable to determine the nature of that something, but I felt it invading the room, preceded by sounds and screams, and slow down absolutely everything around me and in me, creating a void and a suspension. Someone had come in and was spreading that something, but I knew neither what it was, nor how many someones there were—and I was to know that only several days later. I watched Franck drawing his gun with a twofold feeling of hope and panic, but this hope and this panic were numbed, foggy: starting with the moment when Franck's body became the last living image to occupy my visual field, every sensation is combined with the inverse sensation, like Siamese twins who would die if they were separated, like two children balancing each other on a seesaw. I didn't know what this thing was that was enveloping us, but I sensed that Franck was the only one who could save us from it. I sensed that, but at the same time I sensed that he would not succeed and I thought: "You have to draw faster. Faster! Faster!" without knowing exactly why he had to draw his gun. I had never spoken to him, and without speaking, in what might resemble a dream, I addressed him using the familiar *tu*. And while I was beginning to hunch my shoulders and turn toward the right and the far wall and its nonexistent windows as if to escape or no longer see anything, I saw him over and over acting more and more slowly, turning his torso and putting his hand on his gun and looking toward the door through which the sounds were coming in. "Faster! Faster!" But it was

I who was slowing down. Something repeated the scene, slowing it more and more, repeated it and drew it out as if it had
been simulated, or deserved to be, like this text, perpetually
revised. Franck's movement endlessly accompanied my fall, in
order to slow it, to keep what followed from happening. But
what followed had already happened. I heard more and more
clearly the sharp sound made by the bullets, one by one, and,
having curled up, no longer seeing anything or anyone, as if
jammed into a box, I knelt and then lay down on the floor,
slowly, almost carefully, as if for a rehearsal, thinking that I
mustn't, in addition to all the rest—but what rest?—hurt
myself as I fell. It was probably in this movement by stages
toward the floor that I was hit, at least three times, directly or
by stray shots. I had felt nothing and was not aware of having
been hit. I thought I was unharmed. No, not unharmed. The
idea of a wound had not yet made its way to me. I was now on
the floor, on my stomach, my eyes not yet closed, when I heard
the sound of the bullets move completely out of the realm of
practical jokes, childhood, and cartoons, and come closer to
the box or the dream where I was. There were no volleys. The
man who walked toward the back of the room and toward me
fired a bullet and said: "Allah Akbar!" He fired another bullet
and repeated: "Allah Akbar!" With those words, the impression of being the object of a practical joke returned one last
time and superimposed itself on that of experiencing this thing
that had made me see Franck draw his gun again and again a
few seconds earlier, a few seconds but already many more,
because time was sliced up by each step, each bullet, each
"Allah Akbar!," the following second expelling the preceding
one and relegating it to a distant past and even very much farther, to a world that no longer existed. This thing had put me
on the floor, but the joke continued with this cry in a voice that
was almost gentle and that was approaching, "Allah Akbar!"
—this cry, a demented echo of a ritual prayer, became a replica

of a Tarantino film. It would have been easy, at that moment, to understand the fascination inspired by abjectness; to sniff out how those who justify it feel stronger, and those who try to explain it, freer. But it was easier to feel, at that moment, how much this abjectness transcended these disquisitions and these arguments. They belonged to ordinary wretchedness and pride, to common time and logic; no matter how fiery and degraded it might be; abjectness did not. It was a genie that came out of a black lamp, and it didn't matter whose hand had rubbed it. Abjectness lived without limits and by being without limits.

There were more shots, more seconds, more shouts of "Allah Akbar!" Everything was simultaneously foggy, precise, and detached. My body was stretched out in the narrow passage between the conference table and the back wall; my head was turned to the left. I had opened an eye and saw appear, under the table, on the other side, near Bernard's body, two black legs and the tip of a rifle barrel that were floating more than they were moving forward. I closed my eyes, then opened them again, like a child who thinks that no one will see him if he plays dead; because I was playing dead. I was that child that I had been, I was him again, I pretended to be a dead Indian, telling myself that maybe the owner of the black legs wouldn't see me or would think I was dead, and also telling myself that he was going to see me and kill me. I expected, at the same time, both invisibility and a coup de grâce—two ways of disappearing. I still thought I was unharmed. But I was wounded, and sufficiently immobile, with my head probably lying in a pool of blood that was already large enough for the killer, as he approached, to decide that he didn't need to finish me off. I suddenly sensed that he was almost over me, and I closed my eyes, but immediately opened them again, as if, to see a few parts of his body and the rest of the episode, I was prepared to take the risk of suffering the end: it was too strong for me. He was there, like a bull eyeing the immobile torero whom he has just gored, the black legs, the rifle pointed like horns toward the floor, wondering if perhaps he should keep on. I heard him breathing, undecided, perhaps hesitating, I felt that I was alive and almost already dead, both at once, one within the other, caught in his eyes and his breath; then he went slowly away, drawn toward other bodies, other capes, other things; in fact, toward the exit, as I found out much later, because the whole attack had lasted only a little more than two minutes. And everything became silent. Peace descended on the little room, gradually eliminating the threat of a continuation or a return of the killers. I didn't move, I hardly breathed. Silence was fabricating time and, among the wounded and the dead, the first forms of survival.

The dead were almost holding hands. The foot of one of them was touching the stomach of another, whose fingers lay on the face of a third, who was leaning toward the hip of the fourth, who seemed to be staring at the ceiling, and all of them, as never before and for evermore, became, in this arrangement, my comrades. It might have been an image of the *danse macabre*, like the one that I had been going to see now and then for twenty years on the path to my grandparents' house in the Nivernais, in the church of La Ferté-Loupière, or a garland of characters cut out of paper by a child, a sort of round with stopping points, or a Descent from the Cross carried out horizontally, or again an unprecedented and dark version of Matisse's painting *La Danse*. I was one of them, but I wasn't dead, and, in the minutes following the killers' departure, I didn't see them that way at first, since I didn't see them at all. My field of vision was reduced to the void that arose from the event and my own immobility or, to be more precise, from my suspension. I had not yet put the label "killer" on the figure I had glimpsed and didn't know whether it had come alone or accompanied. I wasn't fully conscious of the attack, but it had put its blinkers on and was already turning toward the solitary disasters of childhood: at that moment, I was alone among the others and I was no more than five or six years old.

The editorial office was at first a still in a film that was opaque and mysterious, not yet tragic, neither truly begun nor truly finished, a film in which I acted without having wished to, without knowing what to act or how, without knowing if I was the star, a stand-in, or an extra. The abruptly improvised scene floated in the ruins of our own lives, but it was not a projectionist's hand that had stopped everything: it was armed men, it was their bullets; it was what we hadn't imagined, even though we were professionals in aggressive imagination, because this was simply not imaginable, not really. Unexpected death; the methodical bull in the china shop; the short, cold hurricane; nothingness.

"Nothingness" is a word that we no longer like to use, and I had used it in too many articles because I'd read too much poetry, or read it too late; it's one of those words that swell up in people's consciousness as they grow older, like a dead body in the water, swollen and then split open. It's a state that can be conceived, but is generally used and conceived as one fires a blank, without ever being completely able to apply it to oneself. In that ordinary, relatively ugly room, nothingness could be imagined only as a survivor—ready to describe it or draw it, before moving on to the next text or drawing. But was I, at that instant, a survivor? A ghost? Where was death, where was life? What remained of me? I wasn't thinking about these questions from outside, as subjects for an essay. I was living them. They were lying there, around me and in me, as concrete as a shard of wood or a hole in the wooden floor, as vague as an unidentified pain, they saturated me and I didn't know what to make of them. I still l don't know, and I don't think I'm writing what will follow to discover it or to console myself for having lost, in addition to a large part of my jaw, something indefinable. I am just trying to define the nature of the event by discovering how it has changed my own nature. I try to do that, but I can't. Words enable me to go further, but when one has gone so far, all at once, in spite of oneself, they no longer explore, no longer make conquests; now they just follow what happened, like old, worn-out hounds. They set artificial limits, which are too narrow, on the anarchic crowd of sensations and visions.

On the floor, I took a first look at a few square meters and this world without limits. The rubble consisted neither of dust nor ashes, nor glass, nor plaster. It consisted of silence and blood. I didn't feel the blood, though I was lying in it, I hadn't even seen my own, but I heard the silence, in fact I heard nothing but that. It enveloped me and seized my body to make it levitate above me and the others, levitate blindly and endlessly for a few seconds, a few minutes, an eternity, nearly weightless, weightless, while the earlier man, the one who was already almost dead and who remained lying flat on the floor, said to me: "What happened? Is it possible that nothing happened to me? I'm alive, I'm here? Or not?" Or something like that. The half-dead man added: "He may not have left, the guy who was saying 'Allah Akbar.' Better not move." Everything was still reduced to the appearance of a pair of black legs and the wait for their return.

Otherwise, the words that the half-dead man uttered were quite similar, I think, to those one utters during a dream: simultaneously clear to the dreamer and incomprehensible for the person who, waking at his side, hears them. I was already no longer capable of fully understanding the person I had been, but I didn't know that. I listened to him speak and thought: "What in the world is he saying?"

I was lying on my stomach, my head turned to the left, and so it was my left eye that I opened first. I saw a bloody left hand sticking out of the sleeve of my pea coat, and it took me a second to understand that this hand was mine, a new hand, cut open on the back and revealing its wound between two articulations called metacarpophalangeal joints, those of the index and middle fingers. These are words I learned later, because I had to learn to name the wounded parts of the body, the treatment given them, and the secondary phenomena that developed in them. Naming them was a way of taming them, and of living a little better, or a little less badly, with what they designated. The hospital is a place where everyone's mission is to be precise, in words as in acts.

The voice of the man I still was said to me: "Hmm, we've been hit in the hand. But we don't feel anything." We were two, he and I, he who was beneath me, more exactly, and I levitating above, and he addressed me from below, using the first-person plural. My eye passed over the hand and saw beyond it, a meter away, the body of a man lying on his stomach whose checked jacket I recognized and who was not moving. My eye turned to the head and saw, through his hair, the brain tissue of this man, this colleague, this friend, which was sticking out somewhat from his skull. Bernard is dead, the man I was said to me, and I replied, yes, he's dead, and we merged on him, on the point where that brain was sticking out; I would have liked to put it back inside his skull. I could no longer take my eye off it, because it was through it, at that moment, that I finally felt, understood, that something irreversible had taken place.

How long did I look at Bernard's brain? Long enough for it to become part of me. I had to make an effort to look away and turn my head toward my other arm. I did so very slowly. I don't think we were in agreement, the man from before and myself, concerning the necessity and nature of this movement. There was a discussion. The man from before didn't want to learn the consequences of what had happened, he was wise enough to foresee that the bad news could wait when good news wasn't coming to temper it, but he was nonetheless obliged to follow the man who was experiencing the bad news, he was not in control; without knowing it, he was gradually fading into the new consciousness that was, like sleep confused with existence, emerging.

I turned my head very slowly, again as if the killer were there: like a child who continues to play dead after the departure of the bad guys who were looking for him, and who can't help watching through his fingers what, if he were dead as he pretends to be, he could not see: the dead lying around him after the attack.

I saw in front of me the legs of a man who was not moving and who I thought was dead as well, although he wasn't: it was Fabrice. Like me up to that point, he was probably also pretending to be dead or was waiting for the *coup de grâce*, or he was floating in that space that was not yet completely a universe of pain. My head continued to swivel and came gently to rest on the left cheek. I saw that the other sleeve of my pea coat, the right one, was torn, and then I saw that my forearm was slit from the elbow to the wrist. "As if by a dagger," said the man who wasn't quite dead, and he saw a Rambo-style dagger, long, serrated, very sharp. The flesh was completely open and as he considered the wound he said: "Looks like calf's liver." And he remembered the calf's liver that his grandmother used to serve him when he was a child, on the Rue des Blancs-Manteaux; it had exactly that color and texture, and the man who wasn't quite dead had always greatly enjoyed contemplating it before eating it. "For her cat," he added, "my grandmother bought heifer's liver"—but the blood that was flowing from the wound and congealing in an increasingly dreadful silence, that blood drowned my remembering and I finally thought: "I've been hit in the arm." Farther up, my second hand was also bloody, but I didn't know it, didn't feel whether the blood was coming from the arm or from a wound that I had not yet noticed. All the blood is coming from the same injury, I said to myself, and I wondered if, in this wounding, bones were broken. I ran my tongue around my mouth and felt fragments of teeth floating everywhere. After a few seconds of panic, the man who wasn't dead thought: "Your mouth is full of little bones," and he reviewed his whole childhood through these bits of bone, played out in bedrooms or ash heaps. Then teeth replaced the bits of bone, each had its story connected for the past twenty-five years with my dentist, we had grown old together and, I thought, he'd done all that work for nothing. Panic returned and I preferred to forget everything, the bits of bone, teeth, the dentist, because I wasn't alive enough to completely fall back into childhood or adolescence, into the life that we sink our teeth into, an expression that takes on a comic sense at a time when I was losing the latter, having almost lost the former, and was not alive enough or dead enough to face what awaited me.

I turned my head toward Bernard's body and, looking again at his skull and his brains, I felt for the first time a thorough sadness, thorough because I had the feeling of being each one of his hairs, dampened and stuck to one another by what was coming out of his skull: my whole body, and what remained to me of consciousness, had been put under the microscope. I closed my eyes one last time, as if to erase what had taken place, as if, by not seeing, all that might not have been experienced. I opened my eyes again and Bernard was still there. The person I was becoming wanted to weep, but the one who wasn't quite dead prevented him from doing so. He said: "They've left, now I've got to get up." He said it in the plural, "They've left," as if nothing had happened. The one who wasn't quite dead tried to return to the detail of his habits. He was anxious about only one thing, getting his bag, finding his bicycle, and handing in his pages on Shakespeare. He was looking for his habits and scruples. He was moving from one reflex to another like a chicken with its head cut off.

I gradually rolled over on my side, then rose up with my back against the wall, sitting on the floor, facing one of the entrances. I ran my hand over my neck and noticed that my scarf was still there, but was pierced with holes. In front of me, almost under the table, was Bernard's body, and, right next to it, in the passage and on its back, was that of Tignous. At the time, I didn't see what the police report, which I read eighteen months later, revealed to me: a pencil remained planted right between the fingers of one hand, in a vertical position. Tignous was drawing or writing when they burst in. Tignous died with his pencil in his hand like an inhabitant of Pompeii seized by the lava, still faster, without even knowing that the eruption had taken place and that the lava was coming, without being able to flee the killers by disappearing into the drawing that he was making. Every cartoonist probably drew to have the right to escape into what he drew, just as every writer ended up dissolving himself, for a time, in what he was writing. This dissolution was not a guarantee of survival or even of quality, but it was a necessary stage on the way that might lead there. This time, not only had the right to dissolution been denied the cartoonists, but exactly the reverse had occurred; they had been forced to enter a cartoon they had not imagined, a dark idea of the Belgian cartoonist Franquin, and they never emerged from it again. If the killers were possessed, my dead companions were dispossessed. Dispossessed of their art and their violent insouciance, dispossessed of all life. When Salman Rushdie became the victim of Ayatollah Khomeini's fatwa, the writer V. S. Naipaul refused to support him, on the grounds that the fatwa was, after all, only an extreme form of literary criticism. His sarcasm—far more inspired by his nasty temper and a harsh criticism Rushdie had made of one of his books than by a sympathy with Muslims that he did not feel—was not unfounded: any censorship is indeed an extreme, paranoid form of criticism. The most extreme form could be exercised only by ignorant or illiterate people, that was how things were, and that was exactly what had just happened: we had been the victims of the most efficient censors, those who liquidate everything without having read anything.

The cartoonists hadn't had time to think about the drawing that was closing in on them. Did they think about anything at all? If they did, what did each of them think? I tend to believe that they didn't have time to think about anything, and I, in any case, thought of almost nothing. Fear is perhaps just that: the reduction to the minimum of the gap separating the last second of life from the event that is going to interrupt it, a death administered without advance notice. In this gap, there is not room for much. However, what there is room for doesn't end. All that remains, when one survives, is subject to it.

I don't know how long the silence lasted. But it had settled in to the point that I finally understood that my voices were right: the killers wouldn't come back. I stretched an arm toward my backpack, which was lying on the floor a few centimeters away, I clutched it to me like a little old lady worried about being robbed. Inside were my papers and books, that is, my life at that moment. Later I learned that the room was a pool of blood, but as I said, although I was immersed in it, I hardly saw it. I saw nothing but Bernard's skull, Tignous's face, and Fabrice's legs, without even being aware of the fact that someone else's leg was over me and that Honoré's body was between that leg and the rest, as I was told long afterward. And I saw only my own blood, the natural prolongation of my wounds.

Silhouettes appeared, but I didn't immediately recognize them, they did not come closer, but finally I saw Sigolène, her bright eyes, her delicate fawnlike air. She was trying to approach me, but she couldn't, and I didn't understand why. I believe she was weeping a little, with her habitual discretion, no one is more discreet, and watching her get on her Harley-Davidson was a delicious experience, lightness mounted on power, the whole merged by chic and fragility. But this time we had mounted the *Erlkönig*'s old nag. "Nag" (*canasson*) is a word that might have been found in *Charlie* or in *Don Quixote*. Its fragile trot corresponded neither to the Harley-Davidson ridden by Sigolène, who was looking at me and crying, now I was sure of that, nor to the powerful gallop of an animal that is carrying a child to its death. But that was the word that was appropriate for each of us, for this newspaper, for the old left, for a growing part of this society: nag, nag, they shoot nags, don't they? I noticed that I was short of breath and didn't understand why.

Sigolène finally came up to me. Later, she told me that we had talked a little and that she understood me perfectly. I don't remember what I said to her. I simply recall that she was the first living, intact person that I saw appear, the first who made me feel to what point those who approached me, now, came from another planet—the planet where life goes on.

Her silhouette disappeared, I don't know how, in that murky, noisy, cold beyond located behind the door of the editorial room, and soon located behind the door of the hospital room. It was a beyond where people came and went freely, in a space that was forbidden and far away, they would soon gallop from one vanishing point to another before reappearing before me, for a few instants, like actors on stage, almost immobile, finding their roles and leaving their lives at the door. Sigolène's silhouette moved away and I found myself alone again, for an indeterminate length of time.

In the silence reestablished by her departure, Coco's silhouette appeared. Both of them seemed to have emerged from the coffin into which I'd almost gone. She too is alive! I said to myself. Alive? I looked at the young cartoonist's dark hair and somber eyes as she came nearer, and I was seeing two of her: the man who wasn't quite dead saw her as he had seen her appear, silent, unknown, with her almost Egyptian air, sitting behind the participants in the meeting a few years earlier. The paper's offices were still on the Rue de Turbigo in central Paris. Cavanna was present, with his skeptical chin and his mustache that made him look like a musketeer. The man who was going to have to live looked at her approaching like a creature from another world to which he no longer belonged. She bent down over me. Like Sigolène, she was weeping. I didn't know that she must have opened the door to the killers, who threatened her with their guns and that, although she was not responsible for anything, she had already begun to live with that memory, one of those memories that isolate you and draw you back to a scene that you would like to replay differently, freely, ideally, and that begins over and over in the same way the better to imprison you.

I kept looking over to the right toward Bernard's open skull. Although recalling this image causes me a great pain, I have no desire for it to disappear too soon; I want to live long enough to deny any death and remember this image as long as I can, as best I can, without having to talk about it or repeat it anywhere other than in this text that perpetuates it.

I took my cell phone out of the pocket of my pea coat, entered the password, and ran through the list of contacts. I was in a hurry, but the list was interminable and seemed obsolete. How could I have known so many people whose names I sometimes no longer recognized? And why did these strangers seem to have been joined so quickly, there, before my eyes, by those whom I still knew but who were becoming, second by second, as the names passed by, increasingly vague? Not only vague: painfully vague? The names passed by and the people they designated bid me farewell, and that farewell—silent, as if it had faded away—was like a kind of anesthesia.

Was that the life of a journalist, a man who was fifty-one years old? An existence like that of a comet's tail that went on too long—until I reached my mother's number, under the name "Madre." Who else could I have called, and to report exactly what? Gabriela was in New York, asleep. My brother was in Nice on business. My father almost never used his cell phone. I felt lucid as much· as I felt carried away, without knowing on what that lucidity bore, nor toward what I was being transported. I handed the phone to Coco, and it was then, as I handed it to her, that I saw my face reflected on the screen. My hair, forehead, eyes, nose, cheeks, upper lip—all that was fine and intact. But where my chin and the right half of my lower lip should have been, there was not exactly a hole, but a crater of torn, hanging flesh that seemed to have been put there by the hand of a childish painter, like a blob of gouache on a picture. What remained of my gums and teeth was laid bare and the whole—that combination of a face that was three-quarters intact and one part destroyed—had turned me into a monster. I had a few seconds of despondency, but they didn't last. I put my hand under my jaw, to hold it and to repair it, as if by keeping the flesh of one part pressed against the other the two would join up again, the hole would disappear, and life would continue.

But that's not right: Sigolène told me later, with certainty, that I was already holding my jaw when she came up to me. So I must have taken out my phone and seen my face a few minutes before. Sigolène and Coco are conflated in a ceremony that distributes false memories regarding the event that provoked it. I still cannot bear that confusion: the facts are the only baggage I would have wanted to take with me on the journey that followed; but the facts, like the rest, are deformed under pressure. Violence had perverted what it hadn't destroyed. Like a storm, it had sunk the ship. Memories rose to the surface in disorder, twisted, useless, sometimes even unidentifiable, but with a solid presence. I had hardly experienced the moment before its traces were deposited in disorder on the island where I had washed up, in this little room saturated with paper, blood, bodies, and gunpowder. I had to make an impossible selection, as Robinson Crusoe did with the remains of his ship. In passing, I note that this ship had no name and, on the eve of a hospital crossing and an insular and psychic sojourn on which you may accompany me, dear reader,

I wonder with a certain uneasiness how it was possible for the famous shipwreck survivor to set out on a ship that had not been named. With a certain uneasiness because, at this stage, I don't know how to name my own ship, not to mention my island—or more exactly, my islands. If writing consists in imagining everything that is lacking, in substituting a certain order for the void, I am not writing: how could I create the slightest fiction when I have been myself swallowed up by a fiction? How could I construct an order of any kind on such ruins? You might as well ask Jonah to imagine that he is living in the belly of a whale at the moment that he is living in the belly of a whale. I don't need to write in order to lie, imagine, or transform what traversed me. Experiencing it was enough for me. And yet, I'm writing.

I think I told Coco: "It's my mother's number, let her know!" But she was floating. I started getting irritated, first because she seemed not to understand me, and then because she probably had some reason not to understand me. For my part, I didn't understand what was resisting. Everyone lay dead around us, but that was no reason for the survivors not to communicate among one another. I understood myself, I heard my voice, my words, everything was perfectly clear and I knew what had to be done, but her eyes told me that she was having difficulty following me. My voice was really there, however, where it was supposed to be, the voice that I didn't like and that for once I was glad to hear.

A few bits of broken teeth moved from right to left in my mouth, my tongue played with them like crumbs and I sensed that I might have some difficulty articulating. Coco took my cell phone, looked at the number that was on the screen and repeated: "Is that your mother? I should call your mother?" I said yes. She called and I heard her say: "Hello, it's Coco, I'm a cartoonist at *Charlie*. There has been an attack. Your son is seriously wounded. He's with me, he's alive, he's disfigured."

Did she say that? In my memory, yes, and I believe I remember my reaction: "Don't say that!" Coco spoke with my mother for a few more seconds, I don't know, but she hung up, gasping for breath and weeping. Later, I found out that my mother asked her what had happened and where I was. At first, she thought I was the only victim, and that I had been shot because of the article on Michel Houellebecq. That wasn't true, but after all it wasn't entirely false, either. People who want to eliminate you always have a reason for doing it, and it's interesting to imagine that they aren't wrong.

However, according to Coco, I was the one who said to her: "Call my mother, tell her I'm disfigured!" That's possible. It's possible that having been surprised to find myself, and under the shock of a revelation that left me cold, I asked Coco to communicate what must have seemed to me, in spite of everything, the most important information. If that is the case, Coco understood me perfectly—or, in any case, enough. Why was I to continue to see her hesitating, wavering, as if she didn't understand anything I was asking of her? Was I the one who was wavering, not understanding anything, speaking without knowing it and, like a professional liar but for less presentable reasons, providing myself with an isolating and selective memory? The man who was sifting memories as if a century separated him from the preceding minute, was he the one who was already almost dead, or the one who was beginning to replace him? I didn't know which of the two was living and I don't know which of the two is writing.

The diary my brother kept confuses the retrospective arrangement a little more. He was in a business meeting in Nice at the time of the attack, with his cell phone turned off. He writes: "At 12:10 P.M., the discussion ended, and I took the time to listen to my messages. First, a business message, then the message from 'my brother.' A woman's voice . . . a few seconds of terror: 'Hello, it's Coco. I work with your brother at

Charlie Hebdo. There has just been a massacre. He's disfigured.' For a second, I thought it was a bad joke. It's so unreal. But it can't be a bad joke: the call came from Philippe's cell phone and no one could have made such a joke. I learned later that Philippe, who was conscious, had tried to call us, but not being able to speak, he had handed the telephone to Coco, who had survived the massacre, and pointed to the names of my parents, myself, and the manager of *Libération.*" Did I also tell Coco to inform my brother that I was disfigured? Or did she repeat what she had just said to my mother? Your son is disfigured, your brother is disfigured . . . Why haven't I forgotten that she called my mother in front of me? Why have I forgotten that she called my brother? And why are these questions, which may appear pointless, as important for me as solving of a crime is for a detective who makes his whole life depend on it? Am I simultaneously the detective, the witness, and the victim?

I took my phone back from Coco with a hand that was as nervous as it was hesitant, and looked for Laurent Joffrin's number, listed under the name "Joffrin O.K." because he had changed numbers and I hadn't erased the old one: just as I had trouble getting rid of old things, resembling in that respect my maternal grandfather who accumulated in his outdoor kitchen everything that should have ended up in the garbage can, I found it hard to erase phone numbers that had become obsolete, as if they were going to suddenly be reborn and become useful again, as if everything that belonged to the past was only slumbering and destined, not only to return to life, but also to substitute itself for the lives that had replaced it. Everything was slumbering in a kind of vestibule, in an indeterminate quarantine, and what I had been up to this point might have just rejoined the objects and numbers that deserved to disappear in the gray zone where things of the past, although deactivated, retained certain modest rights to exist. That is what is called obtaining a reprieve.

Among these things, there was my rust-colored cap, bought in New York, and fur-lined gloves that had been given me, a few months before, by an old woman friend. I have never got them back and haven't tried to do so. Eighteen months later, reading the police report written in the hours following the attack, I discovered that the investigators had mentioned, "stuck to the left hip" of Bernard, "an orange-colored cap without any identifying label," and then, "close" to his feet, "a pair of khaki-colored gloves with beige lining lying on the floor and covered with numerous traces of blood": these were my cap and my gloves. Finding them in this report, objectified by it, like little branches cast up on an unknown, hostile shore, a shore whose tall trees hid predatory, armed Indians, stupefied me and literally took my breath away. However, they began to beckon me and pull me toward the existence from which they came and which had come to a conclusion there. So they had ended up like that, near Bernard, like a little, concrete caress along his wounded body. They were the last echo of the presence of things that he would no longer feel. Reading these words, I felt the presence of things as I had never before felt anything on Earth, a presence as intense as it was fragile, established there forever, threatened there forever, destroyed by the event and saved by the sentences in a police report. The gloves and cap constituted a small bridge, made up of the everyday, of words and of perpetuity, between Bernard's body and the life that remained to me. Beneath, there was something else. I reread the police report several times in order not to fall into it.

Next, the investigators noted the presence, between the bodies of my comrades, of a knife of the Laguiole brand that had "a gray handle and a total length of 28 centimeters," and "an aluminum wrapper for a pastry and bits of cake soaked with blood." But where did Cabu's cookies go?

He liked to eat them during or after the meeting, when it

wasn't some stale bread or something like that, wrapped in aluminum foil. Those may have been the only moments when he was not drawing—and yet, even that isn't certain, because he could draw with one hand while nibbling with the other. I often watched him do this with affection and concern, as you watch a child acting until the moment when you realize that he's eighty years old, a phenomenon that means that you are no longer quite twenty years old yourself. Cabu and his bangs were ageless, insofar as he was constantly rejuvenated and illuminated, so to speak, by the drawings that continued and, in a way, justified the bangs. He was like his cookies, his stale bread: his intelligence might be limited, but his genius gave taste to anything. He would always remain an insolent schoolboy, ornery, shy, and extremely talented, who caricatured the fabricators of authority on an old wooden table that was covered with graffiti and who, toward the end of the class, took out his package of cookies to eat one or two, like a rodent in winter, before continuing to remake the worst and the best of all possible worlds, with a sure touch, on one material or another, including his pocket or, why not, the palm of his hand or a shoe sole. In his grotto, everything served as a wall, something on which inscriptions and the shadow of a laugh could be left.

I hadn't eaten anything before the editorial meeting. On that day, Cabu had a pastry, but toward the end he passed around a package of cookies. Were they really his? I don't know. But it was he who handed them to me, and they were my last meal before extinction. A few minutes before the killers entered, I ate one of them, not without hesitation, because I didn't feel I had a right to accept the slightest gift from those with whom I shared so little and among whom I still felt, despite years of working with them, so marginal and so little legitimate, so little capable of waging the slightest combat or remembering the slightest exploit. I hadn't been an adult in the sixties and seventies, I hadn't had to test the freedoms from which I had benefitted. I was a man without abuses among people who had committed some or who, in any case, had recounted, discussed, and drawn pictures of them. This lack of abuses often prevented me from eating Tignous's brioche or Cabu's cookies.

I still remember the smell and slightly buttery taste of this first and last cookie that I accepted. It was on top of my stomach when I arrived in the operating room and it remained there, ready to come up to my lips and end up in the melancholy peacock blue of some basin. Later, every time I went back down to the operating room, there always came a moment when I worried about it, as if having remained stuck there, it was going to come back up into my throat and cause a problem with the anesthesia.

The Laguiole knife belonged to the newspaper. The pastry it was going to cut up had in reality just been bought by Sigolène at the bakery down the street, to celebrate Luz's birthday; we were waiting for him but, fortunately for him, he hadn't gotten up in time to make the meeting. I was so little connected with the paper's everyday life that I didn't know it was his birthday. The attack put lives at the heart of my own life at the very time when most of them disappeared from it.

Coco called Laurent Joffrin, weeping, but his phone was turned off and she gave me a look that said, as if it were her fault: "Forgive me, it's too much, I can't!" I was saddened to the point of tears that Laurent didn't answer, I felt abandoned by my trade. After all, he was my only friend who was also my boss. Once again I looked at Coco's somber, haggard eyes. And again I was irritated, because at that moment I felt nothing other than an impatience to act on the details. I also wanted her to give back my phone: so long as I had it in my hand, I felt autonomous. I was hardly moving anymore, and I was vaguely short of breath, but nothing seemed serious to me, nothing seemed to justify either tears or hesitations. All emotion had disappeared, or rather it was only for others: those who were neither present nor injured. As for the dead, the poor dead, the more time passed, the more I thought with Baudelaire what I have never ceased to feel since that morning: they suffer great pains. And these pains—to which I will return from the point of view of the hospital room where I was soon to land—were not the pains of those who wept over them. They were eternal pains and eternally childlike.

Coco walked away with my phone, as if she hadn't noticed. I would have liked to shout at her to give it back to me, but I no longer had the strength to speak. I saw her put it down on a desk, very far away. Other people came up to me.

Among them was a young journalist from an agency whose offices were next door to those of *Charlie*. Nine months later, he wrote me just as I was finally leaving the hospital to return to what was no longer entirely my home. The subject line of his e-mail read: "The one who looked away." I quote it, because apart from the emotion and compassion that in inspired in me, it reveals how those who have seen things they shouldn't have seen may experience them:

> I take the liberty of writing you this message after reflecting at length about the consequences that doing so might have for you and for me. I am going to speak to you about January 7 and my cowardice. I suspect that it is difficult for you to think about it, so if you wish, you can stop reading this message right here, it won't do you any good. It has been among my drafts for months. Today I'm sending it to you because I can't move on, M. Lançon.
>
> I beg you to forgive me for imposing my account on you, but guilt gnaws at me every day. I write this message hoping—out of pure egoism—to beg your pardon. I will be brief.
>
> On January 7 last year, I was your neighbor.
>
> We were in the office across from *Charlie*'s.

When we heard the shots, we took refuge on the roof. I was the one who filmed the killers running away and shooting at policemen on bicycles.

Once they had escaped, after a few minutes, we went to help the victims. I was, along with my colleagues, one of the first to enter the offices of *Charlie*.

After moving away the tables to make it easier for the paramedics, extricating Simon from his chair, and making the rounds of the editorial offices to guide the young firemen—who were stunned—I saw you. Alone. Out of the way, on a table or a chest, I no longer know. You were in shock, that goes without saying. You couldn't talk, obviously, but your eyes said everything: you were begging for help. Your eyes met mine. And I looked away. Cravenly. I said to myself that I would never get over that image of you, suffering, in my arms or in my hands. I even told myself that you might be going to die and that I couldn't do anything about it. I looked away because I was afraid of you. I chose instead to go help others, those who were less messed up. I comforted Laurent Léger, Patrick Pelloux. I accompanied *Charlie*'s whole editorial staff to our offices. And I left you alone.

Of course, the paramedics were there. Of course, you survived. But no day goes past without my thinking again about my cowardice toward you. Not a day when I don't look in the mirror and see all my limits as a Man. Not a day without thinking of you.

I'm aware that my words are hard and that they might make you suffer more. That is what has prevented me from writing to you up to now. But I can no longer keep this to myself. Forgive me, M. Lançon.

I know that you are suffering. I hope that you will emerge from this murky, gloomy tunnel and return to the light. Life is beautiful, they say.

At first, I was perplexed by this e-mail. I absolutely did not remember him, or our eyes meeting. The preceding months had certainly taught me to live with blank spots of considerable size and of all kinds, and to what point people who approached me might be disconcerted, or frightened, even panicked, by my eyes and my bandaged jaw like a hole into which they might fall. I was not only their friend but also the man who had actually seen the killers and been wounded by them—the man whose simple presence reminded them, in spite of himself, in spite of themselves, without saying a word, how uncertain our lives are, and how bold or reckless it is to forget that. Not remembering anything about this fellow has marked me almost as much as all my memories taken together. I would have liked not to forget anything that I experienced, absolutely nothing, the life of the dead and the rest of my life depended on each detail; but how could I avoid forgetting moments, appearances, that seemed to have been completely erased? How could I live with the attack, if an appearance as important as that one had never taken place?

I wouldn't want to look like a *memento mori* and I don't believe I have the mentality of a priest or a confessor. However, I had to relieve, so far as I could, the man who had written this e-mail, and eight hours later, I simply replied what seemed to me then to be, if not the truth, at least what I felt:

Thank you for your note. There are in fact too many things about January 7 that I remember, but I confess that I don't recall either that you appeared or that you looked away. I was sitting against the back wall, behind Bernard Maris and Honoré. I was not yet completely conscious of what had happened to me. I understood it only when I handed my cell phone to Sigolène, because I saw myself in the reflection. Then everything became clear.

Memory is selective, the more what weighs on it is

violent, the more selective it is, and, I don't know why, it did not select you.

But I sincerely think that you mustn't feel yourself to be either weak or cowardly: it was a horrible situation for everyone, for the survivors, whether wounded or not, and for those who, like you came just afterward. They all did what they could, and if January 7 taught me anything, it's the leakiness of judgments regarding what people do when they are caught up in an event like this one.

After the attack, I was floating in a universe that was both infinitely precise and distant, and at no time did I have the deep feeling of asking for help; I was in another world and at the same time in this one—even if I know, by other testimonies that confirm yours, that my eyes gave exactly that impression.

Subsequently, I experienced two and half months of hell, but in this hell, I was supported and accompanied—by caregivers, family, friends, and colleagues. And I immediately felt myself to be a link in a human chain—and that helped me hang on and finally get through those months in relative peace. Neither joy nor feelings were absent at any time, and since I am a journalist, I had plenty of time to explore and understand a hospital world with which I was rather unfamiliar.

If this message might be of some use, it would be, really, to relieve you. I can't hold anything against you, but I am grateful to you for having written to me.

Cordially,

Philippe

Two days later, he replied:

Dear Philippe,

It's for me to thank you for your message. It touches me in the depths of my being. Thank you for your words and your account. Your absolution is generous and courageous. I find you full of lucidity and—I must say—a rather striking calm.

I won't bother you any longer, I simply hope to have an opportunity to see you again, dear colleague.

As for the rest, I wish you once again all the best.

Thanks.

M.

The calm and lucidity he kindly attributed to me from a distance were, if they existed, merely long survival instincts. As for the rest, had I absolved him? Had I tried to? Troubled, I've reread this e-mail several times. In no case would I have wanted to obtain from the attack, from my survival and experience, a power that their absence would not have given me.

Shortly after Coco's departure, the first aid unit arrived. I didn't see them. I was looking sometimes at Bernard's skull, sometimes at the legs of Fabrice, who I still believed was dead. I didn't see the paramedics, but now I heard their voices: "There, dead! There, dead! There, dead!" This word, "dead!" echoed the cry that the killers had repeated with each shot, "Allah Akbar!" Allah Akbar, dead. Allah Akbar, dead. Allah Akbar, dead. The odiously burlesque couple waltzed within me like lame partners, while the paramedics moved slowly toward me, body by body, following paths that seemed to me as untrodden as they were mysteriously indirect. They looked like mountain climbers planting their pitons, during misty weather, in a crumbling, frozen wall. Their advance, cadenced by the notation, "There, dead!," suggested to me that I was alive, without really knowing either how or why. Would they get as far as me? No doubt, because at no time did I believe that I was going to die—or even pass out.

In the distance, framed by the door through which Franck Brinsolaro had disappeared, his gun in his hand, I saw Patrick Pelloux appear. He was our editorial companion and an emergency physician. He looked at me and said: "Here's Philippe. He's wounded in the jaw!" I no longer know, to tell the truth, whether he said my name. But I remember that I clung like an anchor to his familiar face, tense with the need to act and already crumpled by the rise of sorrow; he too seemed to me already to come from another world, that of people who could stand and who hadn't undergone, as I had, something that they would have to live with from now on. I couldn't have formulated it that way, because everything was limited to sensation, floating, unforeseeable waves of thoughts and reminiscences, and an almost unbearable compassion for the dead and for the living. Weren't they going to be irradiated by the violence that had carried us off? Was it contagious? To what extent was I affected? I didn't benefit from a kind of elevation. I underwent it. Like Baudelaire, who was soon to accompany me like a stowaway during the most difficult moments, I could almost have said:

Derrière les ennuis et les vastes chagrins
Qui chargent de leur poids l'existence brumeuse,
Heureux celui qui peut d'une aile vigoureuse
S'élancer vers les champs lumineux et sereins

Beyond where cares or boredom hold dominion,
Which charge our fogged existence with their spleen,
Happy is he who with a stalwart pinion
Can seek those fields so shining and serene

But only almost. The "stalwart pinion" was weighed down

by an indefinable something, while the paramedics were working on me and, to my great dismay, slitting, with enormous shiny scissors, the sleeves of my beautiful pea coat. I protested, I didn't want to be separated from it, from it or my backpack, or my cell phone, or anything, but the man who was cutting went vigorously on with his work, telling me to remain calm and not move. Once the jacket was off, the man went away and I grabbed my backpack and clutched it to my belly, determined never to let go of it again. I understood that they would soon take me away. On my right I heard moans, at once monotone and insistent, so insistent and so monotone that they seemed false. So someone else was alive there. It was Fabrice, whose wounded legs were hurting. I was relieved not to be the sole survivor, and also something else, but what? I listened to Fabrice's moans and suddenly I understood: they revealed to me that I was not suffering. Neither my right arm nor my hands, nor my face felt the slightest sensation. I looked at them in an attempt to understand this mystery which my surgeon, a few days later, was going to explain with her cheerful, didactic naturalness. I looked at my hands and thought about the articles on Shakespeare and the book on jazz that I wouldn't write that day.

Other men approached. They discussed how to carry me away. The passage was narrow, encumbered by all these dead bodies that mustn't be moved. They took one of the armchairs that was in the room and put me on it, then lifted me up. As I remember it, the chair had legs with casters on them, as is often the case in newspaper offices. Two men carried it, while a third held my legs. I had insisted on keeping my backpack with me. They carried me off slowly, though rather quickly, and for the first and last time I passed over some of my dead companions. Baudelaire concluded his poem *Élévation* with these lines:

Celui dont les pensées, comme des alouettes,
Vers les cieux le matin prennent un libre essor,
—Qui plane sur la vie, et comprend sans effort
Le langage des fleurs et des choses muettes!

Whose thoughts, like larks, rise on the freshening breeze
Who fans the morning with his tameless wings,
Skims over life, and understands with ease
The speech of flowers and other voiceless things.

In being elevated, toward what was I flying? Were my thoughts larks? *Alouettes, je vous plumerai!* I was soaring over my dead companions and understood with ease their voiceless speech. I understood with despair the silence of those whom I was leaving behind, because, at that moment, I was one of them.

I hadn't seen Honoré, who nevertheless lay dead almost on top of me. I hadn't seen Cabu, even though his body was underneath me. But I saw Tignous, lying on his back, his face a little yellow around his glasses, his eyes closed, like a recumbent funerary statue. I didn't see the pencil planted between his fingers, I was fixated on his face and I felt, there, over him, the solitude of being alive. It was the sadness of going toward anything at all, anywhere at all, knowing that he would not be able to follow me. We had never been close, there was only an instinctive fellow feeling between us. The event had bound us together at the very moment that it separated us. We would never be able to benefit from the intimacy that its shadows had forged. To life, to death, as children say, to life in death. I looked at his face as long as I could, and then, turning my head toward the right, I saw Wolinski's body. It was partly leaning against the wall. His face was peaceful, a little sad, his eyes closed, and I thought that he was a splendid old bird, a kind of infinitely civilized eagle, and that the melancholy that he hid so well had caught up with him. The smile had disappeared. The dead don't smile and they don't make people laugh. Georges had joined Tignous and Bernard's skull, and from my flying, jouncing seat I said to them in a certain tone, as if they were alive: "You're lucky, for you it's over. For me, it's just beginning." A little farther on, there was Charb's sailor's sweater, but I hardly glimpsed it before they took me out of the room. This movement spared me the sight of what the killers had done to his face.

In the entrance hall, I recognized my cell phone, lying on a table. I reached toward it and signaled to my bearers, trying to tell them what I was pointing to. One of them looked at me, hesitated, and then said: "What do you want? No time, we'll see about that later," and we went out. I looked at my phone one last time, right to the end, as if my eyes could bring it to me. The moment when it disappeared began a period of four months during which I depended only on others.

I no longer know if I was transferred to the second floor on a stretcher or when I arrived on the ground floor. Outside, it was gray and cold. There were people, noise, and ambulances everywhere, a whole exhausting merry-go-round of the living. For the first time, I felt a sensation that was going to be constantly renewed, with more or less intensity, from one hospital to another: I was emerging from a cocoon where everything was muffled and immobile, where I lived with the dead as I was going to live with the caregivers, deposited in an antechamber with deep, muffled vibrations, in order to re-enter, in the open air, a world that was agitated, indifferent, and incomprehensible, a world where people came, went, and acted as if nothing had taken place, as if their acts had the slightest importance, as if they believed they were alive.

The stretcher was put down in front of a man in uniform, no doubt a fireman. For me, he was a giant. His vertical power and his uniform reassured me. He looked at me, and almost shouted: "That's a war wound!" The word exploded and then resonated like an inward and yet foreign echo, an echo provoked by an episode that invaded me without belonging to me. I was a war victim between Bastille and République, a few blocks from the Russian library, the Italian grocery, and *Libération*, a hundred meters from the bakery where I sometimes bought a croissant after the Wednesday meeting, not far from my bicycle attached to a signpost. I thought: "My bicycle! Like my cell phone, they're going to steal it from me!" I was a wounded war victim in a country that was at peace and I was distraught. I took in the giant's expression while at the same time clutching my backpack a little more tightly, I felt that its incongruity was precious and that I would have to keep it inside and take it with me everywhere like a strange blessing, like a strange curse; take it with everything that it contained that day, my books, my notebooks, my pencils, my papers, my ID photos, visiting cards given me by forgotten people, and even pebbles picked up in a Chilean mine, not far from Gabriela's native town, and that never left me.

In the ambulance, another man sat down alongside me and told me not to move. I didn't obey him and opened the front pocket of my backpack to take out my health insurance card and my identity card: if a few individuals had died or been wounded in me, the one who was an obedient and registered insured person had clearly not. He performed the acts that the administration would have expected of him in normal times, and he performed them with the greatest care, the greatest guilt, as if his registered existence and his administrative future depended on them. While the wounded war victim was taken away, the good citizen Lançon thought: "When I get to the hospital, they'll have to see these papers, otherwise they won't know who I am and they'll take a tremendously long time to reimburse me—if they reimburse me! They'll lose my file and won't reimburse me." The wounded man had not yet entered the hospital before the citizen, that numbered mule, had already left it. I showed the man sitting beside me my two cards, my two master-passes, as if, before the fall of the Berlin Wall, I was going to cross the border through Checkpoint Charlie. He took them and stuck them between my thighs. An indeterminate amount of time passed, I looked at the sky through the window trying to guess, as they do in films, where they were taking me. I wondered if I was going north or south, if I was crossing the Seine. Robinson Crusoe's ship is nameless, and no hospital's name occurred to me.

Later, I was taken out of the ambulance, and the stretcher was rolled into a large room. I—suddenly? finally?—began to gasp and weep at the moment when a brunette nurse with a sweet and concentrated face told me to calm down, it was O.K., I was going to go to sleep, I'd be taken care of and everything would be fine. She placed a mask over my face, she talked to me, I no longer understood her, I felt that I was suffocating, and as panic overcame me, I began to cry, I was five or six years old again, I would always be that age, I was abandoned in the dark and in a faraway land, without parents, without friends, without colleagues, without a wife, without anything, with just this nurse's face, and that's how everything was extinguished.

CHAPTER 6
THE AWAKENING

I woke in the folds of ecstasy, the way I did in Cuba, smelling the fragrance of coffee. I was in my bed, in a good mood. It was dawn. I'd slept well and was going to get up, drink that coffee, do some exercises, take a shower, put on deodorant, read and take notes, and then, after stopping by *Charlie*, go to *Libération* and write my article on *Twelfth Night*. Still half asleep, I saw the day pass before me in the penumbra, as I did almost every morning, but with an unusual precision— an inventory-like precision. It was a day that would never take place and had already taken place.

On the way to the newspaper offices, I stopped at the Monoprix to buy a liquid yogurt that I drank on the sidewalk along the boulevard—and I noticed the yogurt's vanilla smell. I began to mull over the sentences of the article as I breathed in the odors of the city in the morning, the good and the less good odors, to which I am excessively sensitive. A little group of homeless people, always the same ones, was sitting on the bench near the Monoprix. They were emitting husky, violent sounds that were unintelligible for me, and I wondered once again what they might be saying to each other in that tone, with those voices, what their lives might have been like, but I didn't dare approach them or talk to them, out of a concern for my comfort or out of tact, and because I was no longer the twenty-year-old journalist in Lyon whose first significant reporting assignment had been to live on the streets and in the shelters for a few days with a couple of bums. As I tossed the empty yogurt bottle in the nearest trashcan, I remembered those two bums in Lyon, as I did almost every day, as if I had seen them the day before, as if they were there, at my bedside, with their wild-strawberry complexions; one of them was nicknamed "Wild Strawberry," the one who didn't speak. I remembered what they had taught me about begging from the group to which I belonged, the people for whom the city is not a territory of struggle and conquest, a territory without shelter, as it was soon to become for me, for different reasons. I recalled the moment when they had advised me to go home: you're too young and the winter is too hard. They gave me fifty francs to take the train or the bus, fifty francs I couldn't refuse.

I still hadn't moved. In a week, I'd be in New York, at Gabriela's apartment. She'd smiled at me on the iPad's screen just a few minutes earlier, I thought. Her smile was going to return outside the screen, looking out on the East River, and the smell of coffee was immediately merged with that of Gabriela's breath. I smelled them, both of them, one mixed with the other, before I opened my eyes. I will probably smell them until I die, intact, floating, because they've never had as much power or intensity as they did at the moment when they were an illusion and a farewell.

I saw and experienced all that in a few seconds, in twenty years, all brought together by time in a single act, like a bouquet of flowers that one thought had been picked in the fields and that are revealed, in the light of the living room, to be artificial. I was inhabited by the sweet phantoms of love, of the future, and of habit. These phantoms are almost invulnerable, eternity is always behind them and in front of them; but at that moment they were fragile, and suddenly everything vanished: the apartment, the bed, the coffee, the yogurt, the fruit, the bums, the begging lesson, the day, Shakespeare, Gabriela's smile and breath, and everything that had constituted and could have continued to constitute my life.

The man with black legs entered my reverie and began to disturb it, without my being able to recognize or interpret him: I was still the man from before; but something had begun to go wrong. The black legs had moved in everywhere without being invited. They changed the way people looked, their acts, their smells. They put them at a distance, deactivating them like lamp bearers who extinguish their lamps once they have moved away. They pointed me down an unknown path I did not want to take but took nonetheless. One detail suddenly alerted me: I still hadn't opened my eyes when I wondered how I could smell coffee, since I hadn't yet gotten up and my coffee maker was not automatic. It was then, on opening my eyes, that I saw the big recovery room and its pale light, between yellow and green, and when I looked down toward the foot of my bed, I saw, instead of the cast-iron rail and the comforter cover, an unfamiliar yellow sheet on which two bandaged arms and two hands lay. It took me a few seconds to understand that these were mine, and in these seconds that extended beyond the bed all the rest, the attack and the fol-lowing minutes, was swallowed up, and along with it, fifty-one years of an existence that came to an end there, in this return to consciousness, at that instant.

I raised my eyes and on my left, above me, my brother Arnaud's face appeared. Then, and for the first time, I felt that something serious had happened to me, that if the coffee and the rest were a dream, the attack certainly wasn't, and I, the elder sibling, looked at my brother as I had never looked at him before. How thin he was! And strangely pale . . . Had he lost weight and grown pale in such a short time? What was he doing there? All alone? How long had it been since I'd seen him? A few days, at most . . . Now this place's lights had dis-colored him. My brother had been repainted in the colors of my new life and he had been rejuvenated at the same time, out of the very heart of weariness and anxiety, rejuvenated and confirmed in the mission that he accepted and was beginning. This mission was to make him for several months my twin and my practical, administrative, social, private chief of staff. The order for it had been released, despite him and despite me, in this first exchange of looks. I reached for his hand in a twofold demand for consolation: I had to console him and he had to console me, one not being separable from the other, there would be no one-way consolation.

I thought that each of us had only one brother, the other one, and tried to imagine what his life would be like without mine, and, looking at him fixedly, my life without his. Children sometimes do this experiment, in play, to scare themselves and test the limits of their ability to withstand terror—the better ultimately to reassure themselves. The exercise requires indulgence—as when one pushes on a sore tooth in order to verify the pain that one thereby increases, and to have the delicate pleasure of complaining about it by doing it again. What was happening to me was perhaps of the same nature, but it differed in intensity: I wasn't playing, I was being played, and the sight fell on me without my being prepared for it.

When one imagines what is the least imaginable, with unforeseen force and as if detached from oneself, with such force that the scene imagined becomes the only one possible, something bursts in the fragile, sturdy tissue that serves as consciousness: seeing things from the point of view of our twin deaths opened up a field that I immediately sensed, despite my exhaustion, would, if I set out to explore it, drive me just as mad as looking too long at Bernard's brain. I saw my brother dead and watched the rest pass before my eyes: his burial, our ravaged parents, me taking care of them, etc. I saw myself dead and watched the rest pass by, my brother at my burial, our ravaged parents, him taking care of them, etc. In both cases the funeral took place in our village and each of us was buried in our grandparents' tomb, close to that of the writer Romain

Rolland. The scenes detached themselves from me and revolved like wooden horses on a carousel, mixing with one another to envelop and imprison me in their fixity and repetition. The carousel was to return regularly in the course of the following months. It served as the setting for different but recurrent scenes that turned round and round. Some of them made me live through what I feared most; others, the most terrible ones, made me experience what I had lived through and could never live through again: I saw over and over the burial of my past lives; but who exactly was mourning them? I had no idea. It was the field of the worst immediately present, a series of images that cornered me to strangle the remains of my own existence and fill them with uncertainties, with the void. I was becoming what I was seeing and what I was seeing was making me disappear. Just as a flock of crows in a wheat field had one day become, as Van Gogh painted it, the only reality, the reality of the artist with his ear cut off and of the cloud into which he disappeared.

Van Gogh's wheat field appeared for the first time in that moment, during the night of awakening. I closed my eyes to escape it, hoping to go back to the illusion of coffee and Gabriela's breath, to go back to them through reality. But the attack does not allow this kind of fiction: it dissolves any attempt to return to the past. It is the future that it destroys, the only future, its only destruction, and so long as it reigns it is no more than that. I reopened my eyes. My brother was still there and he was alive. I was, too. Van Gogh's field had disappeared. The nurse came in to check my condition and that of the drips. She gave us a small whiteboard and a blue felt-tip pen so that we could communicate.

What relationships do brothers have? What about sisters? How do memories of everyday private life—that of childhood—mix with the gradual drifting apart that generally succeeds it? Arnaud and I got along well, without tensions or conflicts, but without seeing much of each other, except at family meals. Our lives and our friends were as different as possible—two pups from the same litter but of different breeds, who rediscovered their common reflexes only in the doghouse that took them back to the shared time that had been lost. Acquired or innate, this distance was abolished in the recovery room—or rather our intimacy, latent, took advantage of an opportunity to emerge again, an opportunity that we would gladly have foregone. Our parents were still not there, I didn't know whether it was dawn, daytime, or night; Arnaud dealt with my life and my schedule. He did so with the reliability, the diplomacy, and the moral sense that characterized him. Our shared childhood, our vacations, our parties, our inane jokes, our quick, regular lunches in a Chinese restaurant on the Avenue de la République, where we always ate exactly the same thing, the thousand and one ties that linked us without our thinking about them, everything seemed to have taken place only in order to end up there, in that recovery room, the first step in the test that awaited us. The attack weighed on us with such power that there was never any need, over the following months, for commentaries or explanations: its violence and the violence of its consequences simplified everything.

Arnaud had arrived wondering what he would have to cope with. He didn't know to what extent I was affected, conscious, or diminished. He was worried about finding a vegetable or an entirely disfigured man. He found a face that was two-thirds intact. The third part, below, was covered with bandages. One could only imagine the absence of the lip and the teeth, and the hole. The operation had lasted between six and eight hours. The orthopedists waited until the stomatologists finished their work before patching up my hands and right forearm. My surgeon, Chloé, was eating lunch with a friend when she was called. "And do you know what we were talking about?" she asked me two years later. "About Houellebecq! My friend had brought a copy of *Soumission* with her, and gave it to me . . . " Their meal stopped there. Later, she read the book and liked it. What would she have thought of it had my arrival in the operating room not abridged her lunch? When she spoke to me about it, we were in her office, I was no longer in a horizontal position, and we simply laughed about the coincidence, but after all, was it a coincidence? To me, Houellebecq now seemed far away. He belonged to my memories, as he belongs to my book. I wonder who ended up with my copy of *Soumission*, which I lost.

I didn't know what time it was, whether an hour, a day, or a month had passed. Later, I found out that it was midnight. Arnaud said to me in a gentle voice: "We're very lucky, brother. You're alive . . . " It was only on hearing those words that I realized that I could have died, and looking again at my bandaged hands and arms, recalling that my jaw had been destroyed, I wondered why I hadn't. There was neither anger nor panic nor complaint in that mute question addressed to I don't know who. There was only a desire to get my bearings. I was disoriented. I looked at my brother again, felt that I was having trouble breathing. My old body was departing to make way for a mass of sensations that were precise, unpleasant, and unprecedented, but well-bred enough to enter only on tiptoe.

Arnaud was watching me. I found him definitely thin and pale, like the light from which he seemed to emanate. He looked so young, so alone! I was tempted to pity him, take him in my arms; but my arms refused to move. And this time both of us saw ourselves as two brothers who had come close to never seeing each other again and whom the prospect of death had just bound together. I didn't even try to speak. I was not yet aware of the bandages that closed up my face and the tracheal tube (or "trach," as I soon learned to say) or the nasal cannula that was soon going to irritate unbearably my throat and nose, but something warned me that speaking was impossible. The patient senses what he doesn't know. His violated body is an usher. It announces guests, unknown persons, and almost all undesirables to consciousness, which thinks it is the mistress of the house. I made a slow sign to Arnaud, a moribund sovereign's tiny little gesture, and he began to talk to me. About what? It doesn't matter. He was talking to me.

Later I made another gesture. He understood that I wanted the whiteboard the nurse had brought me. With difficulty, I wrote in capital letters: "It's over with Gabriela." With great speed, I'd assessed the situation: she was living and surviving in New York, without money or established status; she was enduring a difficult divorce, which was driving her crazy; her father was slowly dying in the Atacama Desert, reciting to ghosts poems by Pablo Neruda. No matter how strong her love, she would never be able to get through the marathon that was looming. Future events were to prove that I was wrong, at least in part. However, I didn't write that sentence on the whiteboard to ward off what it forecast. I wrote it to relieve myself of the sorrow I felt: to write was to protest, but it was also, already, to accept. The first sentence thus had this immediate virtue: it made me understand how much my life was going to change, and that everything that change would impose had to be admitted without hesitation. The circumstances were so new that they required a man who was, if not new, at least transformed morally, as he had been transformed physically. Everything was determined, I believe, in these first minutes. A mixture of Stoicism and good will defined my attitude for the following months: it found its source in this instant, under that light and in this simple sentence, "It's over with Gabriela." This mixture was not without dandyism: I wanted to appear under all circumstances to be the man I had decided to be, from the operating room to the toilets, from the armchair to the stretcher, from the austere service hallway to the beautiful, shady garden of La Salpêtrière hospital. But insofar as my body was undergoing a sudden and irreversible transformation, this way of being became my second nature, the nature that accompanied it. The necessity of accepting everything, and the duty to accept it with as much gratitude and good humor as possible, with an iron gratitude and an iron good humor, were going to lead me to make immutable the only thing that could, and had to be, immutable: my character in the presence of others. The surgeons were going to help nature repair my body. I had to help this nature fortify the rest. And not to pay the horror I'd experienced the homage of an anger or melancholy that I had so willingly expressed in less difficult days that were now over. I found myself in a situation in which dandyism became a virtue.

I erased the first sentence, and wrote the following: "This little paper that wasn't harming anyone." I was referring to *Charlie*—with a rather flagrant naïveté, the naïveté of a sad, helpless child, but not only that. People like to quote a writer's last words, because they seem to have a meaning that sheds light on his life and circumstances, just as in church. When Chekhov dies saying *Ich sterbe*, "I'm dying," we say to ourselves, "that's really Chekhovian." He says the only thing to say at the moment when he dies. His laconic redundancy liquidates any literary effect. Being in limbo and so little a writer, I was now writing my "first sentences." And since I tend to be pompous and sentimental, the sentence "This little paper . . . " obviously leaned in that direction. So long as our defects follow us, we're still alive, all we can do is shape them. The little sentence followed the channel dug long ago by my paternal grandfather, a charming little man who never meant any harm. He was born in a family of poor peasants in the Pyrenees, near the Spanish border, and he was, as they say, quick to weep; perhaps that came from the melting glaciers across from his village. He was an old radical-socialist, born of the people and remaining there. Although he had died thirty-two years earlier, it was he who held my hand at this moment. He died just as I was beginning the career that was to take me there, to that recovery room, and no one else cold have written, after taking off his black beret and with his cheeks trembling a bit in the smell of strong tobacco, this sentence that is both true and brimming with tears: "This little paper that wasn't harming anyone."

This "little paper" had a great history and its humor had, happily, pained a countless number of imbeciles, bigots, bourgeois, notables, people who took their ridiculous notions seriously. For the past few years, it had been almost moribund; since the preceding day, it no longer existed. But it already existed in a different way. The killers had immediately given it a symbolic, international status that we, as its producers, would have preferred to do without. We didn't want that kind of glory, among that kind of people, but we hadn't been given a choice, and now we had to take advantage of it, of course, and also put up with it. We had become a major newspaper that harmed lots of people.

My brother photographed the sentence and shortly afterward sent the photo to my friends, my colleagues at *Libération*; after all, it was proof that I was alive: I could think, remember, be moved; I could write letters and line up words, therefore I was still among the living. Then I took up the felt-tip pen again and indicated to my brother that my bike was parked in front of *Charlie* and would have to be picked up pretty soon. I saw in his eyes that he was stupefied.

Around 2 A.M., the nurse returned and asked Arnaud to step out. She had to change the neighboring patient's bandages. She took advantage of this to bring me a large salmon-colored notebook from Public Assistance. When he came back, my brother was surprised to see the felt-tip pen attached to the three unbandaged fingers of my left hand and the notebook open on my stomach, on top of the sheets. He kept this notebook and returned it to me a few months later. I open it again and read the big letters shaped hesitatingly, as if written in a foreign language, less by a survivor than by a stranger, an ancestor, almost a dinosaur, on the walls of a cave. The letters, which are capitals, lean every which way on the page. There are only one or two words on each line, as if I were writing in the dark. I take a flashlight and move around the cave through which I returned. I shine the light on these graffiti.

First page: "Who died? / Cabu Wolinski Charb / Riss? / What day? / Who's coming? / My backpack is here with me." I take great pleasure in writing the question marks, in shaping them. They are hooks I cling to. I need to know whether there were more dead than I saw, and who they were. Did I really see what I saw? What didn't I see? I calculate. I check. I'm worried about the idea that my backpack has disappeared, with my books, my notebooks, my papers. I think again about the pea coat ripped apart by the bullets and then by the paramedic's big scissors. The keys to my apartment were in one of the pockets. I think about my bike again. I worry about these disappearances: on top of everything, I may be robbed, dispossessed. I no longer know what my brother said in reply. His own diary indicates that he talked to me, talked to me, about everything and nothing, about what was known regarding the attack, at that point not much, about friends asking for news, about all those who were soon to enter the hospital dance card he was keeping with, I repeat, the mutual understanding of a twin and the efficiency of a superintendent. When he stops talking, I give him a little tap on the elbow. He says: "You want me to talk to you?" I nod, systematically. I want him to talk, about the attack, but especially about the most mundane things, about our parents, his children, for the moment, that's the only thing that connects me to life. Then, even when he doesn't know what else to say, he continues.

He was in Nice on that day, to see customers of the computer company he founded fifteen years earlier. At 11:45, he receives Coco's call from my cell phone, which he doesn't take: he's in a meeting. He is about to go to lunch with his customers when, stepping aside to check to his messages, he listens to the call. Stunned, he looks at the news on his smartphone and learns that there has in fact been an attack at *Charlie*. He calls my parents, who already know. Laurent Joffrin, the manager of *Libération*, has called them. They know that I'm alive, but they don't know either where I am or what my condition is. My brother tells his customers the news and goes to the airport, driving "like a robot," those are the words he uses.

When he lands at Orly, around 4 P.M., he learns from our mother that I was at La Pitié-Salpêtrière hospital. The family has had news through Thibault, a young cousin's husband who had begun his career as an anesthetist in this hospital. His friends are keeping him informed about the progress of the operation, almost minute by minute. The operation is continuing, and Thibault advises my brother not to go to the hospital that night, because I will be too groggy to talk about anything with anybody. In his diary, my brother writes: "It's unimaginable that after what he's been through, Philippe won't see a familiar face and a loving presence when he opens his eyes. I prefer to go there, even for nothing, rather than stay at home." That is the right choice: his presence, by putting me in a state of maniacal and tender lucidity, elicits countless . . . what shall I call them: emotions, reflections? Reflective emotions, rather. I'm emerging from an attack and an operation that lasted from six to eight hours, I'm covered with tubes and bandages, I don't feel anything and I already hurt all over, but I'm obsessed with practical details and the meaning of an experience that I've not yet assimilated, or even, to tell the truth, experienced. Second page: "Cancel / Air France Cancel / Condition jaw / I was supposed to go to NY on January 14 / Cancel Air

France." My brother deciphers these words, repeats them, fills in the gaps as in a dictation. I almost died and I'm thinking about getting my ticket reimbursed by Air France: the petit bourgeois survives everything. Third page, which is probably addressed to the night-duty nurse, because my brother knows Gabriela: "My friend Gabriela is in NY." Fourth page, probably intended for my brother again: "Thanks / It's like a dream / Who is it? / Killer." Here, I can fill in the gaps. I'm thanking him for being there, the first expression of gratitude in a recurrent song that is addressed to everyone and whose refrain was soon to become: "Thanks very much." Until the day when, at the Invalides hospital, three months later, a virulent, comical West Indian auxiliary nurse cut me off, saying: "Why thanks very much? It's too much. Thanks is enough. Be simple, I don't like people who lay it on thick." She's wrong. I'm not laying anything on: I'm trying to be as courteous as possible toward those on whom I depend. And she's right: I had to gradually stop saying "very much," not wanting my courtesy to be confused with the flattery of someone who lives at the expense of those who are listening to him. I'm willing to be a fox, but not so much that I transform my caregivers into crows.

"It was like a dream" are the first words, banal ones, that I used to define the attack. Banal and not entirely true: it was neither like life nor like a dream. It was in a space and a time for which nothing could have prepared us. And this space and this time were not only the contrary of a dream, but its continuation beyond the nerves cut. "Who is it?" refers to the following word, "Killer," which my brother didn't understand at first. It was not yet known who it was, I still thought there was only one killer, the man with black legs, the only one I saw, even if I also thought: "They've left." The following pages inform my brother regarding what he knows (but I don't know yet that he knows): Coco called with my cell phone, and Luce Lapin, the paper's assistant, must be asked to go get it back.

I'm not aware of the fact that this phone has become, like the rest, evidence in a criminal case. Then I return to my backpack: "Arrived here with black backpack / Inside, iPad." And, on the next page: "Marilyn? / They won't be disappointed! / Never lost consciousness." I ask my brother whether my exwife has been informed. The certainty of her sorrow frightens me. How will she handle this? I don't think I'm very important, but I know what unites us. We lived for almost ten years in an almost complete fusion: she's the only one who can understand everything about me that escapes me. "They won't be disappointed!" refers to my parents. The incomplete negation and the exclamation point are not accidental: I am trying to introduce a touch of familiarity into the disaster, as if they were all at the dinner table, a few days ago, with our jokes and good wine; as if I were going to appear with a carnival mask on my face. "Never lost consciousness" is from the outset a circumstance, whether good or bad, which I am proud of. The killer wounded the man, but he missed the witness. So much the better for me, so much the worse for him.

Now, my favorite page:

J'ai touché
Bras et visage Parmi
Les morts et
compris
Adieu Princeton!

I touched
Arm and face Among
The dead and
Understood
Farewell Princeton!

Although I continued to read poetry, it had already been

some time since I'd stopped writing it, other than in the form of verse portraits and occasional doggerel. If you can't become La Fontaine or Rimbaud, the best thing is to apply your residual talent to the circumstances, to pleasure and oblivion. The appearance of text messages has favored this resurrection of a minor mode that has no future. These words written in a recovery room in the depth of the night are perhaps my best poem. They have the merit of being involuntary and, since it's a question of experience, the disadvantage of having demanded a little too much of my life. "Farewell Princeton!", I like this fall that mixes Fitzgerald with Perrette and her milk pitcher, I like it because I wasn't trying to produce it. Farewell Gabriela, "Farewell Princeton!", I wrote that during a sleepless night as a good joke, looking up at the ceiling, whereas I had to say farewell to quite a few things, and the tracheal tube, by drawing attention to its painful existence, was beginning to teach me that I would soon have to accept others.

On the following page, I quite naturally wrote: "Need you / and / Gabriela!" Here the exclamation point has a meaning completely different from the one that follows "Princeton." I'm writing to my family and to Gabriela, who was absent, that I can't imagine continuing without them. But "continuing" is not the right word. I still don't know what it is: it's a matter of a mad series of births—each one crushing the pains of the preceding one under the weight of those that follow them. Moreover, hadn't I written two hours earlier that it was over with Gabriela? At this point, memory is a quickly saturated disk. It erases or modifies what consciousness, which struggles in the present, cannot endure.

The last pages of this first notebook are increasingly covered with words: the mad habit of writing is reclaiming its rights and imposing itself on the wounded body, on the morphine, on every sort of excess, on anything at all. I describe for my brother the moments that followed the attack: "People /

were more / afraid than I was. / I saw it in / their eyes. And my / disfiguration!" Then: "Didn't feel / the bullet. / Played dead. / The guy went by / shouting Allah Akbar!" As I write these words, "Allah Akbar," I feel a dull chill and nausea descending and rising from everywhere. I dissolve myself in it. Allah Akbar stretches out on me just as not long ago Van Gogh's field did, and it is at this moment that I feel how much that expression has become the imitation of a Tarantino character: this religious prayer that I have so often heard in Arab countries, in India, in Indonesia, this prayer that rocked me to sleep and woke me before dawn when I lived near a mosque, this peaceful prayer that broadened the sky when it announced the coming day, this prayer is no longer anything but a cry of death as ridiculous as it is sinister, a stupid gimmick uttered by the walking dead, a cry that I will no longer be able to hear without wanting to vomit in disgust, sarcasm, and boredom. Then: "Didn't move / a bit. / Thought about Gabriela / and parents / Strangely calm." The notebook ends with a statement: "It was ending / I was going to leave!", and this observation: "I saw / the brains / of poor Bernard Maris / under my nose." I weep for the first time at the moment that I write these words in the notebook, this name of a woman that I think I'll never see again but whose presence floated over me, in me, while the black legs were appearing; this name of a companion that I would like never again to write in this context. I was to weep in spite of myself, over the coming months, every time I thought, said, or wrote these names that deposited in me, around me, the presence of the persons whom they designate and who, while the killer was approaching and going away, accompanied me.

My brother left around 4 A.M., and I was able, thanks to potions, to go to sleep. My parents arrived the next morning, just as I was being transferred from the emergency services building to the stomatology building. I hadn't seen them since the preceding weekend. We had celebrated New Year's at their home. Erect and well-dressed, affectionate and a little lost, they came from that other world full of oysters, gifts, memories, and *foie gras*. I looked at them from below and perpendicularly, from the cradle where I could neither cry nor believe that I was going to be reborn, but also from above, like a kind of Buddha levitating over their silhouettes, their pain. They were suffering, I could see that, but I wasn't: I *was* the suffering. Living inside suffering, entirely, no longer being determined by anything but suffering, is not to suffer; it's something else, a complete modification of being. I felt that I was being detached from everything that I saw and from myself, the better to digest it. My parents' faces floated like those of characters I had to create, feed, develop, beings that were intimate and were no longer intimate. I entered with them and through them into this particular fiction that is a sudden excess of reality.

I wrote to them, with a blue felt-tip pen, more or less what I had written to my brother a few hours earlier, with variants that might seem out of place had they not indicated that I was already trying, by every means possible, to take some distance on what I had become. For example: "I played dead / very quickly / I lay down / and didn't move again / All dead around / clear view of the poor man's brain," and here again the name of my dead neighbor and the silent tears that accompanied it. Then I asked them to tell me what was being said. I wanted to be comforted by their voices, as I had been by my brother's, by the tranquil eternity of our relationships, and I became completely what I had never ceased to be, their child. They were eighty-one years old and they were going to enjoy for a few months the extravagant privilege of becoming once again indispensable in the life of their old son, as if he had just been born. I wrote to them, as I had to my brother, that my bank card had to be canceled, the heat shut off in my apartment, the neighbors who had the keys notified, the plants watered in a few days, and so on. Everything involved in daily routines constituted another barrier to the absurd by the absurd: I was the companion of Kafka's poor K's. This tendency was soon to be accentuated. I wanted to do everything well so that I would be irreproachable. I wanted to be in accord with the law. The more extraordinary the situation became, the more I wanted to follow the rules. The more I understood that I was a victim, the guiltier I felt. But what was I guilty of, if it wasn't of having been at the wrong place at the wrong time? That was already a lot, it was too much. I looked at my parents, sturdy, in good health, standing on the right and left of my bed. I was at least guilty of that: of imposing this trial on them at the end of their lives. The killer could have shown a little consideration, if not for me, at least for them. Their old, closed hands, warm and wrinkled, touched me lightly, as if to sculpt me. In their eyes, I felt their strength, their despair, their love, and also, where the bandages were, the blankets in which they would have liked to swaddle me. My father's white beard, carefully trimmed as always, his elegance and demeanor, my mother's apparent placidity and her little affectionate gestures, intensified by her crinkly eyes, all that reassured me. Once again, as in the case of my brother, I would have liked to console them as much as they consoled me. I would have liked to console them for being there, in that big, pallid recovery room where people suffered and sometimes died, alongside a neighbor as tubed up as I was, there and not at home, my mother doing her crossword puzzles, my father reading *Le Figaro* newspaper, a sailing magazine, or an English text, after drinking a cup of coffee while listening to a Bach cantata under the blind eyes of the mask he had brought back from Africa in the 1950s.

I was put on a stretcher. The period of being strictly in the antechamber was coming to a close. This period between dream and sensation, between terror and levitation, the one in which you recall all you have lost and all that is happening to you as if it had been experienced by someone else, but someone else developing inside you like a water lily, this period of cloudy intensity and total submission to what serves as destiny, this suspended *huis clos*, all that had existed for only a few hours, in solitude and with my brother, a little longer with my parents, and was now vanishing.

While I was being moved the pain arrived, the real one, and with it, for an instant, like a red light through a louvered shutter, the perception of the battle I was going to have to wage. I briefly and violently longed for that night in the antechamber, which had given me access to a state that words did not allow me to restore. The last word that came to me was Pilar, the name of the recovery room nurse: it was also the name of the wife of a poet, Jules Supervielle, whose exile's melancholy had enchanted my adolescence, and it was the name I gave, for that reason, to the heroine of my first novel, written under a pseudonym, at a time when I thought myself sufficiently unworthy of publishing to do so under a name other than my own. Supervielle was then forgotten, and my novel enjoyed no success, but that didn't matter because I no longer knew much about the man who had written it. But this name, Pilar, resurfaced with the no-nonsense emergency room nurse. It returned between the pages, between the dreams, between the dead, through the fictive smells of coffee and Gabriela's breath, and through the very real smells of antiseptics and disinfectants. The novel was entitled *Je ne sais pas écrire et je suis un innocent* (*I Don't Know How to Write and I'm an Innocent*). That was a verse by a Cuban poet. Eleven years after its publication, the title was finally justified: I was in a state and a situation that made me an innocent, in the strict sense of the word, and I would have to slowly overcome, if it was possible, the feeling that I didn't know how to write anything about what was happening to me. I would have to do that simply to relearn how to live.

My parents accompanied me in the ambulance that took me to the other end of La Pitié-Salpêtrière hospital. It was a patchwork city, the product of three and a half centuries of architecture and of police and public health policy that seemed intended to justify a course of lectures given by Michel Foucault. I didn't see anything through the blocked windows. The building where the stomatology department was located was at the opposite end from the main entrance, way at the back, not far from the elevated metro line. It must have been constructed in the 1960s. It was particularly ugly. I was moved into a room on the second floor.

On January 8, entering room 106, among the tubes I thought of one of Pascal's sentences. It was a true cliché, but I'd read a lot of Pascal when I was a teenager, at the time when you forget almost nothing and believe almost everything, good or bad, that falls into your hands. You repeat it as a mantra and when, thirty-five years later, you find yourself in the hospital after an attack, that's what occurs to you: "the sole cause of man's unhappiness is that he does not know how to stay quietly in his room." So I must begin by admitting that despite the suffering, the anxiety, the nightmares, the waiting, the disappointments, the sight of my wounds, one operating room after another, and the feeling that I no longer had any future outside my room, I felt a certain happiness in residing here without a telephone, without television, almost without radio, under permanent police guard, and with systematically filtered visits. The orientation of the battle had been simplified.

This happiness was the fragile happiness of a little, power-less king, immobile and improvised, but a king all the same, finally left to himself and to his own resources, without distractions or pointless meetings, and accompanied solely by his caregivers, his family, and a few friends, books, a computer, and music; the happiness of a king who had to render account, ultimately, only to one god, his surgeon, and to a single Holy Spirit, his health. It was almost the happiness of Captain Nemo in the *Nautilus*, but a happiness without bitterness, without anger. My sorrow was sympathetic toward my hosts, and I had no scores to settle with the human race. This was not the happiness desired by Pascal, however, because there is no peace in a hospital. In any case, there was little peace for me and in the department where I was. A hospital is a place with a tight schedule, where everything is action, tension, discipline, and nervous crisis, as in the army; a place where, during the first three months, I became, because I had no choice, a bedroom athlete.

Put under house arrest after a duel, the military hero of *Voyage autour de ma chambre* (*Voyage Around My Room*), the novel that Xavier de Maistre published in 1794, takes his reader on a tour of his room for forty-two days. I quickly counted the number of paces it would take me to cover in one direction and the other the hospital service corridor where I had landed: fifty-two. I counted them until I grew dizzy, but up to that point I hadn't yet counted the days spent in my rooms at La Salpêtrière and then at Les Invalides. I can at least, for starters, count the rooms, five, in which I stayed at this time that seemed to me as recent as it was prehistoric. Recent and prehistoric: you'll have to get used to this contradiction, reader, because since the attack, it's exceptional when, in feeling or thinking something, I don't immediately feel or think the opposite. The closed world of the hospital developed a kind of wild, spontaneous dialectic that survived it and that shatters any horizon line. I can no more rid myself of it than I can of the sensations that trigger it. Fatigue accentuates the phenomenon: it's permanent, dissolving every activity, every ambition that seeks to escape it. In the room, there is no tomorrow. Reality no longer seems to be anything more than a denial of reality. Perhaps the life that I have been allowed to continue merely brought me back to the death that I had rubbed shoulders with. If that was the case, their twinning and antagonism spread their grammar over everything that surrounded me and constituted me.

If I bit into an apple, my teeth were going to fall out and orchards full of apple trees would disappear, until a ray of sun—or a nurse's smile, or a poet's verse, or a melody by Chet Baker—who, now that I think about it, had also lost most of his teeth all at once—restored the jaw, the light, the orchard, and the horizon. But at the hospital, the horizon disappears quickly: the patient is constantly passing from dawn to twilight and he fears like the plague the night that awaits him. He's a strange person, simultaneously assailed by cruel nuances and simplified.

Big Brother's Newspeak in George Orwell's novel *1984* allowed me to formulate, without saying it, what I felt in the first of my rooms: my floating state was that of a "deadalive," and the reflex best suited to it was "yesno." The three categories into which Newspeak divided its vocabulary were adapted to the situation: vocabulary A (words necessary for everyday life), vocabulary B (words created for political purposes, intended to impose a desired mental attitude on the person who uses them, and vocabulary C (technical and scientific words). I could have gone even further: in the hospital room, vocabulary A and vocabulary C tended to merge. As for vocabulary B, it derived from a rather simple mental attitude which the head of the department, standing there in front of me in her white smock and reconstructed face, summed up soon after my arrival: "In a year, Monsieur Lançon, you'll see that no one will see anything!" Naturally, that was false, and naturally I believed it. Hadn't she herself survived a terrible accident? I looked at the skin around her tawny, intense, and slightly mad eyes: no trace. Or else at that point I preferred not to see the traces. It would therefore be the same for me. Many people here told me about their past or present problems, and the moral was always the same: you have to fight, you'll get over it. I believed everything I was told because it had to be believed for it to have a chance of being true someday, later on, as soon as possible. I also invented a word for this: you had to be "betterbetter."

Newspeak also had a word to refer to a little more than feeling or sensing, "bellyfeel"—which means, Orwell explains, "feel with your gut." I gradually worked out its forms, depending on the hours of the day and the points of discomfort—"discomfort" being the word I rather quickly chose to define for others what my body was going through. This was neither an effort to please nor a mere euphemism: by reducing the word, I reduced the pain and pity that accompanied it. Discomfort was sometimes "feeljaw," sometimes "feelnose," sometimes "feelthroat," sometimes "feeleye," sometimes "feelhand" or "feelarm," and during the night, as a final combo, "feelall." Whatever was felt, it hurt, it irritated, it burned, it flooded. I thought all these words, and many others, but I didn't write them down and no one knew anything about them.

Should I have said all this? Not necessarily. On the one hand, I was already talkative enough as it was, even without being able to speak. On the other hand, after entering Room 196 and during the following months, most of my senses seemed to me affected or shut off forever. I didn't see well. I couldn't open my mouth. I had drips and drains in my arms, a drain in my neck, an enormous, complex bandage on the lower third of my face, an uncomfortable stomach tube in my nose— you have to eat to live and not live to eat, as the saying goes. My hands were bandaged, I could hardly touch anything. I could neither eat nor drink, nor smile. Luckily, I hadn't lost my sense of smell and, although I'd become blind, I could have quickly identified the various caregivers by their smell or their perfume. Not being able to embrace anyone, I immediately returned to a childhood reflex: offering my forehead to be kissed by others when they came up to embrace me. Their whole mouths touched my hair. It took me two years to lose this reflex of offering my forehead. The last people to have benefited from it were my parents.

Four in one hospital, one in the other: that is the number of rooms in which I stayed full-time between January 8, 2015, and October 17, 2015. If I make a final count and am not mistaken, that comes to a total of 282 days. It's prisoners, and often the sick, who count the days, because they would like to escape and disappear. I was neither a prisoner nor an invalid: I was a victim, a wounded person, and I would have liked to stay in my hospitals as long as possible. They protected me and rescued me from an evil that I had the greatest difficulty understanding and to which I did not want, nor was able, to oppose any furious anger. Above all, I did not want to escape the way Henri Charrière, a.k.a. Papillon, had escaped from prison. It was only through the everyday routine of the hospital that I was able to come to terms with what had taken place.

During this period, I slept outside the hospital on four occasions: one night with Gabriela at the home of a friend, a weekend in the country at the family home, three weeks of summer vacation with my family and with friends, and an initial return to my apartment for a few days in the autumn, between leaks and repair work, one month before I truly "went home"—an expression that I put between quotation marks because I didn't understand and still don't what it might mean: "to go home" is for me to return to the hospital. These rooms had become my ports, my cabins. I sometimes believed or feared, listening to a nurse's cart passing in the dark, hearing the cry of a patient or an engine backfiring, that the killers were moving through the corridors looking for me. I never believed that enough to get up and hide under my bed—where, I thought when I was tempted to do it anyway, they would in any case have quickly found me. I imagined the scene enough to experience it, but I didn't experience it enough to act on it. To tell the truth, nothing any longer seemed to me completely credible: neither life nor death. But both of them, together, functioned rather well, with the strength and fragility of Siamese twins: if one of them dies, the other follows him.

Room 106 was a small, clean room where I immediately felt fluttering around me a ballet of white and blue smocks. Everything that came into my room was an apparition.

I was forbidden to speak, because of the unfenestrated tracheotomy tube that had been inserted in my neck; my second nature being well constructed, I didn't feel the need to speak. I was still not really experiencing pain that was peculiar to the cannula, even if I had the impression that I couldn't breathe completely freely. My parents were asked to step out while the nurses were dealing with me, beginning the first of their interminable periods of waiting in the bare, cold corridor. There were two chairs near the elevator. The closest cafe was a couple of hundred meters away. They were always treated with consideration in a place without consideration. The patient struggles, survives, dies. The others are there simply as visitors. Their ordinary life and their comfort are out of place. I didn't think much about that; what took place beyond my door and the elevator belonged to a world that seemed to me more than distant, it seemed improbable. People no doubt had lives, outside, but from the first day on, these lives disappeared into the wings, from which they would emerge only to exist here, on my stage, in these few square meters. Those who entered the room had, outside it, less existence than characters in a novel once the book was closed. I could no longer imagine them outside the reduced circle of my own life.

The first of the apparitions that I remember, Émilie, was a little brunette nurse, twenty-one years old. She was stubborn and strong-willed, she closed and puckered her little mouth when she was annoyed. I believe I remember that she was from Brittany. This was her first position as a nurse. She had to make analyses, as one always does when one starts in a department.

But where to give me a shot, with these tubes everywhere? Someone more experienced helped her find a vein. She was irritated. Stretched out on my bed and breathing as best I could, I watched her work, wondering if my life might depend on someone so stubborn and, what's more, so young. But most of the department's nurses and auxiliaries were young, indeed very young, if not stubborn. This sensation was accentuated during the following hours. I noticed that I no longer had any familiarity with people in their twenties or thirties. I suddenly felt old, and for the first time in my life, *dependent on people who would survive me.* I looked at Émilie's concentrated, frowning face, and undertook through her, in her, a vague meditation in which anxiety fought a desperate battle with enthusiasm. Every detail illuminated the struggle, her lips, her eyes, her hair, her hands, her gestures, her shrill, firm voice that said: "Ah! You're really not easy to inject! Your veins seem to have decided to hide themselves." I picked up my notebook with my other hand and wrote with difficulty: "They're shy." She wrinkled up her nose: "Well then, it would be better if they weren't!" We undertook the journey, she as a nurse and I as a patient, hand in hand. Her lack of experience supported my own, and this initial moment, like awakening beside my brother, determined what followed. I was enveloped in her youth as if in a carpet, rough, to be sure, and full of holes, but able to fly and heading, amid instability, toward a country where I would not have been able to go alone, a country where life was suddenly the strongest. And the mistakes made along the way—veins poorly injected, badly done bandages, and all the rest, mattered little: it was all part of journey.

That night, I slept intermittently only thanks to morphine. It was my first night in my new life. I have forgotten everything, but the next day I wrote down this dream under morphine, in hesitant capital letters and in Spanish: "I was in a beautiful house at the seaside. Suddenly, thousands of gypsies arrived to celebrate the watermelon festival." I did not write down the rest, but on reading these words, I remember it: the watermelons were piled up in pyramids, pyramids that were soon higher than the house and that threatened to collapse at any moment. Gradually, amazement was replaced by threat and asphyxia. The end of the dream, which I've forgotten, revealed a childhood memory.

One summer, in a Spanish market, when I was seven years old, my mother gave me an enormous watermelon. I was supposed to carry it while she continued to run errands. I was standing amid adults and the noise and joyful atmosphere peculiar to a Spanish market in those years. The watermelon was in my arms. I was holding it the way you hold a child, or a new ball, or your pillow. I clutched it, I clutched it, I was afraid of dropping it. Then I began to think about something else and, naturally, I dropped the watermelon. It exploded at my feet. The red liquid, full of seeds, spread over several meters around me. People laughed, I began to cry, and watching me cry made them laugh even more. It took more than a whole day to console me. In my hospital room, I relived the story of the watermelon as if I were seven years old. I was once again in the Spanish market. The watermelon, at my feet, had split open and was leaking out. What was I thinking about when I dropped it? I said to myself that existence must be circular, and that in this market, forty-four years earlier, I had thought about what had just happened to me.

The next morning, I still didn't know who the killers were, and I wasn't thinking about that, but I had to get up to go to the toilet and to take a first shower. It was Linda who helped me, first of all by lifting me up. Linda was an auxiliary nurse from the Antilles who was particularly strong, almost sixty years old, tough as steel, and she did not seem upset about nearing retirement age. Life was hard in this department, and some of the patients were very trying: Linda treated them with a sovereign indifference. Even if I'd ever felt like stepping on her toes, it would never have occurred to me to do it. On the other hand, I liked to listen to her and to watch her work. Like many of the auxiliary nurses, she enjoyed a certain power over the life of the patients and the nurses here, but there was something else. She was endowed, in a way, with a martial good will, based on what her work and her own life had taught her, and that reassured me. She had power and a pinch of coquetry.

Like the dream about the watermelon, her sweet perfume plunged me back into childhood. Her curls, which were always perfect, calmed me. They reminded me of those of my maternal grandmother, whose hair was, like hers, gray, fine, curly, full, and always clean. At the age of eighty-four, my grandmother came out of the bathroom in an impeccable state and was preceded by a cloud of eau de cologne that, twenty years after her death, still floated around me in that room. I pressed gently on her hair, which was as light as a breath. She pulled away, laughing with an annoyed air and crying: "Ah! Don't spoil my permanent!" I watched Linda approach with desire. I would have liked to press on her curls, but I could hardly breathe and move, and, instead of the posthumous cry of my grandmother, whose name was Germaine, I heard Linda bellow in a jovial tone: "Let's go, Monsieur Lançon, you have to go to the mouth" (*bouche*). She meant to say "to the shower" (*douche*), and she probably did, but I heard it wrong, and then everything led me back to that ruined orifice from which nothing could emerge. Perhaps it was an additional sign from my grandmother, who, in addition to her permanents, had the characteristic of deforming unfamiliar words and other people's names, as do certain characters in Proust. Being from the Berry in central France, she required foreignness and the foreigner to pay a duty, which consisted in being pitilessly transformed. So it was that *magret de canard*, when she discovered it, was called *Maghreb de canard,* although she had never gone to Africa or to any foreign country, no doubt in reference to couscous, which she had discovered during the same period and which she liked so much, especially the couscous made by the Garbit firm, which she preferred to Buitoni's. I went to the mouth and resumed a sedentary life in which I also had to learn everything, even if it meant deforming it.

Linda took hold of me. Slowly, limping, a two-tone monster with two heads, four legs, four arms, an intravenous solution stand, and several tubes headed toward the bathroom and the anti-skid floor tile that immediately pleased me. On each new stay at the hospital, I return to these long, granulated tiles as Proust does to his *madeleine* or his uneven paving stones. They don't lead me, as they do the little Marcel, toward the stained-glass window of a church, a vest-maker's ass, or a duchess's indifference, but rather toward the amniotic certainty that I am alive. It is in fact I who am heading for the shower, with a burlesque fragility and in the grip of Linda's powerful body. Several times, hardly able to stand up, I almost fell. Linda's chubby, muscular mass supported and enveloped me like a newborn.

In the bathroom, she helped me take off, or rather rip apart, the operating room smock, which spared us the task of passing the tubes through the sleeves, and harnessed me with garbage bags to prepare me for the shower. The garbage bags protected the fresh cicatrices, the bandages, and the drips. It's not so easy to put them in place, and when you manage do it quickly and by yourself you feel a legitimate pride. They also informed me of a characteristic of life in a cutting-edge surgery department: a mixture of technicity, rusticity, and poverty. Linda swaddled my arms. I was forbidden to put my face under the shower. To wash my hair, I had to sit down and lean back as far as possible. Linda handled the shampoo, telling me: "Next time, you'll do it, Monsieur Lançon. You'll see, you'll succeed." I liked her roughness, which was kindhearted. Two and a half months later, entering the room and examining closely a face that she had not seen for a month because she was on vacation, she said to me, smiling: "Let's see? It's not so bad. You're not so disfigured as all that! We've seen much worse!" Here, you always saw people who were worse off than you were, but I couldn't help being devastated by her reaction. I put on a Bach disc, calmed down, and thought that after all she was right. The same remark, or almost, was made to me a month later, in my village, by Ginette, the peasant woman from whom we had bought eggs since I was a child. She made a gesture with her head as if to banish pity and say: "To hell with aesthetics! What does that matter . . . You're alive, you're eating and talking." The wind was blowing. Her geese began to cackle.

Several times during the shower, I almost fell down. Each time, Linda's body served me as a mattress, a corset, and a prop. The more the water flowed, the smaller I became and more Linda grew. If the shower had lasted an hour, I would have been the size of a mouse and she the size of a mountain. At that moment, gasping for air, on the brink of metamorphosis and fainting away, I discovered what this reminded me of: a page in Robert Merle's *L'Île* (*The Island*), which had enchanted my adolescence. The British hero—exhausted, almost moribund, and hidden in a grotto by the natives, who are protecting him from the bad guys—is massaged and warmed up by the giant, fragrant, and naked body of Omaata, a Tahitian woman straight out of a painting by Gauguin. I had read this page ten times, a hundred times, it provided me with the same relief and the same vital force as it did to its poor hero, Adam Purcell. On January 8, during the shower and now dressed, Omaata was reincarnated in Linda.

I watched how she went about removing the garbage bags: she simply tore them to shreds. Then she stood up and, having taken hold of me again, she dried me and rubbed me with an eau de cologne which was not that of my grandmother, but reminded me of it, and which my parents had brought. Linda accompanied me back to my bed, which she had remade while I remained sitting in the chair, trembling, near the toilets. Treatment could begin.

At first, a peaceful and slender African guard had been posted in front of my door. His discretion had moved me, and I greeted him from my stretcher as we came in, with the friendliest gesture possible, as if we were going to live together, and as if my whole life depended on him. He was soon replaced by four policemen armed with Beretta rifles, two in front of the door, two at the elevator entrance. The nurses didn't much like that, but fairly quickly they started serving them coffee and talking with them. After a few days, they were part of the furniture. With their weapons and their bulletproof vests, they were carrying about twenty kilos on their bodies and they were relieved every nine hours. Often, I heard the evening and the morning changing of the guard without having been able to greet those who had protected me during the night. I heard them talking, I heard their radios, but they were voices without faces: the voices behind the door. Since my first room was almost across from the elevator, they formed a small group around it. The elevator door opened and visitors came upon these men in uniform, armed, relatively threatening, especially at first, who asked them where they were going. It took me no more than two days to feel to what extent, just as the morphine relieved me, their presence reassured me. It worried my nephews, aged six and eight, so much that the first time they entered the room, they didn't dare come closer to me. The fear that these armed men had inspired in them followed them right up to the foot of my bed. It wasn't like on television.

That was when Toinette and her companion Christophe came in, as if they'd popped out of a Christmas cracker. It was late in the morning, I was surprised, my brother hadn't said anything about it, and I knew that visits, which were carefully filtered, began only at 1:30 P.M. I was simultaneously happy, curious, and destabilized: with Toinette, my childhood and my village burst into the event that seemed to me to have destroyed them, and they did so at the moment when I was least expecting them. Something exploded, as if two planets had collided on what was no longer, or not yet, a dissection table. I was terrified.

Toinette's long red hair spread over the room like autumn leaves. Her name did not suit her perfectly well, because more than one of Molière's servants, she looked like one of Marivaux's. She was no longer young enough to be a maid, but that didn't matter: with her, you were always at the theater. Toinette had been involved in drama ever since she was a child; it was her passion and her trade, but her temperament inclined her toward worlds other than those of Molière or Marivaux: Elizabethan theater, Grand Guignol horror shows, baroque theater, everything that put death, madness, and blood onstage with the maximum of violence, contrast, and effects. Its in-your-face, morbid comedy came from the burlesque. One of Toinette's closest friends had committed suicide, hanged himself, I think, and another, whom I had known well in our youth, had died of a heart attack when he was still young, while he was running. Death was her neighbor, one of those old widows with piercing eyes such as we had known in our village and who knocked on your door at night, at the moment when you least expected it. It often visited Toinette, I believe, and still frightened her just as much. In any case, Toinette still talked about it, she dreamed about it and found that so intolerable that she liked to invite it to join her onstage the better to tame it—in vain. Then she burst into laughter, because she was sweet, even delicate, and good-natured. Christophe played in most of the plays that she produced. He had probably sacrificed, if not his talent, which was great, then at least a part of his career to Toinette and to their family; but if he had done that, it was with a naturalness and an equanimity of mind that I had always considered admirable. I liked to run and talk with him, and I would have liked to hear him recite, in our village, all the poems that I loved. The preceding summer, I had given him my old copies of Francis Ponge's poems, in the hope that he would learn them.

Toinette was a childhood friend, we had spent our vacations in the same village in the Nivernais, the one where my grandparents and her great aunt lived. It was there, in her attic, that she had begun to produce little plays for other children. I seldom witnessed these at the time, maybe because I was a few years older, and doubtless because then neither theater nor literature really interested me. I preferred cycling on the forest roads, swimming in the Yonne River, playing tarot or croquet in a meadow. It had taken us thirty years, Toinette and I, to give meaning to our friendship. The first time I saw her again, in Paris, near the Luxembourg Gardens, she had become a stage director and I a journalist. She was wearing a spectacular silvery suit that made her look like a cosmonaut in a 1960s science-fiction series without a budget. Later on, I participated in a collective project that she was directing, wrote articles about the plays that she was producing and that I had liked. In the summer, she worked in her house, I in mine; we lived within a few dozen meters of each other. At the end of the day, we met at her home, around her big wooden table, with Christophe, to have a glass of wine or dinner. The evening light filtered through a walnut tree. Inside, there were books and old objects all over. The wine relaxed us. Sometimes, we played Ping-Pong. It was still the beautiful summer, a summer that had begun right there when we were ten years old, and memories thickened the moments.

How did she get there? In the little room, Toinette had hardly looked at me before she took my hand and kissed it as if, I thought as I observed that mouth and that hand, I had a horrible, magic secret that she was looking for and that she had feared for a long time, forever, from bouts of insomnia to *mises-en-scène*. I was still floating between life and death and I was still a virgin with regard to other people's reactions: each apparition deflowered me. Panicked, I looked at Christophe. He was at the foot of the bed, and he, too, was looking at me. His eyes and his attitude, which were sober, should have reassured me, he had always had common sense and a solidity that gave me confidence; but he was caught up in Toinette's emotional whirlwind and his silhouette and his eyes, behind her, were unable to help me. I took my whiteboard and wrote: "miracle!" I felt incapable of making the gestures that Toinette seemed to expect from me, as if I had been an actor, the gestures that would reveal to her the nature of what I had undergone. But was it really those gestures that she was expecting? What did she expect, exactly? Perhaps simply that: that I take a whiteboard and write on it: "miracle!"

Toinette had learned the news on her cell phone, in a train that was taking her to Le Havre, where she was going to a concert connected with the reopening of a theater. Before the concert, there was a minute of silence for the victims at *Charlie*. Toinette wondered what she was doing there, why she wasn't in Paris, at my side. The next day, at dawn, she told Christophe in the train taking them home: "We're going to go, whether not we're forbidden to go there. I want to be there, with him." Christophe replied: "Your choice, I'm with you." When they arrived at the hospital, she encountered my surgeon. Chloé must have sensed Toinette's helpless confusion, because she authorized her to go in. It wasn't the moment, or the hour, or the rule, people were improvising and acting in accord with their instinct. My father had told her that it was too early to come, but she had not been able to wait, she had to be sure that I was alive, she had to see me and touch me. I sensed all that, she was my oldest friend, but her presence, her position, her eyes, her frightened compassion, all became unbearable for me, and I even had the impression—a false one, according to her—that she was kneeling down before me. They left rather quickly, my minutes counted more than double, and they ran into my brother and his wife Florence, who were surprised, at the exit from the hospital. They had just dined at the Saint Marcel, an old-fashioned bistro where the patients' melancholy families ate steaks. It could have been called, like the bar that was across the street from the Fresnes prison: "Here . . . better than across the way." During the following weeks, Toinette acquired the habit of sitting there. She was working right there, near the window, on a translation of Lenz's *The Soldiers*. She saw passersby whom she knew and who were going to the hospital to see me. She wrote me messages to which I did not reply. She was waiting for me to make a sign that did not come.

She was paying, I believe, for having seen me too soon. A year and a half later, at her home in our village, she told me what she had felt at that time:

"If you had died, the village and life would have never been the same again. At first, I didn't understand why you forbade me to come to see you, to help you. Why you put me outside the circle of your friends. If that's how it was, what did our friendship mean?"

"Our friendship wasn't in question," I told her. "But I was in no condition to endure your presence and your emotion. I had the impression that you were going to theatricalize everything, and I didn't want that. I had to make a selection, and that selection had nothing to do, or at least not only, with proximity. I see now that I chose, at that time, those who I sensed would make me stronger. You weren't among them."

"But can you understand what I felt?"

"I can and no doubt I could. But at that point, taking into account what you might feel was for me a luxury that I couldn't afford. It's important that you understand that."

Did she understand it? I don't know, but I don't feel guilty of anything. I did what I could, and what I could on that January 8, in the no-man's-land where I found myself, was to liquidate Toinette, her hand, her eyes, and her genuflection, which I apparently dreamed. I sacrificed her to the person who, from then on, was to simplify everything. I did it without hesitation, almost without thinking about it. Later, I saw her again with a joy that was limited by no shame, no regret. Culpability barely survived the attack.

A little later, the surgeons and the head of the department came into the room where Toinette's presence was still floating. I had not yet identified them. I saw one after the other of these white giants pass through, cold and kindly, as if, from the depth of my coffin in front of the altar, I had awakened to see strangers file by, bless me, observe me, or, why not?, resuscitate me. I didn't know them, but I sensed that my prolonged destiny depended on them. They talked calmly about a man who must have been me and whom I observed as they did, but from within. I fixed my attention on the bright, very expressive eyes of the department head, Christiane, a former reader for *Charlie Hebdo*, whom the attack had particularly shaken, and who was going to make my stay at the hospital a personal matter. I was there, I was elsewhere, I was listening to them, but where was I? I haven't the slightest idea. In the hallway, with my parents, my brother, and my sister-in-law, Marilyn was waiting.

She was coming from Belfort and was supposed to leave the same evening. My brother had met her the day before at a little Arab delicatessen that she and I, fifteen years earlier, had patronized. We knew the owner well, her name was Naïma. When she was still living in Paris, Marilyn was always delighted to go to eat there. I hadn't been there for a long time. I had been close to Naïma. We talked about everything, nothing, ourselves. In addition to cooking, she made shirts for a major couturier and had given me one of them, which I still wear in the winter. I went to have lunch at her shop rather late, when the last customers were leaving. She always reserved a meal for me. One day, a few months after September 11, 2001, Naïma finally said to me: "You know, I learned from an uncle who works for the Algerian secret police that that didn't happen the way people say. Everything was known in advance. It was carried out by Israel. He can't say any more, but it's certain . . . " The newspapers had reported that this paranoid, anti-Semitic scenario was widespread among Muslims. Reading it in the press was one thing, hearing it said in front of me by someone whom I saw frequently and liked was another. It wasn't the first time that I'd heard that theory: an Algerian journalist and an Iranian academic had served it up to me, and, to be fair, so had a French surgeon who was in no way Muslim. I had to put up with these last three only during one evening. Not to forget anything, I must add that most of my Latin American friends had begun by celebrating, whether for a minute or a day, the attack on the World Trade Center towers, on the theme: "Those Yankees, who've been annoying the whole world and putting it to fire and sword in the name of their morality, they got what they deserved!" That reflex didn't last and they quickly recognized the Islamists for what they are, infamous killjoys and a remedy a hundred times worse than the disease. Naïma was not an Islamist, but she was a Muslim, and I saw her almost every day. I didn't know what to say to her in reply, because I already no longer believed that it is possible to convince anyone who talks that way, which indicates a fantastical collapse of intelligence. I stopped going to lunch at her shop, though I continued to walk in front of it, with a twinge of sorrow and without looking at it.

On January 8, Marilyn hadn't seen Naïma for a long time. She told Naïma the story of her life, why and how we had divorced eight years before. Naïma told Marilyn about her own life. Then my brother came, and they began to talk about the attack, and about my condition. Naïma listened to them, expressed her compassion, participated. One of her friends, also an Arab, arrived, and then little by little, Marilyn began to feel uncomfortable. She didn't want these two women to know too much about me, where I was. The killers hadn't yet been identified or found. They were out there somewhere, perhaps only a few meters away. She thought: we can't continue to talk in front of her, she might be a friend of the terrorists. If she knows where he is, they'll go to the hospital and find him. Paranoia, she told me later, had set in. She and my brother left. Outside, he told Marilyn that my wounds were "scratches," that's the word he used. He was smiling, relaxed. He wanted to reassure himself, reassure her. She believed him.

That evening, she returned to the home of some old friends where she was going to spend the night. In her turn, she reassured them. They began to make jokes about me, in the Cuban fashion, with a good-natured black humor. It wasn't so serious, after all. A woman friend said those very words, which Marilyn has never forgotten: "Ah, bueno, el bicho está bien, dejémosle el tiempo de recuperarse y ya iremos a verlo." Which meant: "Oh well, the beastie is doing fine, let's give him time to recover and then we'll go see him." "El bicho," the beastie: an affectionate term, familiar, animal, which put me back into everyday life, in the Cuban past, as if nothing had happened.

Marilyn came into the room alone and we looked at each other. Slowly, she took my hand. We had loved each other so much. What did she think when she heard the news? What had she seen? In the summer of 2016, she wrote to me about this encounter. I reproduce her letter almost without alterations:

On the way to the hospital, your parents told me the day's news regarding your health, and then we arrived at the ward. Arnaud and Florence were there. Six or seven people were visiting you, people high up in the hospital management, doctors. We waited outside. In the meantime, Florence called me and took me to the stairwell. She said to me: "You have to prepare yourself psychologically, because it's not a pretty sight," I think those were her words or something like that. Then: "He's not the Philippe that you saw the last time, it's going to be a shock, he's disfigured," and she showed me which part was concerned. She was very efficient and intelligent in her choice of words. The hospital VIPs left the room, but we still couldn't go in, because it was time for the nurses' rounds. The bigwigs greeted us one by one and we introduced ourselves to them, each in his turn.

Then the big door opened, it seemed enormous to me. Taking a deep breath, I went in and saw you. It was overwhelming, it's true, but what really shocked me and upset me was your eyes and the way you looked at me. They were dark! A deep look, and your eyes were so dark they almost spilled over. I don't know if it was Florence's words before we went in that produced that effect on me, but the wound to the jaw didn't traumatize me as much as the "scratches" on your arms. They weren't scratches, they were a massacre, and I resented your brother for saying that. I looked at the wound to your jaw and was almost reassured, because I said to myself: "That can be repaired." I almost saw the work that the surgeons would have to do, but I was persuaded that it was going to be all right.

Marilyn didn't see the lower part of my face, any more than the others had. What did it look like, underneath the bandage? Two days had passed, and already I was forgetting or believed I was forgetting what I had seen on my cell phone screen after the killers left. Moreover, I had already changed. I had been in the operating room and the long process of repair had begun. A titanium collar had been installed in the hole to keep what remained of the bone in place.

Two years later, seeing me depressed by an interminable and painful process of reeducation, the nurse I was closest to, Alexandra, said to me in a bistro:

"You don't have the right to weaken. Not you! If you'd seen what you looked like when you arrived in the operating room . . . I wasn't there, but I've seen the photos."

"What did I look like?"

"The upper two thirds of the face were intact. Up to here . . . "

She pointed to her upper lip.

"Then it looked like raw a slab of raw meat. You couldn't tell the flesh from the bone, it was just a mess that hung there."

It was like Racine's play when Athaliah dreams that her mother is bent over her to pity her:

Son ombre vers mon lit a paru se baisser;
Et moi, je lui tendais les mains pour l'embrasser.
Mais je n'ai plus trouvé qu'un horrible mélange
D'os et de chairs meurtris, et traînés dans la fange,
Des lambeaux pleins de sang, et des membres affreux,
Que des chiens dévorants se disputaient entre eux.

Towards my bed
Her shadow seemed to bend itself, and I
Held out my arms in order to embrace it;
But only found confusion horrible
Of mangled bones and flesh dragged in the mud,
And tatters soaked in gore, of hideous limbs,
That dogs, devouring, fought for with each other.

After I left the hospital, strangers, often merchants, asked me what had happened to me. I replied: "An accident." That was too vague for them. Many of them, thinking they had the right answer, said: "A dog bite, no?" I said yes. I always answered yes to the hypotheses proposed to me, that reassured those who proposed them, but I ended up liking the one about devouring dogs more than the others, all the more because it was plausible. A good hypothesis never appeared.

My mother came in soon after Marilyn. She said she was going to leave us alone, and, like Athaliah, bent over to kiss me. Only it wasn't her face that was devoured, but mine. I've forgotten her bending over me. Marilyn hasn't: "She kissed you on the forehead. Seeing such a strong woman brought low in a few hours, which eighty years couldn't do, that was truly intense. I had to hold myself back to keep from crying. You got the little boy look that annoyed me so much when we were married, but this one had another tone, you were embarrassed because you didn't want to make her experience what was going on right then. The eighty years and the fifty years weighed heavily on this scene. Especially by the places they occupied." My mother left the room and Marilyn stayed with me.

She didn't know what to say, and neither did I. I took out my notebook and asked her for news about Jonathan. Jonathan was her son. He was born a year after our divorce. His father had become Marilyn's husband. Then I thought of a coincidence that had escaped me. It was here, at La Salpêtrière, ten years earlier, that we had tried to have the child we hadn't had. The hospital where I had gone several times to masturbate at dawn in a little room stuffed with old porn magazines that produced no effect on me; the hospital where I watched other men, engaged in the same infertile enterprise as I, looking at the ceiling and their feet as elements of the disaster; the hospital where some of them went into the little room and never came out, because they couldn't ejaculate; the hospital where we'd had a few dramatic meetings with physicians who served up a psychology for dummies ("if you can't have a child, maybe it's because down deep you don't really want one?"); the hospital where these same physicians, moving our file from one building to another, ended up losing it. The hospital where we had sought in vain to give life was the one where I now had to do all I could to find it again.

A little later they came to get me for the first postoperative scan. The room where the scan would be done was in another building. The orderly arrived. My brother suggested to Marilyn that she accompany me. She accepted without hesitation. A nurse put a mask over my face. I took my felt-tip pen and my notebook, inaugurating a habit that I was henceforth to maintain from stretcher to stretcher. We went downstairs in the freight elevator and in the basement passed through shabby and deserted, increasingly sinister corridors. They made it possible to move from one building to another while avoiding bad weather. Two of the four policemen accompanied us, their hands on their Berettas. They walked, in accord with their instructions, slightly behind us. I had regained consciousness as my brother was watching over me. Now I had the feeling of going peacefully toward death, and to be doing so in the company of my ex-wife—the person who, no doubt, knew me best. She took my hand, caressed my arm. Once, at the most bare point in these corridors, she caressed my forehead and kissed it. Later, she continued to write to me in her imperfect French which had always moved me, and whose secret and simplicity I would have liked to know: "That made me think of the moments of tenderness that we shared when we were married. Tenderness was the only thing authorized between us, and then it calms weariness. In addition, I saw you so helpless, lost, deprotected, that my acts were a short way of bringing you relief." "Deprotected" (*déprotégé*) is a word that doesn't exist in French, a word that comes from Spanish "desprotegido," without protection. It was probably the right word. Marilyn went into the technician's booth while I was entering the narrow white tunnel. I was asked not to move. I thought about the life that we'd led, a relatively good life, and I said to myself that hell was not as bad a place as this was. It was a clinical and discreetly spectacular place, located underground, where killers emerged from nowhere for unknown reasons. They executed those who surrounded you, reciting mysterious and stupid formulas, and they sent you, on a stretcher, to the limits of another world. In the area around these limits, you found, one by one, the people whom you'd loved, whom you loved now. They reappeared like kings and queens of hearts on the table for a game of cards around 5 A.M. They accompanied you as far as possible in the game that you had to play and, at the moment that you entered a box, in a dream, they disappeared behind a door and you could finally give yourself over to everything that solitude, memories, and technology could provide.

But hell doesn't last any longer than the rest. I was taken out of the scanner and Marilyn accompanied me back to my room. On the whiteboard, I wrote what she knew already: in two hours, having come from New York, Gabriela would be there. As in a vaudeville play, the ex-wife had to leave so that the new one could come in, and all the more because the latter was unaware of the former's presence. No one had told her or wanted to tell her, fearing her reaction if she learned that Marilyn had preceded her. Marilyn asked me if Gabriela spoke French; she was worried about her ability to get things done. I said that she did. Back in the room, she told my brother that Gabriela couldn't come in immediately, couldn't come into this room covered with microbes and dirt, that she would first have to take a shower and change clothes at my place. My brother replied that Gabriela was coming here directly and would wash here, in my bathroom. Marilyn cried out furiously: "But that's madness!" She had worked in a hospital for ten years and found it difficult to accept violations of sanitary protocol. My brother calmed her down and, she told me, "I suddenly felt that I was only an intruder in a world of which I was no longer a part, and in addition I had come secretly." That was false: starting on January 7, all the worlds in which I had lived, all the persons whom I had loved began to cohabit in me without precedence or decorum, with a mad intensity proportional to the sensation that was dominant: I was going to lose them, I had already lost them.

Later, Marilyn helped me go to the toilet. She held the tubes while I pissed. For the first time since we separated, she saw me naked. She saw me as she would probably have seen me if we had grown old together, because that was in fact what she had in front of her: a young old man. This old man wanted to pee, go back to bed, go to sleep, extinguish himself, holding the hand of a woman he'd loved. My brother returned: down there, outside, they were asking if I wanted to write for *Charlie*. Marilyn cried out again: "Can't you leave him alone? He needs calm, rest. He's in no condition to make decisions like that." My brother answered calmly that the family had decided to ask my opinion about everything. I listened without listening, I saw without seeing. Marilyn looked at me. She saw in my eyes two expressions that, according to her, meant: "Do something, I'm terrified and exhausted" and "After all, they're kind, but they don't understand anything." What could they have understood? The life of newspapers continued. The news, reactions, the life of others, what must be done and what must not be done. Besides, what good are newspapers if they don't welcome life and reproduce it? While Marilyn and Arnaud were talking to me, or talking in front of me, I was chewing Cabu's cookie, murmuring a joke to Wolinski, seeing and seeing again with hope, with despair, Franck drawing his gun to signal with a shot that the show was over. He didn't succeed and the show was only beginning, the show that gradually put the spectators in a coffin and onstage.

Marilyn got dressed, took my hand again, and kissed my

forehead. It was time to leave. She was returning that same evening to her village, near Belfort. I watched her walk away, thinking I might never see her again. At the same time, outside it was learned that someone named Coulibaly had taken hostage the customers and staff of a kosher supermarket. I didn't hear anything about it. My brother and my sister-in-law walked Marilyn back to the exit from the hospital. She began to cry. Her legs were trembling. They supported her. On the way, they happened on my father. He told us the latest news, repeating "It never ends, it never ends." He uttered the name Coulibaly. Coulibaly is a common name in Mali, and Marilyn remembered a young autistic girl she had supervised, whose name was also Coulibaly. In the same letter written a year and a half later, she told me that "the young autistic girl had a very beautiful, haughty mother, tall and elegant in her African clothes. With the social assistant, we visited her house in the 19th arrondissement of Paris. Mme Coulibaly was difficult. She did not speak French, but understood it when she wanted to. Subsequently, each time that I heard the name Coulibaly I thought of the little girl, so sweet and smiling. Plugging her ears with her fingers and sitting on a couch with a group of autistic or psychotic children from the hospital. I wondered: do the killer and she belong to the same family?" At *Charlie*, we didn't even have time to plug our ears. My father took Marilyn in his arms, repeated "it never ends, it never ends" and they began to cry.

An hour later, Gabriela came in with her big suitcase through the same door that Marilyn had just closed. I had always known her with big dancer's bags and large suitcases. *Libération* had spontaneously paid for her trip from New York. The hospital had installed a small bed for her, alongside mine. She stood erect in her big, dark blue coat. Her long, thick hair fell to her waist. Her dark eyes looked into mine. She was smiling. She was going to live here for a week.

CHAPTER 8
POOR LUDO

One day, I was told there was a demonstration in Paris. It was my brother who announced it to me. He'd already said that it would take place, that most of our friends would be going, that it was an important moment for France and for us, but I must have forgotten it. In the hospital room, news arrived the way light comes from the stars, from too far away, already dead, to end up among bandages and tubes. Everything was implausible and attenuated. From what planet did those who brought this news come? I had neither a telescope nor a vessel nor the energy to find out and to look into it more closely. I was not like the astronomer who, in *The Shooting Star*, is going to have soft caramels bought because the end of the world has not taken place. It had taken place, the end of one world, in any case, mine, ours perhaps. No one had made a mistake in the calculations, because no one had carried them out. Even if this end was provisional, at that moment it was perpetual, and in the fog I couldn't see anything. In the fog of the end, there was neither a renewal nor a breakthrough. There was nothing, not even a show of support. To enjoy or to fear the news, you have to be able to imagine it.

The day before, my brother had come into my room and said: "They've wasted the bastards. Nobody's going to cry over them." That was how I learned of the existence of the Kouachi brothers. Now, the black legs had a name, and they were no longer alone. There were two pairs of black legs. They'd died somewhere out there, in a little print shop northeast of Paris.

There had been other attacks, other killers. A jogger had been attacked on the greenway in the southern suburbs, exactly where my father went to run and where I had sometimes accompanied him. Who were these zombies? What zone were they returning from? From the zone in which I was plunged? A zone where the dead were a kind of living beings and where any kind of vision had the irreversible force of an act?

"Waste," "bastards"—I'd never heard my brother use words like that, it wasn't at all his style. I understood the dissonance, an effect of emotion, but I was shocked. I wouldn't have wished there to be any kind of violence in this room, or in my own life. I would have liked to make it a decompression chamber, one of those boxes through which you have to pass when you surface too quickly from a dive. Everything aggressive or useless that came in was an obstacle to what life I still had. Everything that came out of me also had to be pacified and float in a pacified air.

For the past four days, I had no longer been able to speak. Not only did it very quickly come to seem to me that I had never spoken, but I began to think that because I had talked so long, I deserved my punishment. You don't believe in God, I said to myself, but something is punishing you for having talked so much, written so much, for nothing. Something is punishing you for blathering on, for your articles, your tirades, your judgments, the numbers you did with women, all the noise that you contributed to. If you decide that's how it's going to be, that noise will finally remain outside the door, with the noise of voices and police radios and the nurses' carts. Yes, you're being punished the same way you sinned, even if you don't believe in sin or in redemption, and even if those who punished you did it for completely different reasons. Take advantage of the silence that these stupid killers forced upon you.

Policemen came in and bent over me. They were investigating the Kouachi brothers and wanted to know what I had seen. They were gentle, attentive. There were two of them. I searched the depth of their eyes for an answer they hadn't come to get, and that I was incapable of giving them. With my three fingers, I sketched on a notebook a map of the meeting room. Rectangles represented the bodies I remembered. I thought all that was very poorly drawn and felt guilty for not having much to say. As usual, I said to myself. Even in this affair, you remain a bad journalist, a guy with nothing to impart to others. No info to give, nothing new. Just a few marks on a notebook page. You won't help the investigation move forward.

In the ward, everyone seemed horrified. And I was the victim of what horrified them. I, a victim? A journalist can be wounded or killed while on assignment, but he can't be a victim. A journalist can be a target. He's not a subject. He's not protected from the story he's covering, but he can't be the heart of the story itself. That's a plant that grows in the event's blind spot. This idea was not exactly a credo; it was a sensation. This trade, I'd been taught, required discretion. How can you be discreet when everyone is looking at you but you don't have any control over what they see?

In the ward, there were people who, like Christiane, the department head, mourned the dead cartoonists of their youth, and with them, a very French bit of civilization. She had received my parents with tears in her eyes. Cabu, Wolinski . . . how could they have killed them? My parents had never laughed with Cabu and Wolinski, because they'd never read them. That was one of my pleasures, tinged with compassion: in addition to everything else, my parents hadn't deserved to be forced to enter a world in which they were foreigners: the killers had achieved that marvel. To be sure, my parents were entering that world a little late and without having chosen it. They were backing the dead cartoonists in order to support their son who had been deprived of his jaw. They were going to stay in the cartoonists' country out of solidarity. They would stay there as long as was necessary, longer than others who were in theory more favorable (or less unfavorable) toward *Charlie*. Their politics were right-wing, middle class, they were attached to proprieties and to discreet reserve, to not going too far, and completely immune to the virulent second level of *Charlie* and its battles. They had principles, but they would never have used the word "values." They did not belong to the cultural world and were not aware of its malevolent decorum.

Christiane could have been one of Wolinski's characters, a malicious, sensual creature with the eyes of a tiger ready to pounce on anyone, and perhaps she saw intimate opportunism for caricature and fiction die with Georges. The dead had bequeathed us the ridiculous aspects we had, but also those that we might have had. With her and a few others, my parents learned that it was possible to be serious, at least in accord with their criteria, and enjoy the humor of *Charlie*'s cartoonists. There were not so many people on Earth to make other laugh at everything and anything, to make them laugh by awakening what naturalness they had in them, what was in bad taste, childlike, anarchic, indignant, not socially acceptable, anti-authoritarian, and stubborn. It was fun to let one's monsters speak, and then to leave all clean and well-dressed.

On weekends Christiane often went horseback riding in the countryside. She returned with a backache that she liked to tell me about. Everything that she said about herself, whether happy or unhappy, always had enough interest to distract my attention from myself. For a few moments, her horse's gallop won out over my pains and tubes. It was marvelous, that room, because it was concrete; those who entered fascinated me, provided that they talked to me about themselves, but if they talked about current events, they dissolved themselves in abstraction. I would fall half asleep. I've forgotten Christiane's perfume, but I know that she had one.

When she was younger, she'd had a car accident. Her face, she told me one morning, had been reconstructed. She leaned toward me, pointed to her remodeled profile, and said: "You see, Monsieur Lançon, you can no longer see anything! It will be the same for you!" How happy I was to believe it! Especially since she soon brought me an oil that did miracles, according to her, if it was used to massage the cicatrices rigorously. The oil was so fatty that once it was spread on me, I could only spread it more. It quickly disgusted me as much as the saliva that constant flowed through the hole in my jaw, wetting the bandage that enclosed my face, doubling or tripling its weight until it slipped down and detached itself like an overly ripe fruit. What came from outside was an intrusion: what came from inside was, too.

The physical therapist, Corinne, was as sweet as an angel, and also talked to me as she began to massage (without Christiane's oil) my fingers, which were gradually emerging from the bandages like little, misshapen mummies. She told me about the accident that had destroyed part of her lower face: she had fallen off a ladder. When her daughter saw her, she had hardly recognized her, and then when she did, she fainted. The lower lip hung down, the chin was laid open, a real butchery, she said. I wrote on my whiteboard: "And now?" "Now," she replied, "there's just a little scar, but I feel hardly anything, except when I think about it and, for example, talk with you about it, as I am now." The ward seemed to be full of ghosts meant to reassure me regarding my future. I examined Corinne's face more closely. I looked for the little scar. I was delighted not to find it.

In a few days, this became a habit. Every time Corinne or Christiane entered the room, I looked for their wounds and the traces of their disappearance. Their faces were maps of my future territory. I imagined them destroyed, one by the car accident, the other by the fall from the ladder. I lacked a clinical eye. I saw what I wanted to see and I hadn't understood to what extent the lower part of my own face was broken. Besides, they didn't really want me to understand that. However, a few days earlier I'd seen that hanging lower face, right where the attack took place, but the memory of it had, if not disappeared, at least migrated toward the star where all the useless or harmful news piled up, as in a cellar or a refrigerator. This phenomenon was going to be accentuated over the following months. Memories didn't disappear; they melted into a thick, cold, silent mist, falling indifferently on the day before or a distant decade, like the fog that in *The Vikings*, a film by Richard Fleischer, invades the fjord at the moment when Tony Curtis and Janet Leigh are trying to escape. This was one of the first films that I watched, ten months later, once I was back in my apartment. It was late, I was alone, and as often happened, I couldn't sleep. It had been one of my favorite films ever since I was a child. I looked at Kirk Douglas's eye, which had been plucked out by a falcon, and Tony Curtis's arm, which had been cut off with a sword. They were brothers, I was their brother, and they were going to kill each other. I would have liked to reconcile them at the moment of the final duel, restore his eye to one of them and his arm to the other, and give both of them the contrary of the rage they shared. I wept.

The people in the operating room wouldn't have been surprised to be caring for a Viking if they had worked among the Vikings. But they found this presence unprecedented, a soldier with a war wound in Paris. Some of them had seen and cared for wounded soldiers in Africa, Yugoslavia, and Arab countries. I, too, had seen some. That was elsewhere. The context had prepared consciousness for what happened. This time, it hadn't. But to cope with change, the nurses had this advantage: they were responding to the destruction with precise acts intended to repair, like automatons endowed with reason.

These acts replaced tears, talking, useless compassion, dangerous pity. "We'll have to learn to live like the Lebanese, and I used to pity them," said my surgeon, Chloé, after the following attack, the one that took place on November 13. In her thesis, she'd cited a play by Sophocles, *Ajax*. She remembered it aptly when she was examining me, and quoted a verse that she hadn't forgotten. Since I hadn't written it down, a little later I asked her to remind me of it. She replied in a text message: "Loose translation: a good physician doesn't recite magic formulas over a problem that calls for the sword. That's what Ajax says before falling on Hector's sword. Taken out of context, that's one way of saying: 'When you have to go, you have to go.' Have a good day."

Finally, there were people who, like Aïcha, the Arab auxiliary nurse who read all kinds of newspapers and books, were simply nauseated by the killers' imbecility. On those days I felt how a newspaper like *Charlie* participated in the French social contract—or rather, what remained of it. Most of them wouldn't have signed this contract if it had been offered to them; but it wasn't necessary to sign it to live by it, even in spite of oneself. It sufficed to breathe the air in which its ink had long ago dried. It wasn't the air of gossip, what people say, or even that of shrewdness or competence. It was the air of farce and a lack of respect, the air that put everyone in a state of insouciance and critical spirit.

In the early afternoon of January 11, my brother said to me: "It looks like there's already a huge crowd at the demonstration. If I weren't with you, I'd be with them, down there. Everybody is saying: 'I am Charlie.' Everybody's Charlie. You'd think a tidal wave was sweeping over the country." Or something like that, I didn't write it down. At that time, I wrote almost nothing down, but I didn't lose the habit. The little that I wrote, I wrote on the whiteboard and then erased it, for practical reasons, and as if it had never existed. For three months, in periods during which I had to be silent so that my lower lip and the area around it would have a chance to heal, my fingers constantly went back and forth over this whiteboard and were blackened by the felt-tip pens like those of a careless schoolboy. It was the lesser evil. It reminded me of primary school classes, when we still wrote with an inkwell, in the shadow of Alphonse Daudet or Henri Bosco. I was left-handed and got ink all over the paper, my middle finger, the ring finger, and sometimes my lower wrist. Now I had a big, bloody mess underneath the bandage, between the middle and ring fingers of my left hand. It looked like a pile of mud between two hills. Would that end up going away? My brother continued to talk about the schedule for the national day of mourning. Outside, they were demonstrating. Inside, childhood continued to protest. It was taken out of the trunk, like a spare tire, and the journey continued. But what journey?

In my room, the first whiteboard soon had to be replaced. I've kept it, out of fetishism, with the last words written on it. I don't understand—or no longer understand—what they mean. They're written in Spanish, with the blue felt-tip pen, in capital letters. It's a poem. It must have been written for Gabriela, but I don't know if she read it, and in any case it is not necessarily addressed to her. It might have been written for myself or for one of my best friends, Juan, with whom we liked to exchange by text message Spanish poems that were written sometimes by poets, sometimes by us. These words inform me about the state of mind or soul, whatever, in which I was immersed when my brother told me about the demonstration. I translate:

Profite du sommeil du malade
Dans la paresse du marbre
Recouvert de son drap
De morphine.

Il y a peu tu me dansais
Un poème de Mickiewicz
Qui certainement n'existe pas,
"Rêve d'un homme calme tranquille"
Sur mon bras blessé.

Take advantage of the sick man's sleep
In the indolence of marble
Covered with his sheet
Of morphine.
A little while ago you danced me
A poem by Mickiewicz
That surely does not exist,
"Dream of a calm, tranquil man"
On my wounded arm.

How did the Polish poet Adam Mickiewicz—I don't recall ever having read a line by him—end up there? I've looked for an answer to that question. I didn't find it. I remember only one thing: at the time when I wrote it on the whiteboard, this poem seemed to me to sum up what I was going through. It was written like a dream that you write down when you're half asleep, thinking it crucial, and when you wake up, appears as what it is: the mediocre, incomprehensible trace of a vital but buried emotion; the hieroglyph of a personality that has disappeared.

As he talked about the demonstration, my brother was smiling. He was happy and proud of the general, national support, and happy to announce it to me. However, he had taken his wife and children back to their home in the suburbs. I think he feared there would be another attack, or disturbances in the crowd, an additional source of concern. For the past four days, the family had seen enough of that kind of thing. My room was in the penumbra. I listened, I acquiesced. The tracheal tube hurt and the nasal cannula was beginning to irritate my nose and throat. I wasn't sure that I understood what had taken place and, apart from this discomfort sprinkled with pain, I felt nothing. For the first time I heard the slogan "I am Charlie." The demonstration and the slogan concerned an event of which I had been a victim, of which I was one of the survivors, but for me, this event was private. I had carried away, like an evil treasure, a secret, to this room where no one could completely follow me, except perhaps the person who preceded me on the path I now had to take: Chloé, my surgeon. I was writing for *Charlie*, I had been wounded, and I had seen my companions dead at *Charlie*, but I was not Charlie. On January 11, I was Chloé.

For the preceding two days, I was also Gabriela. Or rather: I was Gabriela's smile. It was exactly the smile that she had had twenty-two years earlier in Paris, when I was introduced to her at a party where I had arrived, with two friends, in drag. I had just returned from Cuba. She was sitting alone along a wall. She was wearing black leather trousers and had the straight neck and back of a dancer, that long, thick black hair, and that smile that took over her whole face, a ballet smile that appears under all circumstances, even torture. Classical dancers are soldiers, and Gabriela was a soldier.

Two days before the demonstration, her smile had entered my room and immediately relieved me. If it had come this far, life was going to begin again. Gabriela was perhaps an apparition intended to console me for everything that had just happened, for everything that was going to happen, for I don't know what, perhaps simply for myself. Through her smile I experienced and reexperienced the moment when I saw her for the first time, and yet the woman who should have accompanied her, although she was present, was dead, like all those I had known and loved before the attack. I was fifty-one years old and had a hole in my jaw. I was seven years old and night was coming on. A pretty ghost with an Indian face was introduced to me in the form of a woman whom I loved and who could not be here, in this room, after the attack, because the man who was looking at her wasn't really there anymore. As Verlaine would have put it, she was neither completely the same nor completely different. She flew into this cramped and somber room full of the smell of disinfectants. Was she going to perform an entrechat, perhaps? I remembered that although I had often seen her rehearsing or teaching in a practice hall, I had never seen her dance onstage. I clung to the smile as to a vision, and, for a few seconds, I abandoned my age and my childhood to return to the year I turned thirty. I held out two fingers toward Gabriela, it's amazing how heavy signs become, almost religious, when they are reduced to almost nothing. I talked to her about Cuba, as we stood along an apartment wall, drinking a mojito. Hers, as always, had no alcohol in it.

That was in 1993. She'd spent three years in a Mexican ballet company and was trying her luck in Paris. We separated quite soon. I didn't find out that she had joined the Opéra, or that she had left it again.

Twelve years later, after dreaming about her and through the powers of the Internet, I tracked her down. I had just divorced. She had a site, and I wrote to her. She took a few months to reply. She was now living in New York, where she was teaching dance and Pilates. She had played the villain— Latin, obviously—in some television series. She was living with an American banker from Chicago who was older than she. They had no children. When I wrote to her, she had just opened a small studio, where many Chileans came to dance. What kind of life do people lead when they have left our own behind? We don't know, and what we imagine is almost always false.

They were living in Midtown Manhattan, in a relatively large and dark apartment near the East River. Her husband had bought it thanks to the brief real estate crisis that had followed the September 11 attacks. On that day, he was out of town, and after the towers fell, Gabriela had walked alone, like so many others, toward the river, in an apocalyptic atmosphere, thinking that a war was beginning. She had spent her adolescence under the Chilean dictatorship and still knew by heart the nationalist anthems that she was taught in middle school. She liked to sing them for me and laugh, History and patriotism being part of a comedy that it was better to avoid. She loved her country like a memory that she returned to with joy, but not without annoyance. She constantly thought about her sick father in the Atacama Desert.

She had left her country at eighteen, to dance. A foreign ballet company had given her a scholarship, but she didn't have an airplane ticket. Her family couldn't afford to buy it for her. When she wanted something, Gabriela would do anything to get it. From Copiapó, her native city, she wrote to Pinochet, whom she detested and feared, to explain her situation. She must have been persuasive: the president's secretary scheduled an appointment for the provincial girl. With her mother, she took the night bus to Santiago. They were seated on a couch in front of a disagreeable assistant who told them that the president's secretary was busy. Time passed. Gabriela's mother, ashamed, wanted to leave. The assistant disappeared without a word. Gabriela sank into the couch, closed her eyes, and as I often saw her do later in my hospital room and elsewhere, began to breathe slowly and enter into meditation. The meditation, that day, had only one subject: "This woman is going to come back smiling. She will have the airplane ticket and, first of all, she will serve us coffee." And that is exactly what happened. The assistant reappeared with a smile and coffee, and announced that the president's secretary was giving them a voucher for a ticket that was to be picked up from the Chilean airline company. Shortly afterward, Gabriela flew to Geneva.

She'd never seen snow and had been told that this city was surrounded by mountains. She got off the plane in a parka, but it was August, it was infernally hot, and she slipped into the airport restroom to change her clothes, as ashamed of her naïveté as her mother had been as she dealt with the president's secretary.

Physically, she had changed little in thirty years. So far as alcohol went, she could tolerate only champagne, and even then, only a few drops to moisten her lips. She did not smoke, and ate little, but she was a gourmet and loved ginger and chocolate. She began to develop a belly as soon as she stopped dancing, but she didn't often stop and exercised regularly at home, on her machines, while doing her e-mail and studying a book. She didn't read the newspapers, didn't watch TV, didn't listen to the radio. Current events didn't interest her and reached her only through what other people said, a little randomly, in a fog of indifference electrified by her sensitivity. She saw in them, I believe, the presence of evil and the uselessness of everything that led people away from the best and the most demanding of their passions—in her case, dancing. She insisted on living in her "little world," that was her expression, just as on the Little Prince's planet the rose lives under a cloche. It was, moreover not a rose without thorns. It had replaced the coquettishness of St. Exupéry's all-too-human plant with a solitary discipline that I admired, even though I found it austere, or perhaps because I found it austere.

When we saw each other again, the circumstances, and an ongoing divorce that was particularly difficult, had cracked the cloche under which she lived. Living without resources in New York, and persecuted by a banker as wily as he was convinced of his right, made her unhappy, and even crazy, because she was imprisoned in a vicious circle. She continued to go back and forth with her suitcases and bags under the cloche, from one gymnasium to another, from one end of the world to the other, from Copiapó to New York, from New York to Paris, and now from Roissy to La Salpêtrière. The cold air of the tragedy, entering through the crack, had made her character more somber, but it hardly changed her bearing or, to use the ancients' language, her sense of her destiny. Her amusements remained rare and rather childlike. Her life discipline struggled with the mental disorder that her imagination, her reveries, and her situation imposed on her. She avoided anything that made her sad, but what she drove out the door returned through the window, and when she no longer succeeded in escaping, it was anger or sorrow that took over. Then her smile disappeared, her face frowned, her eyes hardened or brimmed over with tears, and absolutely nothing of Gabriela's tranquil sweetness remained. I liked her tears, because they allowed me to console her, but I feared her anger, because I couldn't tame it. An hour of dancing somewhere swept away all the clouds, and the smile reappeared.

She took off her coat, bent over me, and, after touching my good fingers, she talked to me while at the same time explaining that she didn't want to tire me; then she took her shower. Later, on my whiteboard, I asked her to tell me about her trip, to talk about her life in New York. Once again, I wrote a few words about the attack, but she didn't want to enter into the details of that particular reality. I no longer know at what point she left to go to a dance practice room to revive. My room was small, we were going to have to live here for a week. At any time, Gabriela might have to step out so that I could be attended to. She would never hear the sound of my voice.

During the night, the slightest of my movements or nightmares awakened her. She jumped. I had the impression of being woken by her jump, which reassured me. From her bed, she stretched her arm out toward mine and, not knowing how to touch me without harming me, she held my three unbandaged fingers or caressed my head. My whole body lived in her hand. For a few minutes I fell back asleep.

The day before the demonstration, she helped Linda give me a shower, and starting on January 11, I took it alone with her. She laughed and held me upright gently and with a certain imagination. It was like a game, with its rules and its challenges; but when my sister-in-law ran into her in the aisles of the superette nearest the hospital, she was crying. In the shower, she said to me: "Don't they have anything but these garbage bags? It's not a big deal. They lend you a certain charm."

They didn't have the means to avoid lending me that charm: outside the operating room, the hospital was flat broke. And I was afforded special treatment. Apart from the parents of children who were hospitalized, no one had the right to spend the night here. But as a nurse soon told me, "you're not an ordinary patient." For the first time since nursery school, I was the pet. Because I hated the cafeteria, the woman who served as the school monitor took me to her home at noon. She gave me the better part of her meal, in particular of her steaks, limiting herself to eating mine. It was the period when my grandfather walked me to school, and I made him cross the street every time a little mutt barked behind a fence. In a city whose prince is a child, the child is almost always tyrannical and ungrateful. He generally ends up being executed, like a prince, before he has had time to gain access to memories. This time, the child had survived everything, better, in any case, than his various successors. He joined me in this room all the time. Enjoy the monitor's steak, he told me, everything you get is your due.

On the day of the demonstration, I got up. Gabriela helped me take the first steps toward the door and my first walk the length of the corridor. There were tubes everywhere. She rolled the drip stand alongside me. We didn't take the 104 steps, the full round trip, that morning, but she immediately treated me as a dancer:

"Stand up straight, raise your head, shoulder blades in, imagine that you're a marionette and that the top of your head is being held by the hair. You're leaning to the right, straighten up!" We walked at a slow pace. Two policemen followed us at a distance of a few meters, their hands on their Berettas. The two others remained near the elevator, standing. I didn't have to do many lengths to learn to live in their company as if they were shadows that followed me without depending on me and without coming too close to me. I was going to cohabit with them, twenty-four hours a day, for four and a half months, and the day they left I felt naked. Their presence doubled that of the nurses, providing a privacy without solitude. It required me to watch my behavior.

As I walked with Gabriela, I looked at the doors of the other rooms. Here, each one was occupied by only one patient. Almost all of them were rather serious cases, lots of tracheotomies, lots of tubes, lots of dribble on the floor. Most of the patients came from a lower-class background. Many had cancer of the jaw or the tongue. They smoked too much, drank too much. Some came in drunk the day before an operation. Others left their rooms without telling anyone. Sometimes the same person did both. Some smoked in their rooms, sometimes even through the tracheal tube, when they could no longer smoke through their mouths: the drive survived the tubes. There were some who took their drip stands with them when they went to smoke outdoors, in the sun, sitting on the low, gray wall across from the ambulance entrance. The most vigorous of them went as far as the benches in the sumptuous garden between the buildings and the great chapel built during the reign of Louis XIV.

There were accident victims of all kinds. There were petty thugs with broken jaws. They were usually brought in on weekends, at night, after a fight. They received many visits by their families or pals, who looked around the corridors like warriors in foreign territory. Their bodies sought the habitual reflexes, but their instinct didn't follow through, and they seemed embarrassed. This embarrassment sometimes gave way to a kind of delicacy. Uncertainty suspended action. Nothing they would have wanted to do was in its place or could be determined. Sometimes, a mother went to the nurse's station to ask for something that she obtained or didn't. She looked tired, almost faded, and gave off a kind of odor of destiny. It was a dense odor, against a background of bleach and antiseptic. Like the humidity of the tropics, it slowed the pace.

I didn't know what was going on behind the closed doors, but I occasionally heard it, and sometimes, as time went by, the nurses or the auxiliaries talked to me about it. Among the petty thugs, there were some who were very macho, and couldn't cope with depending on women. They treated the nurses with rage and scorn. One of them, who occupied the room across from mine, threw his water cup when a nurse entered, screaming, "Pick it up!" From that time on, the nurses no longer entered his room except at the time for routine care.

In general, the doors were closed, and there was no relationship among the patients. For one thing, they didn't stay long. For another, as Corneille would have said, each person is in his night—especially in a ward where everything that required working with the mouth created problems. We sometimes met with our drip stands in the hall, shuffling along without speaking. At best, a gesture or a little greeting. We hadn't watched over the cattle together as children, and didn't want to, the herd moving along the cliff when it didn't fall off it. Each face was deformed, blinded, twisted, swollen, bruised, dented, bandaged. For a day or forever, it was the corridor of the *gueules cassées*, war veterans with serious facial injuries. Some of them would end up looking like themselves again;

others would not, ever. Some of the cancer patients were going to die, in a month or a year. Whatever the future might be, in this corridor each one was the mirror of the other. Only madmen and wicked queens talk to a mirror, especially if it is distorting.

The door to a room was left open in case of an emergency or a serious problem, for example, a respiratory one. The open door often opened onto the beyond. A few steps away from mine, I found that of a patient curled up on his bed, like the hammer of a pistol, immobile and silent, his head turned slightly up. His face was moon-shaped, forming a concave oval that extended from his forehead to his chin. A saw seemed to have cut out the face, leaving only each extremity, and in the middle, in the emptiness, eyes that seemed no longer to see anything. His legs had grown so thin that they seemed as slender as matchsticks, ready to break or burst into flame. He had been in the ward for a year and no longer walked or spoke. They had given him a radio that blasted hit tunes. A nurse told me that he liked that and that he still reacted, with movements. You just had to know how to interpret them. His name was Ludo. He belonged to a different category of patients: those who had tried to kill themselves. Ludo had shot himself in the head because of a woman, but he'd failed.

I saw for the first time this face without a face, this body emaciated by suffering and surviving, and I gestured to Gabriela to say: "Did you see that?" She had seen and signaled that I should turn back. I'd made enough effort already. I didn't need to see that. There was no question of going beyond Ludo, at least not on that day.

After that first walk, I couldn't pass his open door even once without stopping in front of the room of the man I now called "poor Ludo": looking at him was like a prayer. I didn't know anything about him, and I still don't know much more, but he accompanied me. He was the forerunner and he was what I could have been. All it would have taken was for the bullet to strike me a little higher up or for a second one to follow. His solitude—unsullied by any visitor—impressed me. At first, poor Ludo had recovered a few functions. He could almost speak, or at least make himself understood. His family and friends came to see him. There had been a time, as distant and improbable as that of the dinosaurs, when he had walked by himself as far as the nurses' station or the little staff room. His birthday was celebrated, and even if Christiane had taken a dislike to him for reasons no one explained, perhaps simply because he was occupying a bed and was taking a long time to die, he'd become the ward's mascot.

Then, little by little, his condition had taken a turn for the worse and people stopped coming to see him. Now he was alone. He was going away with the nurses as his companions. The lead that remained in his head had multiplied the cerebral, nervous problems. His intestines went wrong. Poor Ludo had stopped walking, expressing himself, moving. He had to be turned over, washed, changed. He was breaking up inside and everywhere. Henceforth he was merely existing: an existence without any contingency, invaded by a suffering that had become mute, in which all that remained of life escaped the living. This presence, from one end of the corridor to the other, determined the lengths I walked and helped me live.

One day Linda, seeing that I was looking at him, said to me: "Ah! Monsieur Lançon. If you want to kill yourself, above all don't shoot yourself in the head or throw yourself out a window. Because if it goes wrong . . . No, the best thing is still a nice big poison cookie!" She said it with an unctuous, almost greedy air, like a cook about to deliver her recipe for custard. I wondered what color the cookie would be, and I thought: you'd still have to have the ingredients. That same evening, I wrote to my brother telling him I wanted to join the Death with Dignity organization. "Me too," he said. We didn't do it.

One night in February poor Ludo died, just before dawn. There was noise in the corridor—a certain kind of noise, a nervous mixture of voices, equipment, and carts that I had learned to recognize. The nurses who cared for me first that morning gave me the news that I was expecting. As I was doing my walking, I knew that poor Ludo was gone, but I looked for him. The door was open. The room was empty, the plastic-covered mattress was bare. It was going to be cleaned. I continued to think of him every day, as I passed in front of this room, which was occupied the same day by another patient, and the door was now closed. Often, I still think about him. I relive the day when, passing slowly by, I saw him for the first time living and letting himself die. It was the day that I was told there was a demonstration in Paris. It took place, I wasn't there, and the next day I went back to the operating room. It was the first time I went there conscious. For a year, for everything, it was always the first time. The operating room was part of my new house. I still didn't know to what extent this room would become familiar to me, and even desirable. It was the room where the body changed and where others, those from outside, didn't follow me. I went there to escape poor Ludo's fate.

Y ou're going to be in first position, Monsieur Lançon."
It was the night nurse who was talking. I was seeing
her for the first time. She told me her first name. I
thought it was that of one of Raymond Queneau's characters,
that it was dated, that she must be about my age, and that I,
too, was dated. When you're dated, it's because you've survived something, or even several things, and perhaps you
shouldn't have. You've survived, but what? Huddled in my
bed, I now believed that the attack had given me an expiration
date. For some time, I'd no longer felt suited to a trade that
was panic-stricken, frightening, and required conforming to a
world that was going much too fast and too savagely for me.
Current events had become a hall of mirrors, filled with over-
heated lamps that no longer illuminated anything, and around
which fluttered clouds of increasingly stupid, moralizing, self-
advertising, nervous mosquitos. From now on, every word,
every sentence made me feel its price. My shattered jaw looked
like a metaphor and that was okay.

The night nurse bore the first name of one of Raymond
Queneau's characters, but it was also the name, I thought as I
looked at her, of a girl I had known when I was eighteen and
who one night had offered me a stuffed toy just as I was about
to kiss her, which cooled my ardor. The day before, my brother
had installed an internet connection for me at the hospital, an
expensive little terminal that was to follow me from one bedroom to another. It was possible to gain access to the hospital's

network at a lower price, but it didn't work well. The TV worked better, it was like the polluted air that one breathes, but I stuck to a decision that I have never regretted: neither television nor radio in my room. I would have felt as if I were being invaded by mosquitos. I wanted to hear or be subject only to noises that were directly related to my own experience, and in the greatest silence possible, even if it meant putting mosquito coils under my bed. When the doors of the room were opened while I was doing my first lengths up and down the corridor, I had discovered without surprise that most of the patients, confined to their beds, and no matter how moribund they were, were watching television night and day, the sound turned all the way up as if to awaken a deaf person, or else the dead man that they might well be in the near future, and particularly the last and most effective of the brainwashing machines, the BFM television channel. I understood why they were doing that, and I wouldn't for the world have judged the way in which each individual confronted the condition that we shared; but I didn't want to add, to the images that occupied me, and that had at least the merit of being private and relatively discreet, that collective picture of hell: news and entertainment repeated over and over.

A little later that night, I continued to think about Raymond Queneau. His metrical and melancholic humor had always consoled me, though I wasn't sure why. Now, I knew. Two lines, just two, came back to me—it's true that I didn't know many others:

Je crains pas ça tellment la mort de mes entrailles
et la mort de mon nez et celle de mes os.

I'm not so afraid of the death of my guts
And the death of my nose and that of my bones.

Stretched out on my bed, my jaw leaked less, but it started to leak again, I drooled at the slightest emotion, and the nasal cannula burned my throat and my nose. A pressure ulcer had appeared inside the nostril through which the tube ran. They were constantly taking it out and putting it back in. I soon understood that to limit the discomfort, I had to accept the tube, welcome it, so to speak, just as when diving, if you're starting to get sinusitis, you have to open the sinuses to the salt water and allow it to clean them out in order to have a chance to go down, and especially to come back up, without damage. The tube is boss: the more you fear it and resist it, the more it punishes and tortures you. What was true for the nose was true for the veins, from blood tests to catheters, and soon was true for the stomach as well. You had to love tubes, because although they violated you, it was for your own good. They brought you water, sugar, food, drugs, soporifics, and finally life itself, survival and relief. They were benevolent despots.

Besides, I felt guilty for feeling these pains, because if I compared the condition of my nose with that of my hands and especially my jaw, the former was, like the effects, secondary. Complaining about it was like a recent amputee who had been blown up by a mine complaining about having a horsefly bite on the tip of his nose. I would have liked to arrange my ills hierarchically with the wisdom of Buddha, but I was incapable of doing so. I didn't live under a banyan tree or near a lotus flower, but rather in a hospital bed, and I felt guilty of not being up to the test. The day before, a male nurse had told me, laughing: "Now there's a hero in the family!" I didn't feel like a hero, but I was ashamed that I was unable to play the role that circumstances assigned to me. It was an initial manifestation of that particular culpability, simultaneously depressing and touchy: the culpability of the patient. He depends on others for almost everything, and he would like to control at least the manner in which this dependency is expressed. It only grew and appeared in all possible ways in the course of the following weeks, to the point that it became a problem in itself, one against which I had to fight, just as my surgeons fought against the loss of weight, the burning of the tissues, the festering of the wounds, the aforementioned leaks from my chin and mouth, and an exhaustion which, as I passed from one operating room to another, was becoming worrisome.

At night, I searched for a trace of the girl who had offered me the stuffed toy. I remembered her broad neck, her androgynous face, her short, blond hair, like that of Jean Seberg. It took me a long time to recall her family name. More than thirty years had passed; she might have changed. Was I already alive, at that time? I surfed in vain, clumsily. The girl's face entered my body and made my head spin. I breathed with increasing difficulty. The effect of the morphine was wearing off. The stuffed toy, I suddenly remembered, was a squirrel, a charming little rodent whose whole purpose is to evoke autumn, trees, a feather-duster, and its own disappearance. When she gave it to me, Mitterrand had just been elected, Europe was a future project that we studied in law school, and that made the officials in Brussels into virtual new adventurers. I searched for the odors of the university cafeteria and the smoky, greasy bars where we went to drink coffee, eat a croque monsieur, talk about a cycle by Bergman or Anthony Mann, and Godard's or Truffaut's last film. I couldn't find them either. I was eighteen years old and I will gladly allow anyone to say that it's the best part of life, but faced by this computer, this search, in this bed, it was an age that had not existed, another one, an age of which the attack had erased, not every image, but every sensation.

"What are you doing?" Gabriela asked me.

The light from the computer had awakened her. I wrote on the whiteboard:

"Nothing. I'm thinking."

"You're not looking at news about the attacks, are you?

You should absolutely avoid doing that. You have to think about positive things, things that do you good. Concentrate on a landscape that you love, concentrate very hard and go back to it."

Gabriela seemed to think that it sufficed to think about the Good to drive Evil away. I have never been able to imagine a lake in the Pyrenees—probably the landscape I like best in the world—to the point of feeling that I'm immersed in it. But I wouldn't have been looking at news about the attacks, either. I repeat: wrongly or rightly, I felt that doing that would devalue what we experienced. The news was for other people now. But Gabriela hadn't traveled six thousand kilometers to learn that while she was worrying about me, I was looking, under the influence of morphine, for a forgotten girl. How could I tell her, moreover, that I had begun to look for traces of everything that surfaced, in disorder, like dead bodies in the water, for some reason or other? Looking for everything, and first of all what had disappeared long ago? There were names, silhouettes, moments that appeared only through a short circuit. I wouldn't have known how to explain it to someone who, like her, lived in continuity, even in the midst of crisis, even with ruptures: what Gabriela would have taken to be an indelicacy would only have fed her anxiety and even her jealousy. We were there, in that little room, as if in the belly of a whale, she with her interrupted life, I with my shattered face, suspended between dramas, and she was not going to change either her situation or her character on the pretext that I had to change jaws and lives.

The night nurse bore the name of one of Raymond Queneau's characters. In this book, rather than Zazie, I will call her Madeleine. Her hair was long, light-colored, and straight. Her square glasses had a light frame that seemed to glow wickedly in the dark. She came up to my bed, passing in front of Gabriela's. I looked to see if Gabriela was there to defend me, in the event that . . . that what? Well, in the event that Madeleine murdered me. Ever since they had turned up unexpectedly at *Charlie*, I imagined that the killers took all sorts of forms and that they were at home everywhere, in particular in my home. Gabriela seemed to be asleep. Her hair moved a little on the pillow. Madeleine's smile and her soft, almost murmuring voice came still closer. A little hard look and a stocky neck contradicted them. I thought that Madeleine was single and athletic, the kind of person who spends her vacations walking without comfort but well-equipped through distant countries, poor countries, without Queneau, without nurses, without health care, countries where people survived attacks much less well than they did here. While she was bending over me and talking to me, I looked into her eyes and wondered if she also traveled in countries where it was impossible to laugh at everything.

She had crossed the little room with the stealthy steps of a burglar. She probably wore, like the other nurses, clogs made of perforated rubber because they squeaked slightly as they touched the floor tiles. She was heavyset, square-shouldered, and while she was changing the feeding bag and injecting me with beneficial and nourishing morphine, I imagined her in a gym, giving lectures on a pommel horse, the parallel bars, the rings, in all the positions, and then in a clinical torture room where she became, with each patient, an excellent torturer. She soon took up this latter job in the sequence of my dreams. She returned every night to take something away from me and to make me admit something, anything. Her imaginary role was to force me to confess and to prolong the punishment. In reality, Madeleine never mistreated me, and like most of the night staff, she generally reassured me instead; but there emanated from her a threat, a lack of affection, and I immediately felt guilty of suffering and of having told her. Was that a bad thing? I'm not sure. With Madeleine, you didn't let yourself go. And she informed me:

"You're going to be in first position, Monsieur Lançon."

The next morning, January 12, I went down to the operating room a little before 8 A.M. It was the second operation, and it was the first time that I heard the expression "first position." I thought of "pole position," of the rumble of race cars on the starting line, like mastiffs being held back, and of an accident that I had seen live, and in which the Swedish driver Ronnie Peterson had died. I was fifteen, and I'd decided to watch, for the first time, a Formula 1 Grand Prix. Ronnie Peterson was my favorite driver. At that time, in part because of Bjorn Borg, the tennis player who dominated the circuit about as much as Everest, the Swedes stood high in my imagination. They were all blond, silent and discreet people, and, if they won in the end like the Germans, they were not as disagreeable as the Germans were. They hadn't occupied us. They hadn't exterminated the Jews. They didn't control the referees. They didn't spread their bellies and their shouts on Spanish beaches. Their language was just as incomprehensible, but no one was obliged to learn it in school. The Swedes were my good Germans, the tall blondes who gave me complexes without being unpleasant. After Ronnie Peterson's death, I never watched a Formula 1 Grand Prix again.

In pole position for my second operation . . . I have had seventeen operations at the time that I am writing these lines in August 2017, in the Scottish hinterland. It's raining, it's sunny, the weather here changes much more quickly than the heart of a mortal, without ever giving the impression of being capricious or inconsistent: it's up to humans to adapt. Further attacks have occurred far from here, in Catalonia, on Barcelona's Rambla, and in a popular vacation spot. I have rather unpleasant memories of summer. Franco had just died. Spain and its modest pesetas offered cheap vacations for Northern Europeans; today it's Greece. I was an adolescent and I was horrified by the vulgarity of the vacationers, and first of all by the Germans. I had the impression that my parents were yielding to the atmosphere, that their courtesy was becoming submission to the brutes. I was no different from them.

On the beaches near Cambrils, I sometimes read Balzac, sometimes Gérard de Villiers's *SAS* novels. I was very fond of Vautrin and Félix de Vandenesse, much less of Rastignac and Rubempré, and I liked Malko, Villiers's princely spy and pornographer, who defended the West against the Reds. Balzac's monsters joined those of Villiers very naturally among the bellies and bikinis. I'm not nostalgic about those years, which were marked by malaise, but I am nostalgic about at least two things, the solitude that reading procured under all circumstances and the absence of good and bad taste: the mind was no more finicky than Balzac's appetite or my stomach, filled in the late afternoon, when the sea breeze warmed the air, by a paper cone of nice, greasy churros.

I'm writing to remember all that, too, all I've almost forgotten, all that I've lost, knowing that I have nonetheless forgotten or lost it. It had happened to me as it happens to everyone to lose it and suddenly find it again, without being prepared for it, but the continuity of life protected me against everything that was menacing in these mnemonic lightning bolts. January 7 foregrounded the menace, every day, every minute, in every detail. Since then, each time there's an attack, I'm a little more certain that I will die in a world where Balzac's heroes no longer exist for anyone, where no one will read a vulgar novel by Gérard de Villiers on a Spanish beach in the summertime. Like the earlier ones, the attacks in Barcelona and Cambrils distanced me from a story in which, once the candles were extinguished and the little hearts put away, everyone acted as if nothing had happened—how could they do otherwise?—and as if these killers were not a disastrous consequence of what we are, what we experience.

My second operation, I was saying. I haven't stopped counting the operations any more than I've stopped counting the attacks. I know that the number is not final, and that this accounting has become unimportant. I continue to make it known, not without complacency, to people who ask me about it and to *Charlie*'s readers. It has fed most of the articles that referred to my case, people like statistics and records and most journalists are always prepared to give them, as one would to children, what they are trained to want. This accounting reminds me of something: so long as there's an operating room in the future, there's hope—hope to improve a little, a lot, passionately, madly. Or not at all, but I'm not yet at that point. I'm not, as they say in the jargon of state evaluators, consolidated. Going back to the operating room is no longer a habit, but it remains a prospect, and as soon as I return to it, it becomes both a habit and a prospect. I'm the old nag of the operating room, whose ears twitch and whose nostrils tremble as he descends toward that slightly cold, slightly green room, like an animal heading for the show jumping course after being weighed. Besides, the patient is not cut out for staying in bed. Action takes place in the world below.

That morning, Madeleine woke me around 5:30. Gabriela stirred, but she wasn't really sleeping. As she had the preceding evening, she helped me take a shower. For the first time, I performed the dawn gestures that every regular knows. They were soon to become a ritual, and then, the operations taking place every three to six months, a commemorative pleasure. Going to the bathroom with the drip stand. Ripping up that night's smock and throwing it in the trash can. Making sure the kit is complete: the yellow Betadine capsules that serves as soap, the rough, green drawsheet that serves as a towel, the surgical cap to cover wet hair after the shower, disposable slippers for bare feet. Putting the garbage bags around the bandages and tying them as best I can. Sitting on a chair brought by

Gabriela or an auxiliary nurse, holding my head as far back as possible. Turning on the water and washing myself, making a maximum effort to avoid the zones under the bandages, and absolutely the jaw and the area around it. Taking off the plastic bags. Drying myself with the green cloth that doesn't dry, while performing as few acrobatics as possible. Putting on the operating room smock. Knotting it around my waist. Putting the surgical cap on my head and returning to bed, putting the disposable slippers on the night able. Taking the light sedative that the nurse dilutes in a minimum of water. Then, closing my eyes and waiting for the orderly to arrive.

This time, I didn't hear him coming. I was drowsing and was not yet used to the specific sound of the casters that announces, like a leper's rattle, the coming action. There were several stretcher-bearers in the ward. One of them was from the Antilles, big and strong, very handsome. Later, as he was bringing me back up from an operating room, he promised to make one of his favorite dishes for me someday. I'm still waiting, but that doesn't matter: the idea of this meal made it possible to persuade me, in the freight elevator that was taking me back to my room, that one day soon I would again be able to eat.

The orderly who most often accompanied me was young and pale, with light brown hair and a two- or three-day beard. His surgical cap always prevented me from seeing the exact nature and length of his hair; the people in the operating room never took off their surgical caps to greet the patient on whom they were going to operate, and I could imagine his size only in relation to the walls and the other caregivers, since I only saw him, as I did so many others, when I was lying down. I didn't learn his name, either, so I will call him Bill. Bill had a soft voice, a little desperate, and a sense of derision that would have made him a good character in a TV series, whether it was set in a hospital or not. I take the opportunity to say that though I hadn't watched *ER*, I became a fan of Dr. House. Bill had attached to his locker a phrase from Dante's *Inferno*: "Abandon all hope, you who enter here." Dr. House couldn't have said it better.

Bill was not the only one who accompanied me. The two policemen who'd spent the night in front of my room calmly insisted on following us. Those were their instructions. So there all four of us were, in the freight elevator descending to the operating room. There was not much space between the walls and the stretcher. My nose and the tubes were almost touching the Berettas. Sometimes I looked at Bill's face, sometimes at that of each of the policemen, smiling at them as if my life depended on it: they were there to remind me that the killers were never far away. They smiled back at me. We did not speak. Bill was troubled by the presence of these uniforms. I'd taken my whiteboard and my felt-tip pen. I wrote: "Strange place for a meeting." I had the impression that I was going not to the next floor below, but to an unknown, distant planet, like Pluto. The door opened onto a narrow antechamber full of objects and emergency room clothes, a sort of dimly lit closet. The negotiation between the cosmonauts began. The policemen wanted to accompany me as far as possible. I wondered whether they would be in the operating room during the surgery, if they would watch Chloé tinker with my jaw. It seemed to me improbable that she could tolerate that. Bill explained that beyond the first door, access was forbidden to those who were neither care-givers nor patients. In any case, for reasons of hygiene, even if they remained in the antechamber they would have to put on a surgical cap, shoe covers, and a smock. Embarrassed smiles passed from one face to the other, like clouds over a landscape. We were floating between professionalism and comedy. Imagining the policemen in the operating room immediately led me to imagine the killers entering it. But

imagining is too weak a word. It was as if the scene were projected in front of me. Once again, I was part of it.

A policeman said:

"Are there several access doors, or is this the only one?"

There was another one, Bill said, on the other side of the
operating rooms, but nobody used it. The policeman said that
if there was a door, somebody could use it, so one of them
would go guard it. Then they slowly put their weapons on the
floor and put on, with difficulty, the surgical caps and shoe
covers. The cosmonauts were now floating in an atmosphere
without gravity. Perhaps their weapons were going to fly away,
and they with them, to end up on the ceiling, like Captain
Haddock's solidified whisky. For them, there was no question
of putting the operating room smock over their uniforms, they
would have to begin by taking everything off and we would be
there all morning. It was perhaps for that reason that, weighed
down by twenty kilos of uniforms, radios, pistols, and belts,
they finally remained on earth.

Behind the door, the people of the world below looked at
the scene with a half-mocking, half-alarmed air. It was cold,
but on Pluto we were sort of at the theater and, although I was
breathing the wrong way, I thought that if this was to be my
last vision, it was a success.

I entered the "waiting room" watching one of the two
policemen disappear behind the porthole, his surgical cap on
his head and holding his submachine gun. See you soon! I
thought. Bill put me along the wall and wished me good luck,
telling me that they would come to take care of me. That is
when la Castafiore appeared.

She was the nurse responsible for the recovery room. That
was what they called her in the ward, because it was difficult to
ignore her presence and because for a long time she had sung.
She adored the opera, being a singer had been her dream, and
quite soon, during the following visits to the operating room,

while we waited for the operating table to be ready, that was what we talked about. Her name was Annie. She took my hand or my wrist and gently massaged me, caressing my fingers and palms and thus comforting me, in a way. My whole body relaxed under her firm, strong, plump hands. She talked to me about her favorite arias. Contrary to Captain Haddock, I would have liked to hear her sing, but the operating room isn't an opera house or a recording studio, and Annie could only prepare my entrance on the operating stage, and, if she had time, keep me company all the way to the end. She gladly did it. From one operating room to another, we exchanged views regarding the interpretation of this or that work. One day, she came into the operating room and, to make me more comfortable, tried to arrange the tubes in a certain fashion and give me a drug that would relax me. She was abruptly asked to leave, the operating room was not made for courtesy, and she left mumbling: "All right, if that's how it is, I'm going, I just wanted to help him . . . ."

A nurse-anesthetist came to install the drip. On that day, it was easy: I still had veins. From operating room to operating room, they got harder, rarer, thin and hard to find, rolling and escaping under the long needle, disappearing to end up under the thin surface of the skin. This sensitive reaction accentuated the pain of the injections and the embarrassment of the nurses who, after a few fruitless attempts, called for that first-rate truffle dog: the anaesthetist. A few days later I wrote to my favorite anaesthetist, Annette, to whom we will soon return: "Excuse my veins, they're shy." For me, it was a miracle and a relief to see her appear (she or another, there were four anesthetists, including three hefty women you didn't want to tangle with). She felt my forearm and my hand and discovered, where no one else had seen anything, a lazy vein, a slowpoke, accommodating, that was waiting to be seized and immediately pierced. Unfortunately, the anesthetist came in only when the others

had given up, and the search for a vein, after the fourth operating room, became for me the main hurdle to be cleared, the
other being the recovery period. I liked returning to the world
below and its inhabitants, I felt good among them, but even
though I set an example of the greatest civility for my veins, my
little prostitutes, they persisted in refusing any contact with the
nurses. Between operations, they had only four or five days to
recover. It wasn't long enough.

A month later, I went on one of my first outings. I'd asked
my brother to organize with the policemen a visit to a museum
of which I'm particularly fond: the Guimet museum, devoted
to Asian art. I wanted to see China, which is far away, and I
wanted to see the Seine, which is close: I wanted to see something different, and see the same thing again. There was a show
on the splendor of the Han dynasty. The statues of dancers
were so fluid that they seemed to be moving. One of them had
flared, slit sleeves that hid her hands as if under flowers in the
form of little bells. Their bodies blended with the air, which
became the sleeves. My every gesture had become difficult and
my neck was now no more than a rusty periscope; I was intimidated by these ancient creatures who were so elegant, so supple, who swept away the borderline between immobility and
movement. I circled them painfully, while in the window I saw
reflected the silhouette of one of the two policemen in plain
clothes who were accompanying me, gradually melding with
the statue to give it additional life. The other policeman was
not far away: possible attackers mustn't be given a concentrated target. The horsemen and their mounts, with their little
tails proudly tied up in a bun, seemed to be rising out of the
tomb to accomplish all sorts of dreams and avenge all sorts of
humiliations. There was the statue of Tianlu, who is in charge
of the riches accorded by heaven, and that of Bixie, who drives
evil spirits away. But the one that attracted me the most represented Guan Yin, the goddess with a thousand arms, because

I would have liked, when I arrived in the operating room, to have some of them. For each operation, I would have stretched out an unsullied arm to hold the anesthetist's tourniquet, and la Castafiore, who was always concerned to relax me and distract me, would have said: "Ah! Monsieur Lançon, if all patients had as many arms as you do, nurses would be on cloud nine! And I who dream of going to China . . . " Avoiding a few pains by making the nurses' task easier was exactly the mission that I dreamed of fulfilling. I wasn't a hero, but all the same I would have liked to be one. The fact that Guan Yin is a goddess of mercy who rescues, among others, people threatened by sword and by fire, only added to her charms and her usefulness.

I hung onto the catalog for the show at the museum for a few months, until, to thank him, I gave it to Joël, the hairdresser who came several times to my room to cut my hair free of charge. The first time was just before the most important operation: the grafting of the jawbone. "Well now, it's time you went to the hairdresser! You can't continue going down to the operating room like that!" Chloé had said to me; like all surgeons, she didn't like hair. Joël cut my hair in silence while we listened to *The Well-Tempered Clavier*. He cut the hair of middle-class ladies in Paris's 7th arondissement, actresses, and chic, redone people, but he also went to cut hair in prisons and hospitals, and now he was cutting the hair of a journalist with a face under construction. He arrived with his equipment and the ceremony began. While he was putting the protective paper in place and spraying my head, I closed my eyes, and under that artificial dew, I felt a brief joy. For a few minutes, the pains died away, I shivered, I was reborn a little, and, with Bach's help, I had the sensitive, friendly, almost tender feeling that by giving me a nice, condemned man's haircut, Joël was preparing me to look my best for an execution.

A certain time passed before I was taken into the operating

room. People were fussing around me. Until the last minute, I kept my whiteboard and my felt-tip pen. Finally, I was moved from the stretcher to the operating table.

"Move up a little, Monsieur Lançon!"

My head had to be placed at the edge of the operating table, in a sort of recess that made it lean back, almost into thin air, and that did not make breathing easier: my face was turned toward the surgeon, almost like an animal to be slaughtered. Annette was preparing the anesthesia, after a nurse had placed the electrodes, at the same time telling me what she was doing, with a slight grimace, a little greedy, a little wild, that resembled a smile but might not have been one. She was in her fifties at least, with a wrinkled face and large, bright eyes that looked at you as if from the bottom of a disturbing lake to which you would never have access. I followed her eyes and her strange smile the way a child follows those of a monitor on whom the path depends. She put in place the polyester heating blanket, which was thin and transparent. I thought of camping equipment. A little later, Chloé came in. It was the first time I saw her with a surgical cap on her head. Her blond hair had disappeared. As she often did, she spoke to me with a smile, as if she were not speaking to anyone in particular. Annette told me that I was going to feel a light burning sensation on my left arm, at the point where the anesthetic went in. At that moment, I imagined the killers bursting in while I was under, and I looked at all the faces with surgical caps surroundeding me as if we were all going to die, they in terror and I in peace. A year later, an article informed me that during a bombardment at Homs, in Syria, surgeons had been forced to flee the operating rooms right in the middle of surgery, leaving their patients unconscious. I was so shocked that I immediately mentioned it to Chloé, who replied: "What do you expect, there are times when there's only one thing to do, save your own skin." What does a patient dream about when he's going to die alone, under anesthesia, in the middle of an operating room that is being bombarded? I went to sleep.

I have difficulty recalling the sensations of the second operating room, because they are covered over by the habit that the following ones gave me. Starting with the fifth or sixth operation, I was happy to go back there. I returned like a regular to this greenish world and the people who occupied it. I looked them over one by one, like a man who, after a journey, returns to his village and finds familiar faces. I knew the little I had to do. I knew that each of the team's actions would transform me. I sometimes went there with a book hidden under the sheet: Kafka's *Letters to Milena*. I had started reading it at dawn, just before the third operation, and it was while waiting to go in, lying on my stretcher alongside a wall, with Annie absent, that I took the book out from under the sheet and read a few passages, including this one: "So, you are not well, worse than you have ever been since I have known you. And that insurmountable distance combined with your suffering produces this effect: it's as if I were in your room and you could hardly recognize me and I paced helplessly back and forth between the bed and the window and had no confidence in anyone, in any doctor, in any treatment, and I knew nothing and I would look at the dismal sky and after all the jokes of past years it would unveil itself to me for the first time in its true despair . . . "

They came to get me a first time, and left me right at the entrance to the operating room. I took the book out from under the sheet again and read, a little farther on, this sentence: "The sick man is abandoned by the healthy one, but the healthy man is also abandoned by the sick one." Did that twofold abandonment hold true here as well, in the world below? I was taken away as I was ruminating on another passage about the cauldrons in Hell.

Once I was strapped in place on the operating table, I began to tell a story to the people who were preparing to anesthetize me. About one minute after the little burning sensation in my left wrist, I lost consciousness in the middle of my story. Today, I have forgotten even the beginning. But it must have been sufficiently precise for Chloé to ask me the next morning, during her rounds, "What was the end of your story? What were you trying to say to us? We spent the whole time in the operating room wondering about it." The least that can be said is that over the following days I tried to discover—in vain—what the end of the story might be—just as I am trying, today, to discover the beginning. As I was finishing this chapter, I wrote to Chloé again to ask if she remembered it: she too had forgotten everything. At the time, I consoled myself by reflecting that for once in my life I'd been a good storyteller, someone who held the attention of the people who had put him to sleep and who had to continue to watch over him, but without him; who had, in a way, to survive the end of a story that they were not to know. Then I said to myself that if Kafka was incapable of finding this story for me, at least he gave its disappearance a *raison d'être*. Rather than finishing a narrative whose end would have opened only on the void and more sorrow, I had voluntarily recounted it in a place and at a time when it could only be interrupted and disappear, like a dream. Then I stretched out in the garden opened up by the little burning sensation, the garden whose view enchanted me and plunged me, for a few hours, into a coma.

Most awakenings have been either difficult or dreadful. Some were dominated by physical pain: my throat on fire, an inability to breathe, nausea. The others added to that pain the repetition of the initial awakening, the one on January 7: once again I was at home and an ordinary day was about to begin, once again the pale light and the nurses' voices swept away the well-being I felt, that tailend of the coma, and plunged me back into one of the Kafkaesque cauldrons; wasn't that just what Hell was: the eternal return of a fictive sensation, created by memory, and the abrupt expulsion from the ordinary paradise that it recalled? In any case, that was how it was upon awakening from the second operation. I was at home, happy under the bedclothes, when my throat began to burn horribly. I opened my eyes, saw that light, and immediately closed them again to go back to the sleep that had interrupted my story. But this time the pain came to the aid of the awakening. It heightened it and forced me to stop crawling along in the intermediate zone where there is no borderline between consciousness, perception, and memory. Then the order of requirements was inverted: awake, handed over entirely to pain and malaise, I had to take, as quickly as possible, the baited hooks that that the recovery room offered me. That morning, two nurses, at the foot of my stretcher-bed, were doing crossword puzzles. I concentrated to listen to them, to understand them. One said: "A four-letter word for Madame Bovary?" They didn't find one. My eyes were closing. Wake up! I thought. I made a movement, and they saw it. I heard: "Do you want to tell us something, sir?" I nodded and pointed to their crossword puzzle. "You want to help us, is that it?" I nodded again. One of them took my whiteboard and my felt-tip pen, which had been put with *Letters to Milena*, and the two of them came up to me. "So, have you got an idea? A four-letter word for Madame Bovary? We're stuck . . . " With a trembling hand, I wrote "Emma." And under it: "It's her first name." Had I ever felt so happy to have read a novel and not to have forgotten its title? In any case, I was awake and I thought: Thanks, Flaubert.

Chapter 10
The Anemone

D ear friends of *Charlie* and *Libération*,

For the moment, I have only three fingers sticking out of bandages, a wrapped-up jaw, and a few minutes of energy, beyond which my ticket is no longer valid, to assure you of all my affection and thank you for your support and your friendship. I wanted to tell you simply this: if there is one thing that this attack reminded me of, or rather taught me, it's why I exercise this trade for these two newspapers—out of a spirit of freedom and an inclination to manifest it, by providing information or caricature, in good company, and in all possible ways, even if they fail, without it being necessary to judge them."

Seven days after the attack, I published in *Libération* an article that began with these lines, but didn't feel that I had written it. If I except the unfortunate poems of my youth that I mentioned earlier, this was the only time in my life when I knew the text almost by heart at the moment that I began to type it. I typed it as a dream and as I could, between morphine and waiting for morphine, on the computer my brother had brought me from the dusty shambles called my apartment. The journalist, with his Pavlovian discipline, was coming to the aid of the wounded man, so that the patient could express himself. He was not able to eliminate the passion for pain in which the other two were immersed. It's difficult not to take seriously your emotions and sensations when what you've become is reduced to them. You'd have to keep them at a distance and practice the comfortable art of mockery; but comfort is absent and mockery would be merely a pose. It takes time to pose, and I didn't have any.

It was also the first time in thirty years as a journalist that I'd written directly about myself in a newspaper. Since I was part of the event, I described it from within and from above, but not without embarrassment. Huddled in my bed, I had the impression of doing something forbidden and even disgusting. What was I doing, exactly? I was signaling to others that I was still alive and would soon be back among them. At least, that's what they believed or wanted to believe, what they said to me and wrote to me, and that's probably why I tried to believe and to make them believe: this optimism of the will was, after all, a sign of life. However, at the moment that I wrote it, the text also signified the inverse: it was those who ended up over there, around the conference table and in the hallway at *Charlie*, that I was addressing. A posthumous piano lesson: if the right hand plays for the living, the left plays for the dead, and that's the hand that keeps time.

I certainly wouldn't say that this text was "dictated" to me by a voice. My name is not Joan of Arc, and I've never believed in the notion of the "inhabited" writer. I'm really the one who wrote the article and sent it in all conscience to the newspaper, like any article, but this writing, or rather this fermentation, arose from a state between waking and sleeping, between two worlds in which, from my hospital room, I was actually speaking more to the dead than to the living, because in those days I felt closer to the dead, and even a little more than close: one of them. So I wrote and published an article addressed primarily to readers who could never read it. Their absence attracted me, penetrated me. They had entered a well in which part of myself, out of solidarity, out of compassion, or simply out of pain, would have liked to follow them and felt prepared to do so. So that I couldn't say, even today, whether I wrote this article, this letter, this confession, to join them or to move away from them. Or both. A pair of hands on the keyboard, I said. It's possible that my companions played the left hand, but at no point did I hear their voices. It's even because I could no longer hear them that I began to repeat words, certain words, that were going to become this text. It was not written by Joan of Arc among her white sheep, but it is assuredly the product of a deaf person and a visionary.

There were no flowers in Room 106, either real ones or ones drawn by children, but this text was born one evening when the anemone was throbbing under the morphine a little more loudly than usual. It was two days after the demonstration on January 11. The flower was beating so hard that it threatened to swallow me. The roll-up shutter on the window had been pulled down. Gabriela was working alongside me on the little bed that had been put there for her. Her concentrated face was lit by the glow from the screen. I closed my eyes.

It was a sea anemone—like the ones that I liked to look at when I was young, especially at night, illuminated by the beam of light from an underwater flashlight when I was diving. The slow movement of the tentacles delighted me. Since my arrival at the hospital, the anemone appeared in the evening, at the time when, in the ward, the patients rang the bells placed at the head of the bed. These bells often fell on the floor. Using the bedrail to catch hold of the wire that connected them with the wall and putting them in a place where they could easily be reached, almost without moving, like a computer mouse or a security blanket, calms the life of the disoriented patient: the feeling of comfort and the prospect of sleep depend on it. That is why, as evening approached, everyone used and abused them—but the idea of abuse, here, had no meaning, because everyone had the feeling, in his bed, that he was the victim of an abuse—of the body, of people, or of destiny. It was the hour of pure anxiety, unsullied by any future, and I did not escape it, even if I was aware, in my cloud of dark reveries, that this anxiety depended on the weather, and owed its strength only to the arrival of the night.

When a visitor was there, I sometimes wrote on the white-board or the notebook: "It's the hour when the birds sing." And then he heard them. It had taken me only a few days to become proud of my knowledge about the hospital and to inform others about it, like a child or a parvenu. My ignorance was beneficial: it allowed me not to notice a condition I believed I understood, or the nurses' errors or the things they forgot. Acquiring knowledge of actions and procedures, like all knowledge, was gradually to increase the waiting, the worry, and the feeling of solitude. The moment when the patient believes he has become an expert on his own care is a danger-ous one, because that belief, though exaggerated, is not unfounded: like a little old man or a peasant, he ends up know-ing almost everything about his limited territory. No attention left unprovided escapes him. He lives in the suspicion and ver-ification of negligences. Later on, I came to long for the time when I didn't know anything of what I believed I knew, and when I proudly wrote, as if words could free me from what they designated: "It's the hour when the birds sing."

In reality, I called the bells in the neighboring rooms "blackbirds," but that was my secret; so long as I didn't men-tion them in front of others, not even in front of Gabriela, the blackbirds wouldn't invade my room and I wouldn't have to feed them. Listening to them sing beyond my walls, I said to myself: "You understand those who call for help, but you aren't like them. There are crows out there, you can see them through the window, but there are no blackbirds in your room. You won't ring the bell. No, you won't ring it." I held out for a while, then I rang it, and long before the auxiliary nurse arrived, my blackbird entered the room. He was alone, landed on me, prevented me from breathing. My vision was clouded, my eyes stung, I could no longer read: was he going to pluck out my eyes as well, like the ravens in the Tower of London in the Middle Ages? For weeks, I was afraid, each evening, that I would become blind. I wrote to my brother: "On top of all that, I'm losing my eyesight. I've read enough in my life, read far too many useless books, but I'd nonetheless like to go on reading them. The killers lacked compassion." I was trying to be clever. I would have liked to be an old, sarcastic Spaniard, but they can't be improvised any more than mockery can, and what I wanted more than anything, like everyone else, was relief.

The first evening, I'd closed my eyes to escape the black-bird and the crow's viewpoint, but what appeared, under my eyelids, was Bernard's brain. It was spread out next to me in the conference room, quite cool, now alone: without shouts, without noise, without parquet floor, without black legs, with-out bodies around it, without anything other than it and me to look at it inside me. I was observing it. I was assimilating it. Little by little, it began to move and transform itself. It became a plant, a living plant, a maritime plant, and the sea anemone appeared. Contraction, dilation, contraction, dilation: it throbbed in a liquid milieu, dark red and lethally purifying. It was blood and it was the sea, and more precisely the mouth of a little Cuban river where I liked to swim at dusk in the cur-rents mixing salt water and fresh, with the desire to reach the other bank, mountainous, distant, not so distant, and the childlike fear of drowning or being devoured by a shark in the night.

In Room 106, the sea anemone returned every evening. It rose up from the Cuban past and replaced Bernard's brain. It beat its own rhythm, my pulse. It sent me blood, dark war, interrupted or threatened memories, like images projected on a screen into which the spectator ends up disappearing, and, quite rapidly, this beating attracted me. It projected fewer and fewer images and sucked me more and more toward its own void, toward the bottom. It pumped me. I was becoming the sea anemone, the bloody anemone, and once inside it, in its tentacles, its velvet, its pulsing, I became once again Bernard's brain, an oceanic brain detached from the little parquet floor of the Rue Nicolas-Appert, like a jellyfish in deep water. At that instant, a panic sadness invaded me. It was the anemone's gift, an absolute reality and as inedible as 100 percent cocoa, and yet I had to swallow it. I opened my eyes to escape the attraction, the digestion. If I had continued to keep them closed, the reality of the attack would have closed over what remained to me of consciousness: the anemone born from Bernard's brain would have devoured mine, and if I hadn't died of it, I might have gone mad. I would have gone back to the heart of the event and decomposed there, in it, on that parquet floor on which we were lying. That may be what characterizes the madman: being a perpetual prisoner of the cruel and unthinkable event which, he thinks, he founded.

The anemone was in me, under my eyelids, in my skin. Opening my eyes was the only way to escape from it. But opening my eyes meant not sleeping, not sleeping anymore, abandoning myself to other, more rational fears arising from exhaustion and an obscure perception of the future—or rather, at that period, of its impossibility. I was then entering a no-man's-land from which I could be freed only by the appearance of Christian, the night nurse, whom I called Brother Morphine. I awakened my blackbird and, announced by the auxiliary nurse, he appeared. He was partly bald, middle-aged. He had a gracious, warm, high-pitched voice. He wore glasses and was always smiling. I think he spent a lot of time taking care of his mother. There were quite a few discreetly tragic fates in the night-duty teams, and perhaps Madeleine's was one of them. I sensed it more than I knew it. Sensing it was enough for me and reassured me. Who would want to confide his distress and loneliness to someone who had never really felt any?

Some people said, with a smile, that Christian was generous with the morphine, but if that was the case, I didn't complain about it and I remain solidly grateful to him: he was the person who, by his presence and his injections, drove away the anemone and sleeplessness.

"In the arm or in the shoulder?"

I took my felt-tip pen and wrote:

"Shoulder. As close as possible to the neck."

That way, the morphine acted quicker and more violently. It led to more acceptable visions, if not more appropriate ones—visions distributed by the anemone from which they escaped in the dark lit by Gabriela's computer. The brain and the body, bit by bit, bloomed. The visions didn't cause me to lose consciousness entirely. They gave form to states that were constantly transformed, naturally, producing a slow-motion fireworks show: I watched it live and I lived in it, as if I had been the spectator, the Roman candles, the skyrockets, the fountains, and the night. One evening, after the injection had been made and Christian had left, the brain transformed itself into an anemone and the dead came out of it. I spoke to them, one by one and then all together, as if they were alive or as if I no longer existed. I talked to them about what we had experienced, I asked what they were experiencing, I explained to them where I was. I wasn't sad; I was sadness. Imperceptibly passing from a deep reverie to a moment of double clarity, I began to see them at a distance, as they were, completely dead, and simultaneously as they had been, very much alive. Looking at them from a little farther away, from above, detached from the anemone, I dried my tears. I began to murmur to them a kind of prayer that my mouth with one lip, and the lack of an opening in my cannula, prevented me from uttering. I didn't know to whom I could address it, I wasn't thinking about that. What mattered was saying it. It was addressed first of all to the person whose death had opened my eyes, Bernard, but laughing and living, and then to the person I felt closest to, Wolinski.

Picking up on this quasi-prayer, I reread the article that came out of it to determine by which sentence I had shifted from the former to the latter. It was, it seems to me, this one: "While the paramedics were lifting me onto an armchair with casters in the conference room, I flew over the bodies of my dead companions—Bernard, Tignous, Cabu, Georges—whom my rescuers were stepping over or alongside, and suddenly, my God, they weren't laughing anymore." But what I said first in Room 106, to escape from the anemone, was different. I began by repeating twice, twenty times: "The paramedics lifted me up and I flew over *your dead bodies*, which they were stepping over, and suddenly, no one was laughing anymore." This sentence was not simply a sentence. It was an address and a magical formula. As I repeated it, I flew over the scene once again, as I had when the rescuers were carrying me on the armchair. Other sweeter, more intimate sentences followed, and I repeated them to avoid abandoning my companions to their fate. I repeated them all night, word by word, in one direction and then in the other, like something confided, without yet thinking that it might be an article intended to be read. I tried to speak to the dead so that they would not disappear, as one advises soldiers on the battlefield to do with a wounded man— at least in films: "Talk to him! Talk to him! Above all, don't let him fall asleep!" I didn't want the dead to fall asleep and I didn't want to fall asleep without them.

In the morning, after I'd taken a shower and the nurses had made their rounds, Gabriela left to exercise in one of the dance practice rooms that structured her geography. I continued to repeat the sentences, but they had changed in nature. It was no longer a little prayer, nor a formula, nor an address, nor a confidence, but it was not yet an article; it floated among all these. The sentences were in the middle of a ford. They didn't know which bank of the river to head for. I don't know exactly when "the paramedics lifted me up" became "While the paramedics were lifting me up," or when "and suddenly, my God, they weren't laughing anymore" became "While the paramedics were lifting me up," or when "and suddenly, my God, they were no longer laughing" appeared, but it was the change in syntax, the appearance of "while" and "my God," that suggested to me that I was now addressing others, those who might read me. I write *suggested to me*, because I was still not aware of what I was doing in writing what I spent the night chewing over, ruminating, to distract myself from the pain or to accompany the visions modified by the morphine. The anemone had opened out like a menace; I reopened it like a thought, liquid and then verbalized, and the matter that seemed to flow through one of my tubes to reappear transformed into a kind of intimate and political discourse was the beginning of a return to the living. Where could I have made this known better than in the places and by the means that had given me so much freedom? The person the killers had failed to kill worked, like those they had liquidated, for newspapers. It was in newspapers that he had to reappear. At the end of the day, the prayer to the dead had become an article.

The last word I hesitated on was one of the first: this "my God," which resembled a lament, but was written by a nonbeliever, an infidel if you wish, who was apostrophizing the dead who were no less unbelieving. I deleted it, put it back, deleted it, put it back. It didn't suit me, but it suited the situation. I finally left it to represent a sigh, a pause over those whom I had left six days earlier, and whom I was leaving again by ending this text.

That evening, around 6 P.M., I handed the computer to

Gabriela and my brother, and asked them on the whiteboard what they thought of the text: was it too intimate? Was it an article? Should I send it to *Libé* or to *Charlie*? Or keep it to myself? I had no idea. What I had written was essential for me, but was it interesting for others? Both of them told me that they didn't know and that it was up to me, but it seemed to them that neither of my newspapers would be embarrassed to publish it. I wasn't so certain about that. In my hospital room, in that isolated chamber where life outside reached me muffled and deformed by the silence that had been established in me and around me, any public statement was regarded as a matter of indifference and vanity, any public statement, starting with mine. Words now lived only in the most intimate, the most concrete, field, it was there that they could live, and two and a half years later that sensation, though it has lessened, has still not left me as I write these lines, whatever their worth. I always feel that I'm writing alongside myself, when I write for those who have not known that room and the silence that enveloped it. The room is the place where words die, flicker out. I have not left it. I still have the impression that what I write is superfluous.

On January 13, shortly before 7 P.M., I e-mailed the text to *Libération* with these words:

> Dear friends, I wrote this little text in the hospital, it's my way of thinking about you, and especially about my dead companions, over at *Charlie*.
>
> Do with it what you think best.
>
> I have written at too great length, as usual; even killers don't change bad habits.
>
> I am, of course, sending the text to *Charlie*.
>
> Decide with them what you want to do.
>
> I'm going to rest: a third operation, a long one, is possible (but not certain) on Thursday.

Tell everyone I'm doing better, and as well as possible. Hugs to all.

Stéphanie, an old friend who is the editor in chief at *Libération*, replied:

Dear Philippe,

After discussion, it seems best to publish it. This evening, for tomorrow's paper. Seeing that I had left for the hospital, Michel got suspicious, and saved a whole page, just in case, even though I hadn't said anything to him.

So, no, for once you're not too long.

If, however, that doesn't suit you, let me know right away, through Gabriela. We'll substitute a full-page self-advertisement.

I embrace you as well

And I'm going to drink to your health (as I have every evening since they've been there) with the *Charlies*.

Stéphanie

I read Stéphanie's e-mail, smiled, and thought: "That's the second time she's helped me at an important point." She was recovering from a bout with cancer, smoked as much as always, and drank, I think, hardly any less. In hospital matters, she had a few lengths' lead on me. If I went down to the operating room with a book hidden under the sheet, she must have gone there with a package of cigarettes hidden in the same place. I even imagined her drinking whisky or beer in her room, shortly after returning from the world below, and, if I imagined it so clearly, that was because it had to be true. I was relieved to learn that for once I wasn't too long. That was one of my journalistic sins, and when I wrote an article, I often thought I saw Stéphanie's cheeks puff out with irony as she said to me: "So, Lançon, too long as usual? You're a pain in the ass."

We hadn't hung out together in a long time. But we have several lives in us, and in one of ours, we had liked each other very much. Twenty-three years earlier, in midsummer, following a love affair that had gone sour, I had half passed out in a street in Lyon. Only half, the other half being destined for a comedy that a passing doctor quickly dealt with: there's always a doctor passing by where you'd prefer that there wasn't one. Recovering from my fainting spell more quickly than from my shame and chagrin, I'd called Stéphanie in a panic, gasping, from a telephone booth, there weren't any cell phones at that time. I knew that she was in this city, the city of her childhood, visiting her parents. It was August. Lyon was broiling hot and deserted. Stéphanie was twenty years old, she was a university student, we were friends. She came to get me and took me to her family's home, where she cared for me with a sweetness, a delicacy, that I have never forgotten. She ordered pizzas. We ate them while we watched a summer television series that she adored and that was a hit: *Les Coeurs brûlés* (*Burnt Hearts*). It suited the circumstances: Mireille Darc was perfect in the role of an aging, duplicitous bitch who ran a luxury hotel on the Côte d'Azur. *Les Coeurs brûlés* was better than a hot bath to vaporize all the tragedy that I attributed to my own life. Later on, we left to hike around the department of Ain. The treatment had succeeded.

I reread Stéphanie's e-mail and thought that, all things considered, she'd been an excellent nurse. I would have liked to see *Les Coeurs brûlés* again and eat pizzas with her, in that room, as if we weren't twenty-three years and a few lives older, she with cancer on top of everything else and I with thirteen teeth less. Like every reminiscence, this one moved me insofar as it took the form of a subtraction. The fortuity of the situations continued the anarchic inventory of what I had loved, and lost.

The next morning, the article was published. It had a strange impact. Those who knew me were pleased to know that I was so alive. Those who didn't know me seemed to be equally pleased. After all, more than a man, I was now, for an indeterminate time, probably quite brief, a symbol. I received an enormous amount of mail. I read it only little by little, at random, sometimes one or two months later. Time no longer mattered, and I seldom answered: I didn't have the energy for that. The e-mails and letters were for the most part sympathetic, encouraging, full of good feelings . . . and amazingly unrealistic. Everyone seemed to believe that in a few days I would be out of the hospital, hale and hearty, and that I was going to go back to work as spotless and enthusiastic as a lamb: everyone was dreaming. Everyone except the other victims, the regulars in my room, and the caregivers. To be sure, writing elicits and maintains this kind of misunderstanding, but this benevolent blindness was nonetheless strange. People wrote to me less to reassure me than to be reassured: how could a person whose legs have been amputated be reassured by a bunch of blind persons who explain to him, with many doleful sighs and cries of joy that soon he'll be on his feet again? Rise, you imbecile, and you shall walk! I began to feel that for victims, the punishment was twofold: they were responsible not only for themselves, but also for those they mustn't disappoint. Victims had to welcome and put up with the weakness of others, those about whom my rough physiotherapist said much later, as she tortured my neck with the pincers that served her as hands, before offering me a cup of hot chocolate or coffee: "Don't listen to them, they're not living in reality." However, they lived in a world that celebrated the cult of that reality through all its political and cultural orifices. In real life, as always, it was phony. The difficult reality of others was one of those uninhabitable planets that people love to see in images, listen to on the radio, perhaps even read, but in which one cannot breathe for a minute. This wasn't the last of my surprises in this area, but I could discover it only by exploring the surgical and mental labyrinth that I had just entered. For many people, it was like the cinema. In scene 1, I was hit in the face by a bullet. Since my jawbone was made of cardboard, I returned almost intact in scene 2. In scene 3, I was eating the scout's apple with the discreet grimace of a wounded but composed man, what composure, what dignity! Equipped with these certificates of resilience and decorum, the film could continue because people's lives continued. Naturally, the film was a flop.

The anemone survived the article, but not by much. For ten months, it had visited me less and less often, less and less intensely, until the next attack, the one on November 13, which acted like horse medicine, transforming me from one minute to the next into a war veteran. Until that event, that accentuated aftershock, the anemone had set up a kind of intermittent terror. It tugged at my sleeve to remind me from whence I came, who I was no longer. However, it was in and through the anemone that I began to write again, first this article, then others. It's the first step that counts, right? Or the first word. Maybe it was Bernard's last gift: an ink sac.

L et's leave Room 106 and make, if you're willing, a slight jump ahead.

On January 6, 2017, around 10 A.M., I sat down once more in a booth in the stomatology department across from a woman whom I did not know well and who had taken on an outsized importance in my life: Chloé, my surgeon. The weather outside was almost the same, gray and cool, as it had been when I arrived at La Pitié-Salpêtrière hospital two years earlier. The first time, I came in an ambulance. This time, I came on foot. I'd acquired the habit. I still felt least bad when I was walking—as when I was doing my "lengths" of 52 paces in the ward's corridor. And it was when I was going to see Chloé that I walked the best.

When I entered her office, I was Pangloss. Everything was for the best in the best of all possible worlds, everything would end up being all right. When I came out, one time out of two, I had reread *Candide*: Chloé's realism punctured my illusions. As I was complaining about this one day, she said to me: "I understand your impatience. But if I tell you things that aren't going to happen, that's what you'll never forgive me for." It remained for me only to cultivate my garden: in other words, to do each day my labial and mandibular exercises while waiting for the next operating room, in a month or in a year. Life was punctuated by the discipline that reconstruction demands.

Someone cried out in a neighboring booth. It was the peculiar cry that anticipates the pain feared more than it expresses

the pain felt. It was a man's cry. It could come from a child or
an adult: it merged ages. It's like that with teeth, I said to
myself. First, you're afraid of suffering. Then you play the suffering in accord with the registers that pride offers, and which
are available to the voice, passing suddenly from the bass to the
soprano. Finally, you feel this suffering, because the nerves
take their revenge on a comedy that, by anticipating them, has
stimulated them. The three stages—fear, play, pain—are sometimes so close to one another that they can't be distinguished,
but by experience, the ear gets more discriminating; from one
consultation to the next, the invisible sources of these cries
gave me—me, the toothless guy—almost a piano tuner's sensitivity. Other people's pain calmed me. Their cries came out of
a bad theatrical piece of which I heard only voices in the dark,
a radio drama with excessive sound effects. I fell asleep in the
middle of their narrative with the blessed certainty that I had
not participated in it.

On that day, a new stage of reconstruction was beginning.
As always, Chloé was at work. Shortly after the attack, she had
said one evening in my room: "The surgeon's temptation is to
go as far as possible, to approach, from one retouching to
another, the ideal face. Obviously, we never succeed in this,
and one has to know how to stop." I told her that the same
goes for a book. You try to bring the book you're writing closer
to the book you imagined, but they never merge, and there
comes a time when, as you say, one has to know how to stop.
The patient remains with his twisted face, his scars, his handi-
cap more or less reduced. The book remains alone with its
imperfections, its ramblings, its defects. We banally concluded
that the limit is not made to be attained.

Since then, I have been unable to think about Chloé's
work without thinking of my own. Her precision and
patience, the way in which she had overcome or evaded the
obstacles connected with the state of my cicatrices and my

lower lip, everything took me back to what I should have done when I wrote, and to the day when a nurse said to me: "She's completely mad. She can't bear to fail!", I thought that this madwoman who was saving my face, could have made me a man whom writing saved. All I had to do was reread myself to know that this wasn't true. My writing was some distance behind my jawbone. The former wouldn't catch up with the latter either in its fall or in its progress.

Two years later, Chloé still had ideas and doubts regarding what had to be done, and I, though I hardly had aesthetic and literary fantasies anymore, continued to have a few mechanical hopes: I would gladly have given up writing the slightest article to be able to bite into a piece of fruit or a sandwich without pain and without spilling it all over, to drink a glass of wine without putting my tongue in it as if I were half dog, to be able to feel entirely the lips that I was kissing. We still weren't at the final point.

Chloé preferred to be described as a surgeon. I called her Chloé in the hospital, and, when I talked about her to people who didn't know her, I called her my surgeon. It was exaggeratedly possessive, I admit, but what else could I call the branch to which a shipwrecked man clings and finally carries, once on the shore, like a trophy? Chloé, my surgeon . . . and yet, it had taken me months to write her family name correctly. I always added a "h" in the middle, as I did to the word "hospital," a place outside of which I have never seen her—except for one time.

On January 6, 2017, I looked at her again: blonde, smiling, bright eyes, always erect, rather pale with ruddy spots, seeming taller than she was, holding herself straight despite her backache, with plump cheeks that could have made her the heroine of a comic strip, but which her spiky character made one quickly forget. Very ironic and tonic, almost joyous amid disaster, radiating a health she may have had, or not, seeming to me all the taller because I was lying down, all the more strong-willed because I had to be strong-willed, all the more cheerful because I clung to her mood to get out of my own. If it hadn't been for her smock and the context, she would have looked like what she was, moreover, a pretty bourgeoise from the 7th arrondissement, slightly combined with a tomboy; a cultivated bourgeoise, dominant and quick to get impatient with the slowness and weaknesses of others, a handyman who detested carelessness and an absence of cleanliness. She could have been arrogant, and some people thought she was, if, like so many women who have had to make their way in a man's world, she hadn't had a pride without vanity: the humility that her profession imposed on her had not been destroyed by the power that people had ended up granting her. Her somewhat haughty, very direct temper protected her from others but also, to a certain extent, from herself. She expected much from them, probably too much, but in the end less than she demanded of her own strengths.

She knew her value and was not sparing with her scorn. She knew her madness and was not sparing with her reason. She knew her hardness and was not sparing with her attention or even with her tenderness—at least, at certain times, and without witnesses. She had devoted her life to surgery, but without proclaiming it: her dislike of bombast and sentimentality was immediately perceptible and obliged me to play the role of the stoic, even amused, patient. To a young surgeon who complained one day about his work hours, which were in fact dreadful, she replied: "What are you complaining about? In any case, we'll all be dead before we've gotten old." She had said to me, one day when I was comparing the ward to an asylum: "But what do you expect? You have to be mad to believe that you can save people and spend your days in the operating room repairing them!" A medical student whose professor she had been told me that she could terrorize students. At the beginning of the school year, she had said to them: "As for those who will fail, I don't ever want to hear them mentioned again." An expression she often used when someone enjoyed a pleasure was "lucky devil!" She often repeated it to me when I began to go to art exhibits again. I felt indebted to her and sent her photos of Poussin and Picasso, like a child who wants to please his absent mother. "Lucky devil!" she wrote to me, as she had sometimes said it to me in my room: and I heard the exclamation point resounding like the vibration of an arrow. She was so serious about her profession, so scandalized by carelessness, that she could not endure the appearances of self-importance. Once, I sent her a photo of a burlesque bird sculpted by Picasso. She replied: "What a likable chicken! I believe that though he was very conscious of his genius, Picasso never took himself seriously." I: "In any case, he's funny." She: "Can you be funny if you take yourself seriously? I mean, funny without it being at your own expense?"

In the summer, she often went to a Greek island that she had known, I think, since she was a child. As she was talking to me about it one evening, I wrote on my notebook, "Do you know the correspondence between Henry Miller and Lawrence Durrell? They spoke so well about the Greek islands." I had read an article about this correspondence and I would have liked to have it at hand. She knew it. I thought of Durrell. A writer who had known him down there, on another Greek island, had told me how he drank alcohol straight out of the bottle. Were there alcoholics in Chloé's family? Her father, an engineer, had created electrical networks in several countries. Her childhood seemed to have been magical and nomadic.

The nurses were inspecting my wounds. I was not allowed to speak. She said: "Durrell had been a diplomat in Greece, moreover." I wrote: "In his youth, yes. But not in Greece, in the Balkans." She stuck to her guns: "No, in Greece!" The team had hardly left before I checked: it was in fact in the Balkans. I would have drooled with joy, but I didn't need to feel any emotion to drool. The next morning, when she was to examine me, she came in with her team and before anything else, in front of the stunned nurses and interns, and just as I was going to triumphantly hand her my notebook, she said, looking up: "Yes, I know, I know, it was in the Balkans!" She had checked, too. That morning, through this detail, I understood that she carried the lives of her patients around with her—and, in any case, mine. Would she carry it as far as her Greek island? "Oh! I'd spend my life there," she told me, but it was in the operating room that she spent her life—and she laughed at her own regrets. Chloé had only a few characteristics in common with Emma Bovary. I was told that she had a cat, but I didn't dare ask her what its name was.

She sometimes dressed like a retired person, and a nurse who was fond of her, and at the same time feared her as almost everyone did, had told her one day that she ought to make an effort not to "look like an old lady." I don't know what she said in reply; I think she must have smiled and walked away.

She was in her early forties. She had played the cello, but her schedule had become so full that she had to give it up, like the surgeons passionate about cars who, according to Proust, stopped driving the day before they performed an operation. I am not quoting Proust by accident: *In Search of Lost Time* followed me from room to room and I constantly found in it something to meditate on, or to laugh about, concerning my condition and Chloé.

Jean Giono had visited her family in the Dauphiné, but she was bored by Giono's books, just as I am now, whereas I used to like them so much, I thought as I read the e-mail in which she mentioned this to me. I liked to draw her onto literary terrain, the only one where I might not feel dependent and dominated. When you're lying down and covered with oozing wounds, it's always good to talk about a writer that you love to those who are examining you. During the summer of 2016, she had read Koestler's *Scum of the Earth* and books by Annie Ernaux, Philippe Djian, Delphine de Vigan, and, for the first time, Le Clézio's novels, about which she wrote to me: "What fakery! What a lack of life! How did he get a Nobel Prize?" I hadn't the slightest idea.

Since she had first entered Room 106, two years and a century had passed. She had discovered, examined, and operated on me twenty-four hours before we could become acquainted. Our relationship had begun on bases the inverse of those that determine most human relationships: first the body, in a state of the most complete abandonment, and the rest afterward. We didn't have an appointment, but my face immediately depended on her and continued to depend on her long after the period that this book is about. The intimacy that linked us was vital, and yet it didn't exist. I could send her photos taken while I was traveling, what she called my postcards, but I would never have dared to talk to her about my private worries—even if she divined them. There was a framework that must not be exceeded, any more than my balls could hang out of my underwear while she was examining me, which one day caused her to say in front of the nurses: "Try to put those away, that'll be better for everyone." I'd gotten old, my balls hung down, and I couldn't, after all, ask her to do a lift-job that was not part of her specialty. I felt like Reiser's Gros Dégueulasse ("Big Disgusting"), plus shame, but also with a certain irritation, since if they hung out that day, it was first of all because I had to leave my legs bare and my underpants folded so that the open areas where the graft had been taken, on my upper left thigh, could be protected from any rubbing and examined: a hospital is often the site of contradictory injunctions. Irritation, but also gratitude, because in matters of dignity, she seemed to be telling me, I was expected to do the impossible—

or, in any case, in the absence of a negligée—and, like the aged Hegel, to transcend contradictions in practice. Chloé was close and distant, fair and unfair, benevolent and severe, all-powerful and all-distant. She finished the sentences that I began. She was the imperfect fairy who, perched on my cradle, had given me a second life. This second life obligated me.

In the booth, two years later, I still saw her as if she were about to pull out a magic wand and annihilate my problems, when she said in an exasperated voice: "Not those syringes, they're much too big and they'll wreck the valve! How many times do I have to tell you: for that, we need the little orange syringes! The little orange syringes, you understand?" Soon afterward, the nurse returned, as phlegmatic as a gnu. I looked at these syringes in order to memorize them, like a worthy student-patient who thinks: "If they make that mistake the next time, and if Chloé isn't there, I'll be the one to correct the problem." If I didn't want to end up in the whale's belly, I mustn't be like Pinocchio. I had to be equal to the fairy's concerns. Besides, it wasn't my nose that was supposed to grow longer: it was my neck that was supposed to swell, as much as possible, day after day, in the month that was starting.

I will recount in the following chapters the first stages of the reconstruction. For the moment, and to ensure the comprehension of what will follow, it suffices to know that my lower jawbone having largely disappeared, a graft was taken from my right fibula, along with a bit of skin from the leg, called a "skin paddle," which served as a substitute for my chin. Two years and many operations later, they were going to inflate the skin of my neck, thanks to an expander made of silicone that had been installed and that would be slowly filled with saline. Then this bit of skin would be stretched to put it in place of the beardless, peach-colored skin that transformed the lower part of my face into a patchwork. Thus I would once again have a chin more or less knit together, with a beard intended to mask the scars, and not a few long, sparse hairs like the ones on my calf.

Chloé stuck the little orange syringe in the silicon valve that was located behind my right ear, at the center of the so-called retroauricular zone. It was from there that the expander would be inflated. Since the skin that should have covered this valve was necrotic, I looked like an extraterrestrial or a hero of the *Matrix* type: seen from this point of entry, my whole skeleton seemed to be built in a half-opaque, half-transparent manner, which could have made me an immortal. An immortal is not necessarily a god, or even a hero. It can be someone who has sensed all his mortality and who has the fragile feeling of surviving this sensation, but in the form of plastic matter. Once again, I felt absurdly prolonged. A few weeks earlier, for a professional conference at which she was to give the introductory address, the subject of which was the smile—the smile is important, in particular for those who can't produce it anymore—I had given Chloé Bergson's book *Le Rire* (*Laughter*). In the end, she wasn't able to go to this conference, and I don't know whether she read the book. What I know is that now, I too was something mechanical superimposed on something living; but that was less comic.

At first, I felt nothing. Slowly, Chloé injected twenty cubic centimeters of saline. The liquid gradually cooled the tube that passed under the skin. Then it entered the expander. A slight burning sensation circulated, as if it were alive, under the chin. It felt like a skinner was carefully stripping off my skin. I thought: what crime do I have to confess?

The expander, or expansion prosthesis, had been installed two months earlier. As is often the case, it had begun by getting infected: the neck is a sensory intersection and a culture medium that isn't fond of foreign bodies. The bacteria must have entered through the valve. They had invaded the folds of this prosthesis, which was still mainly empty, as they do in the folds of a deflated buoy, and they had waited for their moment to strike. The infection had appeared abruptly, while I was writing an article about Arnold Schoenberg's paintings. Suddenly, I felt an intense burning in my neck. I felt as if I were being strangled. I looked at myself in the mirror. My neck had doubled in volume and it was the color of the couch on which I was sitting: bright red. I was less hideous—or less disturbing—than Schoenberg's self-portraits, but I had reason to hope that I could soon compete with them. The night was short and unpleasant.

At dawn, I took a selfie that I sent to Chloé. She replied: "Can you come in this morning? It's time to have a look at that, I think." An attempt to save the prosthesis had to be made. Afterward, I was on antibiotics and the infection, following a few ups and downs, seemed to have been stabilized. However, Chloé said to me: "Anyway, if that doesn't work, we'll try again later on the other side." I looked at her, overwhelmed. Two more general anesthesias, and more months of permanent discomfort, not to mention the artificial goiter and the daily nurse's care: I would never have the courage for that. But I didn't say anything. Surgeons live in a world where everything that is technically possible ends up being tried.

Now, day after day, the prosthesis had to be inflated. The goal was a prosthesis of a minimum of two hundred cubic centimeters, to obtain the additional skin necessary for "draping" the chin. "Draping" was the right word: they were going to pull the skin from the neck as far as the lower lip, and even beyond it, because the skin retracts, as the sheet does over Captain Haddock's beard. Until that operation, the expander was going to make me look like a pelican or a toad, and cause a few serious pains in my neck and in my back, some resembling burns, others driven in like nails, but that's another story, also posterior to the one I'm telling here. Surgery is a book that doesn't end.

After the injection, Chloé sat down on a stool, facing me, to see how I reacted. It was then that I said to her: "Tomorrow, it will be two years since we met." I had been thinking about that since the day before, and I had resolved to say it to her. I don't like anniversaries, and this one even less than others, but I would have preferred that this first injection take place on January 7. "Yes," she said, and I understood that she had thought about it, too. "Do you know what I was doing when you got here?" she asked. I replied: "Hossein told me that you were eating lunch. He called you and he put me on ice while I waited for you to arrive. Hossein was a young surgeon, who had been on call on January 7, 2015. Later, he also became a friend: the day when, changing hospitals, he no longer took care of me as a patient. The gods keep their distance, and so do surgeons. The gods are said to have created man out of clay. For surgeons, there's always a moment when you become once again a pile of flesh and bones to be reshaped.

She sighed: "This guy, he always has to talk." I had difficulty imagining Chloé eating lunch on a weekday. As I saw her, she was always standing, more or less leaning over me, like a goddess over the destiny of a Greek sailor, certainly not sitting and eating a salad or a plate of couscous. She continued: "I was having lunch with a woman friend of mine, which I almost never do . . . " Ah! So I was right. And it was there that she told me how that friend had given her *Soumission*, a book she still found premonitory. Was it premonitory, I wondered, while the nurse was placing the bandage on the injection valve. I said to Chloé: "You know that *Soumission* was the last subject we talked about at . . . " She finished my sentence: "the editorial meeting?" It's nice to be understood implicitly by your surgeon, especially when you have trouble speaking.

In the booth, an intern and two externs were listening to us. One of the externs, young, dark-haired, with a little, thin beard, watched me attentively, without reacting to what we said. I wondered whether he was an Arab and what he thought. It was perhaps to find out that I repeated once again: "On that day, we had both read *Soumission*, Bernard Maris and I, and we both defended it. Those who attacked it hadn't read it. It's almost always like that." Smiles passed over their faces, except that of the young extern with dark brown hair and a beard, who was even more attentive and serious. Was he going to leap into this booth and cut my throat? I continued: "We weren't in agreement. Then the killers came in and they put everyone in agreement." When I talked about the attack, I now did it as if I were talking about a practical joke—since after all it was one. I wasn't sure that Houellebecq's book wasn't one as well. It had at least had the merit of not killing its readers. "There might have been other ways of arriving at a consensus," said Chloé in the same tone. We hadn't had time to find them. We hadn't had time to have imagination, and now, at a time when it was preferable no longer to have any, I sometimes had too much. Everybody continued to smile, except the dark-haired extern. The nurse had finished putting on the bandage. I stood up. As she filled out my prescription (antibiotics, probiotics, paracetamol, the good old trio, which this time lacked the element that completed the quartet, vaseline; I had several tubes of the stuff at home), Chloé began to speak in English with the mysterious and disturbing young man. Until that instant, I hadn't sensed that he didn't understand French. He was a Syrian, a dentist. He had just arrived from Damascus. He had fled a country where, he said, everybody's future was far behind him. Chloé introduced me to him. I shook his hand, wished him welcome, as if he and I were ministers—of what? "There," she said, "now the introductions have been made."

When had the introductions been made between her and me? Between her world and mine? If I except my uncle Pierre, a mischievous obstetrician with a Belle Époque style mustache who was now retired, before January 7 I'd had no relationship with the world of surgeons. My eardrums had been operated on when I was a child, my appendix had been removed the year I graduated from lycée, and I'd had surgery on a thumb I broke skiing two years later. These mediocre adventures had glided over me.

About the first operation, I remembered a big mask made of disgusting brown plastic that smelled bad and put me to sleep as if in the vomit that it made me want to produce. I awakened weeping with pain, as after a bad sore throat. People said I was a softie.

About the second operation, I recalled fainting in the bedroom of my third grandmother, my great-grandfather's second wife. He had died in 1937, at her side, in a car accident near Angoulême. She was young and had never remarried. She lived in the suburbs of Grenoble, where she preached the Gospel to the children of the poor in her city. A ferocious faith had allowed her to survive her husband, to survive everything. With a mushroom-shaped black hat on her head, and despite an almost entirely decalcified spinal column, she walked erect and for a long time: the doctors seemed not to understand how she managed to stand up. Every morning, she put a Bach cantata on the record player, took a large calcium tablet, which I watched dissolve like a communion wafer in a large glass of water, then she did calisthenics on the floor with a pillow and a broomstick. She moved slowly, like a lady, tall, lean, elegant, and had a dry sense of humor. Her chin trembled slightly under the effort made by the will. She never complained about anything. It is possible that her extravagant discipline prepared me for what, thirty years after her death, befell me. As lawyers say, the dead hold the living in their grasp. Moreover, she was not the only grandmother whose destiny, or example, followed me as far as the hospital: I will return to this in the next chapter.

I remembered another difficult awakening in the hospital in Grenoble and an enormous appendix, ready to explode, that the surgeon had brought me in a flask, like a monster or a trophy, without giving me the slightest satisfaction. And I remember the ruined Easter vacations and a baccalaureate exam badly prepared because of fatigue and indifference, a gloomy condition that was crowned by the slightly porcine face of a mathematics teacher who scorned those, including me, whom he did not succeed in enlightening. I belonged to that recent period, allegedly blessed, in which most doctors didn't explain anything to their patients, and in which a nonnegligible number of teachers who lacked teaching ability, sympathy, and patience considered their students to be imbeciles.

About the third operation, I remembered a local anesthesia, still a little pain, an enormous, heavy cast that I hauled around for weeks at the university without anyone writing anything whatever on it, though that was the custom, and a thumb that festered for two months before there emerged from it one morning, in the family bathroom, a long, slender piece of blackened metal, the remains of a surgical pin: no X-ray had been made to check, and I had been through reeducation with that little thing inside me. Now I understood better why I had suffered, without daring to complain. Having seen this little pin appear on the side of my thumb after a shower, I took a pair of tweezers and pulled on it. The pins at La Salpêtrière reminded me how much the bathroom is the site of all kinds of shame and a few discoveries—the place where, from wounds to masturbation and grimaces on the toilet, one has, usually under a cold light, the most sensitive experiences of one's own body. It is the place where everyone is a patient. After pulling a centimeter of the pin out of my thumb, I decided I'd better stop there and go to the nearby clinic, where a doctor removed the thing, which was quite long, and this time made an X-ray, hardly embarrassed: "You know, these things happen." From these tiny surgical adventures, I have two scars. They are still visible, but they seem to be, like so many memories, erased by those that have joined them since January 7 and, in a way, covered them over. They are my scars of a carefree man.

I don't remember the faces of any of my earlier surgeons. They merely passed over secondary wounds, and in my life, like occasional divinities. I had no idea of their trade or their character, but my affection for my uncle Pierre, his humor, his ostentatious lack of sentimentality, the memory of our hikes in the mountains, and a memorable tour of his clinic in Tarbes— all that made surgeons likeable by retrospective assimilation— even if their profession's reputation suggests instead that they aren't very likeable.

The tour of his clinic was memorable because, moving from area to area and surgeon to surgeon, I quickly came to feel that here a comedy, all in understatement with regard to suffering, decomposition, and approaching death, was becoming the contrary of the indecency that it might have signified anywhere else. Like Dr. House, some of my uncle's colleagues—and he himself, first of all—affected a certain ferocity as a way of defending themselves against what bodies were revealing to them and against the bad news that had to be given to those who were going to die. This callous attitude seemed to me the only right one. It corresponded to what I liked when I read a book, a sort of comical stoicism with regard to the stumbling blocks and insufficiencies of life: the glazed manifestation, like a pound cake covered with a thin coating of sugar, of repressed anger. The only way of confronting pain and death was to act as if nothing, ever, could have been shocking. It was armed with these slim memories and Uncle Pierre's implicit teaching that I began my own tour of the hospital, a little less simple than a game of Monopoly. It was, moreover, he and his son-in-law, Thibault the anesthetist, who kept my parents informed concerning my condition during the first hours after the attack.

Ten years before the attack, it was already he who had given my parents, by telephone, a direct, minute-by-minute account of the death of my other uncle, André, the one to whom my brother and I were extremely close. The last precise memories of my childhood are almost all connected with him. He went on the operating able for the second time at the age of seventy-seven, to replace part of an artery. He had gone into the hospital with his habitual calm, his silent pride, without informing anyone, not even my aunt, of what he knew perfectly well: his blood vessels were in such a deplorable state that he was very likely not to come out again. We found out later that he had told his surgeon: "If it goes badly, don't resuscitate me. I don't want to be a vegetable." Did my uncle say exactly that? Or did the surgeon transform his remarks to justify, after the fact, the operation's failure? When you open up a body, you never know what you're going to find inside, and we'll never know. But it was very like him. He wouldn't have wanted to emerge from the operating room a perpetual cripple. He didn't want to be dependent on anyone, or complain about anything. As a result, we didn't know what was going on, like most people close to the patient.

I was at home, sitting at my desk, arguing violently with Marilyn, when the telephone rang. It was my mother. Ordinarily, she has a steady voice, a little severe. This time, it was trembling: "I'm calling you because, you know, I don't know whether Tonton is going to survive this. They're still operating on him, and it's going badly . . . " She was calling me from her landline. I looked at Marilyn, hesitating, dumbfounded. I couldn't imagine that my uncle was going to die and I still didn't believe it. My whole childhood, so pale, and all the good times he had given us appeared and then disappeared, and I felt once again, but with unprecedented force, that we die countless times in the course of a life, little deaths that leave us standing there, petrified, surviving, like

Robinson Crusoe on the island he didn't choose, with only our memories to improvise what comes next and no Friday to help us cultivate it.

For some time, we had noticed that my uncle was pale and tired, but we didn't want to acknowledge it. Two years earlier, he'd had to give up on a little hike in the mountains after a few hundred meters, his body covered with sweat and his face stoically distraught. I was with him, and I thought it was a transitory thing, it's hard to believe that the heroes of your childhood might be weak. In the same way, I believed that this was a major operation, but had no serious consequences. He had gone into the hospital the day before. Like others, I hadn't gone to see him, thinking I'd go there sometime in the next few days and laugh with him about everything and nothing. I still couldn't imagine him on a hospital bed, his eyes bright, reading a history book, shrunken and lying prostrate.

I listened to my mother tell me that my uncle was dying. Marilyn saw my eyes change. A bewilderment that was not yet clarified must have wiped away the anger. At that point, we'd been arguing about an in vitro fertilization that we were supposed to do and that, weary, concerned, pessimistic, and discouraged by the failure of our earlier attempts at insemination, I continually postponed. As I was listening to my mother explain my uncle's condition, I said to Marilyn: "Tonton's operation is going very badly." Marilyn was enormously fond of my uncle. I saw her frown with a sorrow that must not have yet covered up my own. I was hesitating between anger and astonishment. For the past year, sorrow had been continuous at home. Not having a child was slowly killing our marriage without our being entirely aware of it. The failure had destroyed our desire and what self-esteem I still had. And then suddenly, as in the theater, a man whom we loved, someone who had given us strength and humor, this uncle whose sarcastic pride had marked us to such an extent, was dying at the very moment that we no longer knew how to give life. Moreover, we could have laughed about this with him, since he had experienced so much trouble procreating and had taken it hard. Our argument now echoed his death. It had a bitter taste and it was as if we were responsible for what he was going through, as if our argument had had plunged us into an indifference that we already regretted. Developed by anger, our energy and our sadness reversed themselves, like the engine of a jet that is landing, and set us down in a devastated land where we had not planned to go.

I heard a telephone ringing in my parents' apartment; it was my mother's cell. "Wait," she said to me, "it's Pierre . . . " She said "yes" several times, and then I heard a sort of sigh or cry: "Well, there it is, this time it's over, Tonton is dead . . . " Then I heard another sound, like that of a telephone that has been dropped, and the dial tone humming in the void. I was sitting with this news, I wondered if my mother had fainted and if it wasn't a dream, and I looked again at Marilyn. She was standing in front of me, her arms alongside her body, her little, solid body and her dark eyes shining intensely, and I said to her in Spanish: "Tonton ha muerto." She gulped and began to cry. I stood up and took her in my arms. A few minutes later, Marilyn went into the bedroom to inject the hormones in preparation for the in vitro fertilization. There was no longer any question of hesitating. That was very much her manner: a life in exchange for a death, and as fast as that. We never had a child.

I don't know if Chloé came back to see me on the night of January 7, after the first operation. I saw her for the first time on January 8, in my room, her straight neck, white smock, and a smile on her lips: it was like an apparition—and I use that word in the literal sense, because the person who was looking at her was nothing more than a child ready to marvel at anything that might help him live. Although she knew nothing about me, she already knew everything about my body that could be of use to her—about its mechanics and its state of health. Using the whiteboard, I asked her if she wanted an old photo of me to prepare for the operations. I wanted to be *useful*. She shrugged her shoulders and smiled: "No, I don't need one!" I was surprised. I would have liked to ask her, "How do you expect to reconstruct my face if you don't know what it looked like?" I thought I was still in the realm of Photoshop. However, it didn't bother me that she knew so much and so little about me, and I stopped thinking about it, yielding for the first time to that dangerous and necessary feeling: confidence. I knew nothing about her, but it very quickly became essential for me to learn about her, from her. I had to get closer to her to forget to what extent I was dependent on her. I had to know all the imperfect fairy's secrets.

In addition to confidence, I had an immediate liking for her. This liking was not due solely to the fact that she was my savior, or more exactly the commander in chief of the team that was going to give me back, gradually, a mouth, a chin, and a jaw. It was due, more than anything, to her lack of indulgence. Her cheerful severity reassured me.

Her visiting day was Thursday. The first times, when I was going down to the operating room with the frequency of a subscriber with an unlimited card, she came to see me every day. Often, she showed up in the evening, when her workday was over, forcing those who were visiting me, starting with my parents, to leave the room. It was only for a few minutes, I told them. But it could last thirty, forty minutes, sometimes an hour. The visitors waited in the chilly hallway, not far from the policemen, sometimes standing, sometimes sitting near the reception desk on one of the two chairs, sometimes sitting on the floor, exposed to the drafts. I forgot them: I was listening to Chloé talk about my case and about herself. The women I've loved have all accused me, sooner or later, of not paying attention, of floating, of being elsewhere, I don't know where, while they were talking to me. One of them summed up what they had apparently all felt: "Living with you would drive me crazy. I have never felt so alone as I do when I'm with you." Chloé benefitted from an additional attention that wasn't due to love, but to the circumstances. When she came in, I usually handed her a list of written questions bearing on my surgical fate or on a literary or musical point we'd discussed during an earlier visit.

I turned off the music. She sat down next to me, took my tablet and my pencil, and explained what she planned to do in the coming days. She drew schemas, explained the disadvantages and advantages of each surgical option. It's a great relief, when you're in such a condition, to be treated like a strong, intelligent person—a gifted student, in short, rather than a patient. Decisions were made, of course, by the staff, among surgeons, and I quickly understood that Chloé gave me only the explanations that she considered possible and necessary; but she did it in such a way that she seemed not to be concealing her hesitations from me.

I quickly learned, thanks to this private lesson, that surgery is both a great art and a way of making do with what one has: a combination of technique, experience, and improvisation. The choice was usually not between two solutions, a good one and a bad one, but among several possibilities, all of which had disadvantages. The latter had to be weighed against the advantages. The scale was balanced by a beam composed of an alloy: the physical and mental state, postoperative care, and cellular uncertainties. I rather rapidly became my surgeon's roombound chronicler . Since she was making me a man with a face again, everyone who dealt with me had to make her a heroine. Her function was to act, mine to provide the narrative. Surgical romances are chivalric romances.

I liked to compare her, in the presence of my friends, to an excellent chess player, Fischer, Kasparov, or Capablanca. She knew all the maxillofacial combinations; she calculated her moves in advance; her technique was sure and her passion for what she did was exaggerated, like all passions, but she was also obliged, when confronted by cases such as mine that presented a surgical as well as a social challenge, to show intuition and imagination. I was as much a danger as a challenge. Before the graft of my fibula onto my jawbone, she told me calmly: "It works in a little more than ninety percent of the cases. If it doesn't work, we'll try again with the other fibula and with a different team. There's never a complete failure." The department was in fact famous for its "fibulas"; it does about ninety of them a year. But long after the success of this graft, she said to me on one consultation day: "Do you know what you've been through? When the graft of the fibula was done, we were worried. If it had failed, we'd have all gone down with you." I looked at her, stupefied: that expression made me feel the violence that this affair had imposed on her. I saw them jumping, one after the other, into the hole in my jawbone, all of them and Chloé first of all, and, aspirated between the destroyed mucous membranes, disappear along with the energy, the know-how, and the illusions that had motivated them, whereas triumphant in and by ill will and stupidity, the K brothers emerged from it with their supporters and all those who didn't yet dare weep, in the name of the class struggle, over their orphaned childhood.

One day in April, at the time when the secondary grafts were failing one after the other and when I was constantly drooling from my lower lip, she came in with an almost radiant pride and said to me: "I thought about it all night, and I believe I've found the solution . . . " I listened to her, thinking that I was soon going to stop drooling. But I rid myself of that notion, which infantilized me, in order to concentrate on the explanations, which educated me. I was once again the patient,

the pupil, and the observer, a threefold position that her
friendly requirement helped me hold and which had immediately flattered what remained of the journalist in me: I was
experiencing, finally, the pains and the stages of a reconstruction which I was observing, which I had to understand, and
which I would someday have to describe.

That evening, I went to her Facebook page for the first
time. She didn't use it much. She had posted an "I am Charlie"
dated January 7. She had posted symbols of mourning on the
dates of the following attacks. I never asked to be her "friend."
She would no doubt have refused, considering my request out
of place. She would have been right. I was looking for traces of
her feelings, of her life. I was always satisfied to understand
that I wouldn't find them.

CHAPTER 12
THE PREPARATION

The day Gabriela left, I moved from Room 106 to Room 111, which was bigger. The numbers awaken memories. Gabriela left after the nurses' rounds, late in the morning. I accompanied her as far as the elevator. I looked at her big suitcase, her long hair, her long overcoat, she smiled and, as in a film, the elevator door closed. There was a smell of disinfectant and bleach in the corridor. I returned to my room and waited for the nurses. I knew that it would be more than a month before Gabriela came back. By that time, I would have changed—even if I didn't know how much or in what way. The man who watched her disappear would not see her again, insofar as he would no longer exist. I was sad, but I was also almost relieved. I wasn't sure what to do with my feelings. The body and its desires, all of them absent, were no longer there to make my feelings live. I had the impression that I was involuntarily forgetting them, diminishing them, like a fire that you turn down under a saucepan, in order to concentrate on something else—but what?

Christiane, the manager, had planned to put me in the biggest room of all, Room 102, all the way at the end of the hall, near an emergency exit that had been blocked. I went into it with the two police officers on duty and my friend Juan, who had come to visit me and who quickly came to play the role of a participant more than that of a visitor. Juan and I immediately understood that Room 102 was impossible: the window gave onto a flat, gray roof the size of a tennis court, to which anyone could gain access, and from there—why not?—shoot me. I shivered. Juan saw, I think, the shadow of panic in my eyes: looking out on that roof, I saw the killers again, any killers, all in black, with hoods, spraying the room with submachine gun fire then and there. This was not a product of my imagination: it was a genuine scene that was bursting in on the one we were living in and pushing and shoving to replace it. For a few seconds these phantom killers were more real than Christiane, Juan, the policemen, and I myself. Or rather: we were real only under their fire, some of them hiding under the window or under the bed, the rest dead, and I was in the bathroom with my tubes, waiting to be finished off. On that day, and for several months afterward, the bathroom in my hospital room, whatever else it might be, became my "querencia," the place where the bull goes to die, exhausted, his tongue lolling out of his mouth, ready to be given the deathblow. It was there that I ended up when the killers entered.

"I don't think that's going to be possible," one of the policemen said with a faint smile. "Or else we'll have to be in the room twenty-four hours a day. That may not be ideal for Monsieur Lançon."

I wanted to get out of that room as fast as possible, but my panic was going away. There was a moment of hesitation. As in a Western, at the instant when the conflict is going to break out at the trading post, we were looking on like china dogs, not knowing which gunslinger was going to draw first. It wouldn't be me: my bandage was beginning to leak. Christiane was embarrassed. Not only had she thought she was doing the right thing, but now she was going to have review her organization. She opened her bright eyes wide. In such cases, she looked like she had emerged from a sinister bas-relief. The ward had patients under surveillance, prisoners, but it wasn't set up to hold patients who were in danger. Should I be put there all the same? Silently, she weighed the pros and cons. I foresaw the moment when, if the killers didn't come to finish the work that the K brothers had begun, I was going to live night and day with the policemen, witness their discussions and changing of the guard, not to mention their radios, which, behind the door, rarely allowed themselves to be forgotten. The policemen would be there, at the foot of my bed, like servants at the foot of the king's canopied bed, like stone lions at the feet of a recumbent statue. I was already hardly sleeping. I was afraid I would no longer sleep at all. Christiane stopped holding her eyes wide open, the bas-relief returned to the Asian jungle whence it came, and she said:

"O.K., we're going to see what can be done."

We returned to Room 106. A few minutes later, I moved into Room 111, which was actually as spacious as the one I had just been spared, but did not look out on a roof. Moving to another country would not have been a more epic adventure. Every time I moved, I had the same sensation again. To change rooms was to change worlds; thus it was to change lives. The window in Room 111 looked out on a pine tree on which crows perched from time to time. From my bed, I observed every morning and every evening its shape and its shifting colors as if my life depended on them. Often, it seemed to be black. When I wept, all alone, a few weeks later, I was looking at the pine tree. I remained in Room 111 until the day of the big graft, on February 18. My parents took away some of the things that had accumulated. Christiane piled others in her office. The whole floor was going to be closed for a week for a major cleaning. I felt lost when I left it, at dawn, for the longest operation. I was afraid I was going to change my skin, my suffering, my memory, my life.

The day before Gabriela's departure, Chloé removed the cannula without an opening. This was a little ceremony, and there too, a change of life. In the hospital, in accord with the strictest routine, there was only emergency, disorder, and learning at the heart of habit. Chloé said to me:

"You're going to be able to speak, but not too much, O.K.?"

She'd never heard the sound of my voice, but she seemed to know that I was talkative, and there was no need to tell her that. I was going to be able to speak again? The body forgets nothing, but consciousness forgets quickly, and it had taken me less than a week to lose even the memory of the spoken word. I had become used to my whiteboard, to my fingers blackened by the felt-tip pen, to my silence, to my notebook.

Chloé asked Gabriela, who was standing at the foot of my bed, to step aside, "unless you want to end up at the dry cleaners." Then, as the team watched, she removed the cannula. I coughed violently. Blood mixed with mucus spurted through the hole and spattered the wall across from my bed, like a gob of spit. For once, I aimed right. But what was I aiming at? Gabriela laughed. My nose smarted. Chloé cleaned the point of entry and then installed the cannula with an opening, which was going to allow me to speak. I tried to say something, but nothing came out. I took my notebook and wrote: "I can't talk." Now that I was supposed to be able to talk, not being able to worried me. Chloé stood up:

"There's no reason why you can't. A little patience . . . "

I tried again. Little by little, purer and more articulate sounds appeared, sounds that seemed to come from the deepest parts of me, somewhere, even if they signified almost nothing. Gabriela's and Chloé's kindly and amused faces were looking down on me. I've forgotten the first comprehensible words that came out. They must have been as simple and as concrete as those of a child.

Later, with Gabriela and my brother, we listened to the comedian Coluche's sketches on the Internet. Gabriela was writing a paper on French humor, I think, for one of her courses. She didn't know anything about French humor, and understood it poorly. She found the French too bitter, too aggressive, she didn't know Coluche. I took out my notebook to explain the context of the jokes that escaped her, but these jokes, their context, everything remained in a sealed room from which I myself had been extracted. I knew the codes for opening it and returning to it, but what was inside it no longer corresponded to anything. Someone had cut the connection with the meaning of the memories that continued, more or less, to inhabit me. We listened to "The Cop," "Gérard," "The Student," "Journalists." I fell asleep, slightly nauseated, saturated by the excess of words, laughter, and Coluche's accent combined with the vapors of my youth, dissipated by the piece of the world that was no longer my own and that acted on me like a few glasses too many. Coluche belonged to a world in which people could have laughed at an attack like the one on *Charlie*, because it hadn't happened. A third operation was approaching.

"So, here . . . "

Chloé took my notebook and my pen and launched into a lecture whose subject was me. It was rather late in the evening. She had asked all the visitors to step out. They waited in the hallway for fifty minutes. My parents were unhappy and tired. Other visitors left. No one dared say anything. It was that evening, I think, that she talked to me about her family and, with that smile that put everything at a distance, about some of her sorrows. The hospital room is also a confessional, a place for secrets. I will say nothing about it.

She still hoped to be able to save the tissues and the bits of jawbone that remained intact. She wanted to gradually reduce the size of the wound and make grafts. The "loss of substance" was extensive, but that did not seem to be an insuperable obstacle. And then Chloé always preferred to help nature rather than do violence to it. She told me: "Nature is a better surgeon than I am." Following this process, she continued, there would be months of operations, pumping out ichor, and healing, but she seemed confident. Ten days after she explained it, that option was abandoned: the bullet had burned too much tissue and bone to avoid having to replace them. Chloé laid out at length, with little drawings on my notebook, what was involved in the other option, that of the "fibula." She explained how the decision would be made by the staff, after closely fought arguments. Grafts from the fibula had been done for several years, first on patients suffering from cancer of the jaw and mouth, who constituted most of the patients in the ward. This kind of graft also had a different name, and another evening I heard Chloé use for the first time a word that was henceforth going to describe me to a large extent: the flap. They were going to perform a fibular flap on me.

I return to the explanations given in the preceding chapter. The fibula is removed from the patient's leg and grafted onto what remains of his jaw to replace the missing bone. A vein, a piece of artery, and skin from the calf connected with the fibula removed are also grafted, as a kit, in order to vascularize—to irrigate, in short, like a plant—the grafted bone and allow it to adapt to its new surroundings in the company of familiar elements. The skin taken from the calf is replaced by a piece of skin taken from the thigh of the same leg (in my case, the right one). After scanning, the strongest and best vascularized of the two fibulas is chosen. The operation lasts around twelve hours. It requires two surgical teams: one works on the leg, the other on the face. The whole fibula is not removed: the joints at each end are left, to allow the articulations with the tibia—and thus the leg—to function. The principle is that of an autogenous graft: the body accepts it much more easily than an exogenous graft. The patient provides the material. He saves himself by his own means.

Why the fibula? Because by nature and by form, it is one of the bones most compatible with the jaw, and because it is not indispensable for walking and balance: it is a support whose absence can be compensated by months of reeducation. If I understand correctly, the ideal would be to graft bone from the cranium, but it can be used only for small surfaces. You can live without a fibula, and you can live without using your brain too much; but you can't live without the cranium that contains it.

Chloé hesitated. It was Professor G, the head of the department, who told me one evening which solution had been chosen—it was, after all, his responsibility. G was a man in his early sixties, solid, even massive, with a soft and comfortable voice, and of medium height, who had the habit of listening to radio stations like NRJ while he operated: that is what I was told, but I was unable to verify it, because he never operated on me. He came to the hospital on a motorcycle. His eyes were his strangest feature: he would look at you with an attention that was total and totally cold-blooded, his head leaning over the wound, and in the depths of his eyes there was a kind of absence, a little frosted star that seemed to indicate that a part of him was elsewhere, distant, perhaps dead. I called this part the G star. I liked to see it again, because it objectivized my suffering and my fear, and by objectivizing them, drove them away for a few seconds. The G star shone with attention and indifference on the surface of his face, like an overhanging asteroid, and then a slight smile and a deadpan remark made in a good-natured tone expelled it into some sort of void, while the head withdrew to resume its initial position and an amused, human look settled in again in the cold light of the operating room. A nurse had told me that G himself had come close to dying, as a patient, and that this episode had changed him. Frequenting the operating table with such assiduity didn't make me a surgeon, but it had brought me closer to them, and since the nurse had talked to me about G, I couldn't look at him without a special sympathy, that of fish looking at another fish in the opaque, muddy estuary that serves as their environment.

G met me unexpectedly. I had returned from an operating room a few hours earlier and I was having a particularly hard time breathing that evening, sweating and immobilized in my bed with the side-rails raised like that of a newborn in a cradle arranged by a witches' benevolent association: it was one of those times when the following minute seems as inaccessible as the most distant El Dorado. G planted himself on my right and, in that warm voice that calmed me, told me, as if in good fellowship and without seeming to notice my state of suffocation:

"Fine. We discussed it this morning in a staff meeting, and that's enough, no more beating around the bush! We're getting everything ready and we're going to go for the flap, the fibula and implants, off you go, we'll do it all at once and we'll say no more about it!"

G spoke to me as if I had been sitting or standing in front of him, perfectly healthy and taking notes, and not a damp, emaciated mummy with rings under his eyes who was looking at him with eagerness and relief: a decision has been made, the future was becoming clearer, the adventure would go on! In a hospital, nothing is worse than an absence of action and visibility: it's a place made for decisions. I tried not to cough, not to sweat, and even, yes, not to suffer, in order to be up to the news that G had just announced to me—to adopt the same tone, in short. I concentrated on his last words, "and we'll say no more about it!", which resounded like an "open, sesame!", like the magical formula that my whole body was waiting for. There was no G star that evening, only Professor G and his vigorous lack of affect that I found so reassuring. An absence of psychology could be discerned in it For my part, I sensed the implacable and marvelous that lie beyond any psychology—the abolition of the latter by the actions and troop movements that were being announced around my modest body. I had just witnessed Professor G's annunciation.

He left just as massively and naturally as he had come in, after offering a few amused comments on this and that, on an official visit that had just been made to me: "So, it seems that you're receiving important people, that you're a famous man, Monsieur Lançon!", whereas, as I started suffering pain again, I was wondering if I was going to survive the night and get a brand new jawbone, or if I had just witnessed the resurrection of Dr. Cottard.

Later in the evening, calmed by a dose of Tramandol and waiting for Imovane, I took up the second volume of Proust's novel in Clarac's old Pléiade edition, and reread the pages on the grandmother's illness and death, in which the famous Proustian physician appeared again, but this time in the certainty of his diagnosis, rather than in his imbecility. I had to immediately check how close he was to Cottard—and how close I was to this grandmother about to die, whose end had traumatized me every time I reread the passage.

Three deaths survived my youthful reading: that of Coupeau in Zola's *L'Assommoir*, that of old man Thibault in *Les Thibault*, and that of the narrator's grandmother in Proust. I reread these passages regularly, as one focuses on a memory in order to feel the pain. There were quite a few alcoholic patients in the ward. When I met one of them while I was walking up and down the hallway, I sometimes wondered if his feet, like Coupeau's, would start wriggling about at the crucial moment, at the time of poor Ludo's death. Old man Thibault's death had impressed me even more, his attacks of uremia and his screams when he was plunged into a hot bath, but Proust's grandmother was more likeable than he was, and it was she, with her own attack of uremia, whom I had chosen to accompany me from my room to the operating room and back to my room. Her descent toward death made her almost a roommate,

I was with her in her bed, with her absent or renunciatory eyes, near the window that she was trying to open in order to jump out. When my cannula, badly placed or too long, hindered my breathing and formed a cyst in the trachea, it linked up with the leeches that, to the maid Françoise's great joy, moved over her body and skull. I had the feeling that familiarity could arise only from the silence of books; a few lines sufficed to exhaust me and I fell asleep before I had established it.

At this point, it's time to go back two or three days, to January 20, to be precise, in order to discuss the visit of the person to whom Professor G had alluded and who was still president of the Republic: François Hollande. The security personnel had informed my brother the preceding evening, while I was coming back upstairs from the operating room where Chloé was beginning my "reconstruction." She had been able to work on the lip, but hadn't been able to make the planned graft: the tissues were more damaged than she had thought. I had returned accompanied by the two policemen in surgical caps, smocks, and shoecovers, to the great amusement of my brother, who was surprised and delighted to witness a comical scene. His pleasure hadn't lasted long because in my room I was coughing, gasping, and was already no longer able to breathe correctly. The nurse was called, and then the intern, who understood nothing. The little clothespin known as a pulsimeter was put on my finger. The oxygenation was almost perfect, 96 percent, and they began to repeat this figure to me as if I were guilty of dissembling or of simply not corresponding, for some reason as mysterious as it was annoying, to the data that characterized me. "You say you can't breathe, but that's just your impression, in reality you're breathing!" I was shown the figure that contradicted my gasping, no doubt to convince me that it was time to stop gasping and correspond to what the figures indicated. Feeling more capricious with my cannula than a child refusing a toy, I tried to satisfy my caregivers and to prove their instrument correct, like a man who, on the day when the planet disappears, continues to read the Bible and to listen to priests in order to believe in the existence of God, but there was nothing to be done, the planet had disappeared and breathing was not coming back. Then they put electrodes and a mask on me. There is nothing more detestable than this mask made of translucid plastic. It seems to have to make you pay in advance for the good it will do you—if it does you any good; it is sometimes a prelude to death, and no one familiar with the domain, even if he is out of danger, can completely ignore that fact. It usually begins by suffocating the person it is going to help breathe. That was the moment my father chose to arrive at the hospital, and I had to see my apparent condition, that of a dying man, in his handsome, distraught face, the face of an elegant old sea dog with a white beard who reminded me sometimes of Captain Nemo, and sometimes of the Spanish actor Fernando Rey; in short, the boss of a submarine or one of El Greco's characters who had nothing to eat other than a clove of garlic, a drop of oil, and a crust of bread. A brief thought for the proud *hidalgos* of the Prado did not console me for the pain that I was causing him. I looked at my brother, who was there, with paralyzed composure. He saw in my eyes that I thought it was pointless to impose this spectacle on our father any longer, and I saw in his eyes that he agreed. He gently took our father out of the room and I learned much later that he was weeping when he returned to our mother.

During the night, I dreamed that New York had been flooded by freezing water so dirty that one couldn't put a finger into it. I walked along the rivers without being able to cross them, as I would have wished: all the bridges were out. The dirtier the water covered with black ice, the more the city was deserted. I woke up when the dirt contaminated me, in the greatest solitude. I rang for the nurse. Christiane gave me a morphine injection. I fell back to sleep and the dream began again. The dirty waters were rising in the city to which Gabriela had returned.

In the morning, around 10 A.M., everyone was waiting for François Hollande and his entourage. I didn't know to what extent the staff was excited, as Chloé told me later with an amused condescendence: "Seeing a president is an event that won't happen often in their lives!" She was partly right, but less than she seemed to believe. Twelve days had taught me that the lives of those who took care of me were full of micro-events, insofar as these lives proceeded from earlier lives that had often been marked by tragedies.

For the occasion, I had put jeans on under my hospital gown, and, not wanting to receive him in bed, I got up to welcome my visitors when the policemen announced their arrival. I had never met the president. He came into the room accompanied by Emmanuel Hirsch, who seemed to be there to play the role of royal chronicler, and the manager of *Libération*, my newspaper: Laurent Joffrin. My brother was present. Close up, François Hollande was much more elegant than he looks from a distance, and the first thing I noticed, apart from his pleasantly pink complexion and his light makeup, was the perfect cut of his dark suit and his amused, almost impulsive eyes, which behind the delicate glasses kept at a distance, like an efficient but discreet guardrail, all feelings. Hirsch's eyes, also behind glasses, were those of a courtier: pointed, wild, and wary—slightly thrilled to be where this was happening. I don't remember either the pen pusher or the director of the hospital, but I have not forgotten Laurent's eyes.

I'd known him for thirty years. For the first time, I saw his eyes slightly stinging, red-rimmed, misty with emotion. Laurent, the recurrent target of right-wing brutes and intellectuals who take delight in working-class fury, had the reputation of being an indifferent notable, an acrobat of compromise. In reality, his talent chose its passions and left the rest to what, once you came to know him, made him almost childlike: his thoughtlessness. Political choices are often the result of character. Laurent was a social democrat by nature, by conviction—and because he rejected the violence that his father had incarnated. He loved debate, and even duels, so long as they stopped as soon as blood was drawn and, once the adversaries had left the dueling ground, they parted on good terms. He believed in progressivism, negotiated arrangements, conciliation, a kind of civilized carelessness, and although he was not necessarily highly educated, he breathed civility. His beard led the way for his ideas and feelings: it announced them, attenuated them, ornamented them. His many enemies called him a class traitor, a hypocrite and a weakling. On the contrary, he was clear about his battles and his values, which had scarcely changed and which were unrelated to purity. His moral code was suited to a calm war, in peacetime, in which the bad actions of one side did not entirely destroy, massively, the other side's lives. He preferred long, drawn out twilights to revolutions.

He wrote with spectacular ease. Thirty years earlier, he had corrected, line by line, one of my first articles, badly written, badly constructed, about a child who had hanged himself in the wilds of Brittany, in front of the family pond, because he had been accused of a theft he hadn't committed. Once the article was written I sat down with Laurent in the newspaper's office. He asked me questions and proposed different formulations, clearer and simpler. He deleted adjectives, and even more adverbs, saying: "When adverbs are used, it's often because there's a lack of logic in the sequence of sentences. Chateaubriand almost never used adverbs." His hair was still a little long.

Now, he had before him this journalist whom he had helped train, whom he had often received at his home, and in whose presence he had recounted one of the battles of Napoleon, his hero; this journalist with whom he had sometimes had heated arguments about literature and criticism, and in particular regarding Houellebecq and *Soumission*; this colleague and friend whose present condition was the result of everything he abhorred: an ignorant, stupid, and bloody fanaticism. I looked at these slightly reddened, friendly eyes, suddenly less protected, and I found in them the strength to recount the attack for the first time, as precisely as possible, but as if it were a scene in a comedy. It was not just a matter of receiving these people standing around me and cutting a good figure, but also of entertaining and informing them, as Laurent and a few others had taught me to do. Besides, the attack had also been a theatrical scene, a little drama, and it would have remained one in part had the killers used firecrackers and fired blanks while reciting some surah from the Quran. Death was an ending that shouldn't prevent us from laughing at the comedy of the situation that preceded it.

I gazed at Laurent, then at François Hollande. At that moment, in that room, with their slight smiles, the restrained emotion of one and the benevolent and impulsive glow of the other, these two men, so often vilified, lent me strength, reassured me, and, so to speak, reimmersed me in what I could expect from civilization: a curious and courteous distance, sensitive to the other person without excessive emotionalism, a compassion that abandoned neither the needs of lightness nor the benefits of dispassion. While I was talking, my large bandage was becoming heavier and, as it was saturated by drool they couldn't see, detached itself imperceptibly from the chin, like a curtain on a stage. I emphasized the fact that I felt no anger toward the killers and that I did not connect them with Muslims. My "politically correct"—or, one might say, "evangelical"—period had just begun. From the vantage point of my little hospital Golgotha I didn't want to think ill of anyone, and since then I've always missed, even at the price of a certain silliness, that state of complete, inmost suspension of hostilities. François Hollande made a few witty remarks that I've forgotten, but which were well-timed, and then said: "You're right, you have to show restraint, distance yourself, and not make generalizations or speeches." At that moment, Chloé came in. She was wearing her white smock and was probably returning from a small operation: long ones were performed on Monday and Thursday. Holding herself very erect, looking mischievous and ironic, she had come to see how her patient was flying over a nest of notables and, naturally, to rub elbows with them while reminding them that they were on her territory. We were standing and suddenly in a salon, making witty sallies as if nothing had happened, because something had happened. François Hollande was looking at Chloé, and a certain pleasure, like a cloud's shadow, passed over his smooth round, relaxed face, an almost princely face that reminded me, beneath resemblances to Louis XVI, of the Regent, yes, of the sensualist Philippe d'Orléans, and his peacefully relaxed morality. I would have liked to stop this momentary pleasure, or more precisely to cut it out, like a stencil, and spread it over what remained to me of life. The visit lasted forty minutes, then everyone left. I took off my jeans and collapsed on my bed. The bill for the act I'd just put on had to be paid.

A few weeks later, visiting me again, Laurent said to me: "Hey, your surgeon caught Hollande's eye. He talked to me about her again the other day!" We laughed, but that was all, because I was going through another period in which I was forbidden to talk.

The end of this story took place in June, in the first of my ulterior lives. The president was awarding the Legion of Honor to Patrick Pelloux, whose face and body remain for me framed in the door where he appeared a few minutes after the attack, and escapes from it no more than a child does from a land where he has been put under a spell. In the meantime, I had landed, like my friend Simon Fieschi, in Les Invalides hospital, where I was to spend six months in reeducation. It was from there, accompanied by my police escort, that I went to the presidential palace for two hours on my first "official" outing. During the cocktail party that followed the ceremony, I began to do what was to become a rule of life in society during the outings that took place in the following months: drinking a flute of champagne or wine from a glass with a small circumference, to accommodate my lip, anaesthetize my mouth, and drown my fatigue, while continuing to stand and looking at the petits fours I can't eat. The cocktail party and the dinner have become reeducation exercises and combat sports. Each time I return to the hospital exhausted, with the satisfaction of having fulfilled a mission that no one assigned to me, if not my own body, whose imperatives escape me. Their mission accomplished, the silent, muscular policemen take me back to the elephant cemetery. I'm in a hurry to rejoin the nurses, the disfigured veterans, the amputees, the stroke victims, my companions in the operating room, the hallway, and the gymnasium, all the silence and all those whose lives seem to me more solitary and, ultimately, more just. The hospital is the place where an accident quickly produces a sense of failure.

François Holland approached me, smiling, and said: "Ah! You seem to be feeling better . . . And your surgeon, are you still seeing her?"

Surprised, I replied:

"Yes. And I'm going to be seeing her more again."

"Well, then! You're lucky!"

My first reflex was to reply: "I'd just as soon have foregone it." But I didn't, because at least in part it wasn't true. Five months had gone by and I'd come to terms with the event and the surgical program; they had made me what I had become. I couldn't forego what had also so violently transformed me.

Over the following days, I recounted this anecdote to a few

friends. Several of them were indignant. That man, they seemed to think, is really frivolous and inconsistent. Doesn't he have anything else to say or think when he sees a wounded man again? When they're young, most people judge everything. When they get old, it's the same. Between the two, there may be a moment when they might not judge anything, abstain, take seriously only their own misery, but that moment is the one in which they act, build, have a career or fail to have one; the moment when they have great self-esteem, and rarely have the opportunity or the desire to step away. Is it unworthy of a president to remember first of all the beauty of a woman he saw in the hospital room of a victim of a terrorist attack, a few months or a few minutes earlier? Regarding women, François Hollande's reputation is by now certainly established, but his reaction seems to me heartening and even desirable. The best part of life, I said to myself as I looked at his shining, almost slanting eyes, is in fact that: not forgetting what has pleased us, even for an instant, and, if possible, to forget as much of the rest as we can, starting with everything poignant about a situation. His insouciance did more than pay homage to my little calvary, which I don't give a damn about, it relieved me. "Well then! You're lucky!" I ruminated on this little remark as I returned to Les Invalides in the police car. It became as dear to me as the little phrase from Vinteuil's sonata: a private, profound, and frivolous signature tune that opened to me a door that was joyful, even though it led nowhere. Not only was this amiable president right regarding me—I was lucky to have fallen into Chloé's hands—but he was also right regarding himself and the two of us: nothing could better bring us back to life and to pleasure than the elegant figure of this dominant and probably temperamental woman, positioned between us on the occasion of an unforeseeable and discreetly organized encounter, a woman whose professionalism returned one of us to his desires and the other to his wounds, and imposed herself, when she was absent, on the occasion of melancholy social pleasantries exchanged within the paneled walls of the Élysée palace. Charm is really the last thing, after the last drop of blood, that should abandon us.

After François Hollande's visit, a new period began: the one that would take me toward the graft of the fibula, which was set for February 18. I was going back to the operating room, under general anesthesia, every four or five days, accompanied by policemen in surgical caps and shoe covers. The world below had become my second home, my country house. I was happy to see there again those who seemed not to have to come back up any more than did the creatures of the mythological underworld. La Castafiore was Orpheus. She hadn't confined herself to singing. Like Chloé, she also played the cello. She would end her life on the lower floors, remembering that in former times, on Earth, she had played in Sainte-Cécile. And I—what would I remember? The more the days passed, the more I was entering that no-man's-land where an opaque fog and ferocious, unprecedented sensations were deposited on the minutes, the hours, the days, the visits, the awareness of my body and of my past life. The list of people authorized to enter my room was getting longer every day. The day was punctuated by the nurses' rounds, my walks up and down the corridor, the daily visits of my parents and my brother, and friends' appearances. For the night, a "watch" was organized by five of my friends along with my brother: they were permitted to take turns sleeping in my room. The nurses had placed a small, rickety bed at the foot of my own, a child's bed, under the drawings made by children. The friends on guard slept little, awakened by my problems, my resounding snoring, the nurses' visits during the night, the policemen's radio and their discussions, the last rounds in the evening and the first one in the morning. My brother worked in the armchair at my right, typing on his computer. Odalys, an old Cuban friend, massaged me—as did Alexis and Blandine, who also worked: in off hours, Room 111 was ideal for reading, writing, dreaming, thinking about one's own life. I watched a film or listened to jazz with Juan. Marilyn came twice from eastern France. Everything took place in silence, more and more slowly. The pain, more or less permanent, was diffuse, and always surprising. Friends left in the morning, early; the nurses offered them a cup of coffee before beginning their rounds. Some of my friends took showers in my bathroom, others did not. I watched them go off toward a world that no longer existed, a world where they lived, moved, and got older, while here, we had all stopped. The room was my kingdom and we lived there outside of time.

Every morning and every evening, sometimes even at noon, the nurses came to change the gauze bandages, which were getting bigger and bigger. After wrapping the whole lower part of my face, they were knotted around my head to hold them in place, and they now transformed me into an Easter egg. I was suffocating as if I were in a straitjacket. One day, to give me some relief, one of the nurses, Alexandra, took scissors and slowly cut away the gauze over my ears. Their slightly hairy tips emerged up the way little mushrooms do from moss. Laughing, Alexandra handed me the mirror so I could see them; they looked like the edges of a *pied de mouton*, the mushroom I liked to find in the woods of my childhood because I found them as beautiful as a toy. I felt relieved: I was breathing through my ears. For its part, the bandage was becoming saturated with saliva, faster and faster, as it had begun to do the day of François Hollande's visit. It weighed on my head, my neck, my spinal column, it weighed on my whole body until the moment when, the adhesive tape no longer holding, and despite the bands of gauze that mummified my head, it slipped down like wallpaper on a wall that is too damp.

The following scene was repeated, with variants, a hundred times. The nurses entered like the ballerinas in the Kingdom of the Shades scene in *La Bayadère*, in slow motion. Gabriela had often talked to me about this ballet, which she had rehearsed as an understudy without ever appearing in it onstage. Although, unlike Solor, I had not taken opium, I was in a state similar to that of the unfortunate prince, in a dream: it was the most *realistic* way of assimilating my sensations. Before the nurses came in, I checked the condition of the floor. I got up and, using brown paper tissues, cleaned, to the point of making myself dizzy, the slightest stain. Then I cracked the window, which could not be opened further, and perfumed the atmosphere with an eau de toilette with a dominantly citrus fragrance that a woman friend of mine had brought me. Like Solor, I'd made the room's walls fall. The nurses arrived, one behind the other with the cart, smiling, two of them. A third followed. She looked at the foot of the bed while the others did their chores.

"Do you want some music?"

I did, but not just any music. I put Bach on my nephew's boombox, either *The Well-Tempered Clavier*, performed by Sviatoslav Richter; or *The Goldberg Variations*, performed by Glenn Gould or Wilhelm Kempff; or *The Art of the Fugue*, performed by Zhu Xiao-Mei. Bach's music, like morphine, relieved me. It did more than relieve me: it did away with any temptation to complain, any feeling of injustice, any strangeness of the body. Bach descended on the room and the bed, on the nurses and their cart. It enveloped us all. In its sonorous light each gesture was detached and peace, a certain peace, was established. A poem by John Donne, read many years earlier, took on meaning: "there shall be no darkness nor dazzling, but one equal light; no noise nor silence, but one equal music; no fears nor hopes, but one equal possession; no ends nor beginnings, but one equal eternity: in the habitations of thy majesty and glory, world without end." The changing of my bandages could begin.

The nurses gradually removed the bandages from my skull to my chin. They freed my ears, took off the soiled compresses, cleaned, prepared the sterile compresses with a pair of tongs by dipping some of them in saline solution and smearing the others with Vaseline. Their movements were slowed by Bach's clavier. When all the bandages had been removed from my face, one of the nurses asked:

"Do you want to see?"

It was the ritual question. I said yes. She took the little black-bordered mirror that lay on my bedside table, the one with which Alexandra had shown me the tips of my hairy ears, and held it out to me. I examined the hole, right in front of me. To see what it looked like. How it was developing. If it was getting smaller or bigger. In what way it had changed since the preceding day, since the day of the attack. I looked at it coolly, in Bach's notes, as one descends into a well. No one, apart from me and the nurses and the people who discovered me on January 7, saw it. Amid the shredded flesh, there was now this little titanium muzzle that held the remains of my jawbone, of which I saw, for the moment, four links. It was a chain, but also the staff from which the notes we were listening to arose. My lip and most of my lower teeth had disappeared. I saw once again, at the bottom of the intact face, and with a masochistic satisfaction, the familiar monster. If I had been a painted portrait, you'd have to conclude that the artist's hand, as sure as Raphaël's, had devastated about ten centimeters toward the bottom to remind people that this harmony was nothing other, neither more nor less, than paint. My earlier face was a convention that had disappeared. At that moment, it was Bach and the nurses' gestures that restored its unity to it—without erasing its monstrosity.

One morning, I glanced up from the mirror and saw the

third nurse, Ada. While the others were working, her dark eyes stared at me. She had just joined the staff; she was twenty years old. Her boyfriend was a croupier in a casino. She was half French, half Senegalese, but she looked like an Indian princess with her long brown hair, her way of always seeming a little indifferent or imperceptibly annoyed to be there. The veteran nurses said of the new ones that they no longer had a sense of vocation, that they didn't give a damn. For my part, I was very fond of Ada. Bach, like all classical music, bored her, but she told me that only later. I gazed at this perfect face, with its nervous, unblemished beauty, looked again at the hole and the flesh, looked again at Ada's face. I was the beast, she was the beauty, and it was she, here, who had the keys to the castle. Her long eyes smiled slightly. Were they made up? I couldn't see very clearly. I raised my eyebrows as if to say: "That's how it is." She made a face that probably meant: "Yes, that's how it is." Then, slowly, the two other nurses began cleaning the wound, around it, and putting the Easter egg around my head again. That day, Gladys had forgotten to leave my ears free, I was already suffocating. I pointed this out to her. Like Alexandra, she took scissors and began cutting slits in the gauze, without being able to see what she was doing and fearing that she would cut me. Under the Easter egg, she couldn't tell exactly where the edges and the lobes of my ears were. I guided her as best I could. We were hunting for the mushrooms beneath a carpet of moss, and she finally found them. My ears emerged from the gauze, and I unfolded them. I wouldn't have felt freer emerging from a box.

Around that time, Alexis came with a big black-and-white photo he'd taken in Cuba fifteen years earlier. It was taken in a village in the Sierra Maestra, squeezed between the sea and the mountains, at the end of an almost abandoned road. He went there regularly during that period. Once, I had accompanied him. Alexis is a photographer. For him as for me, Cuba had been the country where we had reflected and changed our lives. In the light and the laughter we'd begun to grow old: he by ceasing to be an orphan, I by ceasing to be a bachelor. It was the island where you shed immaturity while experiencing it for the last time. Cuba was the enchanted, difficult terrain of our renascences.

The Sierra Maestra was a zone forbidden to foreign journalists. Permission to go there was doled out sparingly, with precise propaganda goals—at least, the Cuban bureaucracy seemed to find them precise. The beneficiaries of these permissions were monitored. You could violate the prohibition and just go there, and then it was a cat-and-mouse game. If you lived in Havana, as Alexis did, it was also to risk being expelled from the country.

The name of the village was La Bruja—The Witch. It had the status of a "model village" (*aldea piloto*). Alexis knew why the state had suggested, through the mediation of a friend, that he visit this Potemkin-like place; but he wanted to work in the Sierra Maestra, and he knew that everything on the island had broken down enough to prevent a varnish of propaganda from lasting very long. He just had to be patient, speak Spanish, and win the confidence of certain inhabitants. He wanted to depict these women and men in their mountain setting; he wanted to capture the impoverished and austere life that they led. They owned nothing or almost nothing except a few ragged clothes, and sometimes one or two pigs, three scrawny chickens, and some mismatched crockery. Most of them went barefoot in the mountains, which were very steep, and where they cultivated, with difficulty, a few acres on the side of a hill. And yet, from all that poverty swelling considerable pockets of pettiness and jealousy there arose a splendor—a spontaneous, mute splendor, which was summed up in the photo Alexis brought. There was an electrical generator, a television set, and one idiot for the whole village. For a long time, I had kept the photo of the idiot on a wall in my apartment.

The one Alexis silently hung on a wall of my hospital room showed a little girl. She was dressed in a white top that stopped above her navel, and was standing in a field of flowers up to her waist. I took the flowers to be tobacco; they looked like carnations. In the photo, they were white. In reality, they were orange. The little girl was looking straight at the camera, with an indefinable air, perhaps serious, perhaps amused; children generally elude the psychological categories we try to put them into. Now it was me she was looking at. Me, my bandage, and my hole. She was holding one of the flowers in her left hand. I didn't ask Alexis why he had chosen this photo of Eden among so many others he had taken with which I was familiar. I didn't need to ask. We had common memories of Cuba, and in that hospital room, they linked up with the ones that were beginning to be born here. In Spanish, didn't he and I call each other *hermano*, brother? But there was something else: the very nature of the place, of the photo and the little girl's gaze. It was impossible to imagine a more beautiful or more rugged world than the upland of La Bruja, and that little girl, who was so imposing, with such a natural refinement, made me a present of nothing other than a charm produced by the harshest reality. I often talked with her during the following weeks, preferably at night. Her gaze bloomed during the hours of darkness and said to me, like Ada—like what I thought I'd seen in Ada's eyes: "Yes, that's how it is." To look at her was to look at the opposite of the hole: a plenitude without affects and without apt words, a naked eye confronting a naked man. I looked at her and continued looking at her as the night went on, and as, my eyes blurry and stinging, I saw less and less. I saw myself back in Cuba, fifteen years earlier, also during the night, wading into a slightly cool river with Alexis, but very quickly my body and the memory of my body disappeared into the river, then into the image, and I found myself, frightened, close to tears, in front of that little girl, who said to me:

"What are you complaining about? Yes, that's how it is."

Later, I learned that her name was Yarima. Amarillo, a man who lived in La Bruja with whom Alexis and I had remained friends at a distance, finally found her. He took a photo of her and sent it to me on Facebook: now a young woman, sitting on a bench, smiling broadly, wearing skintight black pants and ballet shoes. She didn't remember me, Amarillo wrote me, but she wanted to hear news about me. I had been discharged from the hospital and I didn't send her any news.

I'd gotten to know Alexis in the early 1990s, after returning from a reporting assignment in Somalia. He had followed the civil war a little more closely than I had. We'd published a few of his photos in the newspaper I was then working for. I no longer remember whether they accompanied one of my articles. I didn't keep records of anything. Articles, and most books, are made to be forgotten. Alexis and I had lost contact when, a few years later, I happened by accident to run into him on the sidewalk. He was leaving to live in Cuba. I had just come back and had married Marilyn. Our friendship started like that, on a sidewalk. It was also on a sidewalk, where he was walking with his daughter, that he learned that I'd been wounded in the attack. Like everyone else, he didn't know whether I was alive or dead. He stood there on the sidewalk, motionless, and went to pieces in front of his daughter who'd never seen him cry.

At the hospital, we once talked about the multiple wounds we'd seen in Somalia, about those injured people whom the lack of postoperative care led inevitably, with a smile on their lips, toward gangrene and amputation. What I remembered about Somalia, as about the rest, existed only insofar as it was not private—as if the attack had taken the whole blanket for itself. One evening, alone with the Cuban girl looking at me, I made an inventory of my memories of Somalia.

I smelled the powerful odor of shit that had spread through the looted palace of Siad Barre, the Somalian dictator. I saw the goat that was wandering around amid thousands of official documents covering what remained of the floor. Everything had been destroyed and dismantled, even the plumbing, because everything could be useful or be sold. I remembered the lasagna made by the cook who worked for Doctors Without Borders, the shooting sessions with Kalashnikovs and soccer games on the beach, the dark water in which the threat of sharks floated, the delivery of khat at the airport, and men returning at top speed in pickups to sell it at the best price in the city. I remembered bullets and rockets gone astray, which usually hit women and children. I remembered the copy of Stendhal's *The Red and the Black* that I read in a hotel in Mogadishu where I was the only occupant, by the light of a small candle, while shots grew more frequent outside and a group of cats was howling inside. I remembered the little cake of soap and the carefully folded white towel that the people who were protecting me had left on a stool at the foot of my little, perfectly clean bed. I remembered that they had closed the hotel's gates after greeting me and stood guard all night, before making tea for me in the morning. I remembered the surrounding violence, the people's beauty and their courtesy. I remembered the elegance and the stylishness of General Aidid, who quoted Virgil in Latin and had not yet trapped the Americans.

I remembered the gangrenous wounded who laughed, flies in the operating room, classes given by a French anesthetist to ravishing Somali nurses who had been infibulated. I remembered above all, facing the little girl through whom so many things came back to me, the Kalashnikov that was pointed at me in Mogadishu's arms market. I remembered the moment when, in the reddened, absent, and drugged eyes of the man who was holding the Kalash, I saw that for him, it didn't matter whether he shot me or not. I remembered the way he looked at me, the mortal sensation of fatality, I'd often talked about it with Alexis, but now I knew that the journalist who had been subjected to it, his legs trembling, had no idea what it meant, because fear merely announces the event. I remembered that instant and simultaneously saw it from above, from afar, from up close, as if born around another person, because I was absolutely no longer the one who had experienced it.

What lives had I lived, was I going to live? What meaning could this experience possibly have? One day, a nurse asked if I would agree to see the hospital's chaplain. He'd said that he would like to visit me. Why not the imam, I thought. But no one proposed that, and I didn't say anything; after all, it was better not to overdo it. However, I could have listened to the imam, even if at that time every Arab I met in the hallway—and there were many of them among the patients' friends and family—initially seemed to me to be a killer, an impression that I erased almost immediately with a greeting and a smile that were, almost always, returned. Yes, why not the imam? Being blessed by killers who must have known next to nothing about the religion they were claiming to defend, wasn't that a good opportunity to become familiar with that religion by talking with a man who might be eager to explain it to me? There were three copies of the Quran in my apartment, each of them had gone with me to one Arab country or another, and now they were reposing in peace on the philosophy shelf of my bookcase, which was in great disorder. My parents had just returned to my apartment to pick up a few things and my mother, once again, complained to my brother about the abominable pileup of books. I didn't dare ask her to bring me a copy of the Quran, the big green one translated and introduced by Jacques Berque, and, forgetting the imam, I agreed to receive the chaplain.

I was not a believer, the idea of making confession seemed to me comic, but I finally felt ready to welcome almost anything, as if my condition had stripped me of everything except curiosity. As never before, I felt virgin and kindly, like the lamb who has survived the wolf. The chaplain was a fellow with priest's glasses, cheap, and a kind smile who wanted above all to avoid embarrassing me. His presence immediately stimulated me, and I saw him twice. Since we wanted to talk in peace, the first time we met in the storage room, the second, in the worrisome sentry box. Beyond my room there was a last room, as I've said, where detained patients were held. They had to be under twenty-four-hour surveillance. The worrisome sentry box, which looked down on this room, had smoked glass windows. The second time, the room was empty. We set up in the sentry box. The policemen protecting me didn't follow us there.

About the first conversation, I remember the pharmaceutical products that surrounded us from floor to ceiling, and discussing forgiveness while looking at compresses. I had nothing to forgive men who were dead and who had not, moreover, asked anyone to forgive them, but I didn't accuse them, either. To tell the truth, I didn't give a damn about the Kouachi brothers, just as I didn't care about the arguments that condemned them or that, on the pretext of sociology or thought, were already trying to understand them. I was beginning to read the newspapers again, a little, on the Internet, and I was stupefied—I, the journalist who shouldn't have been stupefied—by the contemporary world's prodigious ability to generate explanations and commentaries on anything and everything. The brouhaha regarding the K brothers was like Dostoevsky's epidemic: everyone thought he was the epileptic novelist, and everyone wanted to understand and narrate the action of the two possessed men. The chaplain, for his part, maintained a worthy timidity and silence. He was not wearing a cassock, and walked on eggshells with ease. "You don't believe in God," he murmured to me at the end of our first talk, "but perhaps a form of prayer might be able to help you anyway?"

"I'll think about it," I said to him, "and I'll talk to you again about it. In any case, thank you for coming."

The second time, in the worrisome sentry box, I said that for the moment, my only prayer passed via Bach and Kafka: one brought me peace, the other a form of modesty and ironic submission to anxiety. Reality, right now, no longer had anything to do with the Hegelian morning prayer. As he was talking to me, I looked through the window at the empty bed, that of the absent detainee. I saw myself in that bed and sensed a kind of menace in the air. Then we talked about the nature of evil, the name "Job" was uttered, perhaps also the expression "dung heap," and finally the word "rose" must have grown, flowered, designating something rather simple that he called faith and I, ultimately, beauty, but I no longer remember exactly what we said about it and I never saw the chaplain again.

Shortly afterward, two instruments entered my life, one for two and a half weeks, the other for four months: the VAC and the gastric feeding tube. The VAC (Vacuum-Assisted Closure) is a small vacuum cleaner with negative pressure which is used chiefly for patients with extensive burns, in order to reduce the wounds and allow them to heal more rapidly by removing the pus and bodily fluids. A foam pad of an appropriate size is attached to the wound that is immersed in a jelly with a bitter taste that one doesn't notice so long as the instrument doesn't leak. A tube comes out of the wound and the foam pad, through which bloody scoria are vacuumed up. They go into a small case where they are filtered and accumulate. The VAC works night and day, the patient hears the motor running. The filter has to be regularly changed. The case I had looked like a handbag. A strap allowed me to move around with it and take showers with it, but I was not allowed to make abrupt movements or get the device wet. Like everything that helped me get out of my situation, like my own body whose bones and skin were soon going to permit me to reconstitute myself, it made me pay a high price for its help. It is suitable primarily for large, flat surfaces, the back or the buttocks. Making it adhere to the face, as Chloé had decided, was not a simple matter: the chin is small, narrow, and full of bumps. The VAC started to leak at the first opportunity, generally at night. I put the case underneath the sheet, between my legs. Its alarm immediately woke me, a few minutes after I'd fallen asleep. I would have liked to drown it like a cat and I called it "the cat." It was the nasty little Proustian VAC, the one that woke me just after the narrator turned off the light. Only it wasn't the thought that it was time to try to go to sleep that kept me awake, it was another leak in the process intended to reconstitute me. Then I called the night nurse, for example young Marion-with-cat's-eyes. She came in with her big smile, laughed a little, and tried, by pushing on the foam pad and adding bandages to bandages, to stop the leak. She didn't succeed, or only for an hour or two, and this time, it was in fact the thought that it was going to ring again that kept me from going to sleep. Every three or four days for the next two weeks this exhausting comedy took me back to the operating room to "redo the VAC." The fuzziness of awakening was almost immediately punctured by a burn on the chin that ended up, once I'd returned to my room and taken painkillers, giving way to anxiety about the leak. What texts Kafka would have written, I thought, on the basis of this anxiety! For the second time, I felt guilty, guilty of leaking as I was already guilty of no longer offering a vein to the needle. I would have liked to be the ideal patient, asymptomatic, the beetle that is retransformed into a human or that never falls from the wall, never ends up on its back, the melancholic and meritorious monster. "Dream on!" the VAC said, and it interrupted its humming and started to ring. Everyone was happy when it had held out for forty-eight hours without piping its little song. Every time, I hoped to beat the record, I thought of nothing else, and my father even more; the idea of a leak put him in such a state that, like me, he no longer slept at night.

However, this VAC reduced my wound day after day, and it had another advantage: it allowed me to call Gabriela on FaceTime at night, when I was alone and depressed. Seeing her smile appear reassured me for a minute. Then, answering her or listening to her talk to me, sometimes about her problems, sometimes about the marvelous life that awaited me, all that wore me out. I called her less often, and although I wrote to her, I rarely answered the phone when she called: either because it was not a good time, or because I was in no condition to be given a lesson in desperate optimism. The difference in time zone didn't help, any more than my lack of enthusiasm for images at a distance, which had always seemed to me to deepen the absence that they were supposed to fill, but those were only secondary explanations. The truth was that everything that wasn't present in my hospital room, there, before my eyes, was moving farther away. I expected almost nothing from those who weren't there. Their absence didn't help me, didn't nourish me. It didn't provide me with anything, and I forgot them. Gabriela's face, appearing on my computer screen, emerged from the limbo to which I hastened to send it back. Her dark, almond eyes touched me, but I would gladly have put one of my bandages over her mouth. None of the voluntarist speeches that came out of it could repair the VAC, or help me to breathe, or relax my neck, or drive away the phantoms of the killers that were reappearing. The exemplary life of others was useless, neither she nor I could do anything about it. I would have preferred Gabriela to disappear until her next visit, after the graft.

N ow that the VAC has been presented, here's part of the calendar corresponding to our common life: the gastric feeding tube joined us the day after the installation of the VAC to form a delicate *ménage à trois*. This calendar is not a diary, because it is reconstituted. I wrote numerous e-mails at that time. I noted down facts, first of all practical details, physical phenomena, but I didn't keep a diary. The only diary consists of the account I gave my visitors, with a slight delay, when I was able to speak, and when I was not able to speak, of my questions and remarks made using the whiteboard. I exhausted what I spoke about, I erased what I wrote. I resembled the artist Marcel Broodthaers in the little silent film in black and white that he made in 1969 entitled *La Pluie (Rain)*. Broodthaers is seated behind a box on which there is an inkwell and a blank sheet of paper. He's writing something or other with great earnestness, and he's writing it in a pouring rain. The sentences are immediately washed away, but Broodthaers calmly continues writing others, which are immediately erased. It's one of my favorite films.

The death of a grandmother continued to determine the rhythm of my descents to the operating room. I refer not to my maternal grandmother, who was born a peasant in Berry and had died twenty years earlier, thin and as light as a doll, six months after fainting in my arms, at her home, like a romantic heroine, and thus undernourished. Nor do I refer to my paternal grandmother, who was born in Rio, the daughter of a more or less unscrupulous businessman-adventurer and mythomaniac. She had died thirty years earlier of a heart attack suffered as she sat at her dining table, alone, and her deformed face, which had been reworked twenty times following an accident, had accompanied me as a scout and a competitor ever since January 7. Nor do I refer to my third grandmother, who was born into a bourgeois family in northern France, the young wife of my great-grandfather. She died the same year as my paternal grandmother and had, as I said above, an ironclad religious faith. Each of these grandmothers visited me during these months in the hospital, depending on her mood or on my vagaries. I consulted them regarding what they had experienced and what they were. Sometimes they answered me. They belonged to a noiseless world, in that room they were closer to me than most of my contemporaries. Every day that went by brought me closer to their smiles, their smells, their eaux de cologne, their gray and white, neatly-combed hair, plucked eyebrows, their century, their minuscule lives. Like me, they lived in a dense universe with rarefied air, where the little that entered was subjected to multiple procedures and had to obey habits. But the one who prepared me for the operating room was once again the narrator's grandmother in Proust's *Recherche*. All the same, contrary to Kafka's letters, she did not follow me, hidden under the sheet on the stretcher, to the world below. Her death was too long for the time on the stretcher. She no more left my night table than Madame de Sévigné's letter left hers.

On January 23, I read the grandmother's death and then went down to the operating room. Chloé tried to stop the "leaks," but failed to do so. A difficult awakening, a difficult return to my room. Later on, Véronique the psychologist came to see me. Since I couldn't speak, I communicated by means of the whiteboard. It's amusing to write sentences that you erase long before you've forgotten them, and to write them as correctly as possible: Marcel Broodthaers was right. I was under morphine that evening, and my brother and I began to watch *The Party*, with Peter Sellers. The film no longer made me laugh. I didn't know what I was watching, I mixed everything up, and fell asleep long before the scene with the elephant that the hippies wash in the Hollywood producer's swimming pool.

Saturday January 24, a friend from *Libération* brought me some of the mail that had piled up at the paper. For a long time I had received almost no mail: the cultural journalist was able to gauge the decline of his profession, of his newspaper, and of his "specialty." The victim that I had become rediscovered the ephemeral joy of stamped envelopes. From this first delivery, I mention a letter that came from Limoges: that of Marie-Laure Meyer. I had written a profile of her for the newspaper in 1997, when she was elected to the city council in Nanterre and was a candidate, under the Socialist label, in the legislative elections. She had no chance of being elected; she'd been chosen to fill out the quotas of female candidates to which her party had committed itself. Up to that point, her life had been itinerant, spent abroad, and then had been suddenly transformed: her husband lost a leg and his autonomy following an accident in the operating room. My profile was quick, light, sympathetic and ironic; that was the paper's tone, or any case it was mine at that time. You wrote for today, without thinking of tomorrow. Profiles were sketches. Marie-Laure did not react and I did not see her again.

Five years later, she was injured in the Nanterre massacre. A man in the audience at a city council meeting, Richard Durn, stood up near the end of the meeting, around 1 A.M. He took out guns concealed under his jacket, approached the officials, and shot them one by one. Eight were killed, nineteen wounded. It lasted fifty seconds. The surprise, the closed space, the brevity of the drama, the modus operandi: it is the massacre that most resembles the one at *Charlie*. Richard Durn was not an Islamist; there were few of them at that time. In a letter he left behind, he wrote that he wanted to kill as many as he could of the disgraceful people who were members of a "local mini-elite." Why? "I'm going to become a serial killer, a mad killer, because I'm frustrated and don't want to die alone, because I've had a shitty life. I want to feel powerful and free just once." You'd think he'd read the psychologists and sociologists who write in the newspapers, since he applied their tunes to his own case. He committed suicide by jumping out a window during an interrogation.

I wasn't in France at the time of this massacre. I didn't know the details and I didn't know that Marie-Laure Meyer had been caught up in this. I had forgotten her. Her letter made a figure reappear from a past with which all communication seemed to have been cut off: it forced its way through. I read it in my bed:

Dear Philippe,

I take the liberty of addressing you in this way because we have already met and we have two things in common:
—an article that you wrote in 1997 in *Libé*'s profiles and that was the first time I'd been interviewed personally by a journalist;
—the fact of having survived a mind-boggling massacre, you the one at *Charlie Hebdo*, I the one at the city council meeting on March 17, 2002.
Consequently, I dare write you even if we know each other no more than that.
First, to tell you that I hope you will rapidly be able to benefit from all the talents of French medicine to repair the damage done by a Kalashnikov (the .357 Magnum is more precise); and second, to tell you what you already know, that it is not

easy to be a survivor, divided between the happiness of being here and the guilt of having made it through . . .

I felt only a little happiness at being here, and, contrary to some of my friends at *Charlie* who were not injured, I felt no guilt for having survived; but I understood what she might have felt.

. . . that the nightmares last a long time (even after twelve years I still don't know if they will someday disappear), that they attack you at the most unforeseeable moments and that crises of panic, anxiety, or despair can transform you into a wreck at the very time when the people around you are congratulating you on your strength of mind.

How far she is right about this, I was to discover, little by little. Those who celebrate the "strength of mind" of a victim who has become a patient are afraid of what its absence might reveal to them. She goes on:

And then to tell you that many of us learned with joy that you had survived and that we are convinced that a *gueule cassée* allows you to continue thinking and writing, and that, even if you are probably going to drool for a while, the body and medical science have unsuspected resources. Your article of January 14, showed me that you had already begun to fight, I'm happy about that and my thoughts accompany you (they may be of little use, but I haven't much else to offer you at this point).

And afterward? How does one move from being a survivor to being a living being? I can only tell you my own experience: first by allowing many people to embrace you and tell you that it's great that you're still here, emphasizing their affection and even their compassion, even if they go a little overboard; and then by finding useful causes outside yourself, ranging from your family to political activity, and including, of course, comforting those who have lost someone close to them, widows, widowers, and orphans who are shattered by the violence of a tragedy, and then exhausted by administrative paperwork, pettiness, and financial problems. Finally, by the whole reflection that can be elicited by the acute suffering of having been powerless during, before, and afterward. It's a mighty crucible.

She reminded me of a review I'd written, a few years before, of a novel in which one of the characters was based on Richard Durn. My article was entitled: "The Carriage of he Humiliated." I no longer remember the novel, the review, or the title. "Like Richard Durn," she wrote to me,

The Kouachi brothers are among the humiliated; that does not give them, however, the right to kill. Like him, they live in a society that rejects those who are not golden boys; like him, they have not moved beyond the desperate need for recognition felt by adolescents unhappy with themselves or timid people who are highly frustrated.

Here, I no longer agree with her. I tend to think that present-day society is a poison that makes people crazy, and I have no doubt regarding the mental disasters that its constant, contradictory injunctions provoke. But I can't do social psychology with the assassins who come out of it. Like Inspector Columbo, I still think the first principle of civilization is: "Thou shalt not kill." Nothing excuses the transgression whose result I saw and suffered. I harbor no anger against the K brothers, I know they are products of this world, but I simply can't explain them. Everyone who kills is summed up in his act and in the dead lying prostrate around me. On this point, my experience goes beyond my thought.

Marie-Laure Meyer broadens her reflection:

Today, should we speak of war? Personally, I think not; these acts are far more a matter of suicide, because war is not simply destruction but also conquest. Should we speak of a failure of the Republic? Yes, of course, by creating ghettoes, by discriminating . . .

Here, I cut in. The argument is too long to read and to copy out. It's not that I find it false; and it remains more fitting than a complacent snigger that sends the killer, all alone, back to the hell that he experiences and spreads around him. It's just that for thirty years, perhaps a century, these humanist arguments have led to nothing. My room rids the air of words that float in clothes too big for them and make them empty. The arguments end up in the tubing.

Then: The problem is not the cause they are fighting for, these causes are in the climate of the time, but rather our collective inability to clarify these subjects through coherent arguments and actions, through respectful political and media practices, and as a result we feed their madness.

I don't disagree with these correct banalities; but they bring me neither consolation nor enlightenment. What helps me is the connection that this letter establishes between the writer and me—the personality of this woman, which expresses itself and which I feel. I therefore prefer the personal gift that concludes it: a poem by Paul Valéry, *Palme* (Palm). It helped Marie-Laure Meyer the way Bach, Proust, and Kafka help me. I liked Paul Valéry very much when I was seventeen or eighteen years old. I learned by heart passages from *La Jeune Parque* and *Le Cimetière marin*. I forgot it all. From *Palme*, I copied out four lines that circulated in my morphine-induced visions: "*Ces jours qui te semblent vides / Et perdus pour l'univers / Ont des racines avides / Qui travaillent les déserts.*" ("These days that to you seem empty / And lost for the universe, / Have avid roots / That disturb the deserts.")

On Tuesday, February 27, I read the grandmother's death and went down to the operating room. It was 11 A.M. Chloé installed the VAC. Morphine had eased my night. Once again, it was necessary to shave me. The nurse aides, Hervé, Cédric, did the job with a delicate concern. Shaving whiskers around a wound is a task for a seamstress. They didn't want to damage the wound, but they had to obey Chloé. As for myself, I was in a panic at the idea of putting a razor on what skin was left to me.

I woke up with a new tube that started from my face and ended in a handbag that hummed. The tracheotomy cannula was irritating more and more. It seemed too long, or too wide, for my trachea. A cyst formed. A suitable cannula had to be ordered, because there was none on hand. In the afternoon, I underwent a scan to determine which fibula was to serve me as a jawbone. Lucien, the ward's handyman, pushed my wheelchair through the basements leading from one building to the other. Lucien, or Lulu, resembled a henchman in *The Godfather*. He was bald, plump, heavyset, not very tall, and he spoke like one of the secondary characters who steal the scene from the stars. That's fine with me, I don't like stars. People who hog the spotlight, wherever it is, make me want to turn it off. When I ran into him in the corridor, Lulu shook my hand firmly and I felt solid and in solidarity with him. I talked with him, in a friendly way, about the time we still had to live. He had a pacemaker, his heart was failing, but he continued to smoke: "We have only one life, and other people aren't going to live it for us." When I went out to take a little walk around La Salpêtrière with the policemen, I always took pleasure in seeing him having a smoke leaning against a wall, like a stubborn cancer patient, near the trash cans whose thunderous rumble awakened and worried me at dawn. He waved to me from a distance, squinting his eyes. Lulu reassured me.

On Wednesday January 28, I felt faint as I came out of the shower under the watchful eye of Juan, who had slept (or tried to sleep) in my room. I saw him go pale, he opened the door and called the nurse, while a policeman came in and held me up. I was put back in bed. I was sorry to impose that on him.

Later, I went to a different building and a different operating room where the gastric feeding tube was supposed to be installed: I could no longer tolerate the nasal feeding tube. Once again, Lulu rolled my wheelchair toward the building's basements. The two armed policemen followed us, a few meters behind, as silent as angels. I'd brought *Letters to Milena* with me. The VAC was humming between my knees. I felt a desire to caress it. We ended up in a narrow, gray corridor that reminded me of the garbage room in the suburban apartment building of my childhood. It was closed, like that space, by a heavy steel door that opened onto the outside. From there, pushed by Lulu, I rolled in a fine rain toward a nearby building, that of cardiovascular surgery. We waited in a small, cold antechamber with yellowish lights. It served as a security entrance. Regularly, an automatic sliding door opened on a nurse in a surgical cap and shoe covers who was passing from the inside to the outside. Through the open door, I saw sleeping patients, lost under tubes, who seemed to be making an interplanetary voyage: the Hal 9000 computer might be going to unplug them. They had just come up from the operating room. This was the recovery room. A fat woman was slowly breathing, monitored by a nurse. There was less eye than flesh, and less flesh than plastic. The door closed, opened, closed. The nurses passed through without greeting us, then greeted us. Again I had the feeling that I was moving toward death, but in an odd way. Each time the door opened I counted the tubes on the bodies I caught sight of, and tried to determine their source, their endpoint, and their use. I couldn't do it: it was like a labyrinth of wires to be untangled. The monitors set the rhythm. The policemen remained silent. Lulu had left; he'd probably gone out for a smoke.

A relatively hairy beanpole about sixty years old exited the phantom vessel and took a seat on the bench, in our vestibule. He began by staring at me, then said: "With what you're going through, you need courage!" I don't know how he recognized me. Had there been photos of me after the attack? He told me that he was a painter, that his liver was shot and that he came regularly to have transfusions. Then: "So, now you know what to think about Muslims! We've been talking about them for twenty years and nobody wants to listen to us. During the war in Serbia, I served as a human shield on the bridges, facing the NATO bombardments. The Serbs understood. Maybe now the French will finally understand, no? In any case I'm 100 percent Charlie." I looked at the policemen, half with a look that said, "Can't you get this madman out of here?" The other half was curious to hear the end. Anyway, my guardian angels were there to protect me from everything, including imbeciles, weren't they? I still sometimes think: the cops; but I have trouble calling them by that name. Who would have said that a journalist at *Libération*, a columnist at *Charlie,* would end up having such warm feelings about the uniform? It is true that they protected me with patience and discretion. Most of them come from the provinces, the suburbs, from modest backgrounds. There are whites, blacks, Arabs, tall redheads, beautiful blondes, little brunettes, all kinds. One of them came into my room and said: "My wife prays every day for you." Then he went out again. They were the shadows behind the door.

I didn't know what to say to the pro-Serbian painter and I pretended to acquiesce, cravenly, giving the policemen another meaningful glance. They smile and remain silent. Finally I'm taken away. I'm relieved. I find anti-Muslim rhetoric just as intolerable as pro-Muslim rhetoric. The problem is not Muslims, it's the rhetoric: leave the Muslims alone! "Good luck!" the pro-Serbian painter cried, "and don't forget that nothing good can be expected from Muslims!" A nurse settled me on a stretcher. I helped her because of the VAC, which I didn't want to disturb any more than I do a newborn, because I don't want to spend the night listening to it cry. I landed in an operating room with dim bluish light. The nurse prepared me and put a breathing mask on me, it was difficult, and then, as in the theater, frisky and speaking in a loud voice, just when I felt like I was suffocating, the surgeon made his entrance, accompanied by an extern who had come for the anatomy lesson. He said to me: "OK, now we're going to do a gastrostomy, you'll see, it's very simple, we'll put a needle in your stomach, to guide the tube. You won't feel anything, or not much, but you have to avoid resisting, right? Because if you contract your muscles, then of course you're going to feel something!" The nurse put a tube in my mouth and injected air into my stomach, so that it would inflate and become clearly visible. I caught my breath and listened to the surgeon's black humor about stomachs that explode. I looked at his brown hair, his glasses with black earpieces, and concluded that he was Lebanese; I found out later that he was Brazilian. A video screen placed above me, on my left, allowed me to see my stomach. The surgeon put a cold gel on my belly and, by means of a series of injections, anesthetized the abdominal wall that he was going to cut through. He acted between suspense and surprise: "I inject? I inject, there? Yes? Yes? No, not yet! And bingo! There I injected! Ah!" The VAC was placed next to me. It was humming a little too much. Would you have few scraps for my VAC? My paternal grandmother gave calves' liver to her cat, Stanislas. She'd found him in a metro station where she worked at a newsstand. One day, he scratched me below my eye, no one knows why. It was the extern who inserted the needle. I breathed to relax myself and, as they say in the hospital, to receive it. The pain was bearable. Then I saw the needle moving around inside me like an insect, looking for the stomach that the extern couldn't find at first. Was that really my body up there on the screen? "No!" the surgeon said to the extern. "Not this way, that way! Don't you see the stomach? It's right there in clear sight, you can't miss it. Anorexic starlets have ridiculous stomachs that hang down like old rags, because they don't work enough. But here it's very visible!" After the operation, I asked him: "How is my stomach?" He looked at me: "Your stomach? Slightly oblique, perfect." As I was moved from the operating table to the stretcher, the VAC started ringing. Damn thing. It was going to have to be readjusted.

On Friday, January 30, I awoke with excruciating abdominal pain: an effect of the incision made the day before. Between the pain and the tubes, getting up to go to the toilet was like doing acrobatics without a net. I mentioned it to a nurse. She smiled and said: "That's how it is after a caesarean. Now you know a little better what women go through." Later, I received a group e-mail written by Simon, my colleague at *Charlie*. It was martial and ironic. I learned that he wrote it as best he could, with one finger, when he emerged from a coma: "I couldn't be bothered to die."

The preceding day, I'd read a volume of *Blake et Mortimer*, just as I used to do when I was fifteen years old, until I felt nauseated. I'm trying to remember the name of the person who introduced me to these two heroes. I can remember only his first name, Jean-François. The last time I saw him, he was at Sciences Po. If I remember correctly, he was wearing braces on his teeth. He also liked *Valérian*, *L'Incal*, and *Blueberry*. What happened to him? Is he still alive? An ordinary disappearance of memories that the situation makes extraordinary. A violent melancholy that the body immediately expresses in the form of another attack of nausea—which does away with the melancholy: long live the physical.

In the afternoon, my nephews visited me for the second time. The first time, they'd been scared of the policemen, my tubes, and my "Easter egg," and they didn't like the hospital's odor, "it smells bad." This time, they came up and embraced me. I showed Hadrien, the elder, the gastric feeding tube and the plastic collar through which the tube enters the stomach. "It's my little flower," I told him, and I explained it in detail, showing him the nutrient infusion bag, and how it worked. Henceforth I had to hook myself up to swallow four bags a day, over twelve to sixteen hours, depending on the rate of ingestion that I chose and that my stomach could accept. I went out to walk up and down the corridor with the drip stand, to which the bag and the drip are attached. I straightened my back and walked at a regular pace to avoid any awkward movements. I also showed Hadrien how to expel air from the tube and how to clamp it before attaching it to the nutrient bag. His eyes shone with interest, almost with greed. Since he doesn't like to eat, he was delighted to learn that one can get along without it. He left with the volume of *Blake et Mortimer*, which I hadn't finished reading. I hardly ever read anymore. I only reread the grandmother's death, a few of Kafka's letters to Milena, and the beginning of *The Magic Mountain*. When he saw these books on my night table, the physician I call "Dr. Mendelssohn," an excellent surgeon, raised an eyebrow and said: "Don't you have anything more amusing to read?" "No." I added: "Kafka is very funny, you know." He gave me a frown that meant: "the patient should do his part." The psychiatrist and the psychologist didn't find me depressive. It was perhaps Dr. Mendelssohn, that excellent surgeon, who needed a psychologist; but surgeons don't need psychologists: they are Greek heroes, all action. Basically, I listen to Bach and drift, that's all.

On Monday February 2, I read the grandmother's death and went down to the operating room in the afternoon. Since the wait was going on and on, I also read a few pages of *The Magic Mountain*, the ones where the dead are brought down in the snow, on bobsleds. I closed my eyes. I was each of them. The snow they were sliding on had an odor composed of hot wax, diesel fuel, and linden and mint tea. Shortly after I'd come back up from the operating room, there was panic all around me: my oxygen saturation was falling, my pulse was racing, I was sweating like melting snow, I couldn't breathe, and the intern didn't know what to do. My father and my brother were looking at me with their arms dangling at their sides, very pale, literally struck dumb. I felt as if I were descending into a damp, warm, airless well. It was terrifying *and* intoxicating. It was mysterious *and* interesting. By playing tricks on me, my body was initiating me. By escaping me, it belonged to me. I observed the descent I was undergoing, I felt that I was my father's father and the ancestor of the brother on whom I depended.

Around 9:30 P.M., Chloé stopped by. When she came in the evening, she was gentle, as intelligent and sensitive people know how to be when they stop being exasperated. She said that the bone was ready to receive the graft. She talked about the possibility of making an excursion of an hour or two to see the outside world. My brother suggested the Luxembourg Gardens, Chloé the André-Citroën park. As always, I followed her suggestion. "As always": I had the impression that she had directed my life since birth. I gave her a signed copy of a little offprint that I'd just received, one of my columns by a non-smoker that appeared in *L'Amateur de cigare*. She was delighted. Alexandra, the nurse, passed by. Her hair had come loose. I made a little gesture, without saying anything, to let her know. She put it back up. In the evening, my brother put a damp glove on my forehead, which he changed regularly. We went to sleep around midnight, after the nurses' last round, listening to melodies by Bill Evans.

On Wednesday February 4, Blandine spent the night in my room. She read American newspapers and short stories by Alice Munro. She read them all, methodically, for pleasure and to improve her English. Blandine is a fighter, a regular in hospitals, and it was the fighter, and the friend, that she had come to help. She did it with gestures, with a presence, without effusiveness, almost without speaking. She knew, from experience, that words were useless. She took advantage of the room to concentrate, to clear her mind, to allow friendship to breathe. I looked at her: two years before, we'd been in Castile, in Soria, with Juan, in the middle of the winter. Like most memories, this one immediately plunged me into a sorrow that was very difficult to bear. I drove it away by returning to her bony, peaceful face, to her hands on the book. I cut them out to glue them, as if in a notebook, outside time.

For the first time since January 7, my brother didn't come to the hospital. I was exhausted. So was he. The VAC was leaking again. The alarm on the case awakened me several times during the night. It also woke Blandine. I hated it. A vision when I was half-asleep: I'm living in the *Nautilus*, the sirens are blaring, the octopus enters, I look for the axe to cut off its tentacles and for the sea lion, to play, like Kirk Douglas, the ukulele. Will I have a dimple in my chin, like his, when it has been reconstructed? In the meantime, we're sinking.

On Thursday February 5, I read the passage on the grandmother's death and go down to the operating room in pole position to change the VAC. At 6:30 A.M. having showered and fully equipped myself, wearing my surgical cap, I wrote to my brother to tell him that the salary from *Charlie* had not been paid and that I was worried. I was not ashamed of my concern and I had no sense of its absurdity. In the evening I watched, with Juan, Howard Hawks's *The Big Sleep*. It was the second film I'd seen since I'd been there, after *The Party*. *The Big Sleep*'s almost incomprehensible plot seemed to me as clear as if I'd dreamed about it: I understood that this film was a dream. Now, since I'd been in the hospital, dreams seemed to me less opaque than life is. I had the impression that I was floating in the fuzziness that this film emanates, in the cigarettes and the whisky. Very soon, as always, I was saturated. Bogart's smile put everything at a distance. It limited the saturation and allowed me to overcome my very little sleep. When the film was over, I was exhausted.

On Friday February 6, three women friends were in my room at the same time. Two of them knew each other, but did not know the third one. The conversation had to pass through me, and I was oversalivating. Moreover, Chloé had told me that I should talk as little as possible. "You're a blabbermouth, and that doesn't help at all." Hossein, the young surgeon on duty that evening, talked to me good-humoredly about patients as silent as peasants, who drooled as they ate their soup and didn't say more than three words a day for the rest of their lives. "Don't they suffer from their condition?" "No," he replied. "They live like that and they accept it." Later, I spoke about this with Véronique, the psychologist. She gave me a knowing smile: "I'm not sure they don't suffer from it."

To my three women friends, I presented the VAC as a sample of Gucci's finest work. Silence flowed into the holes. The third friend, Hortense, who was the first to arrive, had tears in her eyes, which were large and bright. She made me think of a somewhat heavy flower from the South, loaded with dew and feelings. The room became a greenhouse. I'd met Hortense in Cannes, eight years earlier, on a terrace, at night. Nearby there had been a hermetic Mexican film director accompanied by a superb woman with short, straight hair: his wife. I saw only this woman's neck and I have never returned to the Cannes film festival, which is summed up for me in this apparition.

Hortense had come here for the first time. She took me by the hand and said: "You're my *miraculé.*" That was the first time I heard that word. It embarrasses me a little, not much, nothing really embarrasses me, and it reminds me of the title of an anticlerical film made by Jean-Pierre Mocky.

At the end of the day, I took for the first time a turn around La Salpêtrière's garden with the two policemen on duty that day. They were supposed to stay a few paces behind me, but I felt like talking with them about the beauty of the buildings, whose history went back to Louis XIV. The assistant in the ward had given me a small book about the hospital that I read attentively, with devotion. I learned about the past and the extent of my chateau. It had not been taken, like Versailles, from the marshes; but every day that passed, as my walk grew longer, it was taken from the territory left fallow by my quasi-death. It was warm in the ward. The cold outside did me good.

On Saturday February 7, the nurse I call the Marquise des Langes (the Marquise of the Diapers) redid the VAC's dressing, all by herself, for forty minutes, with dexterity and meticulous care, as two other nurses who hadn't been able do it looked on. The Marquise des Langes was the nurse I was closest to at that time. She watched over me and found practical solutions to all my problems. As she redid the VAC's dressing, she said: "It's like a puzzle, and I like puzzles." And in fact she cut bits of bandages into all sorts of forms that she gradually assembled around the foam pad and the tube, with virtuosity, until it held. In the evening, several of my friends and my brother dined at the home of Juan and his wife Anne, near the Luxembourg Gardens. Their apartment became the center for the reception and conviviality of the little group that was supporting me. The bibulous annex, in short, of Room 111. From my bed, I tried to imagine the party: the people, the places, the meals, the sound of the leather couch, the music they listened to, everything that I knew perfectly well and had known for a long time. I couldn't do it.

On Sunday February 8, the first sally outside the hospital, for about two hours, to the Jardin des Plantes, which is quite close to La Salpêtrière. Two policemen in mufti from the SDLP (Protection Service) came to get me. They took over from the policemen in uniform who had been assigned to guard me in the hospital, 24 hours a day. Several friends were waiting for me at the entrance to the garden: my brother had organized everything. I was wearing a big, taupe-colored overcoat that I hadn't put on for twenty years and in which I disappeared, a very soft beige cashmere cap, and matching gloves given me by Hortense. The bandages covered the lower part of my face. The VAC's tube connected it to the case, which hung on a strap over my shoulder, like a handbag. I felt like a phantom. The crowd panicked me, even though it was small; it lacked drip stands, solitude, and *gueules cassées*, and it *didn't move the way patients do.* Yesterday, the cold did me good, but today it surprised me as if I'd never experienced it before. I asked to visit the cactus greenhouse. I looked at the cacti one by one, and felt close to them: they needed very little to live, only heat, and they brought me back to reality, to this intense desert, with lots of spines, stones, and very few flowers. My brother's sons were playing in a labyrinth of greenery. Paul, Juan's son, came along, and that touched me: everything that comes from youth distances me from the feeling of destruction. We finished our walk at the garden's belvedere. The VAC hadn't rung.

On Monday February 9, I read the passage about the grandmother's death and was waiting to go into the operating room by 8 A.M. Around 10 A.M., it was decided that I was not going to go in after all, and that the VAC, which was leaking again, would be redone in my room. Several nurses worked on it for an hour and a half but did not succeed. The intern was called in, and with a confident air, he set about trying to do the task, but it didn't hold. Nurses like to laugh at the clumsiness of surgeons who think they're more adroit than the nurses are. When they used their hands to compress the skin so that the pad would act like a suction cup, I felt like someone was twisting me and burning my face. I wasn't unhappy to have avoided another general anesthesia, but they shouldn't have made me wish I hadn't. I finally murmured that they might call in the Marquise des Langes. A nurse reminded me that the day before, Christiane, the manager, who couldn't stand the Marquise des Langes for old reasons I didn't know about, had transferred her to the second floor and forbidden her to visit me. Faced with the repeated failure of everyone else, I insisted, smiling. "All right," said a nurse, "I'll go get her, but you won't tell, right? It will remain our secret." I agreed, all too happy to share a secret with my friends in the Kingdom of the Shades. The Marquise des Langes came in, a little uneasy, but smiling all the same, and as all the others watched, she constructed, with more virtuosity than ever, her puzzle on my face, explaining what she was doing as she went. I watched her work with gratitude and relief. Her task completed, she slipped off to the floor she wasn't supposed to leave. The manager never found out.

That afternoon Joël the hairdresser, one of Blandine's friends, came to cut my hair. Chloé and Annette-with-the-bright-eyes, my favorite anesthetist, the one who had given me a little rubber monster to strengthen the muscles in my hand by squeezing it, had told me that it was time for a trim, that I couldn't go in for the graft like that. Surgeons hate hair and whiskers. What would they do with Islamists? But Islamists would refuse to be operated on by Chloé and Annette-with-bright-eyes: death to the idiots. Joël prepared his tools in silence. I said to him: "Would it bother you if I put on some Bach?" It didn't bother him. I put on *The Well-Tempered*

Clavier, this time by Richter, and sat down on one of the two gray chairs. He put a black rubber shield over my shoulders, sprayed my hair with water, and began to cut it with scissors. A sensation of coolness and of nerves awakened one by one, like a flower opening. Time was suspended. I closed my eyes. Joël was preparing me for a mass or for the guillotine. He was as silent as a priest, as delicate as an executioner. I will come back to life and he will return.

That evening, I was unable to sleep because of the pains in my throat and my jaw, all sorts of discomforts. Marion-with-cat's-eyes, the young night nurse who came from Le Havre, tried to administer an analgesic to me through the feeding tube. The liquid flowed back like a little geyser. I had it all over me. "Ah," she said, giggling, "that means that your stomach is full. These things always happen to me!" She said that when a patient has a hemorrhage or dies, she always gets blamed. One day, I was to hear a nurse use another expression: "I smoked two more of them tonight. I hope it's going to stop there." It wasn't Marion's bad luck that watched over me: it was her laugh and her feline airs. That night the VAC held out.

On Tuesday February 10, Alexis brought me a pea coat just like the one that the first aid unit had cut off me on the day of the attack. I slowly tried it on, with his help. It was a little complicated with the VAC. I'd lost weight, but the pea coat looked good on me. For a minute, I had the impression that I was putting on the costume of my preceding life. It was a minuscule, supplementary ceremony in the series of those that made up my days. I was touched by Alexis's sweetness.

Juan sent me a text by Nietzsche, "Wisdom in pain:"

There is as much wisdom in pain as there is in pleasure: both belong among the factors that contribute the most to the preservation of the species. If pain did not, it would have perished long ago; that it hurts is no argument against it but its essence. In pain I hear the captain's command: "Take in the sails!" The bold seafarer "man" must have mastered the art of doing a thousand things with his sails; otherwise he would be done for in no time, and the ocean would swallow him. We must learn to live with diminished energies, too: As soon as pain gives its safety signal the time has come to diminish them; some great danger or other, a storm is approaching, and we are well advised to "inflate" ourselves as little as possible.

True, there are people who hear precisely the opposite command when great pain approaches: Their expression is never prouder, more warlike, and happier than it is when a storm comes up; indeed pain itself gives them their greatest moments. This is the heroic type, the great *pain bringers* of humanity, those few or rare human beings who need the very same apology that pain itself needs—and truly, one should not deny it to them. They contribute immensely to the preservation and enhancement of the species, even if only by opposing comfortableness and by not concealing how this sort of happiness nauseates them.

I replied: "As usual, Nietzsche gives strength to those who have it."

That evening, the tracheal tube was removed. An almost immediate relief. I discovered that I was not a real softie, a word that has little meaning here, but to the heroism that seeks pain, I prefer pain that goes away. Especially when I know that it will return: the tracheal tube was to be put back in seven days later, during the graft. Heroes have a mission people don't talk about enough: sparing themselves.

On Thursday February 12, they redid the VAC in the morning, again with the clandestine help of the Marquise des Langes. Lying immobile in my bed, I looked at the children's drawings and the photo of the little Cuban girl, and suddenly I felt an enormous sorrow, a real well. I began to weep in silence, without a spasm, without anything. One of the young student nurses, Fernando, noticed and said: "There are a few tears, Monsieur Lançon . . . " He took a compress and dabbed my eyes. I had the impression that my whole life had leaked out in these few tears that Fernando wiped away, as it waited to leak out through the VAC; that it was going away with them to some peaceful place where there would no longer be room for anything but the nameless flowers that surrounded the little girl and sorrow. Fernando continued to dab away my tears, the Marquise des Langes pressed on my wound, and little Émilie looked on and learned. They must have seen the tears, but they were concentrating on the dressing. At that moment, the psychiatrist appeared, a head, a smile, a bit of body, then went away. The VAC was more important. That was the first time I'd wept, I think, since January 7. I would have liked to go on weeping until I fell asleep.

In the afternoon, Gabriel, a friend who was a violinist, a member of the Thymos Quartet, came to play Bach's *Chaconne* in my room. I sat up in the chair. He spread out the score, which was immense, on the bed. I had told Hossein, the young surgeon who had been on duty on January 7, and who, though he was not yet a friend, was no longer simply a caregiver. He came to listen. He took advantage of the opportunity to give me a collection of Persian poems, *The Oasis of Now*, by Sohrab Sepheri. Some nurses were there. Chloé was unable to come. Gabriel followed the score, slowly moving toward the head of the bed. The strings squeaked, I heard his breathing, the sound of his feet on the floor. Nothing is as physical as a violin. Its body seems to suffer all the beauty it produces. Bach resounded almost savagely in the silence of the room and the ward. I began to salivate underneath the dressing. My nerves tensed and relaxed, the violin's strings squeaked. My hands hurt. I looked at the ugly scars that littered them. My whole body was occupied, like that of the violin, by the difficulty and by the music. All feelings, all emotions parade by in the *Chaconne*; Gabriel communicated them, sometimes one by one, sometimes all together. He made his way as far as the pillow and finished with his hand almost paralyzed. For a few minutes, I had the impression that I'd survived only in order to be there.

On Saturday February 14, accompanied by the policemen, my brother, and my friend Sophia, who had become expert at massaging hands, I visited the exhibition on the Han dynasty at the Guimet Museum. There as a small crowd; I controlled my panic. After leaving the museum, we went to a café. I couldn't drink or eat. I looked at their lips and their glasses of beer, their fingers and their peanuts, without the slightest longing, without any feeling. Outside, it was raining. That night, Odalys was sleeping in the room. I watched her carefully fold her clothes, take out a nightgown, eat a piece of fruit: I was in Cuba. She massaged my feet, my legs, my hands, my arms. I fell asleep during the massage, then abruptly woke up and said to her: "Are you going to massage me?" I'd forgotten. During the night, the VAC rang. Marion fixed it up as best she could. It rang less. I had to avoid moving at all. Around 5 A.M., she injected me with Lysanxia to relax me. This time the catheter didn't overflow.

On Sunday February 15, I took a walk with several friends and the policemen in the Luxembourg Gardens, going all the way around and stopping in front of Baudelaire's statue. Then we went to Anne and Juan's home, where I hadn't set foot since early January. Everyone drank champagne, except for me, of course. I had no desire for it, anyway: all my desires had disappeared. As with Gabriela on the computer screen, as with all the women I'd loved, who, for the most part, visited me during those days, emerging from a more or less distant earlier life. I was happy to see them: their presence reminded me that I had lived. But the nerves connecting my memory with my heart, and my heart with my body, seemed to have been cut. Everything floated and was extinguished, for me, in a shared good will. For them, I think, it was different. They entered my room as if it were a place of truth. The attack had split the tree within which people lived, loved, separated, found each other again, remembered, grew old. It broke the whirlwind of life. Those who had almost died, as a result of illness or attempted suicide, those who had a familiarity with death, had natural impulses, almost frantic, as if I had joined them where they had already been living for a long time. They testified at the foot of the bed of a returning companion. None of them did anything useless or inappropriate. None of them stayed long. I wonder whether you have to have experienced that in order to obtain from the world this kind of grace, freed of anything passive, anything active, simply connected with a few movements, a few looks, a few words. My brother organized the visits to avoid overcrowding or awkward encounters.

At Juan's, the VAC started to ring on the couch. I felt, in my mouth, the bitter gelatin that melts like lukewarm ice cream, as if to say to me: "Shut up." We had to go back. Juan joined me a little later and spent the night in my room. We watched John Ford's *The Searchers*. I'd seen it twice, twenty times. John Wayne's solitude, his anger, nothing spoke about me and everything spoke for me. The patient took all the credit for what the imperfect hero did. The lights in the room were turned off. I wondered which of the nurses resembled Natalie Wood the most. We didn't talk.

On Monday February 16, a masseur, a friend of Alexis's, came to work on my feet. I was writing the first article since the one I'd done for *Libération* on January 14. It was for *Charlie*. It was entitled: "A Hole in the Jacuzzi." "In the Jacuzzi of the Waves" had been the name of this column for seven years. I decided to keep it, even if I no longer talked about television or radio, since I no longer watched or listened to them. I kept the Jacuzzi, without the DVD, but with a hole in it. I will henceforth speak about my life as it is, or rather, as it filters what comes from outside. What escapes my experience, what it can't deal with, doesn't interest me: I have nothing to say or think about what I can't directly experience and describe. All opinions are beginning to seem to me vain, shameful, if they are not immediately reframed, qualified, clarified, even destroyed, by the experiential context of the person who expresses them. Marilyn, coming from the East, spent the night and part of the next day in the room with me.

Tuesday February 17 was the day before the graft. It was high time that it was done. I was leaking more and more. No matter how thick they were, the dressings no longer held. All they did was suffocate me. The best thing was to lie on my back, inclined at a 30-degree angle, the sleeping position. An uninterrupted parade of surgeons, nurses, nurse aides. Corinne the physical therapist and Véronique the psychologist also came by. Annette-with-the-bright-eyes, who had put me on iron to build up my strength and had followed closely my recovery after the major operation, seemed satisfied: the athlete was ready for the test. Everyone checked the condition of the body, the armor, the helmet, the horse, the mind, and, as it says in *Le Cid*, the heart. It was time to see *Ivanhoe* again, but the video was at my parents' house, where my nephews had watched it. My brother spent the last night with me. That evening, an old journalist friend, Yves, wrote to me:

I know that you're supposed to have an important operation tomorrow (although I can't find out exactly what constitutes a major operation for you). I always wonder whether the words are quite appropriate, because what's happening to you seems unreal to us. As if we had remained on the other side of the Earth.

We'd met in Romania in the spring of 1990, at the time of the first so-called democratic elections. I close my eyes and see him, short, broad-backed, in his big room as chic as it was dilapidated, next to a round table and the bay window. We met again in Jordan, Iraq, during the riot in Vaulx-en-Velin, and elsewhere, and then friendship occupied all the space that our profession had left. It was he who, after the hurried return from Iraq, told me: "You came back because of the carpet."

I continued to read his e-mail:

> You'll admit that if it weren't for the abjectness that we're experiencing, it would be rather comical. What should we say about today's France? I don't know and I no longer see it. These days all I know how to talk about is the past. Speaking of the past, do you remember the day we covered the riots in Vaulx-en-Velin near Lyon? I remember drinking a glass of wine with you in the old village, in an old-fashioned café, with a tree out in front, on the day before we left. I had a curious feeling arising from the juxtaposition of the old village with what we had just experienced for two or three days around the housing blocks and the burnt-out cultural center, and that was only the beginning of what we're living through now. I'd completely repressed those moments. It seems like only yesterday. In short, let's leave the memories where they are.

The memories left me where I am.

My experience does a number on my memory, making incisions in it and anaesthetizing it by turns: from this hot and cold arises the sorrow that constantly envelops me, as if I were suffering from everything, having lost everything. Only exhaustion can put a stop to it. Among my friends, my experience seems to awaken memory. I have become an ice core sample cut out of their lives by the attack.

I replied to Yves:

We do in fact have the same memories and reading them coming from you gave me great pleasure. Vaulx-en-Velin, if I recall . . . what happened? And the boy whom I took home and who was getting high on glue in the back seat of my car . . . Scenes unimaginable today. What did we miss? What were we unable to do, to write? I often ask that question, but I have no answer, and the bullets that I took didn't provide one, either. I'm writing to you in haste, in a few hours I'll be going down to the operating room. When I come back up, I'll be missing a fibula but I'll have a new jawbone. What will I look like? I haven't the faintest idea. A big violet-colored pear, I'm told. Or a boxer hammered by Joe Frazier. There will be months of alterations, grafts, and then the teeth, once everything is stabilized. The operation tomorrow is supposed to last seven hours. Afterward, I'll be in the resuscitation room for two days, under constant monitoring, to be sure that the graft is taking and that everything is "vascularized."

I'm learning the moves and the vocabulary of this place. Nurses lavish attention on me. When they lean over my wounded face, I look them straight in the eye and try to come up with a little joke to make everyone chuckle. Sometimes I put music on before they come in. I hand books around. The other day, having permission to go out for a few hours, I went to the Guimet Museum in the car of the cops who protect VIPs, very nice, very refined cops. I wanted a little beauty and I've always loved that museum. I brought back a postcard for the nurses that showed a Buddhist statue with a hundred arms, writing to them that this was the dream patient: no more hassles trying to find a vein—mine are getting increasingly refractory and hard because they've been injected so often. This kind of little gesture they return to me hundredfold. There's one jovial, straight-haired nurse in her thirties whom I like a lot. One evening, she told me that she'd lost all her hair in one night. It had been blond and curly. When it grew back out, it was red and straight. What event had she experienced? I haven't any idea.

CHAPTER 14
THE COOKIE BOX

The day before the graft, Marilyn came into my room with an old cookie box. It must have been cold outside; she was as covered up as a cosmonaut visiting a planet too far from the sun—no doubt mine. Watching her enter, I saw her again as she was twenty years earlier, an onion enveloped in layers of fabric when she was confronting, not without sometimes weeping with loneliness and fatigue, her first European winters. She had landed in Galicia, then in France. When you come from Havana, A Coruña is so grim that it seems to be shedding all the tears you're holding back. As for Paris, it was a City of Light without light. Its beauty distances it from the immigrant.

For a few seconds, the cookie box reminded me of other, earlier times when I sometimes ate too many cookies, and then put the nearly empty package back with just one cookie, or maybe two, either to avoid feeling guilty, or, on the contrary, to make myself guilty twice over, as a glutton and as a hypocrite. These memories made me weep without shedding tears, and it became a mania; something leaked out with them through a dry hole, perhaps not as large as the one in my chin, perhaps larger, a hole in consciousness, because they were no longer entirely my own: they belonged to that man who had suddenly detached himself from me. I had become the product of a subtraction. I had also become a receptacle. My determined absence of religious faith prevented me from making it a stoup. I'd told the chaplain that in the worrisome sentry box: no beyond was going to conclude the trial that I was going through.

I'd acquired the habit of devouring cookies in the family kitchen, when my parents were away, generally walking barefoot on the cold tile floor: the cookies remained associated with that sensation of hardness, coolness, and the forbidden. At that time, a large map of Vietnam was pinned to the wall of my room, alongside my bed; I'd read the books by Jean Hougron, Lucien Bodard, and Michael Herr, and I wanted to go live in Southeast Asia, as if the war were continuing and as if I could, by escaping from the French suburbs, lose myself in a jungle of whose horror—and of whose antipersonnel mines—I remained unaware. I had no experience of either violence or Asia. These books made Asia shimmer on the horizon. Looking at this map, I imagined several novels set over there, novels that I didn't write, because they had been written by others. I was fifteen years old, and all these books ended badly.

I looked at the floor of my hospital room, the lukewarm linoleum on which I'd been advised not to walk without slippers. In the stomatology ward, patients' saliva covered the floor and, after all, part of it was mine. I left my black leather slippers at the bathroom door, perfectly parallel, the tips toward the outside so that I could slip my dried feet into them with the least possible effort. Every morning, my feet felt the rough, anti-slip surface of the floor with a pleasure that anticipated that of the shower, however complicated taking it might be, as we have seen.

While Marilyn was hanging up her coat in one of the two armoires, I wondered whether I might someday eat cookies again and feel that frivolous and childish culpability. The answer, for the moment, was no. And the moment was all I had. I would never again eat cookies, I would never again walk on a cold kitchen floor. I would never again do the things I used to do, from the most to the least anodyne. Each instant closed in on itself before the following ones entered. Inside, there remained only a certain version of myself and the medicated echoes of a vague experience. I closed my eyes and tried to see the adolescent I'd been, the protracted pet with his bangs, his pimples, his stomachaches, his taste for instant mashed potatoes and his first jazz records. He didn't appear. My face was enveloped in the usual series of bandages heavy with saliva. They made a kind of big pipe of white gauze from which emerged my recently shorn head. The VAC's fragile hubbub lulled what could, two days before the major graft, only be called my exhaustion. Marilyn looked at this mummified Droopy who used to be her husband, and then she put the box of cookies on the bed, on my thighs. She opened it and I saw, with a certain dread, one of those old photos. There wasn't enough space in that room for the person I was and the one I'd been, even and especially in the form of slightly outdated photographic traces.

At that moment, the VAC started to ring. I called the nurse, knowing that it would be impossible to redo it at that hour. Once again, a temporary fix would have to be made. A nurse aide came in, soon followed by a nurse, I don't know which one—not Marion-with-cat's-eyes, in any case. It was time for the end-of-day care, cleaning wounds, changing bandages, checking bags and tubes. I told them that Marilyn could stay. They set about reattaching the pad into which the tube was inserted to reestablish pressure and prevent it from bothering us—me, and then the nurses—as long as possible. While one of the nurses was sticking the foam pad on my jaw, the other was trying to attach the bandage more securely. Now that the VAC's days were numbered, I was accustomed to the burning of its pressure: what should have been, I imagine, an acute pain had ended up becoming a sensation curious enough not to be entirely unpleasant. There was even a pleasure in accepting it, as when you anticipate a call that will nonetheless lead nowhere: I felt I was, through the pain that I believed I was provoking, the master of the remnants of my destiny. Masochism had still not become my vice, a vice that I sometimes envied, but it could occasionally be a necessity. And despite everything, I established—involuntarily—an equivalence between the pain I felt, or anticipated, and the success of the procedure that the nurses were carrying out. Even if they tried not to cause it and frequently reminded me that it had to be eliminated before it grew more intense, cutting it off at the root like a poisonous flower, a certain suffering was the price to be paid for efficacy.

It was the same with the tubes: they had penetrated me so much since January 7 that I'd learned not only not to reject them but, as the Brazilian surgeon had told me regarding the needle guiding the feeding tube, to welcome them. Tubes were friends—encumbering, capricious, but friends. They repaired, put to sleep, relieved, fed, disinfected. They maintained and provided life. Their being as intolerable as possible was the proof that everything was functioning. Chloé would have been irritated by this psychology applied to tubes: most of my comparisons struck her as occasionally amusing, but always inappropriate. Her bright eyes opened to emit a ray of irony, and she scolded me for playing the writer so much and the scientist so little—even if here I was neither one nor the other, simply a patient. It was just that psychology was, along with the instinctive quest for metaphors, one of the forms taken by what little imagination I still had. I adapted it to all situations, all objects, all actions, answering in the affirmative Baudelaire's question: "Inanimate objects, have you a soul?" And what a soul! Carefree, inconsistent, simply left to itself . . . We sow psychology where we understand nothing, I said to myself. I watched it blossom in my anechoic chamber, like a carnivorous plant in a greenhouse. I escaped into the hallway to do my lengths, with the VAC and baggage, before it caught me.

When they had performed their tasks, and the VAC was momentarily pacified, the nurses left and I found myself alone with Marilyn, as in the good old days. She began silently arranging her things and mine, like an industrious Cuban aunt who knew that in thirty-six hours I would be descending to the operating room and would not return to this room, which was going to have to be emptied. I no longer remember whether I put music on. It's not certain: I believe I recall that I preferred silence and simply watching my ex-wife move around in this space that was limited and as if emptied by time. This time was descending on us like a cloud. Once we were in it, everything that was ours would be wiped away by the perceptible eraser of the lived instant, everything, the event, its consequences, our past, our future, and everything we had succeeded or failed in doing.

When the caregivers came in, Marilyn had put the cookie box in one of the two narrow cupboards whose Bordeaux color relaxed and reassured me. Now she silently took it out, opened it, and we began to look at the disorderly piles of photos of our life in Cuba. I hadn't been aware that after our divorce she'd taken them with her and kept them. My apartment was in such disorder, saturated with so many memories, that I sometimes came across objects whose provenance I didn't know, texts I'd written that described scenes and people, especially women, whom I had completely forgotten. But I had written about them with such precision and such energy! I stopped keeping a diary when I understood that I no longer realized what was disappearing. What good did it do to register instants whose traces themselves were no longer meaningful?

I'd forgotten next to nothing about Cuba—at least about the Cuba reflected by Alexis's little girl looking at us, or about these photos. Landscapes, friends, love affairs, my Cuban family, a joyous, tropical Ali Baba's cavern, the colorful and slightly passé vestiges of the most important of my earlier lives—if I except a childhood that had, I don't know why, long since disappeared as well, a childhood for which this second, belated youth had been substituted: you are also born where you decide to be reborn. I looked at these photos and made poorly articulated commentaries on the scenes that they revealed, commentaries that Marilyn understood no better than I did. Commentaries or exclamations? Perhaps onomatopoeias . . . I was having more and more difficulty breathing. I came across a photo taken fifteen years earlier on the Iznaga Tower, in the Valle de los Ingenios, beyond Trinidad and at the foot of the Sierra del Excambray.

This tower made it possible to keep watch over the slaves working in the sugarcane fields and immediately sound the alarm in the event of an escape. Guards and dogs were sent in pursuit. It had long been a historical monument. Its form was so refined that it was hard to imagine its original purpose. It was lacy, as if it had been necessary to conceal an excess of brutality by an excess of delicacy. It reminded me of the flamboyant Gothic church of Saint-Père-sous-Vézelay. The top, from which the slaves had been kept under surveillance, had become a tourist attraction. Marilyn and I were in the photo. We were smiling at the camera; a friend had taken the picture. We were floating in a happiness marred more by excessive heat than by the invisible memory of the slaves. But this smiling, tanned young man, simultaneously plump and thin, this young man who was essentially innocent, was no longer I. Nor was he someone other than I. Who was it? And who was the person who, in this room, was looking at him with terror, with pity?

In the children's amusement park in the Bois de Boulogne, there are distorting mirrors in which, as a child, I used to like to look at myself. In the mirror of the Iznaga Tower I saw images distorted not by time, but by the sudden break in time. The man who had died was greeting me. He was smiling at me, a gladiator without being aware of it, like a reflection of the sun in a mirror. Except that I was no longer capable of responding to him, as I had to the mirrors in the park, by laughing or screaming with pleasure to scare myself. I could respond to him only in a silent panic and with tears that, once again, flowed a little. I tried to repress them, I hated to impose them on everyone coming into the room, and especially on Marilyn. In a few seconds I'd seen twenty years of trips to Cuba pass by, twenty years of love and friendship, of voices and smells, and I felt them saturating me. I drove them away as soon as they rose up, I drowned them in the void, taking Marilyn's thick, pale little hand, because I felt that they were going to make me explode. If I joined them, if I entered the photo and stood on the Iznaga Tower, I would go much faster and farther than any fugitive slave, to a place where no foreman, no psychologist, no friend could find me—a place where I would need no dog to devour what remained of me. For the first time, I felt, in a very concrete way, that I had to go backward in order not to go mad. And I closed the cookie box.

I learned later that at that time Marilyn was spending nights on the telephone with other Cuban friends, as they used to do in Cuba on hot nights, sitting on rocking chairs, on the slightest occasion. Overcome by fatigue, I was going to go to bed and, stretched out as I was today, sinking into a sleep that was weighed down and deepened by the heat, as it was by now my condition, I listened to their voices carried by a humid warmth as they remade the world, explored their world, and above all revived their memories of childhood and youth. In the tropical aquarium memories were spread as easily as sounds are underwater, as if the thickness of the air had created a silence as favorable to inactivity as it was to recollection. Words almost had flesh and smell. They turned around and around, ricocheting from one chair to another, between rum and coffee, taking on weight.

I fell asleep like that, with the sound of the fan in the neighboring room and the turning wind of female voices, perhaps as I had fallen asleep a first time on that evening, after looking at my shadow in these photos; as I was falling asleep listening to the voices of the policemen behind the door, of the nurses in the corridor, all those voices that extended the voices of the Cuban night, which had extended their nights into those of exile, thanks to the new means of communication. Cubans scattered by destiny were talking about me on the telephone, on Skype or FaceTime, from one neighborhood, city, or country to another, and this net of wintry or nocturnal attentions and voices supported me without my knowing it, protecting the tightrope walker with a muzzle of gauze and adhesives that I had become—this net of distant friends whose familiarity and joviality had so long made my life easier. It was precisely because this insular people had so thoroughly explored melancholy through colonization, slavery, dictatorships, exile, separations, and the inner dissociation caused by political and social control, that it had been able to cover it with a thick layer of farce and joy. It acted like the layer of animal fat that keeps nomads warm in the Arctic. As I saw it, no one could extend childhood into the mass of disillusions that follow it as well as Cubans could. Marilyn was telling our friends about the situation and they were reflecting on the different ways of putting me back in the saddle: "I couldn't bear the idea," she told me later, "that five minutes of horror could annihilate so many years of memories." I myself could no longer bear the idea that so many memories could survive a few minutes of horror. Because at that point, those minutes, and not the memories that had preceded them, constituted my life. To go on, I had to choose, choose in spite of myself. I no longer had the right to the slightest drop of nostalgia.

I'd read books explaining the links that connect photography with death. In general, they seemed to me too long, and could be summed up this way: what was recorded no longer exists in the following second; what we see is the immobile trace of an instant, of a life that is over; and this trace will itself disappear. What we end up seeing is a condensation of all these phenomena. Thus it is neither a reality nor a memory, nor a fantasy, nor a reverie, nor a ritual of resurrection, but all those at once. Like anyone else, I'd been able to verify this by looking at photos of childhood, youth, and even, finally, of the day before; by looking especially at photos of my mother and father when they were young, which I'd found in their home or in that of my maternal grandmother, and kept; I had glued some of them on sheets of paper and attached them to poems which, at the moment that I was writing them, allowed me to appropriate these lives that had preceded me. I carried out these little operations at a time when, my grandparents being dead, I was beginning to feel that my parents would finally join them. The more I went back to their time, the more slowly they would disappear. These were little magical operations. And it was I, ultimately, who had almost preceded them in the memory photo.

In one of these family photos, my mother appeared at the age of twenty, a university student in a light-colored dress, with a book bag, smiling slightly alongside the railings of the Luxembourg Gardens. At that time, these railings had no posters on them. It was the 1950s, my mother resembled me strangely. Until the attack, at least, she had resembled me. Her face was a mystery: if I looked at it long enough, she became my daughter, and it was I who was growing old. Now the mystery had become mine.

I felt the same sensation on looking at photos of strangers dating from twenty, sixty, a hundred years before—strangers who, by means of a simple family picture found in a used book shop or a secondhand store, became fathers, brothers, friends, or dead companions whom I'd almost joined and whom I had, in short, accompanied a little further than ordinary life permits. Part of the phenomenon was due, naturally, to the presence of the photographic paper. Without this material support that was so fragile, and thus so well-suited to recording the fragility of experienced moments, if it floated on a screen that could be turned on and off at will, or that could no longer be turned off for lack of will, the photo lost part of the implicit threat that made it, by the same movement, resuscitate and destroy people and things.

I'd known that for years, but I knew it as a man who, contrary to what the photo told him, knew he was living in the constant flux that it halted, that it denied. Since January 7, everything had changed. I understood this on that evening, as I opened the cookie box. The photos no longer referred to the poorly sifted grain of experience. They referred to memories that the attack had led, like a flock of sheep, into a dead end, toward a cliff. I experienced interrupted experience. I had entered the photos and disappeared into them.

Marilyn sensed my panic, whose cause she guessed, without completely admitting it to herself. She looked disconsolate. Her face swelled and wrinkled. She would have liked to call me back to life, not send me toward death. It was too soon. She said to me:

"You don't have to look at them now. I'll leave them with you, anyway."

She left me the cookie box, a magic lamp that I was forbidden to rub.

I told Marilyn again that when I returned from the operating room and the resuscitation room, I was going to a different floor of the hospital. This news continued to depress me. I'd become attached to a room in which I had experienced and survived so much—where one month had been as important as an entire life. This place had become my kingdom and my submarine. I had neither subjects nor crew, but I was Louis XIV and Captain Nemo. Especially Louis XIV, because although like Nemo I had taken with me on my adventure a limited crew of friends, I had not, like him, declared war on humanity. On the contrary, and more than ever, I wanted to declare peace. I would have liked to love everyone who came in, and I more or less succeeded in doing so. Through the window, I saw no ocean, no monster, but only that pine tree on which crows continued to perch, as on a gibbet. I sought to accept the implacable hospital ritual as a kind of grace, that of Bach.

I understood this a few days later, as Gabriela and I watched, in my new room, Roberto Rossellini's *The Taking of Power by Louis XIV*. Since Gabriela had to become familiar, for her examination in New York, with the cultural politics of this reign, I had suggested that we watch this film, which is exemplary in its rigor, meticulousness, and simplicity: the best of the reports generated in the time machine. We had watched it one evening after the nurses' rounds, which were repeatedly interrupted by further respiratory problems, nurses bursting into the room, and the calls Gabriela made, always at predetermined times, to talk with her family in Copiapó. Her father, who had worked as an electrician for mining companies, had a weak heart, and was also going blind. Soon he would no longer be able to see his only daughter on the screen.

The way in which the young Louis XIV lived constantly, from getting up in the morning to retiring in the evening, under the watchful eyes of others, has always struck me as admirable: that evening, it became a model that, in addition to its psychological effectiveness, allowed me to laugh at myself. I was an invalid reconstituted under the tubes, with a leg bone in place of my jawbone, a figure rather unworthy of appearing in the memoirs of Cardinal Retz or Saint-Simon, but perhaps worthy enough to radiate a fellow feeling without which this room would have quickly become unbearable. The king's power is a heritage that he takes absolutely and that imposes obligations on him. In all circumstances, he has to show decisiveness, distance, and dignity. He has to show that he is the king. He has to show it rapidly, so as to impose his status on everyone, and first of all to impose it on himself. That is how he becomes what he is supposed to be, making this second nature the only true one, the one the circumstances require. In my room, it was similar. I had to be equal to what had happened, from the attack to the successive operations, and also the visits, and I had to do it at first alone, with as much naturalness as possible, without mendacity, without artifice, drawing on the best part of myself. I had to shit on the throne and piss in the urinal bottle with a maximum of dignity, humor, politeness, and attention, without any complaint or familiarity, even if the urine went all over the bed because I'd failed to aim correctly, as almost always happened. It was not a matter of taking myself to be a king. The situation was crazy enough for it to be useless to add a funnel—or a wig—on my head. It was a matter of taking, from the king's example, everything that could allow me to take control. What in the case of Louis XIV was required by a power of a divine nature was in my case required by an all-too-human context, which made me a man struggling along with others—along with those who were saving him. It was exactly what Sartre wrote at the end of *The Words*: "A whole man, composed of all men and as good as all of them and no better than any." But who, to be as good as anyone, and so that everyone in this room could be as valuable as any other, had, at every moment, to justify and reward their presence, their acts, everything they did, so that by surviving, one man, who could have been any one among them, could hold the torn tissue that bound them together. It was the modesty and gravity of my condition, not its grandeur, that had to put me back on my feet.

Marilyn finished arranging things in the cupboard and on the little bed that had been put at the foot of my own, under the black-and-white photo of the little Cuban girl. The girl looked at me again, like a statue, straight in the eye. Marilyn remembered La Bruja; she had been on the trip, but had stayed outside the village with her brother, in a small hotel full of mosquitoes. She followed my eyes and observed the photo. I told her that most of the nurses loved it.

That evening, as Marilyn was sitting beside me, the girl said to me, "You've come here. You've laughed, walked, eaten, talked, listened here. You've taken notes here. You've bathed here. You've been bored here. You've run on a deserted road with Amarillo, who followed you barefoot because his sandals were worn out. You've seen Alexis buy a pig for twenty dollars, because he wanted to eat decently in this village where that was so rare, you've eaten part of it without hesitation. You've looked at the green, dark mountain that falls over the village, that mountain where you are not allowed to climb. You've looked at it as you're looking at me now, constantly dreaming of going up there and never coming back down. For the moment, you believe that you will never come back to that mountain, and I, I'm there, in your past, like the tobacco flowers, and I'm not expecting you." By turns, I looked at Marilyn's dark eyes and the girl's dark eyes, as if her strength, her childhood, and the flowers would take me to a clean, inclined, solitary, aerial place as violently somber as it was abruptly illuminated, a windless place where you heard nothing other than birdsong and the sound of an agouti running through the trees.

Marilyn stood up. Her petite, strong, stocky, simultaneously plump and agile figure moved easily around the clinical, limited space that it had taken her less than five minutes to inhabit. From her former condition as an immigrant, she had retained this quality: she settled in without difficulty, and immediately, wherever she was, as if she had carried her house on her back and her valise—big, cheap, held together by straps—between her hands. As if at any moment she was going to have to leave. I saw her again at our home when she returned in the evening, tired, on edge after a day at the hospital, completely saturated with the affectivity and aggressivity that had been deposited in her by the autistic and psychotic children she cared for. She went into the little room at the back, "*el cuartico,*" her face closed, and silently emptied out the disorder of her day, of her bag, and of her clothes. I heard her arranging, or rather disarranging, spreading in the middle of the fabric her feelings and memories. She exhausted her fatigue and anger by multiplying things. This noise and this movement reassured me. And they reassured me once again that evening. Her presence reminded me of the ordinariness of a life that had been lived. But as when we looked at the photos, it reminded me of it in a context which, once the first gust of sensations had passed, took me back me to the fact that it was all over.

What was over wasn't my life with Marilyn. We'd long since lived through that end. We'd learned to accept one another, like any couple once united and now separated, and that end itself had since been abolished by the pacifying recrudescence of memories and the reconversion of feelings. But as when I looked at the photos, I was no longer the man who had experienced, accepted, and overcome that end, because I was no longer the man who had preceded it. I sought in vain, in this room, while Marilyn was taking out a thermos, a sandwich, mandarin oranges, and a bottle of Coca-Cola, the man who had been, to use the Hispanic expression, her "half-orange," *media naranja*. He was there, he must have been hanging around in a corner, near the trash can or at the base of the red lamp a friend had given me, perhaps in the operating room kit that had been brought to me a little while earlier, but I didn't find him.

A little later, a nurse aide came in to attach the day's last nutrient bag and to remind me of the protocol: to prepare for the operation, sometime between then and the next morning I had to shave the whole of my right leg, from which the fibula would be taken. Then my parents came in. My mother had met Marilyn earlier in the day and had given her the sandwich, the oranges, and the Coca-Cola for the night. They talked about me for a while, in the habitual tone that sounds so odd in a place that is so little habitual, and then Marilyn offered to shave my leg herself. I wondered whether my mother would allow her to do that. But my mother was tired and distraught. She'd spent enough time massaging the scar tissue on my hands and arms, and caressing my head, to leave to Marilyn what I wouldn't call a privilege, but the benefit of a shared task. At certain times, everything in this room was part of a ceremony that went beyond any of us.

I sat up and put my leg on top of the sheet, freeing it from the gown. Marilyn went into the bathroom. She filled a basin that my parents had brought, took my razor and shaving cream, and then, as my exhausted parents watched in silence, shaved the hair off my leg. I was ten years old, I was a hundred. Sometimes I watched her work, sometimes I looked at my parents, sometimes I looked at the little Cuban girl: we were the same age, this unknown girl and I, an age as ancient, as floating, as that of a Khmer statue in a forest. I remembered a bit of advice I'd been given by a woman friend many years before: "When things are going very badly, when the sadness becomes unbearable, you have to find things that will relieve you. In those cases, I run a hot bath, get in, and shave my legs. Very slowly."

My head remained imprisoned in the damp, white bandage. I was immobile, my throat on fire. I felt as if I were being prepared for a journey of a thousand years to a place that was still much farther away than the place where I was—a place from which I might never return; and those who were slowly and meticulously carrying out the indispensable ritual, like priests preparing a young girl before handing her over to the thaumaturgic gods, were those who loved me.

My parents left around 8 P.M. Night had fallen a long time before. The window was slightly open, to limit the heat given off by the radiator, which had nevertheless been turned off. Before leaving, my father complained about the cold. I was drowsy, dulled by emotion and drugs. My leg had become as smooth as that of an Olympic swimmer. Marilyn had taken her shower, as is done in Cuba, always in the evening. I asked the little Cuban girl: "Do you think nothing has changed?" Her silence was a reply that relieved me, though I couldn't interpret it. Marilyn came out dressed in thick cotton pajamas. For her, it was dinnertime. She took out a thermos full of coffee. I put on a jazz disc. I was finding it harder and harder to breathe. Marilyn came over to me. Without speaking, she put the sandwich under my nose: its smells invaded me. Then, after eating it, she peeled an orange and, still silently, put a quarter of it under my nose. Again, I smelled everything and, looking at the Cuban girl, I said to her: "I may not be able to eat them again, but I'll always smell the fragrance of mangos." Marilyn peeled another orange, pouring coffee in her thermos's cup, very strong coffee, in the Cuban manner, and, with this blessed smell that seemed to rise from the streets of Havana, the smell that woke me every morning over there and whose hallucinated memory had accompanied my awakening on the night of January 7 to 8, it seemed that I had rediscovered for first time one of the senses I thought I'd lost.

Marilyn had brought two meditation discs. On one of them there were Tantric Buddhist chants. I fell asleep, awoke, fell asleep, awoke, plunging into the repetitive vibrations of their voices, which carried me off somewhere. With the help of a sleeping pill, they made me immortal—I'm not sure whether immortal with peace or with sadness. They substituted for the morphine that the nurses had been told not to give me any more of, no doubt because I was beginning to like it too much. Some part of me had leafed through *Tintin in Tibet*, had followed Tintin setting off in search of Chang in the Himalayas, Chang who was sick and had been taken in by the good Yeti. The voices came and went like waves, sometimes I was Tintin, sometimes I was Chang, and I knew that sorrow, like the attack, like the Yeti, would have an end. These monks mustn't stop chanting. They vibrated, vibrated, they had to continue vibrating. They were massaging my body and consciousness and making them revolve in the void opened by the wound. The lights had been turned off. There remained only the pale lantern that illuminated my bed. Marilyn had stretched out on the little bed, under the Cuban girl who was now disappearing into the shadows. In a few gestures, she had just warded off the spell of the cookie box.

CHAPTER 15
THE FLAP

I awoke in the pale light, across from a kind of counter that was perhaps cream-colored, perhaps green. Two nurses were standing behind the counter. For a minute or an hour, I felt nothing. My eyes closed, opened, closed. I looked at the nurses. They were doing strange things. Sometimes they spoke slowly, about people, about beds, about surgical procedures, and their even slower movements constantly slowed further and thickened the light in which I was bathed. Their ordinary life seemed to accompany me toward the extraordinary sleep from which I had come. I would have liked to cling to that ordinariness to escape from it and I did not succeed in doing so. Failing to succeed bothered me. I tried to go back to sleep and couldn't. A kind of Jiminy Cricket told me that I mustn't do it. He jumped over the counter, like a cowboy, and joined the nurses in their activities, which were becoming clearer. One of the two was dark-haired. I wondered what she was doing behind that counter, *as if I didn't exist*. Suddenly she raised her head, looked at me with mechanical attention, approached to check something close to me. I thought of the server in Manet's *Bar at the Folies Bergères*, the one who conflates viewers and her customers and observes us from the counter with a clear and indifferent eye, her mouth closed, facing us, without empathy, without compassion, without aggressiveness, without anything. Pilar—that was the nurse's name, the same one as on the night of my first awakening—had no relationship to her, or to any other of Manet's creations, she was smiling and sweet. However, it was the server who imposed, or superimposed, herself on Pilar, with her blond bangs, her button nose, and her indeterminate air. She said to me: "You're almost alive, that's amusing, and now go back to sleep." She was pitiless.

I did not go back to sleep. Before I began to feel faint, Pilar went back to the counter and another woman took her place: my paternal grandmother and her reconstructed face. I had learned part of her story only when I was about thirty years old, vaguely, and I had to wait until I was forty-six to know it a little better. As a child, I didn't know that she had a destroyed face, or what her life had been like. I saw that she had a kind of bump on her forehead, over her eye, and a big forehead full of irregularities. For me, this bump and this forehead were normal. Fantastic, but normal. All faces are asymmetrical, a perfect symmetry would make them unbearable, but in the mirror hers was particularly asymmetrical. One of her eyes was much lower than the other, as in a painting by Picasso entitled *Mémé* ("Old Lady") that I saw later and of which I immediately sent a photo to Chloé, telling her that like my grandmother, Mémé could really have used her help. "Why?" she replied. "She's so cute!" Mémé had little round glasses and a mischievous smile. My grandmother wore big glasses, at least when she was reading. As I remember her, her smile wasn't mischievous. It was tender, discreet, with something painful about it that I don't understand. Nor do I understand why, in the mirror, one eye is lower than the other—almost on the cheekbone. Are the mirrors magical?

During childhood nights, sometimes, I dreamed of her: she's a monster who emerges from a tapestry and, with a big, cruel, greedy smile, violates or devours me. The monster is wearing a tall wig, like a permanent wave. The scene always takes place on an old, flowered bedspread in my maternal grandparents' gloomy bedroom in their village in Nièvre. I

305 - PHILIPPE LANÇON

sometimes slept there when I was a child. I fell asleep while they were playing pinochle in the living room, hearing their voices announcing trumps in the silence. This nightmare wakes me up, but it doesn't bother me. There is no connection between this grandmother whom I love and the monster based on her, except for that bump, the strange face, the fact that she was constantly weaving a tapestry on a black background, as if waiting for Odysseus. And perhaps the fact that since childhood I had called her "Papy," as if she were a man or someone between two sexes, someone who enchanted me by day and worried me by night. This name, "Papy," was adopted by the whole family, including her; she wasn't called by any other name, and never by her first name, Marguerite. I don't even know whether, in my childhood, she was called by that name. I never knew my paternal grandfather, Gabriel, who died in 1959 of a heart attack in a hotel in Angoulême, worn out by the war. They had divorced while he was in a prisoner-of-war camp in northeastern Germany. He returned from captivity only in the summer of 1945. He was then thirty-eight years old. In a photo that I looked at on the eve of the attack, he looks like he's about the age to be my father. But what does one photo mean? And what do I look like in the photos of my face that Candice, the stomatology department photographer, will soon be taking?

In the studio apartment where Papy lived alone, in the Parisian neighborhood of Le Marais, which was then still working-class, she initially had two fennecs. They hid under the bed when visitors came, and their eyes glowed in the darkness. They were wild, and if you tried to approach them, one would try to bite you. I loved to lie on the floor, watching them. I listened to Gérard Philipe read *Le Petit Prince* and I loved these animals like the fox who comes out of the desert to preach morality, but I was unable to tame them. The apartment smelled bad. Under pressure from the family, she got rid of the fennecs. At that time, she worked at a newsstand in the Les Sablons metro station, and took home a young stray cat that had forced a train to stop: he had finally taken refuge under her little counter without her noticing it. She named him Stanislas, called him "Staniii," and, even though she had no money, gave him calves' liver to eat. When I went to her home, she often bought a live trout, so that I could play with it in the bathtub; then she killed it and ate it, because I didn't like fish. Perhaps I ate, like Stanislas, calves' liver. I liked to watch it being selected and eaten, and I liked being finicky. My grandmother had lots of imagination and talked to me about Egypt, where she dreamed of going; that was to be my first trip, paid for with my own money, and probably made so I could tell her about it. Her apartment had a high ceiling and smelled like fennec piss, then of cat piss. You got there by a steep, dark, little staircase. The bay window looked out on the Blancs-Manteaux church. On the ground floor, there was a cabaret. I was happy there.

The accident had taken place in May, 1940, on the road between Pau and Bagnères-de-Bigorre, where my grandparents lived. My grandfather, who had been called up for military duty, was stationed in Pau. My grandmother came to see him one last time with their two children: my father, almost seven years old, and my aunt, who was four. My grandfather was soon to be taken prisoner on the Loire, at Sully or Gien, and they were never husband and wife again. On the way to Pau as on the way back, my grandmother sat in the suicide seat. A friend was driving. His name was Georges. My father and my aunt were sitting in the back seat. They drove back to Bagnères at night. The car had blue headlights, as was required for passive defense. They illuminated the road badly, you couldn't see anything.

It was my father who at my request recounted the story, on August 13, 2009, as we were completing a hike in the Pyrenees that lasted about ten hours. We were approaching Gaube Lake, which came into sight, little by little. My father had great difficulty in descending an immense talus slope. I helped him, stone by stone. I was afraid for him. For the first time, I felt myself to be my father's father.

A truck had stopped on the road to Bagnères. Georges, the driver, saw it too late, and the car plowed into it. My father told me that my grandmother's body *disappeared into the engine compartment*. He got out of the car, uninjured. In front, Georges was motionless, his ribs crushed, his legs broken, his tongue cut. A car stopped, two men got out, approached, and pulled my aunt, who was stretched out in the back seat, out of the wreck. Like my father, she was uninjured. Then seeing nothing else, the men told the children to get in their car, they were going to drive Georges to the hospital. My father, terrified, said to them: "But my mother is still in there!" They looked and found her *in the car's engine compartment*, her face shapeless and ravaged, covered with blood, *broken everywhere*, my father said, and he added, as the wonderful Gaube Lake appeared in its totality: *I recall her perfectly, her body*. They were taken to the hospital in Pau. The stretcher was set down in a large room. A nun passed by and, looking at my grandmother, covered her face with the sheet, thinking she was dead. At that moment, according to my father, a surgeon came by, looked at her and said: "She's still breathing . . . We're going to see what we can do." When my aunt saw her a few days later, she came out of the room screaming: "That's not my mother!" A hole was bored in my grandmother's skull, just as in the case of the poet Apollinaire. Over the following years, she underwent about thirty operations. The bone structure was stabilized with steel plates. Maxillofacial surgery had made great advances during the First World War as a result of the disfiguring head injuries suffered by soldiers. However, it was not yet the surgery that I was beginning to benefit from.

Hossein told me that the Iran-Iraq War had allowed French surgeons to improve it. All her life, my father told me as we hiked past Gaube Lake, my grandmother suffered from terrible sinusitis and neuralgia.

I was thinking that I'd never seen Papy complain about anything whatever when an intense, total feeling of faintness swept over me from head to foot. It was, to use Marguerite Duras's expression, an invasion of my being, and my grandmother disappeared. There was not enough room for two.

I was duly covered with tubes and was breathing with increasing difficulty. The knife in my throat was gradually returning. My whole body became my jawbone, that unknown that was tearing me apart and seemed to be full of short circuits. This time, the jawbone seemed also to have grown on my right calf and foot, which, when I moved a centimeter or two, silently signaled their discontent. Clearly, they must have removed my fibula. But did I at least have a new jawbone? Had it worked? The inside of my right thigh burned. The tracheal tube had been reinstalled, and I couldn't talk. A nurse aide came in to wash me. I was unable to roll over on my side. He took hold of me and flipped me over like a long crepe. With one arm I tried to hold onto the edge of the bed. I was gasping, I wanted to help, to roll all by myself, to be a wholly imperial baby. I felt guilty for not succeeding and wondered if that was how babies were treated, if they felt the same impotence and the same distress when they were traversed by internal, hostile forces, manipulated—the same condition, but deprived of consciousness and memories. The nurse aide was rubbing my back with a glove moistened with lukewarm water. I thought the way he did it was vigorous, and that adjective, "vigorous," suspended and even civilized, for a second or two, a situation that made me an indeterminate something-or-other without fat and without breath. I could hardly breathe anymore, but I sought the slightest pleasure, and I felt, for a second or two, in the contact with the luke-warm glove, aided by "vigorous," a trace of well-being. The sensation of being nothing more than a body appears when the latter completely escapes our desires and our will, like servants who come to life on the day when, upon being summoned, they all revolt at the same time in order simply to say: I exist. The body is fine so long as it serves the carefree, proud master, so long as it doesn't draw attention to itself. The malaise that invades it makes it autonomous, and thus more alive, but we're not used to this life that we don't control, don't foresee, to this uprising of the organs that expresses itself in an incomprehensible pileup of sensations. Chloé had told me often enough: "It takes time for the brain to understand and translate the messages that the panic-stricken nerves are sending it; the patient has to be patient, and he has to do it as quickly as possible." The time had come for me to remember this lesson; but no matter how often I repeated it to myself, while the lukewarm glove continued to rub my skin, it did not allow me to consider my body from outside, as an observer, as I would have liked. However, I managed to do this to some extent: the mere fact of remembering the lesson and trying to apply it slightly detached me from the pile of flesh covered with tubes and wounds that was called Monsieur Lançon; but it was not enough, and even added a certain peevishness to the situation.

The nurse aide turned me over and cleaned my chest, then the upper part of my face. I began to pant, Chloé's lesson had disappeared, and the pains began, sometimes cooperating, sometimes competing, without any one of them being able to hold the inside track for more than a few minutes. Soon, the first bout of nausea came on. To drive it away, I concentrated on the pain in my thigh, and then, once its mission had been accomplished, the thigh pain was driven away by my open, stiffened foot, until the point where the electrocuted jawbone *jumped inside* and erased the foot. The jawbone thought it reigned alone until a ball of needles located in the trachea overcame it, resting on its laurels until an old bedsore on my buttocks, which dated from before the operation and had been waiting, like the tortoise, for its time to come, crossed the finish line by a head. Time expanded in the merry-go-round, then my bed was moved into the large room, far from the counter. A few meters away, a man was groaning. As was often the case, his groans sounded false. I listened to him with relief, proud of remaining silent. When you keep quiet, you sound right. I asked for a felt-tip pen and my whiteboard, which, like Captain Haddock's adhesive tape, had followed me that far. Later on, the parade of caregivers began.

Annette-with-the-bright-eyes was the first person I remember. She had handled the anesthesia. She must have just come up from the operating room, because she was still in scrubs. Her green eyes looked straight into mine, her lips drew back over her teeth, and she said to me: "Do you feel like a freight train has hit you in the face?" I nodded. "That's normal. But you'll see, in a month we'll drink a glass of pinot."

She walked away, dragging her feet, slightly stooped. A glass of pinot? Why was she talking about pinot? Was Annette from Alsace? What was pinot like? I no longer even knew how wine tasted.

My parents arrived shortly afterward and took up positions, one on my right, the other on my left, each one holding one of my hands and caressing it. I took the tablet and wrote: "Mirror?" They had brought one. I was going to find out how I looked. I took the mirror and discovered, in the place of my chin and the hole, surrounded by thick black or dark blue sutures a large, blood-streaked slab of meat daubed with Vaseline; it was light-colored, between yellow and white, with a smooth, hairless surface as flat as that of a plastic toy. Was that my chin? Was that the result for which I'd been operated on for ten hours, a bone had been extracted from my leg, and I'd been put in this state? I was devastated. I almost missed the VAC, and it was at that moment that I realized it was gone. The parade of caregivers continued. I don't recall seeing Chloé, but Dr. Mendelssohn, who had performed the surgery with her, did appear. I looked at his bright, sad eyes, his slightly balding forehead, his somewhat old-looking youth, his firm, prematurely dried-out face, halfway between a comedy film and an attack of melancholy. He told me that everything had gone well, and that it was, really, a very beautiful wound. "Beautiful wound" (*belle plaie*) is the expression surgeons use in these cases; they see what it will become in what it is. Dr. Mendelssohn must have sensed that my enthusiasm was not as great as his, and he asked:

"So, are you pleased?"

I raised my eyebrows and shook my head a little, as if to say: not really.

He looked surprised, or irritated, or both:

"Why not? You've got a chin, don't you? You didn't have one anymore: it's better than nothing."

I raised my eyebrows and nodded a little, as if to say: "Certainly."

He gave me a cold smile, verging on sarcasm, and explained to me that someone would come every four hours to see if the graft was taking hold. That was the added bit of suspense: for forty-eight to seventy-two hours, the patient who had undergone a graft was in danger of necrosis. In a case like mine, it was unlikely. As Chloé later told Jean-Pierre, my implant specialist, who was amazed by the quality of my dental arch and the wounded tissues: "So what? He's in good shape, my patient. He doesn't have cancer!" Nonetheless, the piece of meat had to be checked every four hours to see if it was living its life or not. The first squad came in not long afterward, two interns. They took out their little tongue depressors and used the wooden tips to touch the thing, with little movements, as if to evaluate its flexibility and texture; everything was going well. And they left, smiling and telling me:

"We'll be back in four hours!"

The nausea returned. A pile of gray cardboard kidney cups had been placed on my night table. I kept my eye on them and threw up black bile several times as my parents looked on. My father had brought me a copy of *Libération*. I didn't read it. Other caregivers came by, friends of cousin Thibault who had been an anesthetist in this same hospital and who asked for news. They all looked at me and said, "Really, it's a very beautiful wound," like Dr. Mendelssohn. I clung to the expression and got through the day on this buoy, trying to move as little as possible.

Chloé had made a fuss in order to get permission for me to spend twenty-four to forty-eight hours in the resuscitation room. It had been recently remodeled, and there were very few bedrooms; those were reserved for emergencies and the dying, and I belonged to neither of those categories, but for Chloé it was essential that patients who had undergone grafts be constantly monitored: not only in order to react in the event of a problem, but also to establish precise bases for protocols. In the resuscitation room, the visiting hours were shorter: from 1:30 P.M. to 3 P.M. and from 7:30 P.M. to 9 P.M. My brother arrived just as an orderly was taking me to that indeterminate antechamber. Two policemen had appeared and were accompanying us. The doors opened right on time, and we went into what had seemed to me to be a spaceship. I had a big bottle of oxygen between my thighs; it resembled the ones I'd used back in the days when I did diving. The orderly had tried to put it at the foot of the stretcher, but in vain. I was breathing more and more poorly, but that wasn't all.

A few minutes before the orderly had arrived, I'd begun trembling all over, from head to toe, without being able to control anything. I'd immediately thought of a night spent at a friend's home near the Place de l'Étoile, thirty years earlier. I'd just separated from Muriel, the woman with whom I'd been living for the past five years, and while waiting to find a studio apartment, I'd been crashing with various friends, coming back during the day to change clothes in what was no longer my apartment, coming and going like a criminal looking for the traces he'd left behind. In the evening, I often returned to my friend's apartment, where the atmosphere was more than convivial. He lived in an apartment belonging to his father, who was a prefect and was not there. In the entry hall, there was a glass-fronted bookcase full of Pléiades, and that was the first time I'd seen so many in one place. Here, the table was open. We ate and drank in the kitchen, like Russians. Those who were too tired or too drunk to leave slept there, wherever they could. That night I slept in the same bed as a girlfriend of my friend's sister. I didn't know her, and all I remember about her is her rather deep voice and her button nose. When she turned her back to me and tried to go to sleep, I smelled her fragrance and wondered if she expected me to try something. For the past year, I'd been living through a terrible relationship crisis, and although I don't believe I felt frustrated, I was sad and exhausted. I listened to the girl's breathing, to discern in it sleep, tension, indifference, or invitation. I didn't hear anything. Should I move closer to her, reach out with a foot or a hand, touch her? Her slightest movement was a sign I couldn't interpret. This fogginess awakened a kind of vague, nervous and humiliating desire in me, and suddenly I began to tremble, a little, a lot, tremendously, somewhere and then all over, like a leaf and then like the whole tree. Shame banished desire. Up to that point, I'd thought: if only she's not asleep! Now I was thinking: if only she's asleep! The more I tried to stop trembling, the more I trembled. I ended up getting up to go read in the adjoining room. I took a Pléiade out of my friend's father's bookcase, a volume of Saint-Simon. The memoir-writer's sentences stopped the trembling. At that hour, reading is effective and sinister. Before long, I felt cold. When I returned to bed, the girl was snoring.

In front of the orderly who was strapping me on the stretcher and attaching the oxygen bottle, I trembled in exactly the same way, but I could neither get up nor go read Saint-Simon, and whereas the girl hadn't noticed anything or had pretended not to notice, the orderly didn't wait to ask, with a benevolent air:

"Are you cold?"

I shook my head.

"Are you scared? That happens."

And he smiled as he took me off to the resuscitation room. My brother arrived at that point. He took my hand, and we set off through the corridors toward the elevator that took us to the resuscitation room. I pressed my thighs against the oxygen bottle to keep from trembling again, but it was my brother's hand that finally calmed me. We arrived in front of the opaque door, and it opened right on time. My brother had to stay outside. The orderly, the policemen, and I entered a dimly lit, apparently new corridor, a true spaceship corridor. On the walls and ceiling, there were luminous stars, very clean, the patient who passed by contemplated the false starry night. The nurse, young and merry, guided the orderly toward the room where I was going to spend the night and part of the following day. This room was big, very clean, and there were machines everywhere. A sliding door led to the hallway where the two policemen were sitting with their Berettas. When it silently opened, I looked at them, and this vision reassured me, even though I could hardly breathe anymore. Electrodes and tubes were attached to me. My body was living down there, quite near, here, elsewhere, in the machines full of little points of light that merged with the stars in the corridor beyond the uniforms and the guns.

"Ah! Surely you're not going to do that to me?"

It was the nurse who was speaking: my catheter and the drip had just come loose. My veins were increasingly absquatulating, in medical jargon I think they are said to be "positional," the drip stopped at the slightest movement. For long minutes, she tried to find other veins but was unable to do so. The nurse-anesthetist came in. I'd forgotten the nurse's first name, but not his, because she said it when she called for help: Serge. Serge was black, rather handsome, no longer very young, with somewhat long curly hair, and as calm as a statue. The nurse was on the left, next to the drips. He stood on the right, looked at me, and then, putting his arm on the bed near mine, said:

"You can take my hand."

He had a warm, deep voice, and I took his hand as if my life depended on it. The nurse tried in vain to find a vein, but they were just not there. The warm, deep voice said to her, over a pointing finger:

"There, maybe?"

Serge was right, the vein was there.

My brother, who had been left outside the ward, joined me when everything had been installed. A photo that he took shows a thin, hirsute, bare-chested man covered with wires, drains, and tubes, his face bloody and swollen, lying at a thirty-degree angle. He is reaching toward the apparatus as if to greet those who were to see it. Did Papy look like that after her accident? After her tenth, her fifteenth, or her twentieth operation? How I would have liked her to be there, at my bedside, to tell me in a peaceful voice what she had been through! In the photo, the blankets are yellow. A small spiral notebook, a larger notebook, a pen, a felt-tip pen, and a bit of green mattress protector can be seen. An hour and a half later, my brother left and I believed I was going to completely stop breathing. I rang for the nurse. She reattached the oxygen mask to the tracheal tube.

"You're going to keep this on for at least an hour, otherwise it won't do any good."

She left, and the situation with the mask got steadily worse. I felt I was no longer breathing. I knew I had to calm down, concentrate, give the mask time to work, that the mask, like all the rest, made people pay a high price for the services it rendered; but knowing that, when one is undergoing it, doesn't take you very far: scientific certainties dissolve in the uncertainties of experience. The policemen had arranged for the door to be kept open. I looked on them as the last point of contact with life, tranquil emissaries of reality, and I beckoned to one of them. He finally came over to me. I took my notebook and wrote, as best I could, the word *nurse*. He set out to find her, but she didn't have time, and I heard her say:

"The little gentleman who has just come in is at least eighty years old, and I'll be surprised if he lasts through the night!"

In the spaceship, it was just as it was in the spaceship in *2001*: the cosmonauts who fell asleep were in danger of not awakening again, and HAL 9000, which I saw glowing and acting all around me, had nothing to do with that. I looked at the policemen, shook my head, I could no longer endure this mask. I wondered how they would react if killers came in here, and, as I did each time I asked myself that question, I saw the scene and was afraid it would immediately take place. If I was afraid, then it must be because I wanted to live? Finally, the nurse came back. She saw that I had moved the mask in the hope of breathing without it, and she put it back in place, saying:

"Keep the mask on, or you're going to stop breathing altogether!"

She left again and the sensation of suffocating increased. For the first time since the attack, I said to myself that I was dying, but since that was a physical view of the mind, the mind went to work and I recited internally lines from the last stanzas of Baudelaire's *Voyage*:

Ô Mort, vieux capitaine! Il est temps! Levons l'ancre!
Ce pays nous ennuie, ô Mort! Appareillons!

O Death, my captain, it is time! Let us raise the anchor!
This country wearies us, O Death! Let us make ready!

It was a little too monochrome, and the artifice of the procedure did not escape me; but breathing and breathing these words was more important, because it had become the same thing, and then there was something good about the artifice, it made the instant a little false, and thus less painful, and I preferred to go on. Since the following lines didn't come to me, I tried again, and again, but memory resisted me: the voyage that I was making obviously did not authorize any more than these two verses, beyond which it was excess baggage. I contented myself with them. I repeated them ten times, fifteen times, twenty times, and breathing came back, and with it, sleep, and just before sleep the last verse:

Au fond de l'inconnu pour trouver du nouveau!

If only to find in the depths of the Unknown the New!

During the night, on two occasions, men with small lamps on their foreheads awakened me. They looked like miners at the end of a gallery. It was the interns, who were coming to determine with their tongue depressors whether the graft was taking. I felt too exhausted to experience the suspense that their appearance presupposed. The following hours disappeared into a hole from which I emerged, eighteen hours later, only to return to the stomatology ward. A new room, on the third floor, was waiting for me. A bed next to mine had been prepared for Gabriela, who was going to appear any time now. My brother was waiting for me and had arranged the room, helped by Christiane. I had hardly moved in before Gabriela arrived. I was happy to see her again, but too devastated to show it. She came from a world without any relation to the one into which, since her prior departure, I had been plunged. She'd scarcely set down her bags when Chloé entered, forcing her to go out. In the corridor, Chloé had met my brother, who had left me alone with Gabriela, and she had said to him, very proudly:

"Did you see how beautiful it is?"

He hadn't known what to say in reply. If he had grimaced, would she have responded more or less as Dr. Mendelssohn had: "So what? He's got a chin, hasn't he?"

After Gabriela left, Chloé explained to me that everything had gone well with the exception of an implant that she and Mendelssohn had not been able to secure. On my notebook, I wrote: "Why?" She replied, sighing:

"I don't know. It was probably defective. We tried once, twice, then we stopped, it wasn't important and after all, we had other things to do!"

As she was leaving, in the corridor she said to Gabriela, who repeated it to me, laughing, only a year later: "Do what you want with him, but don't touch my scars!"

The attack infiltrated the hearts that it bit, but it can't be tamed. It radiates around victims in concentric circles and, in atmospheres that are often pathetic, multiplies them. It contaminates what it has not destroyed by underlining with a clean, bloody pen the secret weaknesses that unite us and that we do not see. Rather soon, things began to go badly with Gabriela.

I was happy to see her again, but while she was gone I'd acquired habits, and more than habits: rules of life and survival. I'd woven my Little Prince's cocoon, oozing, fed by catheter and covered with Vaseline, around a brother, parents, a few friends, and caregivers. I no longer wanted to leave the cocoon, and I felt incapable of doing it. The mere idea of leaving the confines of the hospital frightened me. It was not the place where I was all-powerful; it was the place where my experience was livable. I had set out to read *The Magic Mountain* very carefully, very slowly, as slowly as I would cauterize. From the beginning of the novel, the reflections of Joachim, Hans Castorp's tubercular cousin, had gripped and arrested me. Castorp has hardly arrived before he is already thinking of leaving again, "in three weeks." Joachim replies:

Oh, yes, you are already on the way back home, in your thoughts. Wait a bit. You've only just come. Three weeks are nothing at all, to us up here—they look like a lot of time to you, because you are only up here on a visit, and three weeks is all you have. Get acclimatized first—it isn't so easy, you'll see. And the climate isn't the only queer thing about us. You're going to see some things you've never dreamed of—just wait.

I reread this passage and a few others each morning after my shower, Bach, and my walk, while the first of the nutrient bags was nourishing me for four hours. I reread them as an overture and a prayer: Joachim and Hans had become much closer to me, more intimate, than the people who, entering here, I don't even mention others, came from the "world below" and quickly returned to it. The "world below" was the world of people who soon would be saying to me, I felt it, "Still in the hospital? When do you get out? More operations? But until when? Still in reeducation? You must be tired of it. Still on leave from work? But for how long?" And finally, because it would be the same thing, always the same blind and impatient relationship to time: "What about your book, when are you publishing it?" Like Joachim, like Hans Castorp at the end of a few hundred pages, I had the sensation that I would never leave and that not leaving was going to provide me, if it was possible, with a little wisdom. I had to leave neither the hospital nor the book, the latter being the instruction manual for the former. To be sure, death was not at the end of the road, in any case of this road, but *I had things to learn and experience here* that I could not have discovered elsewhere. My rooms in the stomatology ward were my sanatorium at Davos, and I was not far from thinking that just as the First World War ended Hans Castorp's adventure, another war was on the horizon, a war of which the Islamists were only a symptom and that would oppose humans to themselves, a social, sexual, psychic, ecological, total war that would lead, in a relatively short time, to extinction. I was not claiming to be a prophet, nor was there any narcissism in what I felt; I really had no qualms about it; besides, I didn't mention it to anyone. I simply felt a silent compassion for the people who came to visit me, for their activity, their problems, their children, for my colleagues who were continuing to write their big or little articles. That was the meaning of my reply to Dr. Mendelssohn when, seeing Thomas Mann's novel and Kafka's letters to Milena on my tablet, he said to me sarcastically: "Don't you have anything more amusing to read?" Dr. Mendelssohn had a cold melancholy. I later learned that he played the violin.

Those who entered the cocoon that winter lived in a world apart, that of the weavers who helped me repair the torn tapestry and who, whether they knew it or not, released me from the pressure of time. The list of their first names is not a roll call of the dead, but a roll call of the visitors, constantly renewed, constantly in suspension: Alain, Alexis, Anne, Anne-Laure, Anne-Marie, Arnaud, Aurélien, Benjamin, Blandine, Caroline, Céline, Claire, Éric, Fernand, Florence, Florence, Françoise, Gérard, Giusi, Hadrien, Hadrien, Hélène, Hortense, Jean-Pierre, Joël, Laurent, Laurent, Lila, Lucile, Marc, Marilyn, Maryse, Monique, Muriel, Nadine, Nathalie, Nina, Odalys, Olivier, Pascal, Pascal, Pierre, Pierre, Richard, Sophia, Sylvie, Sylvie, Teresa, Virginie, Zoé. Their first names form a garland and a day never goes by without my thinking of one or another of them. *They are in the tapestry, they are outside time.* Some part of them does not emerge from this limbo, immobilized at the heart of the motif, caught in the cocoon like the cosmonauts caught by Alien, mixed with my states and sensations by a multitude of acts, threads, silences, waiting to be fertilized by a memory that is much more fragile than the jawbone and the dart of Ridley Scott's creature, and whose blooming could only signify an additional uncertainty, friendship, life. This part of them is locked in a very small pocket of eternity. Eternity doesn't last too long, but perhaps there is some wisdom in the shadow it casts, the one that makes Hans Castorp say, after staying in the sanatorium for twenty-four hours: "And yet, in another way, it seems as though I had been here a long time, instead of just a single day—as if I had got older and wiser since I came—that is the way I feel." Other people, no matter how close they might be, lived in a world where the wheel turns, one day after another, one meeting after another. It was the world where the attack had taken place without having taken place.

Gabriela had been living outside the cocoon for more than a month, and it didn't take me long to sense that even though she had once again been at its center for more than a week, she couldn't find her place there. I had feelings for my friends; I no longer felt love for anyone. Gabriela had gotten on the hospital train on January 9 and gotten off a week later to go back to New York and her multiple problems; it was no longer possible to get back on, at least for the moment, and get the love engine going again. The situation had changed, my body had changed, I was metabolizing the attack through the reconstruction of my face, one month was equivalent to ten years, and all the seats were taken, even if everyone had initially left the car, the women first of all, when Gabriela got on. The woman I loved had become unwelcome.

The first sign that I was moving away preceded her return by several weeks. With my brother's help, I had created an e-mail address reserved for my family and close friends—a kind of private channel for the patient Philippe Lançon. This address alluded to the bicycle I'd left in front of *Charlie* on January 7, with which I was obsessed. I had ended up asking the policemen to whom I felt close to go see if it was still there, on the street, attached to its pole. One of them had gone to check, and the next time he was on duty at the hospital, he told me with pleasure that a month and a half after the attack my bicycle hadn't budged. So long as it's there, I thought, the past is where it's supposed to be. The old bicycle at *Charlie* was the sentinel guarding the passage between my life before and my life afterward. I hadn't given Gabriela the new e-mail address. The few decisions I made at that time were instinctive, connected with a condition that could change at any time. I was afraid of bringing her into what my life had become, and I didn't know why. An element of Platonic vaudeville was involved; comedy is never so effective as when it feeds on the tragic.

The presence of Sophia, a friend I'd made not long before the attack, had become essential. After teaching at a university, she was now doing market studies for companies that made luxury products. She went to all kinds of countries to ask all kinds of women about their images of love, of men, of beauty, of luxury. She was about to leave for Shanghai to question Chinese women, who had rather rudimentary conceptions of love. Later, she reminded me that I had called her ten minutes before the attack. I didn't remember that, and I still don't know why I called her at that point, during the editorial meeting. To confirm a rendezvous? To go to the cinema? She'd gone out to walk her dog and called me back a few minutes later, too late. At my request, two and a half years later, she e-mailed me a description of the following days as she had experienced them. I reproduce this description here because it shows how the attack created a chain of abrupt suffering, shared or individual, in which each friend of the victim seems to have been suddenly branded, like livestock, with a red-hot iron: rape is collective. That's why, starting on January 7, my life no longer belonged to me. I became responsible for all those who, in one way or another, loved me. My wounds were also theirs. My ordeal was joint property.

Sophia was in her garden, with her son Pierre-Camille, when they heard the news. She called her brother. He and I had friends in common, and it didn't take him long to learn that my face had been wounded. Here is the rest of Sophia's account:

In the early afternoon, I called two of my clients for whom I was supposed to conduct studies, one of which was supposed to begin on the afternoon of January 7, the other the next day. I told them I couldn't do it, and said why. I was devastated. The day after the attack, I remember calling one of my closest women friends, very early in the morning, at 7 A.M. I don't remember anything about that day except feeling terrible.

Friday morning, I went to Milan, for one of the studies. I see myself again in Terminal F at Charles de Gaulle airport, in the café in the basement, next to the Air France lounge. There were television screens everywhere that were broadcasting, over and over, an account of the attack, a list of the dead and wounded. I watched these reports, and tears were running down my face, I couldn't stop crying, I didn't care what the people around me thought. They probably understood that I knew someone hurt in the attack. Then a woman came up to me; she was quite beautiful, she had children and also a husband, I think. She talked to me, tried to comfort me.

In Milan, I worked with two groups in Italian for eight hours. My Italian friend and partner was there, ready to take over. I held on, but when I left the conference room, I was unable to speak. I couldn't even whisper. It was January 9. I lost my voice, totally, for ten days. I got it back, in part, when I returned from Shanghai on January 19.

On January 14, I left for Shanghai. I see myself again in the Air France lounge. My brother called me to find out how I was doing. I still had no voice, I whispered to him, and he understood me. It was an immense comfort to hear him. I cried for ten days, I've never cried so much, I don't cry often, or easily. I remember having told him that I didn't know how I would ever be able to laugh again someday. However, I'd already known great pain, that of losing my father when I was fourteen years old. The person I loved most in the world, at that time. But the violence of what I felt then was of a different order. My brother comforted me, he was great with me. In Shanghai, I briefed my Chinese partner by whispering and writing down what she couldn't understand.

At the hospital, starting in mid-January, and after having hesitated, I had received Sophia and she had little by little taken, not exactly Gabriela's place, but part of her place, taking care of me in Gabriela's absence, deluging me with gifts and attention, writing to me when she was traveling, bringing me a book on Goya from Madrid, a shirt from Italy, finding the words and gestures that were needed, when they were needed, with a generosity that bordered on saintliness or masochism, and which was, perhaps, simply love and a desire to feel whole again. I never proposed that she join the little "club" of those who slept in my room, but I didn't hesitate to let her help me and love me. There is something vampirelike in the long-term patient; I took what I needed; like others and more than others, she gave it to me. But that wasn't all: I was living in a world attached to nursing and to the phantoms of the attack, and in this world, everything was fiction, and therefore everything became possible. However, I wanted peace. I didn't tell Gabriela about Marilyn's visits, or about Sophia's presence, nothing about what constituted a closed world from which the circumstances had excluded her. Everything that spared me tensions justified what might be described as cowardice.

Often, Gabriela called me from New York on FaceTime. Either I was trying to sleep or I was receiving medical care, or I had a visitor: it was never the right time, or the right words. She continued to preach the desperate optimism that she herself thought she needed to cope with her husband the banker, her sick father in Copiapó, and her loneliness. She tried to

teach me ways of healing that made no sense to me: I'm hermetically closed to positive thinking and meditation. She told
me about a guy whose arm had been eaten by a shark, and
another who had been seriously burned in an accident. Both
had written exemplary books, in the American style, to recount
their "battles," to celebrate will, and explain how much
stronger the ordeal had made them while making life more
beautiful. The books were, of course, dedicated to their families without whom, etc., etc. American podiums and televisions
were full of these survivors who transformed a disaster overcome into an evangelical show. This voluntarist nonsense
annoyed me all the more because I could hardly speak. I
watched Gabriela's smile appear on FaceTime, the smile I had
loved so much, that I still loved, and then, thinking about the
man whose arm had been eaten by a shark, I substituted
Kafka's smile for it; and while she was talking to me about
these model survivors in a state of prophetic resurrection, I
thought again about a sentence by the writer who had become
a companion in the operating rooms: "It is only in death that a
living person can be reconciled with nostalgia."

In my new room, I was nothing but malaise. I hardly read
the newspapers anymore, I still hadn't subscribed to the television, the radio annoyed me like the noise of an outboard
motor coming from the other side of a lake. Reading, in a
weekly someone had brought me, an interview with a French
intellectual who was indulgent toward violence and obviously
fascinated by its element of stimulation and revolution, had
confirmed my reflex—here, one can't speak of will or
thought—to escape the merry-go-round of commentaries,
whether they were prophetic or didactic. There was something
abject about thought when it believed that it could give immediate meaning to the event to which it was subjected. It was the
fly pretending to be an eagle, but it wasn't a fable, just reality,
the dreary reality of intellectual pride: these people thought

they were Kant replying to Benjamin Constant or Marx analyzing Louis Napoleon's coup d'état. They were making a premature abstraction.

I had been covered with organized wounds. This multiplication was in no way miraculous, but it had put me under the spell of the concrete. Current events had become, like so many things, a useless passion. Perhaps I now resembled my paternal grandparents, who were reduced to a narrowly limited world and busy living inside it as if the exterior could only distract, affect, and especially harm. They lived in obscurity, turning off all the lamps in the rooms they left, leaving only one lit in the room where they were. In my room, I no longer needed useless lamps. I wanted only real lamps. There was the cold neon light, the slightly less cold nightlight, the red table lamp Caroline had brought me, the salt lamp Florence had sent me, the accordion-shaped Lumio lamp that another Florence had sent me. I lit them all by turns, like the lamplighter, that was my task, which was determined only by my moods and the image of the woman who had brought it to me, and about whom, as I lit it, I thought of as an amiable fairy. All of them gave off a soft, warm light without for all that allowing me to read any longer, especially in the evening. My eyesight had abruptly declined after the graft, as it did after the attack, or else I could no longer concentrate. I asked Chloé about this one evening. She replied that after a family row, the same thing had happened to her: "I could no longer see anything." That was how I learned about this row, and it was the only time she talked to me about it, briefly. I was in no condition to understand how unexpected and exceptional such a confidence was, how much it revealed about what the surgeon and her patient were going through at the time. I listened to her and accepted what she said; I was curious, surprised, moved, grateful. I felt and, as with Sophie and others, I took. Everything that came from Chloé strengthened me in a special way. It was not a matter of love, but of dependency. It didn't take Gabriela long to feel jealous about this connection. She was wrong, insofar as what bound me to my surgeon was of a vital, not a sentimental nature; but she was right, because at that time, this connection had acquired priority. Chloé came first, before even my brother and my parents. She was the only person on whom my jaw and my future life depended. She was a woman and a principle of action. The other prisoners in the cocoon were all, more or less, in the waiting room.

Gabriela had left the cocoon at the time that it was being formed. Was I becoming a different person, as she soon alleged? The patient is a vampire, I said, and he is selfish: I had only very little to offer, to give, but all my reserves were consumed by the mental and surgical battle. I did not immediately understand that Gabriela was no longer at the heart of this battle, and after I understood that, I was not able to tell her: how could I explain to the woman who had traveled 6,000 kilometers to see me and live with me in a hospital room for ten days? Especially since the truth was even more twisted: the multiple scenes that she was soon to provoke had a power that it took me longer to divine: they transformed the victim of the attack into an ordinary protagonist of a couple's crisis.

Three days after she arrived, we were on edge. I was relieved when she left to teach or to practice for an hour, and I was nervous when she returned. She couldn't stand watching me write e-mails and my first articles for *Charlie*. We knew that the night would go badly, for her as well as for me. The nurses I was closest to sensed all this before I did. They came into the room with their usual brusqueness, but they felt awkward, and we began to communicate as we always had, I with my notebook and they with their gestures and mouths, as if Gabriela weren't there. But she was there, exhausted, her face sullen, sitting on the bed facing her computer, with her glasses on her nose, answering business e-mails, working on courses that she'd taken up again when she registered at NYU. I watched her and recalled something she'd said to me in New York two years before: "You make me a queen." Here, I was the king.

That said, it all started well. She had scarcely arrived before she stretched out on the bed and held my hand while the beautiful Ada changed the bandages on my face and legs. Ada had a tattoo on her arm, in memory of her grandfather. I liked to look at it while she took care of me. Her father had been a groundskeeper, and she'd grown up on an estate. I closed my eyes while she removed the scabs that had formed around the stitches on the hunk of flesh that was to be my new jaw, and I imagined her on the grounds of the estate or on Lake Enghien. On that day, it took her half an hour to clean everything, put Vaseline on it, and protect it. The wound where the fibula had been grafted was long, rectangular, and bright red, like a beef cutlet, ringed with stitches. The skin that had been taken from the inside of my thigh replaced the skin that had been transferred from my calf to my jaw. At the same time, on the inside of my thigh there was a kind of small, rectangular pad that was also bright red and oozing, like the cutlet, and that burned me day and night. I was still on a drip, and was being fed through a catheter again. A drain came out of the incision in my neck.

The next morning, I was supposed to go to the scanner to check the graft. The scanner was in a neighboring building. Gabriela decided to accompany me, as Marilyn had on January 9, during the first check. I'd put on a mask to protect the cutlet, as I would from now on, during the day, for six months. Lulu guided me, the two policemen followed us. No wheelchair had been provided. Gabriela was surprised, and so were the policemen, but we said nothing and set off in the cold air, under a light rain, through streets that were very little hospital-like. Quite quickly, I began to feel weak. Gabriela was holding me by one arm, and a policeman came up and took my other arm. Lulu saw this and suddenly understood: "But . . . no one told me that he was in this condition! They could have warned me, goddammit! What a mess! On the way back, you'll have a wheelchair!" The people we met gave us strange looks: was this masked patient surrounded by so many people dangerous? After taking walk after walk, I'd become accustomed to these looks. With my policemen, I was living in a world parallel to that of the people I met. Gabriel was discovering this parallel world. She later told me that she'd had the same impression as I. She was playing a scene from *The Godfather*, the one where Marlon Brando is hidden by Al Pacino in the hospital, in order to escape the killers. In our story, the killers had already come.

The next day, she took responsibility for part of my reeducation. The nurses and nurse aides had warned me: when you're short a fibula, you have to start walking almost immediately, but you mustn't do it just any old way. It was heel-toe, heel-toe, slowly and with a straight back, not trying to avoid the pain that the movement causes because avoiding it dooms you to having a limp. For this kind of exercise, Gabriela was ideal: a dancer and a high-level professional. Starting the next day, she helped me take my walk up and down the corridor, without being either harsh or indulgent. She walked a meter behind me to check my posture, and the policemen walked a meter behind her. Their mission constituted a *mise en abyme* of ours and vice versa. At first, everyone was smiling.

"Stand up straight! You're leaning to the left! Forget the pain and put your heel on the floor! There, let the movement unfold! Slowly, more slowly!"

And she laughed as she corrected me.

Walking my lengths had become painful, I felt as if I were walking on a bed of nails; but once again, pain had to be welcomed as an ally showing me the path to be followed.

Six years earlier, my parents and I had visited some elderly cousins who lived in the Pyrenees, in Bagnères-de-Luchon.

Monette, who has since died, had been an English teacher. Her husband Jean-Marie had offered me lemonade, as if I were a child. At one point, Monette, who was twisted, hunchbacked, and half blind, went out to do her exercises. She moved very slowly, using two canes, and insisted on walking back and forth in the garden, from the catalpa to the gate, and from the gate to the catalpa. It was in the summer. You'd have said she was a very old animal, a mixture of a mole and a snail. I followed her to help her, as Gabriela was now helping me. When she got to the gate, she turned toward me, her nose level with mine, to see what she didn't see, and said to me in a fragile voice: "I have to do it, don't I?" I replied: "Of course you have to! You have to do lengths, as in a swimming pool, and maybe put a chair near the gate to rest a little and then do it again." She answered: "Ah, yes, I have to do it, I have to want to . . . " Then, once again turning to me: "What's your name again? My memory isn't so good anymore . . . " Her husband, on the other hand, remembered everything: names, ages, family situations, birth dates, all the way back to the most distant member of the family tree, who seemed to live, irrigated by his memory, next to the catalpa. In the corridor with Gabriela, I now repeated to myself: "I have to," and I would have liked to have Monette's husband's memory to irrigate what seemed to have dried out.

Six days after Gabriela's arrival, I resumed with her my walks through the whole hospital. I was happy to show her the recesses of La Pitié-Salpêtrière, as I had shown them to the policemen who accompanied me. Follow the guide, he's a patient! During the month that I'd been walking through it, it had become my domain. Its architectural jumble, its layers of buildings that had lived alongside one another for four centuries, its little invisible places, its streets, its noises, its odors, its façades, its dead ends, its porches, its passages, its unexpected viewpoints, everything made me once again the child-explorer that I had been, though without audacity, in the time when, swimming in the Yonne, the foliage on the opposite bank was more mysterious than the Amazon. *Apes were going to fall from the trees and Indians come out of the forest.* Here, each façade gave exoticism to my melancholy.

First, I went to the big garden between the buildings Louis XIV had had constructed, and then to the big, empty chapel, where I hoped to find the chaplain. I got there either by a stairway or by a small ramp: the latter immediately helped me re-educate my leg without a fibula, heel-toe, heel-toe, along with Gabriela's correction. Then I went under the large building, reached the exit closest to the Gare d'Austerlitz, climbed a long ramp that ran parallel to the outside railings that marked the limits of my domain. This ramp led to a part of the hospital that was less frequented, between the old psychiatric building, called La Force, and another that was equally old and perhaps equally beautiful in its formal simplicity, which housed the laundry. The patients' sheets were regenerated inside walls four centuries old, as classical and perfect as one of Malherbe's verses. By providing me with limits, these *beautiful buildings of eternal structure* reassured me.

On the path between the two edifices, there was my cabin deep in the woods: an old, crooked lane, still paved with stones and called the Rue des Archers, where, in small, two-story buildings covered with dormers, were located syndical offices that looked as old and dilapidated as the period to which they seemed to be relegated: here, it was no longer the seventeenth century of the neighboring buildings, where women of loose morals and madmen had been confined and even chained up, but rather a nineteenth century that looked provincial and Balzacian, in the manner of Eugénie Grandet. The disjointed paving stones are not particularly evocative of memories, but they do make it possible to work on your sense of balance, and the old-fashioned harmony of this minuscule place, outside time, as if abandoned, established a context in which I felt at home and outside myself, in the countryside, in the house of my grandparents when they were still alive, between the time when I had measles, spent on a folding bed of dark blue canvas, and the time when I read *La Comédie humaine* in my bedroom with a red tiled floor or on the bank of the river. I had floated down there in a silent world, full of insects and reserved for magic, a world where those to whom I was close were either in their old age or lived within the pages of a book. This world returned through this crooked lane, discovered by accident, and it was almost as effective as a time machine. In the Rue des Archers, time no longer existed.

A little farther on came my second magic place, located on the Rue des Petites-Loges: a long, one-story building with a pointed roof, bordered by a covered walkway along which benches arranged in a half-circle had been installed at regular intervals. They had forged iron feet and were covered with mnemonic inscriptions. It was a building devoted to neurology. I systematically walked down its walkway as if I were leaving for the seaside, and it seemed to me that if I sat down on one of these benches, I would quietly disappear into this or that memory, as if into a cloud. Then I had to climb a stairway to return to the area around Charcot's building.

On that day, the whole walk took us approximately one hour. Gabriela helped me face the obstacles with a discipline and good humor that, once I was back in my room, were going to disappear. I insisted on having her make the grand tour, and we finished it with the hospital's most recent buildings, which were built of bricks, and some of which were in the Art Deco style. We went down the ramp that ran along the tall modern building of the Brain and Spine Institute. It was there, I told her, that the best cafeteria in the hospital was found. And at the same moment I asked myself what coffee might taste like; the coffee that Marilyn had had me sniff had disappeared, and

I wondered whether someday I'd be able again to enjoy a cup of coffee with, why not, a *pain au chocolat*. Words designate things. In my case, foods and sensations seemed to disappear to the extent that words landed on them. As we arrived in front of the stomatology ward, I thought I saw Pascal, a friend from my village who was a sculptor; I hadn't seen him since the previous summer. It was in fact Pascal, with his eagle-like profile and his simultaneously hard and sentimental, lost and passionate eyes. He had been waiting for me for some time, sitting on the low wall where patients who smoked came to light up, a pack in their hands. He saw me, got up, and gave me a hug. Since I couldn't speak, I looked at him in every way possible. Nurses had told me that my mute way of looking at people had become so expressive that they could discern the nuances of my moods. Pascal had brought me a gift: a book sculpted in alabaster. He embraced me and then left immediately. He feared effusiveness and didn't want to bother me. In my room, I put the sculpture on the wheeled table and felt that once again, Gabriela thought I was too sensitive to the consideration that my friends accorded me.

She'd brought a little coffee maker and communicated at night, by video, with her father or with her class at the university. These conversations deprived me of the little sleep from which I could benefit. She was nervous, anxious, and, once she'd fallen asleep, constantly jumped, like a small, tortured animal. Some of her New York employers were threatening to fire her. They had been indulgent in January, saying "Oh, I'm so sorry!" as Americans do so well, but Americans, who don't like the critical labyrinths of interiority, rarely remain compassionate beyond an area delimited by their interests, their hearts are big but never far from their pocketbooks, and this second trip annoyed them: she had to be replaced, she couldn't be counted on, the attack was no excuse for not meeting her obligations to her clients. The divorce from her husband, the

banker from Chicago, was going badly. He was a Middle
Western Anglican, always on the side of Good, and thus ready
to do whatever it took to impose it. He'd had his minute of
compassion in January, just after the attack, showing Gabriela
all the magnanimity that is fitting in the presence of those who
are about to die and to whom it is a question, as in church, of
saying farewell. But I hadn't died, and he was now accusing her
of going to Paris to drink champagne with her lover. One
evening Gabriela had me read a particularly cold and odious e-
mail, one among others, intended, of course, for the judge.
That evening, she nipped out to buy, not champagne, but a
sandwich, at the superette on the corner, where my sister-in-
law found her in tears, alone, among the shelves: she was losing everything—her job, her divorce, her studies, her companion. When visiting hours began, she went out of the room with
her computer, under the indifferent eyes of the surgeons, and
sat down on the floor in the hallway, near the cops with whom
she talked. It wasn't rare for a nurse aide to say to her: "It's
dirty on the floor!" The two chairs were occupied by my
guards.

During the day, when she didn't go out to dance or to teach,
she was increasingly exasperated to see me writing and rereading my first articles for *Charlie*. She always said the same thing:
"I'm taking risks and sacrificing myself for you, I'm here
instead of looking for work in New York and studying, I'm not
dealing with the divorce, and you, you're in your world and
you're thinking only about yourself. What are your plans for
the future?"

Plans? I didn't have any. I had no future. I didn't see it, didn't
feel it. My future ended with the next round of care and at the
horizon of sensations that were increasingly ferocious and
unprecedented. In any case, I couldn't really answer her, since
I couldn't express myself. I responded with a few words in my
notebook, always the same ones, written in capital letters: "I

love you" and "You're marvelous," which merely increased her exasperation. Writing is slow, internal, silent. It corresponds to neither the rhythm nor the nature of conversation. One of the first columns I wrote for *Charlie* at that time, under Gabriela's nose, bore precisely on that theme. This is what I wrote:

For two weeks, I've been reduced to silence, in accord with my surgeon's benevolent but strict command. The sutures, which are still capricious, have to be protected against a lip that she has remade. A mischievous anesthetist and friend told me that a patient, by not respecting instructions, had caused his sutures to explode. Jabbering is a cardinal sin in surgery: here, I believe everything I'm told, so I keep quiet. And then, one would feel almost intelligent if one keeps quiet: the imposed silence is the contrary of the imposed sound (television, radio) that this column is usually about. It is not a question of filling a void, but rather of abstaining from doing so. Silence is established at the heart of dialogues with my rare visitors and caregivers. I live with a notebook and a small whiteboard. They speak, I write. They speak rather little, because writing is slow. What do they think about while waiting for responses that take their time, like local trains or kept women in the bathroom? The whole business would be less comic if I weren't ordinarily such a dreadful chatterbox. I prefer the whiteboard to the notebook, because everything that is written, like unrecorded words, is immediately erased. For someone who has written in one way or another for more than thirty years, it's not easy to imagine his life without the traces left by fingertips that the felt-tip pen soon blackens. Especially since I try to concentrate. Even if it means writing on the sand of a whiteboard, one might as well do it in correct, precise sentences ripened by the moment and the emotion they inevitably contain, sentences that are, so to speak, mute and destined to join the oblivion from which the event causes them, for a minute, to emerge. We have to believe that the sentences that have been erased have their pride: it is enough for them to make themselves missed when they are replaced by others. Is that a kind of masochism? I don't think so. The point is only to test writing in the moment, whether or not the latter appears, to restore it to the silence offered by the occasion. This concrete silence of writing regarding everything, from "it hurts here" to a discussion of *The Magic Mountain*, has another virtue: it changes the perception of dialogue and of time. It forces words to be delivered more slowly, alters the nature of the exchange. It is born, literally, from what cannot be said in order to join what will not be said.

One morning, I wrote to the head of the stomatology department, Professor G, as he was making his rounds: "I've become a Trappist. Words have the weight of their absence." He laughed heartily. That evening, I wrote something like this to my surgeon: "In Trappist monasteries the monks could be silent, they had God to listen to them. I have doctors." She wrote, above: "And you have to listen to them . . . " I wrote, underneath her words: "And, as monks believe in God, I believe in doctors." Above, she wrote, as she was working on my lip and taking a photo to show it to me and to explain how it was developing: "Because you believe them, in addition? That's Stockholm syndrome! It's time for you to get out of here." As always, she's right.

After reading this column, Chloé told me, in front of everyone and at the beginning of her visit: "So, just like that, I'm always right! Last evening, when I read that to my companion, he said: 'Here's another one who's understood it all!'" Everyone laughed, except me, because I couldn't, and Gabriela, who didn't want to. That day she was working on a paper on Machiavelli, and went into the hallway to continue it. An old friend, Éric, had given me the corresponding Pléiade volume so that she could use it. He had come by while she was away. It was the second time I'd seen Éric since the attack, and since he is more reflective, more cultivated, and more rigorous than I am, we talked about an old problem that I was thinking about night and day, or rather that I was living, in the hope that he would help me understand it a little more clearly: the nature of contemporary evil. Éric is a publisher, specializing in great philosophers and good sociologists. On the question of Evil, he was dissatisfied with everything he read. The world had moved on much more quickly than those who claimed to enlighten it by running after Evil with their concepts and theories. Something, far ahead of them, escaped the analysis of its new manifestations. Neither sociology nor technology, nor biology, nor even philosophy would explain what excellent novelists had been able to describe. Perhaps there is no satisfactory explanation of the taste for death given or received. We looked at each other, in that room, like two fools without oars lost in the middle of an ocean. My dialogue with Éric lasted a good hour. It was a slow, silent dialogue, as if delayed by the foggy, threatening notion that we were trying to penetrate. He spoke to me more and more slowly. I wrote on the whiteboard my reflections and questions, erasing them one after the other. He read them and the cadence of his replies seemed to be determined by mine. I'd never been as intelligent as I was then, silently, but I don't remember it. Since he was ill, he ended up falling asleep. I remembered him, one summer, when we were slowly swimming in the cold water of Normandy and talking about women we'd loved. I told him about a former lover with a precision that must have been such that he finally said to me, in his warm, discreet voice that he never raised, with the elegance of a king who knows he has no clothes: "I can't get out of the water now, there are children on the beach and your story gave me a hard-on." Would I someday get a hard-on again? Would we ever go to swim in Normandy again? I looked at him, drowsing in the chair, with a sensation unprecedented in this room: for a few moments, I was the friend who was watching over him.

After more than a month of interruption, *Charlie* had just appeared again. New columnists and new cartoonists had joined the survivors. It was out of the question that I would not be present in these pages, and I wrote my first column for the resurrection number, leaking everywhere, on the eve of the main graft. What else could I write about in that room, other than my voyage around it? Writing about my own case was the best way to understand it, to assimilate it, but also to think about something else—because the person who was writing was no longer, for a few minutes, or for an hour, the patient about whom he was writing: he was the reporter and chronicler of a reconstruction. I was, as never before, grateful to my trade, which was also a mode of being and ultimately of living: having exercised it for such a long time enabled me to take a distance from my own sufferings at a time when I needed it most, and to transform them, like an alchemist, into reasons to be curious. If the dead returned, I said to myself without saying it to Gabriela, who was working on Machiavelli alongside me, that was perhaps what they would do: describe their life and their end with a precise enthusiasm and a sorrow that was just as distanced. Maybe I had spent thirty years training myself by writing about others in order to arrive at this point.

Gabriela saws things differently. She thought these columns focused my attention on my condition and were leading me into a labyrinth that I should have left behind. In my view, it was exactly the contrary: by describing my condition in this way, I was escaping from my condition. I'd had to land in this place, in this condition, not only to test my craft, but to feel what I had read about a hundred times in other authors without completely understanding it: writing is the best way of getting outside yourself, even if you don't talk about anything else. At the same time, the distinction between fiction and nonfiction was empty; everything was fiction, since everything was a narrative—choice of facts, framing of scenes, style, composition. What counted was the sensation of truth and the feeling of liberty given to the writer as well as to his readers. When I was writing in bed, with three fingers, then five, then seven, with my jawbone full of holes and then reconstituted, with or without the ability to speak, I wasn't the patient I was describing; I was a man who was revealing that patient by observing him, and who was recounting his story with a good will and pleasure that he hoped to share. I was becoming a fiction. It was reality, it was absurd, and I was free. Of course, I paid a price for this activity. I finished each column exhausted, sweating, coughing, weeping. The patient was resuscitated between the words and regained the upper hand.

The slab of meat constituting my reconstructed chin had become, for several months, the chief site of this battle. After writing for a few minutes, it was flooded by a nervous cataract that electrified the lower part of my face and made the skin bloom from inside, as if an anthill were freely circulating there. The chin contracted in countless places under the impact of emotion or thought, but people who have not had it redone are lucky not to know it. All I needed to do was to concentrate a little too much, move my tongue a few centimeters, or be disturbed by an image and this anthill would be awakened. It caused a kind of itching I'd never experienced before, a subterranean itching that would have deserved to have a specific name and that forced me to stop all activity. This itching slowly exploded, like fireworks or like the beating of Bernard's anemone. I left my computer, lay down at a 30-degree angle, closed my eyes, and tried to make the itching go away by breathing. I still couldn't use the best remedy, which is called the "pufferfish": you puff out your cheeks. That had to wait a few months.

Every Tuesday, a courier now brought me copies of my column, which I distributed from my bed, some of them to visitors, the others to my caregivers. This annoyed Gabriela, who repeatedly told me: "You were the victim of an attack, and now you're becoming the victim of your celebrity!" Her annoyance reached its peak the day when a nurse and a nurse aide came in, each with a copy in her hand, and asked me to sign them. I graciously did so. Once the door was closed, Gabriela exploded. "Who do you think you are? You're no longer the same person! You take yourself for a king! You take pleasure in your pain and your notoriety!" I got up, barely able to breathe, to take her in my arms. I emitted a sort of muffled cry, but she pushed me away, saying: "Shut up! You know you're not allowed to talk." We were now close to the window, looking out on the dark pine tree and the gray sky. She looked and me and went on: "Yes, you take pleasure in it! You no longer pay attention to me. You received a bullet in your jaw, but I received a bullet in my heart! I've been violated, my life has been taken away, and I'm not forgiven anything. You're lucky, the newspaper pays you. France is a beautiful country! In America, it's different! If I don't work, I don't get paid." Then, looking at me from closer up, she concluded: "As for your problems, they're merely aesthetic!"

Over the following days, the situation only further deteriorated. Gabriela was so exhausted, so nervous, that she spoke English to the nurses without noticing it. Many of them didn't speak English: I'd heard her do that the day when I was called, before the graft, to help figure out what a young man from Sri Lanka had swallowed that was burning his mouth, his throat, and his stomach. It was caustic soda.

I came to feel that I was to blame for everything that Gabriela was experiencing. Her glasses were no longer right for her eyes and one day I wrote to my brother, from whom I concealed almost nothing: "She's blind as a bat, I can't speak, and between visits and the nurses' rounds, its one scene after another. Can you imagine us being cooped up together like this?" Her money problems grew, whereas between the lip and the cutlet, the upper part of my chin began to leak. Her father was still slowly dying in the Atacama Desert, I could see him on the screen when she called him. The cannula irritated my throat and prevented me from sleeping. One of Gabriela's bosses, a woman who ran a gymnasium financed by her rich husband, was sending her threatening e-mails. A bedsore had appeared at the edge of my buttocks, near the coccyx, and henceforth gave me no peace. On the verge of bankruptcy, Gabriela wanted me to lend her a large sum, and accused me of not having thought of that solution all by myself. My brother and my friends advised against it, they thought she was taking advantage of the situation and was refusing to consider my condition. She repeated, over and over: "I've risked everything to come see you. I came immediately. I thought this was the beginning of something, of a real relationship. But I see you writing articles, seducing nurses, and I feel alone when I'm with you. I have to find work, support my parents, and complete my studies to begin a new career. You aren't offering me anything, I've abandoned everything for you, as I did for my husband, but it's always the same thing, you're in your world just as he's in his." Was she taking me for the banker from Chicago or taking him for me? Neither of us slept anymore. In my notebook, I wrote things like this: "Truth is a kind of horse medicine, but without it, the horse's gait is off." Or again: "There's a surgical truth, rather reassuring; an aesthetic truth, rather opaque; a mental truth, wholly obscure." And again: "Machiavelli's letters are terribly funny and wicked. Only geniuses are allowed to be bitter." And finally: "Let us pray for Hypnos."

A few days before Gabriela left, the psychiatrist suggested that the three of us talk, in my room. I accepted her suggestion.

It seemed to me that Gabriela needed a third party as much as I did, and a professional, to put into perspective the hell we were living through under the eyes of the embarrassed nurses. Gabriela was unhappy because I'd made the decision without talking to her about it. One morning, the psychiatrist sat down between the bed and the window and said to me: "What do you want to talk about?" To please Gabriela, I wrote "the future," because she always had that word in her mouth. But it was even more disagreeable than talking about the past, which had at least existed, and the conversation rapidly degenerated. Gabriela repeated her complaint regarding her loneliness and my narcissism. Armed with a little smile, the psychiatrist waited until Gabriela stopped to take a breath and then asked her a precise question that she couldn't handle, and she began to cry. The psychiatrist finally said: "I think it's better to leave it there, we'll continue this another time." She left, and Gabriela exploded: "What was that? Those aggressive questions?" I wanted only one thing: I wanted her to go back to New York and get out of my room, of my life. To go wither away alongside her farther in the depths of a mine in the Atacama Desert.

During the night, my head constantly rolled to the side. On that night, I had for the first time a brief nightmare that was going to become recurrent at the very heart of each night: by rolling to the side, my head blew the stiches, the wounds opened up, the graft necrosed, and, worst of all, I was to blame for not having known how to prevent it. My punishment was to experience the consequences of my negligence. The only solution was not to sleep anymore. I almost succeeded, but not quite. It's those who are going to die who don't sleep. For others, hell exists; it keeps them awake and guilt is, as they say about hostages, proof that they're alive.

When I was suffering, I avoided calling the night nurse before 5 A.M., contrary to instructions; I was not supposed to let pain establish itself, it was easier to cut it off at the root. However, one night when I could no longer breathe, I called Marion. She appeared, smiling, and after many attempts, she made an enormous blockage pop out of the cannula; it leapt all the way to the wall, and she burst out laughing. I looked with relief at Marion's childlike joy. Gabriela had just fallen asleep. She didn't wake up.

On the eve of her departure, we took a last walk around La Pitié-Salpêtrière. This time, we went into the big chapel. The policemen, after discussing the matter, agreed to stay outside. They told us not to stay inside too long. The church was deserted. We approached the only furnished chapel, at the end on the right, and once we were inside, she asked me to leave her alone there. I slowly walked around the immense edifice, heel-toe, heel-toe, without limping. When I returned to the chapel, I found her praying, her eyes closed. She looked up and asked: "Do you believe that it's possible to bear such things? Do you think I'm going to find my life again? What have we done to deserve all this?" I didn't know what to say in reply, and in any case, I hadn't brought a notebook. I took her in my arms and we both wept.

She left on a Sunday. For the first time since the attack, I got an erection as I watched her sleep. It was brief, but real, and I felt a gratitude for her that no reproach could have driven away. Later, I asked my brother to lend me four hundred euros to give her. That was in the morning. She had gone out to dance or to walk, I don't know. On her return, in the late morning, I handed her the money. She refused it with a brusque gesture, her eyes hardened, and she began to cry again as she said to me: "You take me for your whore and for your nurse. What shame!" She wanted to print her air ticket and leave as soon as possible: an old Chilean friend, Nicanor, was coming to pick her up. I liked Nicanor a lot; he was a small, slender, chic fellow full of imagination and spontaneity. Like

Gabriela, he'd been a classical dancer. A stroke had interrupted his career. He now walked with a cane and owed his bearing only to his discipline. He came into the ward in the middle of our last scene. Crying, Gabriela printed her ticket in the nurses' station. I limped down the corridor, weeping and holding onto the drip stand with one hand. The nurses were making their rounds, taking care not to look at us. Alexandra was there, disconsolate. A few days earlier, she'd told me that after a rather happy childhood in the Antilles, an illness had suddenly changed her life. She'd almost died. She told me that was how she'd lost, in a short time, her magnificent blond, curly head of hair. It had grown back in the way it was now, red and straight. She'd *carried death within her.* She was almost constantly mischievous and good-humored, but I saw in her eyes a deep well of sadness. She had gradually become a friend, and that, too, was intolerable for Gabriela. I exchanged a look with Alexandra as Gabriela was coming out of the nurses' station and returning to the room to close her suitcase, and then, after rejoining Gabriela in the room *to ask her to authorize me to go say hello to Nicanor,* I found him, sitting near the elevator. He knew what was going on, this little, slender, elegant man, a survivor like us all, and, seeing me in this state, he stood up, leaning on his cane, and hugged me as he trembled. We both shed tears: it was a genuine Franco-Chilean melodrama. I took out my notebook. I wrote for him, in Spanish and in capital letters: THANKS FOR PICKING HER UP. TAKE CARE OF YOURSELF. I ADORE HER. GLAD TO SEE YOU!" Another word appears in the notebook: ¿CUANDO? When? It was the reply to what Nicanor had just said to me: "Don't worry. Be patient. She'll come back."

Gabriela joined us, her face closed. She wanted to leave as soon as possible, to avoid running into my family, or having to hold me in her arms again. She didn't want me to accompany them as far as the exit from the building. A few minutes later, my parents and my aunt, who'd been struck by Parkinson's after my uncle's death, came to visit me. They found me in tears. My aunt, who was having more and more difficulty walking, was saddened by what she saw, this chin, these wounds, these tears, this room, this obligatory silence. In her eyes, I saw that I was five years old, ten at most, but her head that was beginning to droop, her body all atremble, the difficulty with which she held herself upright on her chair, all reminded me that she was now too old to be the woman who was so often able to console me. She thought I was crying because of Gabriela's departure. I was sorry to impose this spectacle on her and didn't want to undeceive her.

I was shaved as fully as possible and went back down to the operating room. When I returned, I changed to a different room. Gabriela had sent me a message from New York: "Good luck." She'd left the day before; I had the impression that she lived in another world and that she'd been gone for a year. In that world, in that time, we had probably been reconciled. In the world where I lived, tears had dried, medical care continued. I was no longer thinking about her, or about the preceding days, except as part of a hospital melodrama that exchanging our misfortunes had darkened, and on which the curtain had fallen. The patient who goes from operating room to operating room is almost immobile, but he is a man of action. Every trial relegates the earlier ones, if not to oblivion, at least to an anaesthetizing fog. The patient depends on others, but he likes to slip away.

In the hallway as in the hospital, I asked questions of the policemen who were protecting me. The questions are in my notebooks; their answers were not written down: here, I was not a journalist, or else I was an inside-out journalist. Most of the policemen came from the provinces or the suburbs. The French always talk about "the people"; the policemen came from "the people." I don't know if one becomes a policeman by accident; but most of them had a sense of order and of their mission. They spared neither governments nor their hierarchies, nor the "young people" that newspapers—including one of mine—are so prone to defend. The policeman with whom I made my long guided tour of the hospital was an Arab who had grown up in Trappes, in a family with eight children. The two of us had discussed the beauty of some of the buildings. The day before I went down to the new operating room, a young policewoman accompanied me in the hallway. She was petite, stocky, and plump, rather tough in look and tone, with cheap glasses and her twenty pounds of equipment on her back. Quite soon, she told me that she was writing a novel whose heroine was a young lesbian, Eva, who taught Spanish and played soccer, as she did: "I like the name Eva, it reminds me of Eve, I find it sensual, don't you?" She continued to tell me the plot. She wanted to write soft but natural porn, without exaggerating, and she asked me if I knew where she could publish it; then, suddenly struck by doubt, she said: "You're not making fun of me, right?" "Of course not!" I wrote on my whiteboard, and it was true. I had no desire to make fun of anyone. I watched and I listened, that was all. The nerve that connected me with judgment seemed to have been cut, just like the nerve that connected me with memory: I saw how I could have judged, and according to which criteria, but the desire to do so had disappeared. I now existed only as a body that wasn't entirely my own, and whose consciousness received without moralizing, without resistance, everything that was presented to it. I hadn't been a very great journalist, probably for lack of boldness, tenacity, and passion for current events, but maybe I was becoming, here, a kind of open book: open to others and for others. I had nothing to reject and nothing to hide.

The young policewoman was beginning to talk about her heroine again when we were interrupted by a little hubbub. Linda came out of the room of my neighbor across the hall. I'd never seen him, but I knew he was a homeless man who called the nurses and aides who took care of him "whores." Linda, who was calmly disgusted, and whose feet hurt terribly, was telling a nurse the insults she'd been treated to. I went up to her and asked her, in writing, what was going on. Linda, frowning and holding her head high, replied briefly: "You really have to want to help people in spite of themselves. I made it clear: I refuse to allow myself to be insulted, except in the psychiatric ward. Or then I react, I know myself, I strike back. Even if I'm not allowed to. That's how it is." She had a cold and was wearing a mask, like many of the outside people that winter.

I returned to my room, and Eva, the little unknown lesbian, made me reflect on the magic spell, always more or less shameful, of writing. How was imagination different from memory? How were they connected? Was it because I had so many problems with my memories that I had so little imagination, and my access to fiction had become so weak? Or had I entered a fiction so intense that it became impossible for me to enter the imagination of others? Now I could read only very slowly, and never to relax or to entertain myself.

In January, Alexis had given me Raymond Chandler's Philip Marlowe stories in an edition that I already owned. I'd read these novels twenty-five years earlier, in a hotel on the shores of Lake Geneva, one summer when I was investigating a minor drama that had taken place on the Swiss plateau. I immediately began to reread *The Big Sleep*, whose film adaptation by Howard Hawkes I was to watch again a few days later with Juan. In the opening scene, I got stuck, like an orchid, in the greenhouse where General Sternwood receives Philip Marlowe to give him his instructions. Sitting in his wheelchair, the moribund Sternwood offers all his visitors, including Marlowe, brandy and cigarettes, then watches them enjoying pleasures he is denied. Sternwood, I said to myself, is almost me. A few days before, I had been given some chocolates, which I obviously couldn't eat, and I liked to offer them to people passing through just to watch them enjoy something of whose taste and texture I had lost even an echo. The problem was that once I'd read this scene, I couldn't continue. The characters grew more distant as they moved away from my situation: I could now enter into a fiction only insofar as it was related to what I was experiencing. It was an idiotic way to read, I knew that, but for the moment I had no other. I gave Chandler's works to Chloé to thank her for taking care of me. She seemed delighted, asked me to write a dedication on the flyleaf, and told me that she would read them on her next vacation. The following summer, as she was about to leave for her Greek island, I wrote to ask her if she had remembered to take them with her. "Already in my suitcase," she replied. I never found out whether she'd read them, or, consequently, what she thought of them.

In my room, I set out again in search of my distant memory, of images of the person I'd been. I did it in light of a sentence of Proust's that I was reading alongside Kafka's letters and *The Magic Mountain*, my three deforming, informing mirrors, dipping into them here and there, in homeopathic doses and not without irritation: "However, you can easily dress up stories about a past with which no one is any longer familiar, just as you can about travels in a country where no one has ever been." This sarcasm throwing a civilized acid on people's masks was very Proustian, but I was making a journey in a country where few people had gone, and I wanted to arrange my narrative all the less because I didn't really know what country I had left behind. The person who had experienced the "past that no one knows" seemed to be unable to explore it except as a tourist, or else by flashes as dazzling as those that James Stewart, his leg in a cast, uses to blind the murderer coming to kill him in *Rear Window*. The past was evaporating or blinding me to avoid being grasped, perhaps to escape this fellow in a dressing gown who was walking up and down the hallway with his drip stand and his feeding tube, in the company of a petite policewoman who wanted to write and publish a lesbian novel. Why?

The time has come to mention the use I was making of Proust, an author whom I had read with passion, both as a sort of Bible and as a form of intense entertainment, at several points in my life. I could enter *La Recherche* anywhere, anytime, as if it were a castle in which I'd grown up, to rejoin characters whom I knew better than most of my friends, because Proust had revealed them to me in their solitude and their slightest recesses, as if he, his characters, and I were all dead, all human, and all a little divine.

When I arrived here after the attack, the only books I had with me were the ones in my backpack: the volume of Shakespeare's complete works in the "Bouquins" series that contained *Twelfth Night* and the first volume of Philippe Muray's *Journal*, on which I was preparing an article I never wrote. Now I'd become incapable of reading Shakespeare, and Muray's pessimism, its bad faith and posthumous resistance to the ambient moralizing, which I had liked, now seemed dreary and irrelevant. He'd died in 2006 at the age of sixty, and I had buried him, as we say in journalism, with affection in *Libération*. He was a baroque writer, in the literal sense of the adjective, a man who never tired of writing about the reasons for his melancholy and his exasperation. At the beginning of the 1980s, as a lecturer at the University of California at Berkeley, he had identified and written what was to become in France the "politically correct"—which was never more than a form of Puritanism renovated by the sirens of progressivism and the anger of minorities. I'd begun to read his book the day before the attack, more or less at random, and today I reread, with a retrospective and amused horror, the passages I'd underlined. They date from 1983 and might put Muray on the Index if he were still alive.

For example, this:

Success of Islam: a religion for the masses. Thus destined to have a great future. Rejection of the divinity of Jesus. Rejection of original sin. Thus no danger, after pleasure and enjoyment, of being visited by a bit of knowledge—the latter being assured only if there is guilt. This guilt is the necessary condition for thought.

Here, Muray was in agreement with Kafka; but was it really true that Muslims, and a fortiori Islamists, felt no guilt? At *Charlie,* hadn't we been the victims of a particularly twisted and mad form of guilt? This prophet, fifteen centuries old, whose rites and commandments had to be followed as if they dated from yesterday—wasn't that a creative and absurd acme of human guilt? Essential imperfection submitted to eternity? Muray concluded:

For centuries, Islamic countries have been countries of absolute non-thought. I remember Arab friends of Nanouk's who gave me funny looks and pretended not to speak to me. Considering her an Arab, that was how they reproached her for having betrayed them by living with a Christian and letting him fuck her. The Quran's surahs on this subject are hellishly difficult.

That was the bon vivant talking. But had he properly interpreted the reactions of his wife Nanouk's Arab friends? What would his attitude have been, confronted by them? Could he have put them under this hat called "Arab friends of Nanouk's"—friends of a woman whose body he appropriated without excessive delicacy, thus resembling more than he seemed to think the image of those whom he was denouncing? These passages and others had made me smile before January 7, smile and even feel pleasure; I also read to ensure that bad feelings, mine and those of others, are expressed. The killers and the hospital had not transformed me into a well of virtue, but these sentences, thirty years after they were written, seemed to bear within them the consequences of a mad stupidity, and this postscript, simply, saddened me: there were more dead and cries, less distance and freedom. In the hospital, I left Muray's *Journal* unopened.

Hardly had I moved into my new room than I asked my brother and Juan to bring from my apartment, along with *The Magic Mountain*, the three volumes of the old Pléiade edition of *La Recherche*. I began by rereading, in addition to the death of the grandmother—which as we know, served me as a preparatory prayer—the scenes in which medicine and illness played a role. Although Proust's viewpoint reminded me to what extent he was a "genius of the place," the place of suffering, his perspective on physicians no longer corresponded to my experience: it was better suited to Molière than to Chloé. However, there was still much to be taken from Proust, and first the fact that whatever the caregiver's quality might be, the patient remains isolated in his suffering, as in a drug even stronger than those that can be given to him. He gleans it and transports it to unknown, wild flowers that bloom at any hour as if it were night.

Nonetheless, I rather soon became annoyed by Proust's pessimism and his perpetual representation of loneliness, of lying and misunderstanding. There was a time when this enterprise of "unmasking" made me feel more intelligent, cleverer: Proust is the one who perceives better than anyone what underlies what others say, and he endows the reader with that twofold viewpoint. Suddenly, this all seemed very artificial to me, even immature. I no longer saw anything but the "tricks," the bias, and even, sometimes, the badly written aspect, especially starting with the next-to-last volume, *La Prisonnière* (*The Captive*), where pointlessly convoluted sentences and questionable grammar grew more common and jumped out at me. Then I got into real little domestic rows with him, silently saying: "Stop pretending to be cleverer, you don't know what you're talking about in your gilded cage, you have a few rungs to climb on the ladder of disaster before getting to the point where, without being an artist, one no longer lies!" He resisted me, with a faint and condescending smile, and I continued to read him with an intermittent, profound passion: exasperation fed admiration.

He had in reality become an antidote to my increasingly ecstatic benevolence (when it was not a matter of Gabriela), but also a negative version of what I was experiencing or thought I was experiencing. When, for example, he wrote: "Indeed nothing is more painful than this contrast between the mutability of people and the fixity of memory, when it is borne in upon us that what has preserved so much freshness in our memory can no longer possess any trace of that quality in life." I thought I was experiencing the opposite. For me, nothing was more painful than the opposition between the permanence of beings—all those people who visited me and seemed forever petrified in the days preceding January 7—and the fragility of memory, when I felt that what was so fresh in life, and so ferocious, was no longer fresh or ferocious in memory. I was experiencing neither time lost nor time regained; I was experiencing time interrupted. The same went for friendship. When he wrote: "And far from thinking myself wretched—a belief which some of the greatest men have held [fucking poseur, I thought]—because of this life without friends or familiar talk that I should live, I realized that our powers of exaltation are being given a false direction when we expend them in friendship, because they are then diverted from those truths toward which they might have guided us to aim at a particular friendship which can lead to nothing."

"You must be joking, Marcel," I added, while Alexandra or Gladys was cleaning the gastrostomy with the feeding syringe and covering my cutlet with Vaseline. I was very happy with this life full of friends, of nurses' eyes and hands, of slow conversations lamed by the silence imposed on me. The powers of exaltation that were expended in friendship, far from being a false direction, led me to the only truth that mattered, at the moment: surviving and restoring a minimum of meaning to this life after death, to this fiction that wasn't a fiction. In my hospital room, friendship was not opposed to regenerative solitude: it shaped the latter's contours and strengthened it. Time lost was struggling against time interrupted.

Regarding what everyday life was after January 7, the Proustian perspective was moving away. I could see no farther back than the preceding day, nor farther forward than the following day, but that state hardened as I left the zone between two shores. At the age of thirty, in a hotel in Cambo-les-Bains, while Marilyn was taking a nap, I'd read a sentence by Milan Kundera that said, more or less: "Nothing will be pardoned, everything will be forgotten." I had nothing to pardon anyone for, not even the killers, those phantoms sent by I know not what destiny, but I didn't need time to forget. Time was beginning to remind me that it existed. I resisted it and this resistance required me to make further efforts, and brought me new sorrows. I dissolved crises and pains almost instantly, as if everything were now saturated with the body's Napoleonic labor: it had no energy to waste on the memory of the rest; it was on campaign, one battle after another, and it took everything, horses and men, from the last of the infantrymen to the first of the generals. The floating states of the first period had gone back to a cellar or attic, and I reread, almost without understanding them, the few descriptions that I'd been able to make of them, for other people, in my notebooks. They were like the questions asked of the policemen or the nurses: you would have thought it was a play in which two speeches out of three, and the most important ones, were missing. Written words were immobile, like the fixed stars in a heaven—or in a hell—to which I no longer had access. Other states, other sensations, other reflexes, drove out the preceding ones, without competition and without hierarchy, and to describe them you would have needed to find a vocabulary as brutal as it was liquid, based on movement, routine, pain, and forgetting; a vocabulary and even a grammar that would be renewed at each stage, to avoid moving from a living language to a dead one.

How should we speak of ourselves and of the world, of ourselves in the world, when what has been experienced the day before is sent elsewhere, apparently very far away, by what is experienced today? When we are *traversed* to that extent? Recalling the sensation of burning caused by the VAC applied to the wound was no simpler than retaining water that runs through your fingers, but it was probably more harmful, more encumbering, and the memory of the sensation seemed rather well formed, even polished, only in order to be suspended or erased. Affective memory followed it along this path. Tinker Bell had turned over a new leaf and the tensions between Gabriela and me, in her absence, had naturally merged with the hole, the VAC, morphine, the anemone, and the dressings soaked in saliva, in a world of obstacles to the new experience being undergone. For lack of sufficiently virgin and fluid words, I constantly reread those of others, always the same authors, Proust, Mann, and even more, Kafka.

I've recounted, in "The World Below," how I regularly went downstairs to the operating room with Kafka's *Letters to Milena*, but I haven't yet said how they'd ended up there. A new edition translated by Robert Kahn had just been published by Nous. My friend and department head at *Libération*, Claire, had brought it to me a few days after the attack. When she arrived, I was in the operating room. Since she didn't have any paper, she wrote on the flyleaf: "Dear Philippe, I'll come back to see you, of course. Hugs and kisses, Claire." It took these circumstances to make her do something that her tact and upbringing forbade, that is, to dedicate a book she hadn't written. This little gesture arising from the circumstances had moved me greatly, and these few words from Claire, together with the letters that followed them, made the book a talisman that has henceforth remained with me from room to room, from house to house, and from country to country.

The day when Claire brought me this book, as I returned from the operating room, half-asleep and nauseated, I took it like a drunk taking an ice-cold shower to wake himself up, and I came across sentences that I have up to this point only mentioned. It's the spring of 1920, and Kafka is in Merano. He's talking about his failed engagement, but we have the impression that he's talking about the world of the ill, and since anyway everything is illness, he concludes by discussing it, and writes: "In any case, it's pointless to reflect on these things. It's as if you tried to break one of the cauldrons in Hell. First, you'll fail, and second, even if you succeed, you'll be burned by the blazing mass that flows out of it, but Hell remains intact in its magnificence. You have to go about it differently. First, lie down in a garden and draw from the illness, especially if it's not really an illness, all the sweetness you can. There's a great deal of sweetness in it."

From then on, these sentences served as my breviary, and even my viaticum. I read them in my room, in the world below, in the hospital garden, and in waiting rooms of all kinds. I would have read them on the operating table had I been able to, and even right up to the moment when the burning of the anesthetic told me I was losing consciousness. They set two limits for me, which in my situation were essential. First, not to try to break even one of Hell's cauldrons, which, like Kafka's, would in any case remain "intact in its magnificence." In this place, the word "magnificence" (*Herrlichkeit*) summed up his modesty, his irony, his superior innocence. There's no escape from a Hell where you are, and it can't be destroyed. I couldn't

eliminate the violence that had been done to me, or the violence that sought to reduce its effects. What I could do, on the
other hand, was to learn to live with it, to domesticate it, by
seeking, as Kafka said, to draw from it as much sweetness as
possible. The hospital had become my garden. And, looking at
the nurses, the aides, the surgeons, the family, the friends in
this emergency department where everyone complained and
insulted one another, where crisis was the natural state of
patients and caregivers, I felt that Kafka's sweetness existed,
but that it was no softer than a stone and that finding it
depended on me.

I return to the operation that followed Gabriela's departure. A graft was going to be made under the lower lip in order
to cover the narrow space that was getting larger along the
edge of the flap: the hole had been closed, but just above it I
was leaking. For the first time since the feeding tube was put
in, the operation would be done under local anesthesia. They
wanted to avoid putting me in another coma and thought I was
capable of enduring this session of facial haute couture, something I was not a little proud of. I was all the less annoyed to
embark on this little adventure because I was finally going to
be able to hear and see, I said to myself, what took place when
I was usually put to sleep. A mistake, since what's said over the
body of the unconscious patient probably has little relationship to what he witnesses when he isn't unconscious. There
were, however, relationships: the surgical act itself, along with
the gestures and words that accompany it. As on the day of the
feeding tube, I would be allowed to witness the technique and
these words that would enlighten me and reassure me almost
as much, I imagine, as an explorer who is able to name, in a
jungle that he is exploring, the plants and animals that he sees.
Witnessing the work on my face was a way of coming closer to
the caregivers, of domesticating their world by appropriating
it, of putting a foot on the other side, so to speak. The better

informed I was regarding the work that my body required, the more I felt suited to participate in it: a patient of my kind was an athlete, I repeat that as it was repeated to me, and the athlete has to understand the treatments that are proposed to him, the endurance that is imposed on him, the uncertainties that accompany matches and training. A maximum of will and a minimum of stoicism come at that price. My instinctive reference points, on this subject, were less *ER* or *House* than Antoine, the medical student son in *Les Thibault*, or Cronin's humanistic doctors. It was literature, not fiction, that helped me. I no longer had much strength to read it, but I was still occupied by its slow memory, I who could no longer feel memories of life. Its distant countries forced me not to submit to anything, neither image nor sound nor body. They helped me to rebuild, along with my face and my body, the characters who inhabited it, and who hardly needed their textual cradle to live here, in my room, like guardian angels.

I was all the more satisfied with surgery without general anesthesia because I was going to be operated on by Hossein, whose presence reassured me. Hossein had succeeded, without particular effort, in virtually everything he'd undertaken, in France as well as in the United States, or at least that was the impression he gave. That impression was necessarily false, since surgeons are nearly always terribly hard workers: they have almost godlike power, and they also appear in frescoes, but their Dionysian aspect seems to me limited, and they have, dealing with a patient so often deprived of free will, more responsibilities. Hossein's beauty, which was not long afterward to delight most of my women friends, had something that was very agreeable at the hospital, but it was first of all his implacable, informative gentleness that attracted me. He said things with a smile, in a soft voice, in an almost amused, or distanced, way, with a curiosity that transformed the relationship, with the courtesy of someone who seemed to believe you were intelligent enough that he could take you into his confidence. It was indeed regarding my own case that he took me into his confidence, like Chloé, but in a different way, more egalitarian, more placid, more cunning as well, and also less directly engaged; he didn't have the same status or the same experience as Chloé, and he wasn't my reference point. His taste for sociability, in my room, had an unexpected virtue: speaking to me as if we were talking over a glass of (good) wine, he gave me a glimpse of the *return to polite conversation*, to Parisian life, to its culture and its indispensable frivolities. In sum, he introduced among the tubes and probes a certain equality and lightness—and a continuity with life outside the hospital.

It took me some time to see that his optimism and his apparently satisfied civility masked, not a pessimism, but a clear awareness of his limits. This awareness was probably not peculiar to exiles and their children, but it was often found among them. Hossein's parents had left Iran at the time of the Islamic Revolution. Household furnishings and family objects had remained over there, in storage. They refused to have them brought to France, though more than thirty years had passed. They sensed that they would never return to live in Iran, but the presence of these furnishings and objects abandoned to memory and dreams, over there, allowed life to float in an uncertainty, in a light that suspended or qualified the irreversible impact of the events. I gradually came to understand that in my own life, things were also in storage and would probably be taken out of it again, but at some later time. For the moment they remained there, between the future and the past, leaving me simply the possibility of floating.

Two years later, as we were talking about the feeling of omnipotence that the new president of the Republic emanated, Hossein's dark, bright eyes hardened and he said to me: "If there's a will there's a way? People who think that are dangerous." He was all the more aware of this because a surgeon can do a great deal, and in any case more than most others. "One of the worst things I've had to do," he told me that evening in a deserted café, "was to remove half the face of a woman friend's father. He had cancer. When I told him my diagnosis, he began reciting poems in Persian. He put up with everything, right to the end. He was an extraordinary man." Then I understood why, in Room 111, Hossein had given me the book of poems. The patients' spirits were connected by the surgeon's gesture.

Before going down to the operating room, Cédric, a young nurse aide who was mischievous and badly shaven, took responsibility for shaving me. Shaving my face around the new scar tissue, first around the hole and now around the flap, was a job for a lacemaker that the nurses preferred to avoid, but Chloé insisted on it: hair is an unnecessary source of infection, and patients had to arrive in the operating room as clean-shaven as possible. My parents had brought me the best of razors, but I didn't dare use it. The first person who helped me was Hervé, the phlegmatic nurse aide to whom I was closest. Hervé almost always had his eyebrows raised behind his horn-rimmed glasses, and a smile that might be seen as amused or warmhearted, because he was both. That was how he distanced his discretion—and difficulty. In his youth, he'd played keyboards, under the name of Xeus, in a French funk group, Malka Family. This adventure had lasted ten years. Like quite a few people here, Hervé lived in the hospital a life he had chosen, in which I sensed, without knowing exactly where he came from, the weight of earlier lives. The old-timers, who might be only thirty-five years old, came here loaded with mysteries that the misery of the patients deepened. They hadn't ended up by accident in this difficult ward that was always on the verge of breaking up, where gratitude was the last thing to be expected. The hair closest to the wounds formed little clumps of black and gray that neither Hervé nor Cédric could handle. I looked at Cédric's three-day beard with a certain envy: not only was he not going down to the operating room, but in addition Chloé wouldn't reproach him for anything.

Down there, Annie la Castafiore was sweeter than ever, she sensed or knew that I was soon going to leave the ward. She accompanied me as far as the operating table, speaking to me, I think, about Verdi. For some time we'd been exchanging discs with Hossein, and once I was placed under the heating blanket, he approached and showed me a CD by an American pianist, Richard Buhlig: it was *The Art of the Fugue*, which I listened to more and more often in the room, in a version by the Chinese pianist Zhu Xiao-Mei. Hossein told me: "I thought you might not know this interpretation," and he was right. Then he explained what he was going to do, showing me a kind of improved rasp called a dermatome. It would be used to remove a thin layer of the epidermis on my right thigh, no thicker than the thinnest slices of mortadella, right next to the one that had been taken for the main graft: "Like that," he said, "we'll leave the other thigh intact." The idea that certain parts of my body might escape scars now seemed to me almost incongruous, and I had a brief moment of relief. Part of the slice of skin would then be put over and sewed onto the graft area, under the lip. It was what is called a "thin skin graft." There are also deep skin grafts, but that was for later, when this one had failed. Explanations had been given. The operation could begin.

Hossein put the disc in a CD player. While my right thigh was being disinfected and anaesthetized, the first notes, so slow, of the first counterpoint passed between the nurses' caps and entered, one by one, like the first drops of a rain, into my ear: *Re, la, fa, re, do sharp, re, mi, fa, fa, sol, fa, mi, re.* It was a winter music, it was winter, my life was in winter. The sound of the old recording fell over the room and over my body. I felt the injections and I concentrated on the music composed by Bach, who, it seemed to me more every day, had saved my life. As in Kafka's work, power was combined with modesty, but it was not guilt that drove it; it was confidence in a god that lent genius and peace to this choleric character. Hossein brought the dermatome closer to my thigh. I closed my eyes and tried to concentrate on the fugue that was now developing its various lines, producing this miracle: the more complex it became, the more it simplified me. I felt a slight burning. The musical landscape was emerging. Counterpoints came one after another, and Hossein began working on my face, which he had anaesthetized. On the face, local anesthesia is an even more outright paradox than it is elsewhere. I felt violently everything from which I wasn't yet suffering. The skin that was being attached and stretched, the lip that was being elongated, the movement of the tissues, and finally, the needle being inserted and reinserted by Hossein to make the suture. Since the sensation didn't correspond to any pain, my perception of my face was once again disoriented. Imagination took over for the dulled nerves, as if it were drawing the craziest conclusions from an incomplete sentence. The slightest movement resembled the tremor of a landslide, but without dead and injured, just the tremor and the panic. So I concentrated again on the fugue. I tried to enter into it, to become the fugue in order to escape the variations of my imagination. I couldn't move or complain in Bach's presence, or, for that matter, in Hossein's. On the contrary, now that Hossein seemed to be ripping open my lip to move it toward the right, beyond the operating room, as people pull naughty children's ears, I had to put sensations that were as blind as they were intense in the service of listening to Bach, and that is what I did while pain was beginning to appear, because the anesthesia was insufficient: I made a sign to Hossein and another injection took the pain away. I went back into the fugue and came out of it only when I left to go back upstairs.

Once I was back in my room, I listened to the fugue again.

While I was in the operating room, Gabriela had written me again. Her e-mail was so violent that I didn't respond to it. I was tired. I talked with my brother about Gabriela's message, and he proposed to write her to remind her that I had not been the victim of "a minor traffic accident," because she seemed to have forgotten that. I told him not to do anything, that it wasn't important, and that she had probably already calmed down. She was alone, shaken up, choked with guilt: on who else could she have unloaded her pain and anger? That she did so at the very moment when I was returning from an operation could only distract me from it, at least for a few moments, and Gabriela and the idea of replying to her message disappeared when Bach reestablished the void, and then filled it. The dressings were no longer holding on my body. Hossein had advised me, as the orderly was taking me away, to degrease them with benzoin. I asked my brother to find some, and I went to sleep until I was awakened by one of the painful and recurrent coughs caused by the tracheotomy tube. Two nurses came in and finally managed to expel two blockages. I was sweating, exhausted, and once again I put on *The Art of the Fugue*.

The next day, Chloé visited me to discuss my release from the hospital. We'd been talking about it for a few days, and it seemed to be scheduled for the middle of March; but where would I go? That was the question. Unlike her, I wasn't in any hurry to decide. I didn't want to leave the hospital, and I had, for the first time, written an e-mail to Christiane, the manager, to inform her of my concern. This e-mail gives an idea of my state of mind and of the ultimately submissive, even obsequious, relationship that I entertained with those on whom my condition depended:

> Since I can't speak at this point, I'm sending you a little e-mail to thank you once again, very warmly, for everything that you're doing for me. The medical team is very profes-

sional, and I am well aware that I have received preferential treatment and beautiful rooms.

I also know that I will soon have to think about leaving. Chloé told me that last evening. Next Thursday, as she suggested, seems to me impossible, almost makes me panic; what would I do with this wound, this exhaustion, these pains? I feel neither well enough nor independent enough to impose my presence on my parents or anyone else. And it will be some time before I'm ready to live alone.

But I also know that the hospital's mission is not to keep people it considers to be convalescent. Would it be possible to arrive at a compromise, for a departure in "good shape" in the middle of March? That is what I have imagined, I don't know whether it's possible. In that case I would arrive at my parents' house along with spring, and later return to my own home, with the help of friends.

It was a worried message, but too optimistic: the sequel was to show that I was not on the way to recovery, at least not in the immediate future, and that the release that was going to be imposed on me was, as often happens at the hospital, premature. Christiane replied with all possible tact that I had a marvelous family and friends, that they would all be able to help me and lodge me. In the hospital, the manager's voice is that of his masters—in this case, by Chloé's voice and Professor G's voice. I had to prepare to leave. An e-mail to Sophia, who was in Spain, emphasizes that this process had immediately begun:

Chloé, my surgeon, thinks I have to leave the hospital to reconnect with life rather soon now, even if it's hard. I know she's right, for example, if I want to go back to work soon: how can anyone take an interest in current events, in television, in anything, when he thinks and meditates in such a cocoon, surrounded by good books and prey to all sorts of fears and bad nights? Everything else seems to be distraction.

It's not easy to set both feet on the side of the living. I had to imagine a future that my body and my consciousness rejected.

Did I want to leave and go back to my "life before," as was wished by those who seemed to want to put between parentheses an event that, in my own life, put everything else between parentheses? Or didn't I want that? Those are the dreams which, at that time, reminded me of the importance that the rituals of friendship—the ones that Proust saw as taking up time needed for creation—had to regain, and would regain, even though they would begin by settling on a heap of ruins; I would have to make gestures as I always had, as I never had, just as here every morning I took a sustaining shower, listened to Bach, read the grandmother's death, the beginning of *The Magic Mountain*, and Kafka's letters to Milena, wrote my columns for *Charlie*, connected my nutrient bags, did my twenty trips up and down the hallway or toured the hospital for an hour.

Now Chloé was once again in my room. I wrote down what she said to me:

It has never before happened here, in this ward, this mixture of tenderness and madness that you inspire, and that's why you're going to have to leave. You have to be protected from everybody and from all the silly things people say to you about what will happen later, about your face that is going to be this way or that way. It was inevitable: you're coming out of a national event that has upset everyone's life, and moreover, you have a very special personality. You've been able to find your strength here, and that's good. You've made this ward a welcoming and attractive nest, everyone has entered this nest, and now you have to leave it in order to escape them.

She was right. Although journalism applied in part to others continued to be effective, the journalism I was applying to myself was beginning to turn against me: everyone had his idea about what I was going to become, about what was going to be done or not done to me, the last person who talked to me was always right, and my anxiety increased as a result of so much uncertainty. In this context, seducing people meant simply attaching them to my case—and accepting anxiety in exchange for connections. Chloé reminded me that such an intense place was not suited to keep too long a patient who was trying to transform pain and medical treatment into forms of stimulus, and had obviously succeeded. Poor Ludo had been a mascot, he was dead, I had more or less replaced him in this role, in a different way, but mascots were not meant to last, and the staff had to forget them in order to care for those who came afterward. There had been a time, not far in the past, when patients remained a year, two years, or more in a hospital ward; that was also the period when people weren't cured. Now, patients could remain a long time, like Ludo, only because they were going to die; and even then, you had to be completely incapable of caring for yourself to become an exception to the rule that was not only a matter of accounting but also of life and death, and that had taken control of the hospital as it had the rest of the world, and in its image. Moreover, most people were scared when they came here. They almost became children again. By what miracle had I so well adapted myself to the difficulties of the situation? Why hadn't I, at almost any time up to that point, felt diminished, reduced to nothing? I owed it to my family and friends, to be sure, but not only: I suddenly understood—or else I wanted to believe—that I had never taken very seriously either my job or a social life whose suspension didn't bother me. Something in me felt light as a feather, abandoned to the everyday discipline as to a passing breeze.

Chloé pursued her thoughts out loud: "Go to stay with your parents? Do as you want, but I wouldn't advise you to do that. There's a convalescent home in Normandy, but you'd go crazy there. I wouldn't advise you to stay here in the hospital, either. At your own apartment, with a nurse who comes every-day . . . ah, but you're alone, Gabriela is in New York, so it isn't so simple. Maybe there's another solution . . . " This other solution, which was discussed behind my back, was revealed to me by my brother as soon as possible; it was a place I didn't even know existed, the military hospital of Les Invalides. It had been suggested by a physician, Dr. S, who worked for the crisis unit at the French foreign ministry. He had come to see me the day after the attack. He was a dark-haired, solid man with lively eyes who made decisions quickly and who had positioned himself in my room like a bull ready to charge, not the first torero's cape he saw, but the one he had chosen. My brother had remained in contact with him, and he learned, at the same time as Chloé, where I was soon going to spend most of my time. If at that time Dr. S had been told that I was going to spend almost seven months at Les Invalides, he would probably have leaped in the air, not like a bull, but like a young goat, so difficult do people who live with emergencies find it to imagine a world where they no longer exist. There is always a fertile contradiction in physicians of this type: they have to reconcile the humanism and patience of the caregiver with the impatience and realism of the politician. They are centaurs who, if they don't end up renouncing their duality, often go mad. Dr. S was my centaur, always on a mission here or there, and it was to this firm, amiable, effective man that I owe the stay that partly saved me.

The departure for Les Invalides was planned for March 9: Chloé wanted to see how the graft Hossein had made, which seemed to be going wrong, developed. Two days after the operation, Corinne the physical therapist came in the morning for the almost daily session. I had slept little and was exhausted. She proposed that I walk a bit, to work on balance and the leg without a fibula. I hadn't taken three steps before I felt a sudden nausea coming over me. I didn't have time to go to the toilet or to grab a kidney cup, and I vomited standing up, in successive flows, a yellowish liquid that flooded the floor and the lower part of the walls. Corinne was petrified in her smock, her feet in the yellow liquid, pale as a corpse. A minute passed, I continued to vomit over her silence and immobility, even as I looked at her and wondered: Where is all that *yellow* coming from? Was Corinne going to drown in it? I finally stopped, and she made me lie down and then went out to seek help, while I repeatedly excused myself, like a servant who has broken a lamp or stolen the silverware. Corinne came back with the Marquise des Langes and I continued my excuses while the latter took my pulse and blood pressure. Then a cleaner came in with her mop, her pail, and that marvelous, silent African silence that, in this nervous ward, calmed me. Since I seemed to be better, I accompanied Corinne and the Marquise des Langes as far as the hallway while the room was being cleaned. "Do you want me to come back a little later?" Corinne asked me. I said yes, and then, once the cleaner had left, I took a second shower of the day and changed pajamas. Corinne finally returned to continue the session. "So," she said, "walking is over for today. I'm going to drain a little and have you exercise your hands a little." To drain, Corinne placed herself behind me and massaged my neck and face is such a way as to cause the lymph that had been piling up since the graft to circulate. A warmth immediately rose from my chin to the top of my skull and I became nothing but a series of pleasant, intense shivers. Then Corinne sat down next to me and took my right hand, the one with the stiff and swollen index finger. She'd been massaging it for a minute when I felt nauseated again. Corinne held out a kidney cup for me, but this time, the yellow substance merely preceded the black and I lost consciousness, plunging my head into the full receptacle. When I came to, I was still in the wheelchair, surrounded by a group of familiar faces. A hand was wiping my face, two others were putting my legs on a chair, and I could already hear the nurse's cart coming. I was lifted up, my torso bared, and laid on the bed, where my blood pressure and pulse were taken, blood was drawn for analysis, electrodes were hooked up, and I was put on a drip. I said to myself, almost with satisfaction, "You're not leaving here tomorrow."

That afternoon, I left in an ambulance for the other end of the hospital complex, where the checks that the situation seemed to require would be made. Was it a bacterium, an ulcer, or simply fatigue, an inability to tolerate an analgesic, or something else? It was cold and, foreseeing a wait before the scanner and the ultrasound, I'd taken *The Magic Mountain* with me. The room where the orderly left me was a motley place full of devastated people, gray, greenish, some of them having waited for hours. A terrible draft blew all through it and seemed to linger with maniacal care on each of us. Since I'd been given no blanket, I was shivering under my sheet, and I shivered even more as I looked at the others shivering. I said to myself that exposing patients to bronchitis was perhaps not the best way to cure them of an ulcer or a toothache, and this reflection satisfied me momentarily: there was no point in protesting against a disorder and a brutality that were inherent in the nature of the place.

I took *The Magic Mountain* from under the sheet and tried to do battle, word by word, against the cold that was making me shiver more and more. I opened the first pages at random and came upon the passage where Joachim is talking to Hans about the Schatzalp sanatorium, the highest in the region: "They have to transport the bodies down by bobsled in the winter, because the roads are blocked." Hans is astonished, becomes indignant, and suddenly he burst into laughter, a violent, overpowering laugh that shook his chest and twisted his face, stiffened by the cool wind, into a slightly painful grimace. "On bobsleds! And you can sit there and tell me that so calm and cool? You've become quite the cynic in the last five months."

"That's not cynical at all," Joachim replied with a shrug. "Why do you say that? It doesn't matter to the bodies."

The patients, not so much, and I felt floating in the air a protest that was stifled by exhaustion and resignation, aided by the draft, which also dried faces "into a slightly painful grimace." One hour later, they came to get me for the examination. The orderly was furious, because he now had to wait for the ambulance. I would gladly have proposed that we walk back, at my speed, but the rules forbade that. When we came out, night had fallen. The results of the analyses and the ultrasound showed nothing. An intern said to me: "They didn't find anything? Good news." During the night, the nightmares began again. Not writing them down was a way of forgetting them.

The day after next, in the afternoon, I was given the right to speak again, but not too much, and once more I didn't know what to say or how to talk. Suddenly Linda came in holding in her hand a strange thing that I thought I'd never see again and that was obviously meant for me: a plain yogurt, sitting on a little tray. For the first time since the morning of January 7, I was going to use my mouth to eat. I immediately called Gabriela on FaceTime, we were thus reconciled, and it was in front of her, over there in New York, that I began to eat again as best I could, very slowly and, like an infant, spilling food all over. She had regained the smile she'd had on the screen on the morning of January 7.

Shortly afterward, I wrote a column for *Charlie* entitled

"The Yogurt." It established a direct connection with Marilyn's visit recounted in "The Cookie Box," and Kafka was on board as usual:

No televised cooking show—and there are some very good ones, though they're excessively long-winded, seeking to make up for what can't be eaten with what is not necessarily worth saying—never gave me so much concrete joy as the first food consumed (with difficulty) through my mouth, after two months of being fed exclusively through a tube. It was a simple plain yogurt, with a little sugar, as in the cafeteria: a sort of hospital *madeleine* outside of time. A nurse aide suddenly brought it to me one day around 3 P.M., with the jovial and sometimes brutal naturalness that characterizes the hospital: as if this yogurt, which had never been there, in my room, had in reality been waiting for me there forever. It's not only the patient who has to be patient. It's the world around him. The nurse and the nurse aide went back and forth between the two periods of waiting. Following the instruction of the invisible physician, they gradually brought back in the outside world, which had become mysterious and remote. The patient, who is of every age, welcomes everything with gratitude, with anxiety. I welcomed the yogurt.

The first person who made me once again smell "the taste of green papaya," that is, the fragrance of everyday foods, was a woman friend, a month earlier. It was during a period when I was having difficulty breathing in the evening. This sensation was due only to the tracheotomy, but sensations make the body, even if objective information contradicts them, and at the same time carry all the rest: where air seems not to be going in, dark ideas—repetitive and rarefied ideas—manage to get through. Life as a whole is filtered through a thick, opaque material that mixes time and night and makes them slip into the funnel. My woman friend came one evening with a sandwich, mandarin oranges, and a thermos of heavily sugared coffee. Rather quickly, she discovered that I'd been given some excellent chocolates that were inedible for me, but not for her. She had me smell, little by little and in silence, everything she ate. One of my nostrils was stuffed up, but not the other. All the perfumes of domestic Arabia went into it. I forgot, for a moment, that I was breathing so badly. Later I was reminded that in the prisoner-of-war camp where my grandfather was dying of hunger along with the other prisoners, up there in Pomerania, from 1940 to 1945, men of all nationalities spent their time exchanging their countries' respective recipes, as if they were dreams made concrete by words, even though they were eating nothing but rutabaga soup.

Now, I was sitting in front of that yogurt. I had to open my mouth, not spill all over, and take care in swallowing. When the nurse put it down, I was in the position and the state of mind that Kafka attributes to tuberculosis patients in a letter to Milena written on July 9, 1920:

How I'll be able to cope with the autumn later on is also a question for later. (. . .) If by chance I'm not writing to you, then I'm lying in my armchair, staring out the window. There's enough to look at, the view is open enough, since the house across the street is only one story high. I don't mean to imply I find this occupation particularly depressing—no, not at all—it's just that I can't tear myself away.

With Kafka, unhappiness is never disappointed by the imbecile that is within us. He carries on his shoulder that devil—light and profound, implacable and smiling—who watches you go astray, fall, and never leaves you even, especially, the resource of complacency—or of pathos. At the hospital, Kafka the humorist is a traveling companion.

The first little (plastic) spoon of yogurt, after two months without any taste, was not comparable to the first little taste of beer, according to Philippe Delerm—even if half of it was set aside. This was not a great little pleasure regained, comfortable, shared: it was an austere and solitary rebirth. One is every age except one's own. The memory of yogurt returned immediately, but it was less important than the life that emerged from it. Any taste whatever would have had the same effect, combined with that lost freshness which, in turn, reawakened an extinguished desire, thirst, and then, connected with a smile still reduced by sutures and the pain of the numbed jaw that was beginning to go back to work, a forgotten feeling: anger.

This anger rose as my departure date approached. Two days later, I wrote to my parents, who were proposing to bring me some preserves:

> The preserves are useless, they stuff me like a goose, I can't finish any of my meals, which take me forever to eat (not to mention the mess). But after all, we're not going to complain, it's a return toward life.

Most of the e-mails over the following days were acerbic, almost furious. Eating again, even though so little, made me aware of my regression and my limits. For the first time, I was becoming impatient. It was time to leave a place where I had exhausted the reasons for fighting and being proud of myself.

The day before my departure was a Sunday. I was served a croissant and chocolate, as usual. In the afternoon, I spent a few hours in the Quai Branly Museum, with the policemen, my brother, and a friend. The weather was fine. For the first time since the preceding autumn, I sat in a sidewalk café on the Champ de Mars, near the merry-go-round where my grandfather used to take me when I was three years old. I thought of him as I drank a glass of apricot juice. The juice leaked out through my lip or through the graft. My friend pointed this out to me. All the same, I smelled its taste. I was seated with my back to the sun so that I could remove my mask. When I returned to the hospital, I attached the third bag of Fresubin to my feeding tube. Chloé thought I was not "hooked up" often enough. Later, Juan brought me some gazpacho he'd made—it was one of his specialties—along with iced coffee. I ate the gazpacho in front of him, silently, very slowly, and drank the iced coffee. My body was no longer used to it, and I pissed every hour all through the night. I reread, one last time, the grandmother's death.

For two days, I'd been going through the ceremony of saying farewell. The nurses, the nurse aides, Annette-with-the-bright-eyes and the others, all came to say goodbye to me, day and night, depending on when they were on duty. Annie la Castafiore informed me that she couldn't come up from the world below and regretted that: we would see each other soon. Hossein and one of his colleagues, Jean-Baptiste, gave me a tour of the hospital's staff room. It was covered with big, caricatural frescos. Some of them were in a medieval style. I thought of the *danse macabre* painted on the walls of the church of La Ferté-Loupière. My guides showed me representations of caregivers I knew. Chloé, on a horse, was a knight. That was a moment of pleasure. I was standing. Friendship enveloped surgeons that I was going to leave.

I felt like the characters in *Corto Maltese* who, at the end of *La Ballade de la mer salée*, after so many trials, disappearances, and deaths, greet one another and embrace before boarding their sailing ship and crying to those who remain behind: "Farewell, friends! Farewell! Farewell! You are the best friends in the world!" I was leaving the island that had been a little more than my home: a second cradle. Before departing, I had written two last e-mails. In the first, I replied to a friend who had written me about Kerala. She proposed to bring back a little Ganesh, the elephant god, so that he could watch over me. I liked Ganesh a lot, I'd attended the celebrations dedicated to him in Bombay. Would I return to Bombay someday? I accepted her proposal. In the second e-mail, I asked my parents to bring to Les Invalides the cologne that I hadn't put on since January 7.

Chloé had intended to come to say goodbye, but she was still not there when the ambulance took me away on Monday morning. I'd seen her for the last time on Friday evening. That was when she had said to me: "Do you know what you've been through? When the graft of the fibula was made, we were scared. If it had failed, we would have all gone down along with you." I'd been responsible for my family, my friends, and also, in the end, my surgeons.

My brother followed the ambulance. The two vehicles were loaded with the objects that had piled up in my hospital rooms. In the ambulance, these objects were all around me. I felt like a minor, depressed pharaoh being taken to his tomb, as if in a bark, with everything he would need in the beyond.

I hadn't been in Les Invalides since I was a child, and didn't know that there was a hospital there. I thought there was only a museum, a large courtyard, and a tomb. The great courtyard was dominated by the statue of Napoleon, and the tomb was his. That was appropriate: he had been my hero until I was told that he'd "put Europe to fire and the sword." He came from a big picture book entitled *Napoléon raconté aux enfants* (*The Story of Napoleon for Children*), and, despite my later readings in history and multiple humanistic injunctions, truth forces me to say that he hasn't really fallen, probably thanks to *La Chartreuse de Parme* (*The Charterhouse of Parma*), *Le Colonel Chabert* (*Colonel Chabert*), and Chateaubriand's description of the fat Louis XVIII and his band of émigrés parading, after his return, among Napoleon's old guard: literature, that indefatigable carriage, makes us travel among intimate desires that resist obligatory admiration. I was not now reading much literature, but I was thinking about it a lot. My parents had taken me to see the tomb when I was seven or eight years old. That was the period when the cemetery at Eylau and Grouchy's late arrival at Waterloo made me inconsolable. I detested the Germans, those Nazis who won in soccer, but I detested the English still more, because they had defeated and imprisoned the hero. It could be said that the child was angry with history. It might also be thought that he understood, better than anyone, to what point history is suspended, repetitive, obsessive, and as chronological as it is circular; to what point it resembles the patient's situation.

My new room was on the second floor of the hospital, at the end of a long corridor lined with old windows. From my bed, I could see trees and, standing out against the sky, the dome over the tomb. I was going to live for seven months in this place, which soon became my *castle*. The visitors were my *guests*. I was concerned to behave like a *chatelain* toward them, to do the honors of the place, like an old Russian noble wearing, in addition to his clothes, an old rifle and the traces of a long-lost era. Wasn't I exiled from my own life?

I was happy to receive these friends at the entrance gates, with my policemen, or, if their names had been announced at the sentry box, at the hospital's reception desk. A few of them came directly to my room, but they sometimes got lost in the labyrinth of corridors. I was happy to hug them in my arms, to show them the fine views, the recesses, the courtyards, and the hidden points of view, the cannon taken from the Turks on which could be read loads of inscriptions. I was happy to introduce them to each other, I who had up to that point tended to compartmentalize my life. They came with bottles, cakes, sometimes little dishes. I liked to watch them drinking and eating and talking at dusk in the foyer's almost deserted courtyard, which was also dominated by the dome over the tomb. The policemen took up position in a corner, silent, smiling, and armed. Conviviality descended on the stone of the old buildings. It was warm, time stopped, for my friends and for me, and, when they went away into the night, I returned, exhausted, to my little room, my Vaseline, my sleeping pill, my ultra-soft toothbrush, and my individual life under the tomb's dome. I was here, I was elsewhere, a phantom of Les Invalides, I was not the only one, and I had a hard time leaving. My little room was the bark on which I was making the rest of a crossing whose end I neither foresaw nor could entirely wish. And I connected my last bag of Fresubin.

The room was in the Ambroise Paré sector; the corridor was named Laon. The first day, when she saw our group coming in, a young nurse, Laura, who had a shrill voice and long red hair, "looked for the bandage" to know which of us was the patient. I had a large and partly transparent bandage that went from my lip to my chin. I saw her gaze hesitate, then focus on me. I soon learned that Laura's husband, a Libyan soldier whose legs had been seriously wounded by a rocket, had been going from one graft to the next for years. She talked about it without going on and on, just as she sometimes talked in the same tone about her religion, Islam, and about the cartoon images of the Prophet, which she'd found pointless and inappropriate. We weren't there to accuse each other, or to complain. The world of the hospital is the world of observation. At Les Invalides, contrary to La Salpêtrière, patients rubbed shoulders, hung out with each other: they weren't in the emergency room but in reeducation. The sufferings of some of them put those of the others in perspective. Solitudes and wheelchairs circulated in silence through the broad hallways and in the shadow of buildings constructed under Louis XIV, ending up in the foyer, the gymnasium, or the workshops. It was a calm, ancient place, empty when it was not visiting hours, a place where the power of the site and of History tempered the patient's lack of tranquility. To a certain extent, it helped the patient heal.

I asked Laura if she knew the Laon cathedral, which is so beautiful, reminded me of Vezelay, and seemed, like the latter, to live between two worlds, the Romanesque and the Gothic, the South and the North, the Muslim and the Christian. She did not know that there was a city called Laon. "I thought it was the name of a military doctor," she said, and after all, I said to myself, that may be true, even if the name of the hallway undoubtedly came from the battle of Laon won in 1814 by Napoleon. I retained an inner image of that cathedral, and also of what Commander Ernst Jünger wrote about it in his *Journal* when he occupied Laon with the German army. On June 11, 1940, in the dark, he entered the city's library through a gate that had collapsed:

We walked through the rooms, where I occasionally turned my flashlight on a book—for example, a priceless edition of *Monumenti antichi*. It filled a whole bookcase. Partly on the floor, partly on a long table, a collection of handwritten documents arranged in about thirty large volumes; I opened one of them at random. It contained letters from famous botanists of the eighteenth century; some in a very neat and gracious hand. From a second bundle I took a letter from Alexander I, notes written by Eugène de Beauharnais and Antommarchi, Napoleon's personal physician. Feeling that I had entered a mysterious cavern, opened by a "Sesame," I returned to my billet.

I, too felt that on entering Les Invalides I had penetrated a cavern that, despite the assonance, its past, and its military administration, in no way resembled a *caserne* (barracks); but this cavern had become my billet.

I arrived on the second floor accompanied by the ambulance paramedics and the policemen. While I was getting settled in my room, my brother had gone to register me at the admissions desk. When he was asked under what name I should be registered, he gave mine. Here, the woman on the admissions desk said, he needed a pseudonym. Taken off guard, my brother thought of our father's origin in the Pyrenees, in the city where our aunt and our uncle the surgeon lived, and he said "Tarbes." That was how I came to be, in the world of Les Invalides, Monsieur Tarbes. My brother's choice delighted me, even if at the moment I didn't understand why. It was in the Pyrenees, traveling to the lakes, that I had come closest to the state to which it seemed to me rather pointless to aspire: happiness. It was a state close to dissolution—in the landscape, light, sound, and air. It was not to be achieved without exhausting effort or anxiety: these rocky lakes, located below the summits, had a perfection and virginity that was similar to death. You had only to look at the clear, dark water to feel that, once you were in it, you would never come out again. That was an excellent reason to dive into it and emerge from it again in order to feel alive, in the sun, like a kind of survivor.

The city of Tarbes has few charms; but in addition to my family ties, in my view it has at least two: the magnificent Massey garden, which dates from the nineteenth century, where I used to like to walk under the big trees after a rain, and the fact that the childhoods of three writers I like are connected with it: Théophile Gautier, Jules Laforgue, and Isidore Ducasse. The first of these, who was born in Tarbes, quickly left it. The other two were born in Montevideo, but like many French immigrants to Latin America, their families had ties with Southwest France and they grew up there. The fact that these two great poets spent their childhood in Tarbes had made it an imaginary place. From it, I could go back to distant countries, to that Latin America I'd dreamed about so much, and now I was to go down the river toward a new life, depending on efforts made and circumstances, under this intimate and exotic flag.

In Les Invalides, I was never called by any other name. Very soon, Monsieur Tarbes was living his own life within these walls from the classical age; he was the phantom of Les Invalides. He was composed of discipline and peace, reeducation and tears in consolation, of walks at dawn and still more at night. Monsieur Tarbes was neither Philippe Lançon nor a pseudonym of Philippe Lançon. He was a heteronym, such as Fernando Pessoa had no doubt imagined in creating his work under different lives, and not only names. Monsieur Tarbes did not speak and act entirely like Philippe Lançon. He was less loquacious, slower, more distant, more attentive, more benevolent, too; probably much older, but of an age relieved of an excess of presence. Monsieur Tarbes metabolized his sorrow under the golden tints of the tomb. He was thin, wore a big hat, could not smile, gobbled down his milky, mashed meals, never in the presence of others, to spare them the sight, plop plop plop, of his spills. There was an element of Montevideo in him, a city where Philippe Lançon had never gone, and he became increasingly attached to this element that made him fragile and uncertain confronted by life, sensitive to the breath and manners of the dead. Monsieur Tarbes was suspended, he floated. He became increasingly attached to a city where Philippe Lançon had never gone.

However, memories of dreams had returned, and with them, Philippe Lançon took another, unpleasant step toward life. Thus during the night preceding my departure for Les Invalides, I had a dream that for some time extended its shadow over the first two weeks of Monsieur Tarbes.

I'm staying at Gabriela's, in a big American house. She has taken me in after I was wounded. Today is the children's party. The neighbors' children come, play, make noise, then some of hem get into an immense bathtub full of foam, after a bath has been drawn for them. I take off my clothes, like them, and sit down across from them at the other end of the bathtub. I feel great pleasure in the hot water and in looking at them. Suddenly, an American "mom" comes into the bathroom and screams, frightened and disgusted on seeing me: "What are you doing *there*, in the bathtub, with the *children?*" I look at her and struggle to speak to her: "But . . . I'm taking a bath, I live here. And it's not bothering them. I'm not a pedophile." I articulate badly, but that's not the problem. She refuses to listen to me and shouts, "You're disgusting! I'm going to tell the other parents and the police. We're leaving this *place* immediately. Children, get out of the bathtub!" I try to speak: "But . . . but . . . but . . . ," without being able to say anything more. They all leave and I remain in the tub, devastated. They're going to accuse me of everything, that's what I think, even though I was just trying to find a little well-being where it was. I hear them talking, slamming doors, roaring, getting indignant, leaving. What will Gabriela think and say? Will she, too . . . A man comes in, *a solid American*, ready to reprimand and arrest me. But suddenly he sees my face, and frightened, he says to me: "What's happening to you? That hole has been stopped up since January 7 . . . " Then I see myself through his eyes: my right cheek is visibly turning black, a hole is appearing through which my last teeth pop out and fall, one by one. The dream ends, and waking, I panic, confronted by my mouth that is leaking and through which my whole body, behind the teeth, is emptying out.

Before the attack, I was thin and athletic; I was 5'9" tall, I had my father's delicate frame and my usual weight was about 160 pounds. When I arrived at Les Invalides, I weighed about 125 pounds. I didn't have a bone to lose, so to speak, but one had already been taken from me, and that was quite enough. The time when the graft of the fibula onto my jaw might have necrosed had passed, and it was not planned to take any more. However, the body hadn't stopped helping the body, like a do-it-yourself survival and reconstruction kit, like the magical hold of Robinson Crusoe's shipwrecked vessel. It had given about all it could. It was at the end of its rope, but reeducation began after the end of this rope. Was there another one behind it? At the moment when I discovered it, I regretted having to inventory it, as the doctors inventoried their patient's ills when I arrived at Les Invalides.

I was beginning to speak again, but I no longer knew whether my voice was my voice: it came from a place in the body that seemed to me mysterious, cavernous, and I didn't recognize it. This nonrecognition worried me. When I spoke, I had the impression that gibberish was coming out of my mouth, mashed up by teeth I no longer had. I didn't understand why people seemed to know what I was saying and sometimes wondered if they weren't feigning. I didn't know, either, if my mouth, which was still not reconstructed, was my mouth: this strange, split lower lip, asymmetrical and hanging down, that slowly and with difficulty pushed toward the toothless inside the few liquid foods that it was given—that lip disgusted me and I distanced myself from it by calling it *the membrane*. The graft on my calf became inflamed and resembled a poor-quality ground beef patty, dripping with grease. The graft made by Hossein was "smoked," meaning that it didn't take. I had to return a week later for another try. As for my right little finger, an X-ray had just shown that its first phalanx had become fused. "An operation will be necessary," the radiologist told me, "there are excellent hand surgeons." I began to feel dizzy when I stood up: my right inner ear was acting up, and I was told that calcium crystals must have moved. Gabriela had started calling me on FaceTime again. Our connection was poor. She suggested that we shift to sign language.

Patients often fall silent when faced with impatient people. I understand them, and I also keep silent; but it seems to me that we're wrong. It would be better to plunge other people's heads in what they can't or won't see, know, or imagine. That has to be done regularly, concretely, gently, coldly, at the risk of seeming disagreeable, self-indulgent, aggressive, whining, oversensitive, and inclined to harp on things—in short, someone who makes others deaf. And it is all the more important to do it because those who listen understand, at most, a third of what they hear—if they listen in good will: words communicate poorly to the healthy people a labor performed by the body that worries them and is, for the most part, foreign to them. Words don't seem to come from the body they're trying to describe, and they have no chance of connecting with it if the patient doesn't persist. Modesty, pride, stoicism? Just so many celebrated virtues that I believe I've practiced sufficiently to sense their limits, their ambiguity, and to what point they allow people to forget the suffering of those whom they pretend to respect at the price of their silence. Proust was ill during much of his life, and that may be why, not without a certain situational comedy, he saw only pretense, solitude, poses, and misunderstandings all around him. Illness is not a metaphor; it is life itself.

Let's continue. Doctor, are you listening to me? My right leg and foot hurt, and my right thigh does too, even more at night than during the day. Simple contact with the sheet irritates my whole foot and prevents me from sleeping. The nerves seem to be raw. The malleolus is particularly painful. Day and night, I put support hose over the dressings: if I forget them, I immediately swell up. My chin tingles increasingly, it's *alive*. I've come to believe that I think through my chin. Fortunately, I don't think much. When I do, it seems to say to me, as the ant says to the grasshopper: shut up and work on your reeducation, getting ready for the winter that's coming. Winter is the return to ordinary life. As far off as it may be, it terrifies me. I know, Doctor: The Les Invalides hospital is intended to limit that terror by bringing me closer to the winter that inspires it. But I will need time, if you will grant it. In the meantime, Malebranche's philosophy will do me a world of good, especially when he writes:

All these things show that we constantly have to resist the effort that the body makes against the mind, and that we must gradually accustom ourselves to not believing the reports that our senses make to us about all the bodies that surround us, which they always represent as worthy of our application and our esteem, because there is nothing sensible that we should linger on, or with which we should busy ourselves.

But I hadn't already read Malebranche when I entered Les Invalides. Even if I had, I wouldn't have been able to accept his view, precisely because my mind was increasingly subordinated to my body, to the extent to which this body was leaving the zone where it had invaded everything. The mind resisted the body insofar as both of them were living in the ruins. Now, the body was waking up to life again, but it did so through unprecedented, unforeseeable, painful sensations that the mind was unable to assimilate, and that it perceived as intruders. It no longer rose above symptoms and signs; it kept an eye out for them, like a shopkeeper.

The areas of the graft were oozing. The failed graft took on a dark color and its odor entered my nose at night. My right little finger, which was still stiff, was painful and its swelling did not go down, making my hand almost impotent. The long scar on my arm didn't stretch well. My forearm was hollow like a dead branch. My neck was a periscope. I turned my whole torso to look to the right or to the left. Except that I lacked a monocle, you'd say I looked like Erich Stroheim in *La Grande Illusion*. I dreamed about putting a geranium in a pot in front of my new window. I would cut it on the day of my departure, which I hoped was as far off as possible. The scars around the flap were fragile. Every time I shaved they were in danger. I spent a ridiculous amount of time in the bathroom dealing with their asperities. I drooled when I talked, when I slept, when I ate. When my pains left me in peace, I was awakened ten times, sometimes by a desire to take a piss, sometimes by snoring that degenerated into apnea. The soft palate must have been damaged; I have regular sniffing fits like an old man's, and they degenerate into coughing, as if my throat wanted to compete with my sinuses. Everything is connected in there, despite good sense. It's anarchy. The melting away of my muscles hasn't helped my back, I who never had back trouble.

And to wind this up, this new phenomenon: hairs from my leg grew out of my mouth and established themselves on my reconstituted lower lip: they looked like minuscule black algae that water has stuck on a seashell or coral. They had been there since the graft of the fibula. Since they were shaved off, it took them some time to grow back in their new milieu, which was liquid and warm. They began to form little tufts that I felt when I ran my tongue over them. So long as they stayed inside, it was bearable. But I didn't much like them to accompany my meals, my outings, and my discussions. On this point, I insisted on my modesty. I didn't want to be, in the eyes of outsiders, an *ape inside*. I had not been warned of this little problem. For the surgeons, whatever is not a matter of treatment or necessity is a matter of comfort, that's the word they use. Leg hair in my mouth is a matter of comfort. It forced me a little more to conceive of my body differently, in accord with the exploded forms of one of Picasso's Harlequins. How should I cope with and feel this insensitive skin from my leg on my chin, this skin from my thigh on my calf, this leg hair in my mouth, this inside-out, poorly vascularized mucous membrane that serves me as a lip, this Integra graft based on horse or pig tissue placed along a substitute gum that is irritated by the slightest contact? Sometimes, I wake up with a milk tooth in my nostril, a fingernail in my right ear, eyebrow hairs on the second navel formed by the feeding tube. I also have a foot incarnated in place of the little finger, and a knee covered with scabs, as when I was a child, between the joints of my hand. I have become a discreet monster with staples on the upper part of my ass, but that is not a product of the imagination: it's the bedsore taking advantage of my skinniness and the delicacy of my skin to grow larger. What's that you say, Doctor? Here you have dressings that are more effective or better suited to the wounds than the ones at La Salpêtrière? The army is better endowed than Public Assistance? I can only rejoice in that: any relief is welcome.

My mental state was no better. I emerged from two months of intensive care as from a long dream, with multiple hangovers at once. The delicate moment, Doctor, is the one when the patient regains consciousness of the metamorphosed body in the living world that surrounds him. It's then that he really begins his rebirth, and this rebirth, which was up to this point manifested by physical shocks of an almost magical violence, is now accompanied by a certain sadness: I'm leaving the cycle of Hell's cauldrons to enter the cold bath of Purgatory, which is hardly better. I weep over my lost life, I weep over my future life, I weep over my obscure life, but you won't see me weeping. There you are, Doctor, that's where I am. I see you're taking notes, that's good. But is it enough?

Philippe Lançon fell silent and Monsieur Tarbes moved in.

The room was small, old, with an old-fashioned charm, and at the heart of my suffering, I immediately felt comfortable there. I'd been told that a writer had lived in it, and I know that Edgar Pisani followed me there. The view was also a large part of its attraction, and probably also the memory of a memory: it resembled a *chambre de bonne* I'd lived in when I was a student, on the Rue Notre-Dame-des-Champs. That attic room belonged to two old ladies who lived together a few floors below, and whom I sometimes went to see at teatime. The window of the room at Les Invalides had a broad sill where I put my books and CDs. It was like the one where, more than thirty years earlier, I sat to read Proust, already Proust, while looking out over the roofs. The bathroom was almost as large as the bedroom. When I opened my eyes, what I saw from my new bed was no longer La Salpêtrière's gray roll-up shutter or its dark pine, but rather, beyond the tall, wooden lattice window, beyond the trees in a courtyard that dated, like the other buildings, from the age of Louis XIV, this illuminated cupola. In the daytime, its gold shone in the sky which, that spring and that summer, was almost always blue. At night, it was even better: the illuminated gold stood out against the black sky and I fell asleep looking at it. I still had neither telephone nor television. One of the policemen sat in front of my door, the other at the end of the corridor. As at La Salpêtrière, they changed every eight hours, and I was beginning to see again the men who had guarded me once or twice in what was already becoming my earlier hospital life. One of them accompanied me wherever I went.

The first policeman came from Cherbourg, and he was very young. It was with him that I slowly explored the main courtyard and all the gardens, in particular the lawns that dominated the grand esplanade. You get there from the main courtyard through a door from which the spectacular view of the Alexandre III bridge and, in the distance, the Grand Palais, opened my heart and my life by dissolving me in a painting by Manet. In the dark, it was even more beautiful. Despite my condition, my fatigue, despite the early March cold and sometimes despite the rain, I did not give up a single one of my nocturnal rounds. I wanted to return to that view, that sky, the Seine sensed beyond the row of trees, the roofs of the great museums, and far on, the slopes of Montmartre, all the centuries of this city that I loved and in the heart of which a handful of cartoonists had been unexpectedly massacred. I wanted to enter into that view, as I had entered a valley in the Pyrenees, and every morning and every night I entered Manet's *Jardin d'hiver*. An elegant woman was sitting on a bench, pensive, and she was me. A standing man was leaning over her, bearded, and he was me. Around them were plants and pink flowers, and they were me. Manet seen from Les Invalides was not solely an atmosphere. The gaze of its figures, that slight absence, that suspension above being, was what Philippe Lançon was looking for and what Monsieur Tarbes, without looking for it, found; but it would soon be around another painter that the union of the two would take place.

For the moment, I was limping across the disjointed paving stones of the courtyard of Les Invalides in the company of the little police officer from Cherbourg. We stopped in front of the two tanks parked to the right and left of the gate. He looked at them attentively and told me their history; he constantly read books about the two world wars and the armies that had fought in them. Several times, I encountered encyclopedic policemen. Then we advanced toward the lawns bordered with trimmed boxwood and were delighted to find lots of rabbits there. They came out especially in the morning and the evening, when Les Invalides was closed to the public. This was then their domain, and they took advantage of it, in all positions, shamelessly. Some stretched out on the grass like Lolitas, their asses in the air. Others remained upright, absolutely immobile, for several minutes, then started running madly around in the absence of any hunter.

Monsieur Tarbes was slowly being born, but Philippe Lançon felt alone and scared. He'd left the world of surgeons, those artists of emergency, for that of the reeducators. The Les Invalides hospital had been, since it was created by Louis XIV, a military hospital, dedicated to soldiers wounded in combat, and now to victims of terrorist attacks; but *gueules cassées*, those soldiers disfigured in the First World War, were no longer to be seen there—even though a beautiful blue poster reminded visitors that there was an association that brought them together. Above all, there were now amputees, paralyzed patients, stroke victims, victims of cranial trauma—and two of my wounded and surviving companions from *Charlie*: Simon, the webmaster, and, more episodically, Fabrice, a journalist committed to the ecological battle, who had already been wounded in an attack thirty years earlier.

When I arrived, Fabrice had gone home for a few days: he had young children and, despite his crutches and his leg pains, he wanted to be with them, I think, as much as possible. For his part, Simon had emerged from a coma and was beginning a slow reeducation. He could speak and move his arms, but he couldn't walk. His room was near mine. One of the first things he said to me when I went into his room was "Now we're blood brothers." Another friend from *Charlie*, Zineb, was there. During the Wednesday editorial meetings, which might also have been called reaction meetings, her bellowing tirades against the condition of women in Muslim countries would have awakened the dead that most of us were not yet. She had been lucky enough to be absent the morning of the massacre. The Islamists had put a price on her head, and like me, she was protected: our bodyguards made a real crowd in the hallway. In Simon's room, she wept a little, not too much. Neither Simon nor I were weeping, at least not in public. Tears brought us nothing except a loss of pride and energy. On that day, he was eating a cake that looked excellent. He offered me some, but my mouth was in no condition to accept it, and I gave it a baleful look, thinking: "You get the cakes, I get the walks!" The paralytic and the *gueule cassée*, observed by our slightly mad Arab Amazon, who was savagely feminist, infinitely alive, and who was soon to go to live in a country on the Persian Gulf: all three of us had ended up laughing at the situation, as if we were going to be in a cartoon.

Looking very small on his bed, Simon was living like a marmot in the depths of his burrow in winter. He was thirty years old, but now seemed ageless, or rather, the bullet that had struck his neck and then slowly made its way through his back had given him every age. He was as young as a newborn and, when he thrust his head out a little, as old as a gargoyle. His intelligence, irony, and vanity gave him a layer of fat that protected him from himself and from intruders. I say: his vanity; but aside from the fact that I was no less vain, I didn't see it as a defect but rather as a quality important for survival that was certainly as good as any other, and did not deserve to be judged. At La Salpêtrière, I myself had redeployed an old habit of seduction, not to flirt with the nurses, but to maintain the best possible relationships with the ward's personnel. That was the alchemy of long-stay hospitalization: survivors were allowed all their defects if they made good use of them. Here, we weren't in a bourgeois salon; we fought with each other without judging, without limits, but with all our little weapons. In that respect the spirit of *Charlie*, the paper that fussy people wrapped in virtue, wherever they came from, had never ceased to detest or despise, was well-suited to the occasion: it allowed us to laugh at everything, and first of all at ourselves, using all available means. We hadn't deserved our fate, but that was no reason to suffocate us with principles or take us seriously. For that, there would always be enough people who didn't like us, and they weren't going to be slow about it.

When he wasn't sleeping, Simon was fighting: against pain, for meditation, seeking out each new movement and, later, each new pleasure. He listened to minimalist music, in particular Steve Reich. His future wife, Maisie, discreetly carried on around him a mad, concrete activity: I sometimes met her in the great deserted corridors with a bag of linen, sometimes clean, sometimes dirty, and good quality food. Simon had necessarily become a tactical hero in his burrow. He could not afford the luxury of ordinary altruism any more than I could. So he obtained from caregivers, friends, and institutions everything he might not have been allowed. Les Invalides was a well-protected harbor, with its unchanging beauty, its courtyards, its gardens, its top-flight centers for physical therapy and ergotherapy, where the hull, the sails, the rudder, and the morale of the albatrosses we were could be repaired; but even here, where good will was the rule and keeping your word was a principle, people, places, teams, and the situation had to be analyzed and you had to learn to fight in order to last. It's unfair, but that's how it is: the victim has to be intelligent, obstinate, unscrupulous, and armed: he doesn't have the right, unlike those on whom he depends, to be weak.

Simon and I quickly understood, together, that we had to avoid either exposing ourselves to or believing too much in the political discourses that sanctified us. What we had to do instead was to learn to use them to strengthen our situations when we could: victims don't live in the short term in which contemporary strongmen prosper. We advised and supported each other almost daily for months, and we flattered each other, of course, and even to excess, but, I believe, without lying. There was no question of failing in our reeducation, either for him, or for me, or for either of us with respect to the other. That is why, having begun as allies, we became friends.

I was now going to be cared for and monitored in accord with Chloé's directives, but in her absence. However, she wasn't far away. Once the initial tests and samples were taken, I opened my computer and found the e-mail that she had just sent me:

Hello,

So here you've gone off to Les Invalides—I got out of the operating room too late to be able to say goodbye. I'm convinced that your new place of hospitalization will be able to meet your need for rest. In any case, we'll see each other next Monday for your new skin graft.

The 20th seems to me doable—to do it, I just have to call in sick for a boring meeting, another one, that is planned for that morning. I'll have to leave the museum by 2:30 at the latest for the rest of the day.

See you very soon.

For me, Friday March 20 was an important date: I was going to visit the Velásquez exhibit at the Grand Palais. Ever since my first days at La Salpêtrière, it had been an obsession. I knew that it would take place in the spring, with the spring, and saw in this the sign of my rebirth. I'd said to myself and to my brother, my parents, Claire, and the caregivers that I'd be up for writing a review of it in *Libération*. It would announce my return, and I'd invited Chloé to go to the exhibit with me. It was, after the gift of Chandler's works, another way of thanking her. She had accepted.

Velásquez was not only a painter whom I would enjoy writing about. He was one of the painters who had fed my imagination. Ever since my first visit to the Prado Museum twenty years earlier, I'd never gone back to Madrid without spending time there, alone, in the rooms with *Las Meninas*, Goya's *Pinturas negras*, and El Greco's paintings. This trio had shaped my way of seeing, fed my love for Spain, illuminated joys, pleasures, and depressions. One day, I'd had to rush out of the room where the *Pinturas negras* were; I was on the brink of fainting, I took refuge upstairs in front of Velásquez's jesters, those intense and marginal samples, intense because they're on the margins of humanity: their infirmities had always reassured me. Now they resembled me. The courts of the kings of Spain, with their suffocating ceremonials inherited from the Dukes of Burgundy, ultimately seemed to me more open to disgraces than the society in which I lived, even if it was in order to transform those who suffered from them into entertainers or pets.

El Greco's elongated expressionist figures, which seemed to stretch unduly toward the heavens, had filled me with enthusiasm for an even longer time. I saw them as figures in a comic strip, but also as a species of extravagant, mystical greyhounds in whose company I could go for walks against a background of tropical green under a stormy sky. I wanted to throw my arms around the necks of his saints, caress their wrists and hands as if to elongate them still further. I wanted to see and see again *The Burial of the Count of Orgaz* and leave, as I did on each trip there, part of myself in Toledo, in that spiritual and physical splendor, among the bouquets of beards and angels. A year earlier, the four hundredth anniversary of El Greco's death had been celebrated in Spain. I'd joined Gabriela in Madrid, and from there we went to Toledo, where works from all over the world had been assembled alongside the ones in the permanent collection. Seeing Velásquez again in Paris a year later, two and a half months after the attack, had become of vital importance for me, without my knowing precisely why. The challenges that we set for ourselves are also issued in accord with our reveries. And this exhibit might bring me closer to one of those moments whose nervous distance caused me so much sorrow; it might bring me closer, through the visit and the article, to my past.

I'd been at Les Invalides for ten days, and the second graft, which Chloé herself had just carried out by making a brief round trip between the two hospitals, had failed in turn. On the morning of Friday March 20 they came into my room one after the other, the people from La Salpêtrière and those from Les Invalides, as if to rehearse a play during a set change: the head doctor of the reeducation department, the intern, a nurse, Chloé, and the woman who, for the next two and a half years, was to become a force in my life almost as dominant as Chloé: Denise, my future physical therapist. I'd chosen her on the advice of one of my physiotherapists at La Salpêtrière, for two reasons. She had more or less created the job in the 1960s and did more demanding work with her patients. Her office was a hundred meters from Les Invalides. She was seventy-two years old, and immediately reminded me of one of my grandmothers, the third one, the one who did exercises every morning with a broomstick while she listened to cantatas. Denise looked at me and, with a cheery air and a booming voice, as the head doctor watched circumspectly, she began to explain the first exercises, in other words, the first grimaces I was going to have to make. Her beautiful face with bright eyes twisted with extraordinary ease when she imitated an ape, a rabbit, a hamster, all the animals that were going to become regular parts of my mandibular menagerie. She was capable of jutting her chin or sticking out her tongue farther than you might have imagined, and her face, in this little room, suddenly resembled the Romanesque gargoyles at Vézelay and Autun.

Chloé had come to accompany me to the Grand Palais, but also to inform me that I was returning to her department the following Monday: "This time," she told me, "we're not going to let you go as long as this isn't entirely fixed." I asked her how long that would take. It was one of those stupid questions that I continued to ask in spite of everything, knowing that I would receive no answer: a surgeon doesn't reply if he's not absolutely certain of the response, and he almost never is. She answered with a sort of smile that drove the question out of the room like a fly: "I don't know, a week, ten days . . . " I looked at the head doctor with concern: could I keep my room until I returned? He understood my worry and said: "If it's a week or ten days, no problem, we'll wait for you, you can leave your stuff here." We continued to talk for a good half an hour. We were all standing, and once we were outside, Chloé said to me: "We all have backaches, except you, standing ramrod straight. Basically, you're in better shape than we are." I said to her: "It's because I do sports . . . " I'd begun the stationary bicycle and the treadmill in the gymnasium at Les Invalides, under supervision by the physical therapists. Resuming physical effort relieved my jaw by distributing the pain. The bicycle was across the room from a machine behind which either a paralytic or very old man positioned himself to strengthen his arm muscles by working a double crank. Our eyes scarcely ever met.

Since the weather was good, though a little cool, I put on my mask and we went on foot to the Grand Palais over the Alexandre III bridge. The gold of the statues shone violently. The air whipped my face. The two policemen walked, as usual, a short distance behind us. Florence, my friend at the National Museums, had had a little difficulty organizing this visit: the officials at the Grand Palais were nervous about the idea of being visited by a potential target, and in any case a protected one, and still more about the idea of allowing other policemen to take charge of security in their domain. Florence had overcome the obstacles and had hidden it from me, of course. At the entrance to the Grand Palais, the head of the security service, a dark-haired slender woman with an ironic expression, was waiting for us: the policemen had told me that she didn't want to miss the opportunity.

Certain e-mails written that same evening indicate that I had reservations about the exhibit. Today, I have no critical memories of it at all: they disappeared in the seminal feeling it elicited. The sensation of being reborn by joining together the two ends, before and after, dates from that visit; and with it, the moment when painting took precedence over literature in the physical thrust toward life.

We were walking in the silent, deserted rooms, far apart from each other, suddenly moving closer to look at one of the portraits of jesters, nobles, or inquisitors that gave you all at once, from birth to death, from farce to tragedy, all that was dull and all that was brilliant, all the perspectives on life. I was drooling a little, my nerves were terrifying my chin, but I felt almost good, as if these men, these women, these animals, who had long been dead, and whose destiny hadn't been rosy, were looking at me and saying: "You're going to live." They were there, I was there, I was looking at them, four centuries were equivalent to a minute and we were living.

The paintings had just been hung. The labels hadn't all

been attached. A restorer was using a flashlight to examine the scars on *Venus at Her Mirror*, which a Canadian suffragette had damaged with a hatchet in 1914. The policemen had taken out their cameras. They were photographing everything they saw and admiring it with the care of an investigator on a crime scene. You'd have thought they were looking for clues. Chloé fixed her lynx's eye on certain details: I wondered what she could discern in these patients who had escaped her. She pointed out that the Bourbons, and in particular the Infanta Margarita in blue, were suffering from Crouzon's syndrome, a genetic illness whose consequences were part of her specialty: an underdeveloped upper jaw, protruding eyes, excessively far apart, a face giving the impression of a prominent forehead, and an oversized clog chin. I told her that these symptoms were accentuated in the descendants of Philip IV's family, who were painted by Goya. They could all have ended up in the stomatology department. She showed me the foreheads, the noses, the jaws, the eyes. The surgeon's eye joined with that of the painter in making an inventory of human illnesses. Farther on, she stopped in front of *Three Musicians*, which had come from Berlin. The painting made me think of the concerts painted by Caravaggio. Chloé showed me a long, slender black knife planted like a pin in a big brown, round cheese. I looked at the stringed instruments, thinking of the visit Gabriel the violinist made to my hospital room. The knife pierced the rind of the cheese and I heard the *Chaconne* again.

The exhibit followed the painter's development, from his formative predecessors to his heirs. The farther I went, the more the portraits gave me life, either because I'd already seen them or because I'd dreamed of seeing them, and because in this way time and my suffering would be abolished. They represented dead people who were communicating their life to me. Of the court jesters that surround *Las Meninas* in the Prado, only *Pablo de Valladolid* had made the trip to Paris.

Dressed like a gentleman, whose role he is playing at that moment, he is an actor seen on deserted stage, like a bull in the ring, as if in the void. About him, Manet said: "The background disappears. It's air that surrounds the figure, dressed in black and full of life." His left hand is folded over his breast in a noble gesture that suggests that he's about to make a speech. Space is defined by his gestures, and nothing else. His direct, dark eyes have an indeterminate expression. Manet was right: I could breathe the air that he displaced, and that blew away, from the Castilian plateau, the air that I had so often lacked. Through the jester's body, I entered into the painting and I came out of it again in the Prado, twenty years before, at a time when sadness was not justified by the event. It led me through the cold streets of the Madrid winter as far as the Retiro park, which was soon going to close. It was through the body of Pablo de Valladolid that I felt for the first time, not the memory, but the presence of a man I had been. The patient was the jester of the monarch executed on January 7, and the monarch of the jester whom he had been up to the same date. This silent and massive jester now told me that the cards had been reshuffled. I had to play my role, laugh about it, *fabricate* the air that surrounded me.

There was a traffic jam of presences, sensations, and another portrait suddenly tugged at my sleeve: that of the poet Luis de Góngora, the master of *culteranismo*, painted by Velásquez in Madrid at the request of his teacher, Francisco Pacheco. It dates from 1622. Half bald, with a long, hooked nose, the corners of his mouth turning down, Góngora looks like what he was: a bitter genius who had gotten old and fallen out of grace. I had discovered his poems in his native city, Córdoba, on June 19, 1994: on that day a Spanish friend, a young professor, gave me an anthology of Góngora's works in which the date appears, written in my friend's hand. Góngora was his favorite poet, and he gave me the book in a bar near the Plaza de la Corredera. It was a friendly but solemn moment; Tomás took the trouble to explain to me the incomprehensible opening of the first of the *Solitudes*: "It was the flowering season of the year / When Europa's false-hearted abductor . . . " Velásquez's portrait was reproduced on the cover. I've never been to Boston, where the picture is in the Museum of Fine Arts. At the Grand Palais, I pointed out to Chloé the detail that attracted me: a large beauty spot on the lower part of the right temple. That is what led me toward the void through which I had to pass. She looked at the beauty spot, then at the man, and said to me: "He doesn't look easy to get along with." He wasn't. In 1622, ruined, his protectors dead, he could scarcely leave home, for lack of a horse and carriage. He thought of returning to Cordóba. Finally, he was driven out of his home, which his great rival, the poet Francisco de Quevedo, had secretly bought. He died in his native city, alone, five years later. I entered his poems as if they were a labyrinth without an exit.

A majestic riderless horse closed the exhibit. I began my article, published a few days later in *Libération*, with a description of this painting:

The tour ends in a dark rotunda where there stands an enormous, matte white horse in majesty, so potbellied he could no longer jump the slightest obstacle, terribly anti-El Greco, his tail long and floating like the end of a reign. He is harnessed, but has no rider. Velásquez made the painting between 1634 and 1638; experts say it is unfinished. In the upper part of the large brown and gray background, one can make out the body of a naked man, a hero or a god—or simply a man. His mass faces the pictural dusk, the abstraction of a power that dominates and is about to flicker out: that of the Spanish monarchy, or, perhaps, the power everyone thinks he has over his life when the sun is not setting on it.

We returned as we had come, by crossing the Seine. The sun was still a little high. It was colder than on the way there. Chloé walked straight ahead, cheerfully, into the wind. On the Alexandre III bridge, we talked about euthanasia. I was still thinking about joining the Death with Dignity Association. Chloé was not at all in favor of euthanasia. She looked at the sky, the Seine, the gilded statues, and said to me: "You never know what tomorrow will bring. If you had been told on January 6 what was going to happen to you on the 7th, and the state in which you'd arrive at the hospital, you might have jumped out the window . . . and you would have been wrong, because, you see, here you are, on this bridge, you've just seen that exhibit and now you're going to write about it." I sighed: "It's going to be rather tight. Monday I'm going back to the hospital and it's off to the operation rooms. I'll have to write my article before I go. I don't know if I can do that." She stopped in her tracks and looked at me: "So what? You've got the whole weekend and you don't have anything else to do: that's more than enough!" I thought: she's right, and she could have been an editor in chief. The man from the security service had left us. The two policemen were now walking with us. They were listening to Chloé, speaking to her a little, and looking at her: she had charmed them. Her little round, red car, very chic, was parked alongside Les Invalides. She took out her keys and played with them as they looked on covetously and obliquely. Then she said to me: "See you Monday!" and got into the car. The policemen accompanied me back as far as the Laon corridor, where the two uniformed guards and the peaceful Monsieur Tarbes were waiting for me.

The next day, after an early walk around the deserted Les Invalides, and after the morning rounds, I wrote a first draft of the article. Philippe Lançon told Monsieur Tarbes what he had seen, how he judged it. Monsieur Tarbes tried to lend weight to his enthusiasm, to keep him from taking off toward phrases in which the words would have overflowed him. He wanted to make him avoid any judgment likely to debase the experience he'd had. I was drooling as I wrote. Every forty-five minutes, I gave the tingling in my jaw a rest by stretching out on the bed and breathing, but the article was soon written, and I sent the more than mediocre result to Chloé, who did not reply: she was my surgeon, not my department head. I finished the article on Velásquez on Sunday, thinking that I could return to La Salpêtrière in peace.

A few days earlier, my parents had come to see me. We'd gone from statue to statue in the gardens of the Rodin Museum, then walked as far as a bar on the Boulevard de La Tour-Maubourg, where my uncle and my aunt from Tarbes were waiting for us. The weather was gray and cold. I was exhausted and worried. I was walking as slowly as a robot. On the way to the bar, I suddenly thought of the Chilean embassy, which was nearby. It was in a splendid house from the 1920s to which I'd gone, if not regularly, at least off and on. Two and a half years earlier, I'd interviewed there the former ambassador, Jorge Edwards, a writer and a man I liked. In the 1960s, he'd often talked with Pablo Neruda and Louis Aragon there. Later on, I had gone there for a few "tiendas de vinos," informal receptions where people met old friends who were artists, writers, and also a few diplomats. Now, Jorge was ninety-two years old. He lived in Madrid and had written me a note after the attack. He was what people call a bon vivant and a humanist: a distant, warm, amused, refined person whom life seemed to cradle and death to forget. I thought of him—where was he with his memoirs? How was he? I felt sad and said to my mother: "Do you remember the Chilean embassy? I talked to you about it when I went to see Jorge Edwards. He's no longer there, now, but it would give me pleasure to show you the place." We walked up the sidewalk toward the embassy. I was telling her Jorge's story when, about twenty meters in front of us, I saw the silhouette of an old man, upright and a little hesitant, who had his back to us and was heading toward the door that I had several times passed through. I thought I was hallucinating, and if I wasn't, I was going to faint, fall into a hole in time. Were we there, in March 2015, on a gray day, or was I there alone in the summer of 2012? I shouted, "Jorge!" and the man turned around: it was he, visiting Paris. We walked up to one another. He looked at my body, my bandage, and it was only on meeting my eyes that he recognized me. His eyes filled with sympathy and terror, in equal parts, we exchanged a few words, my bandage was leaking, and after having shaken my hand and hemmed and hawed, he quickly escaped through the door behind which there was a very small part of my past.

M emories of life after the attack had intact nerves, but both memories and nerves grew back askew, and it has never been long before they disillusioned me for the better. I felt euphoric on returning to La Salpêtrière, that is, on going home. I hadn't forgotten anything of what I'd experienced, but two weeks at Les Invalides, by removing me from the peculiar levitation of the emergency department, seemed to have transformed my ordeal into an almost pleasant epic dedicated to a surgical, amiable, mystical repair. I was happy to rejoin the people who had saved me and to depend on them again, as if the rest of the world didn't exist. I was happy to become again the hospital room fighter and the regular in the operating room, just as I had earlier been happy to return to the reporting terrain of the Middle East after a temporary stop in Paris: when intensity becomes the rule, it's delightful to submit to it, and anything that seems to lack it resembles a slack period that turns you into a phantom. I believed I was all the happier, or more satisfied, because I had no choice: that damned hole that was preventing the grafts from taking had to be filled in. One after another, the grafts took on a cream color that darkened toward black. My grandmothers would have said they were "turning." I could feel them dying; the failure was right under my nose.

The day before my return, I'd written to Chloé:

Dear Chloé,

Almost all the nurses at Les Invalides have reservations regarding the dressing you prescribed (but follow your instructions nonetheless); they think the DuoDerm is too thick, fails to contain the leakage from the orocutaneous fistula, and allows the skin on the flap to macerate, damaging it. I'm conveying the message, which is, to be sure, no longer of great importance, since I'll be at La Salpêtrière tomorrow.

It's true that I'm leaking more and more, essentially when I speak: I'm living with compresses. If I don't move or talk, it doesn't leak.

I hope you've had a good weekend.

Cordially yours,

Philippe

A DuoDerm is a thick, hermetically sealed dressing that resembles a small pancake. Chloé didn't reply. Later I found out that she'd rapidly become annoyed with a team that, as she saw it, was not respecting her instructions with the necessary precision. Within a hospital, there are many communication problems within a department and between departments; there are even more between one hospital and another. Hospitals are more or less deaf planets. Each one has its own atmosphere and seems to be caught up in the movement of its own rotation.

The hole that was to blame was very small, invisible to the naked eye because it was no larger than a pinhead: a fistula called an orostome. It is a tunnel in the flesh that establishes a link between the inside and the outside. The saliva that passed through my orostome had methodically soaked the dressings and destroyed the grafts that covered it. It reproduced, in a minuscule form, the hole that the bullet had made.

The day before my return to Les Invalides was a Sunday. The policemen accompanied me to the home of old friends who lived in Montreuil, in accord with a procedure that would be repeated until September: they dropped me off at my friends' home, looked around the house or apartment, and then went to have a drink, and eat lunch or dinner in the neighborhood; some even went to exercise in a local gym, and then, a quarter of an hour before leaving, I sent them a text message to let them know and they came back to pick me up. In their absence, every meal and every conversation was a pleasure paid for by a trial. At other people's homes, even those of my closest friends, I was on an excursion to a distant country that was no longer my own. I was relieved to see my policemen again and to return to the hospital in silence, my mouth on fire. I liked their peripheral intensity. They were guarding my security door, like two stone lions at the entrance to a loggia. They connected me with the world from which they protected me.

On that Sunday, my friends served me a glass of fruit juice. I was sitting on a couch where I'd sat dozens of times, a couch full of extinguished memories. While I was drinking, the juice followed the saliva into the orostome and fell on the floor, in a thin, slightly sticky trickle, like a snail's slime. I was given a napkin. I saw the embarrassment in their eyes, over the smiles and words. I was glad to see these friends again, but it wasn't the happiness of returning to a known and tested territory, as in the case of La Salpêtrière. They were behind the glass, in another life, where people had intact lips and hearts filled with joy or wounded by the natural course of things. I was invading this civilized jungle without a horse, like a conquistador with cracked armor.

A few days before the excursion to the Velásquez exhibit, Chloé had noticed the resurgence of the orostome when, using a delicate plastic syringe whose extremity resembled a mosquito's proboscis, she was injecting saline solution into the last graft that had been made. After a few seconds of suspense that allowed me to think that the hole had been closed, a salty taste invaded my mouth. Was it like the one that my maternal grandmother complained about in her last years, saying with her Berry accent: "Today, I've got my salty taste"? I wondered. In any case, the feared leak persisted.

At that time, I'd come only for a graft and two days at La Salpêtrière, but these two days had sufficed to make me nervous, and they should have warned me about the sequel. I had the feeling that I was experiencing a bad postscript to the preceding chapters, and for the first time I hastened to get out of the book covered with blood and saliva that I'd entered. I said to myself that I was going to leak for the rest of my life and that the hole surrounded with pains and commentaries was my destiny.

Now, ten days had passed, and we were far from Velásquez's horse. I returned to the ward for good, but I no longer had the ghost's innocence nor the ignorance of my first days there. I'd become what Pascal would have called "half-clever": informed enough to be an impatient and distrustful patient, but not enough to perceive the nature of the problems and the slowness of the resolutions. The little I knew accentuated my solitude. A time always comes when the patient becomes his own worst enemy.

My new room was the one that in February the policemen had found too exposed. It was the biggest, the one that looked out on that large, sinister roof made of gray concrete. Christiane, the manager, had once again prepared it, but this time the policemen didn't have any objections. The situation had changed. The danger was no longer considered so grave. I remained an important victim; I was no longer completely a target. The arrangement, in short, was living on its own momentum. It was beginning to outlive the situation. This slight change in status relieved me but, I have to admit, also upset me a little. As embarrassing as they might be, we quickly get used to measures that make us exceptional. We may end up thinking we deserve them. Vanity eases the inconvenience.

Policemen had told me, with a smile, about the extravagant pretension of VIPs who used them as taxis and, if their protection was terminated, called the ministry to have it reinstated. The most disagreeable of these VIPs were often the ones in the least danger. However, benefitting from an extreme, official protection offered an excellent opportunity to remember, when it diminished, how little one is worth. I was worth exactly what the event that was bearing me and the external memory that prolonged it, which was beginning to die out, were worth. Few people create their own context and are capable of maintaining it. That was not my case—and all the less because, like some of my surviving companions, although I agreed to be protected, I wanted to remain discreet. However, discreetly, I was upset. Proud people have more than one contradiction, and I was proud.

I had scarcely moved into my room before I looked out at the big gray roof and lowered the shutter: my fear of killers in black had suddenly merged again with the vision of their appearance. For the first time, I listened to Beethoven's sonatas: up to that point, I'd found their melancholy, repetitive violence unbearable. As I listened to them, I looked at the room and understood that the euphoria I'd felt was an illusion. It had taken me only a few days at Les Invalides to welcome a different life. I left the room to go out for my evening walk. The hallway where I'd done so many lengths seemed to me narrow, sinister, and closed. I was back home, maybe, but in the surgical box. I was served a light meal, with a yogurt. Part of the meal, like the fruit juice my friends had given me, leaked out through the orostome.

The next day, at dawn, before going down to the operating room, I received an e-mail from an old friend, Philippe, whom I hadn't seen since 2014 and who called me Felipe. He wrote to me:

> Ever since my childhood, my grandparents have been living near Les Invalides. I completed my military service there in 1989, reproaching myself for being such a homebody. It was as if I were advancing on a spiral Snakes and Ladders board that took me back to my starting point. One of my favorite films was then Jacques Becker's *Le Trou* (*The Hole*): with countless ruses, the prisoners in La Santé prison dig a tunnel, but an error in estimating the topography causes them to emerge right in the middle of the prison courtyard. I really had to get older to rid myself of this sensation of a failed escape.

I wrote down this expression, "Snakes and Ladders," in a big notebook, adding: "Three squares forward, two squares backward. Right now, it's backward." Then I thought about *Le Trou*, a film that I liked as much as Philippe did, the implacable account of a failed escape, in fact. Toward the end, two of the four prisoners emerge from the tunnel they have all dug to see where it comes out. Before returning to their cell, they discover at dawn the open city of Paris, the sky, and freedom. Would I one day emerge from the spell of my holes? I replied to Philippe and a few minutes later went down to the operating room in pole position. I liked to do my e-mail at that moment. Ideally, I replied to those I hadn't seen for a long time, or even a very long time. A series of phantom friends continued to spring up, through e-mail, from various layers of my past life. I was late in dealing with my mail, as if before an interplanetary journey or a disappearance.

When Chloé entered the operating room, I was already

anesthetized. It was the first time I hadn't seen her appear over me. At the moment that I lost consciousness I thought: "Why isn't she there yet?" People learn to go to sleep in the absence of their mothers, that's how we grow up, and now I had to learn to dive in without my surgeon's face. Never again have I seen her from the horizontal plane of the operating table.

In the recovery room, my mouth was burning and I couldn't wake up. An unprecedented hallucination rocked me in the interzone and prevented me from coming out of it. I saw the nurse leaning over me, though she was a dozen meters away, and while I was going back to sleep, her hair and then her whole face were gradually metamorphosed. I hear her bellowing down there, from her office: "Monsieur Lançon, you've slept in long enough! You have to breathe! Otherwise I'm going to put you on oxygen!" I tried to obey her, as in elementary school, but I couldn't. Again, I went back to sleep and the ghostly nurse with a transformed face, leaning over my cradle, until the voice, this time closer, said to me: "Monsieur Lançon! Where are you going? Breathe! Breathe!" I'd never had so much trouble returning to the world of the living and I found that almost a relief. Well-being was on the other side.

Later, the orderly left me along a wall, near the freight elevator. La Castafiore took advantage of this to come to talk to me about music, while she held my hand. She gently kneaded it, as she was wont to do, and gave me Les Invalides' musical programs, which she'd brought along for me. My neck hurt: the last zone of the graft was infected. My lip burned more and more. This time, Chloé had pulled on it to cover the hole. After reflecting on it all night, she'd also made a bold choice: to raise part of the flap against this lip and attach it with a dental roll, making a kind of little bundle of greasy cotton in the middle of my chin. Once again, and for an indeterminate length of time, I had to keep quiet and let my mouth rest.

In the evening, Hossein explained to me, in a calm tone,

that I had to give up the idea of regaining the face and the sensations that I'd had for fifty years. "You'll have them," he said, "but they'll be different, and it will be some time before they seem natural to you." Three years later, at the moment I'm writing these lines, they still don't seem natural.

The next day, I made a tour of La Salpêtrière with my father. A young policeman from Bordeaux accompanied us. My father and he talked about the Southwest and the Pyrenees. I listened to them referring to lakes and summits as I watched visitors, patients, and caregivers passing by in the garden. A spring breeze was making the white coats flutter a little. The voices lulled me as we headed for the exit, where my father had to renew his permit to park his car in front of my building. The woman at the reception desk gave us a wary look and said: "I'm not used to seeing weapons here." My father answered: "It's for my son, he was a victim of the *Charlie Hebdo* attack!" There was sadness, nervousness, but also pride in his voice. Life was a catastrophe full of jokes; he was a subscriber to *Le Figaro*, came from a royalist family active in Action française, and couldn't have imagined reading *Charlie*, still less bragging about it, in a hospital or elsewhere. Blood had mixed, simplified, unified everything. Now he clipped my columns from a journal that he didn't find funny and, like my mother, was in contact with several of the survivors. I wasn't surprised. As soon as individuals, concrete lives, were involved, my father's good will and scruples won out over his anger and his prejudices.

The young policeman played the guitar, and he looked a little like a rocker, with his brown locks and round nose. In an earlier life, he had sung in bars. He read novellas by Stefan Zweig and was a cyclist. I wrote to him that my bicycle had remained in front of *Charlie* after the attack. He offered to go see, as soon as he could, whether it was still there. That evening, as I was listening to jazz, he knocked at my door. I let him in. He asked me what the music was: melodies by the Spanish guitarist Niño Josele. He noted down the information and I left the door open so that he could hear the music. From then on, when I was listening to jazz, I did the same. Room 102 had to open to the outside.

That evening, I turned on, for the first time, my new cell phone, a gift from a friend. I had long believed I'd be able to get back the old one, which had remained on the site of the attack, but it had disappeared into the graveyard of evidence in the case. Since I couldn't speak, I used the new phone to send text messages to my brother and to the policemen who accompanied me, and to reply to Gabriela on FaceTime. We'd more or less made up. She called me every day. I listened to her talk about her problems, her work, her husband, her resumption of her studies. I answered her by writing a few words in capital letters in a notebook that I held up to the cell phone's camera. She wasn't always able to read them. Sometimes she tried using sign language, but I was tired and didn't understand anything. We also wrote to one another, but the e-mails were sources of almost constant conflicts and misunderstandings; I was afraid to read her messages and to write to her. She was going to return in about ten days. The prospect delighted but did not calm me. This time she would sleep at Eric's place; he was the friend with whom I had talked about evil and who had fallen asleep in my room. His apartment was about a quarter of an hour from the hospital. All the same, I'd asked Christiane and Chloé if Gabriela could spend a few nights in my room from time to time. Chloé didn't reply and Christiane finally told me that it wasn't desirable. No one wanted to revive the February comedy.

I now had twelve fresh cicatrices. They all had to heal at the same time. They couldn't do it; the body didn't have enough energy. When a cicatrix opens up, it is said to have dehisced. Dehiscence was in the air. Despite the multiplication of

Fresubin bags, putting me at 3,000 calories a day, I continued to lose weight; healing took all I had. New recurrent dreams fought against the sleeping pill. In one, I was being pursued through the streets of Paris with Marilyn and I smelled the odor of the bullets' gunpowder. In another, I went into a bakery and asked for an apple and a *pain au chocolat*, being well aware that I was forbidden to eat. When I bit into the *pain au chocolat*, I felt guilty. When I bit into the apple, I lost my teeth. I woke up in a panic, sometimes with the odor of gunpowder in my nose, sometimes with my mouth in ruins.

The slightest thing could depress me. For example, the reactions to the publication of my article on Velásquez. People thought the journalist was back, and since I seemed not to write less well or worse than before, they concluded that everything was now going well and that I had gone home, my face reconstructed. The kindness and encouragements of these e-mails touched me, naturally, but the blindness of their authors depressed me just as much. They confused, or wanted to confuse, the writer's condition with that of the patient. I had never so extensively tried out the Proustian sentence before; writing was in fact the product of a different self, a product intended precisely to get me out of the condition I was in, even if it consisted in describing that condition. I wrote about a picture by Velásquez in *Libération* just as I wrote about my series of surgeries in *Charlie*, to enter into the former and to escape from the latter. I also wrote to transmit an experience, but most of the reactions reminded me of Céline's cruel remark: "Experience is a dark lantern that illuminates only the person who carries it."

My concern, as well, exaggerated everything. For example, the letter from Social Security asking me in a threatening tone whether, after what would soon be three months, I was still on sick leave. In which case, the official added, I had to prove it as soon as possible; failure to do so would lead to legal proceedings. I sent this letter around to my friends in the ward. Apart from me, everyone laughed about it: the robot-like functioning of the administration was out of a play by Ionesco—one in which, fortunately, I was not cast.

I began my complaints with Véronique, the psychologist whose walk and bearing had reminded me of those of my mother at the age of forty. She was now the only one, with Corinne the physical therapist, who was capable of providing me with relief; she had the time, not to listen to me, but to read me, because I wasn't allowed to talk. I wrote to her in a big notebook begun for the occasion. I started with these words: "Here, it's hard: the face, the Vaseline that drips, the cops who talk loudly behind the door, day and night, the fact that I'm an old patient who is left alone more, and who is helped much less. I sense that my wounds have become secondary. There are more serious, more urgent cases. But it's Chloé who has insisted on my being brought back."

At just the moment when it seemed to me that I needed her most, Chloé began to avoid me. I signaled this to her, at first implicitly, by addressing her by her last name, a rather ridiculous way of pretending to take a distance that she seemed to be resuming in her dealings with me:

I'm sending you a photo taken this morning, after shaving and the first nurses' visit, because blood was dripping a bit.

During the night, while I was sleeping, my unconscious right hand scratched lightly under the lip, probably because the cicatrix was tickling me, as it did during the day. I woke with a start and immediately called the nurse, who cleaned up.

Earlier, the cicatrix on the clavicle had opened, spraying my shirt with blood.

I'm writing you all this because the weekend here is

rather empty, and the ward, for all I sense and learn, is falling apart a little these days, and transmissions of information from one team to the next from sometimes go wrong, which hardly reassures the patient. But I think you know all that.

This afternoon, I'll go to the theater all the same.

I wish you a good Sunday, despite the rain.

Philippe Lançon

The same evening, she replied:

Hello, Philippe,

Don't be scared by the ambient mess: that's the basic atmosphere of a surgical department, but only initiates, of which you are now one, know that. So thanks for helping us keep this disturbing secret.

Is there leakage through the area laid bare by the scraping done tonight? If no saliva is going through, we're on the right track. Your photo confirms what the team said: the transferred skin on the flap has tolerated the maneuver well. That's excellent.

Good luck and have a good Sunday

Chloé

It wasn't just any Sunday. For the first time since January 6, I was going to the theater—in the afternoon, at the Carreau du Temple. The theater was almost next door to the offices of *Libération*. The excursion had been, as always, arranged by my brother with the policemen from the protection service. They came to pick me up at 2 P.M. and Arnaud was to join me

at the theater with Sophia, who had bought tickets. At 4 A.M.,
an initial nutrient bag was attached to me, and a second bag
at 8 A.M., so that I could go out loaded with calories. Toward
noon, I was so constipated that I began to feel ill. I went to the
toilet and did what I wasn't supposed to do: push hard.
Nothing came out, except sweat and stars indicating that I
was about to faint. I almost fell on the floor, and then, after
catching my breath, I returned to my bed and called the nurse.
Pain was sawing through my abdomen with the slowness of a
torturer. No position succeeded in giving me relief. Ornella, a
young woman of African origin who seemed to deposit her
carefree, gracious smile on my wounds, was on duty. She
brought me the usual enema, with an embarrassed air. I think
she wasn't used to seeing me in this state. I was careful to conceal my private acts from my caregivers as much as I could.
She went out and I injected the enema. It didn't work. I rang
again. It was Sunday. It was some time before Ornella
returned. She needed the intern's agreement to move to a
more powerful enema. Time passed. I was increasingly
uncomfortable. The pain provoked by extreme constipation is
unbearable: you have all the disadvantages of a violent desire
to take a shit without the final advantage of succeeding in
doing so; you feel like you're going to explode, and there's no
release. The sensation dissolves all sense of space and time
without sparing you the ridiculousness of the situation. I rose
and started pacing up and down, like a wild animal, thinking:
"You have to shit, you have to go to the theater, you have to
shit, you have to go to the theater . . . " The pain increasing, I
started counting the steps out loud. Ornella came back and
told me that I looked pale. She took my blood pressure, which
was rather low. Finally, the new enema came. I lay down on
my side and asked her if she could administer it to me. She
smiled, embarrassed again, and said to me: "I'd prefer that
you do it alone . . . " I was ashamed, but I felt grateful. She

was recalling me to a sense of that quality which, in this place, might seem pointless, but which in fact wasn't: modesty. Here, modesty was not a question of morals or decorum; it was a therapeutic act. If immodesty could have improved my condition, I would have shown it.

Thus it was up to me to put the little tube in my anus and wait a few minutes for it to produce its effect. Once the fluid has been released, a few minutes is a very long time; it's an eternity. You endure it as an additional pain and a challenge, which you accept because you want to get out of it. In the end I ran toward the toilet and liberation, a little sooner than was recommended. Two hours later, I arrived at the theater, as proud as Pompey after a victory.

When we came out, I told Sophia that I wanted to go by *Libération*, to see the offices from the outside. I hadn't seen them since January 6. But I had hardly gone a few meters before I began to cry. I couldn't go any farther. A wall of sorrow had risen up, but it also might have been a fissure running through this familiar urban landscape, between the bars, cars, bikes, trees, and dog turds, as through the heart of my existence. I took Sophia's arm. She understood. There was a light rain. We left. It was too soon for me to move closer to my future, to my past.

One expression in the play had struck me: it referred to "patients' deep and unformulated hope of brotherhood." I thought I'd formulated that hope. But at the next day's rounds it was a different expression that I showed the interns, asking them what they thought of it: "What is the impact made on the imagination of a physician by the sufferings that he encounters every day and that he cannot relieve by prescribing treatment?" One of them, smiling, replied: "Here, a time comes when as a result of enslavement and exhaustion you no longer have any imagination. Then the impact is directly on the physician's body: eczema, stomach problems, insomnia, extreme nervousness. For example, I constantly quarrel with my girl-friend." In fact, their schedules were horrific and I, the alba-tross, felt sorry for them when I saw them coming into my room in the morning, their faces haggard and as pale as their white jackets after a series of all-nighters. I knew that they sometimes worked beyond the hours that were covered by insurance. The underfunded and poorly organized institution took advantage of them in order to survive. It was becoming delinquent because it was violating the laws to avoid having to pay the surgeons overtime. And yet here these young, inden-tured surgeons who were always on edge and took excessive risks acquired a rock-solid training. They were like Roman soldiers.

After the interns left, I wrote a column about the perform-ance, which was published somewhat later in *Charlie*. I began writing it with my legs and balls bare under a sterile work sur-face that Constance, the nurse with bright eyes, had set up before being called away for an emergency: she didn't return until two hours later. I could hardly move, but I could roll the work surface over my torso and open my computer. It was while writing this column that I became aware of a state that I had, up to that point, more or less concealed: I could no longer describe what I was seeing or reading without overtly connect-ing it with my experience. The latter became the filter, the vesi-cle through which everything circulated. Anything that did not affect it no longer concerned me; but that raised a new prob-lem, new to me: how to avoid becoming the "vendor" of that experience? How could I use it not as a lure, a brand, a loss leader, or a sign of recognition, but on the contrary as a way of detaching it from myself? The only solution was not to harp on this experience, but to isolate what was taking form within it to the point that the person who had lived—or undergone—it was dispossessed of it.

The next day, I wrote to Chloé again, adopting a more

intimate tone again. Her reply on Sunday had pacified me, but I'd just been told that she had left on vacation. How could she have failed to tell me that? I felt I had rights I didn't have and I was distraught to find her resistant to my abuse. I wrote to her:

Dear Chloé,

I'm told that you've gone on vacation: the patient feels abandoned, but the man wishes you a very good vacation, I hope on your Greek island.

Here, I hear anything and everything regarding the buzzing, the lip which is retracting, etc. People should do what I have to do: keep quiet.

I hope you'll have good weather over there, and that the wind will blow away your worries. This evening, I'm going to see the Philharmonia's new hall. A Pollini concert.

Best regards.

She replied:

Not so far away, alas. Treat with contempt what you hear. If we close the orostome, we've won. The rest will follow in due course. I know that the second part of that sentence is not likely to please you. Nonetheless, I remind you how far we've come since January 7.

Pollini, you lucky dog . . . The last time I heard him was twenty-five years ago in Pleyel, he was playing Beethoven's last sonatas. Savor it.

I'll come by the ward tomorrow afternoon.

Until then

Chloé

So that evening I went to the Philharmonia with Sophia and, as usual, the two policemen. Constance had taken care to make me a fine bandage for the occasion. It was my going-out bandage. I had permission to stay out until 11:30. I dressed as well as I could and put a silk scarf over the bandage. Since the policemen had to sit behind me, our seats were upgraded. Pollini had put together a program spanning a century and a half, with a melancholy free of sentimentality. The works complemented each other subtly and without overly obvious echoes. He played Chopin's twenty-four preludes, preludes by Debussy, a sonata by Boulez, and, as encores, Debussy's *La Cathédrale engloutie* and Chopin's first *Ballade*—the one the Jewish survivor plays for the German officer in Roman Polanski's film *The Pianist*. When he made his entrance on-stage, slow, stiff, and hunched, Pollini was an old man made of porcelain. Once he was at the piano, he was a living stock whose musical roots sank very deeply on the keyboard and inside the soul; it was a relief, a simplification, and an elevation. He let his hand fall easily, and his body gently curled to mold itself to the piano. While he was playing Boulez's sonata, I had a blackout that led me to a hallucination: in that large hall that reminded me of the *Nautilus*, I saw blue rabbits descend from the ceiling in cages, as if through portholes. Were they in reality jellyfish, sharks, or other marine animals? In any case I didn't imagine them; I saw them. This evening out was a bright spot in a stay that was growing darker.

I was in the policemen's car when, on the way back, Gabriela called me. I touched the key and her face appeared, smiling and devastated: her purse and all her papers had just been stolen over there, in New York. She'd made a list of everything she'd lost and the steps she was going to have to take as a result of this further stroke of bad luck. I listened without being able to answer her. That was our situation: a woman alone and fearful was recounting another small disaster, through the mediation of a screen, to a man who was six thousand kilometers away, in a police car, with a bandage on his mouth. It wasn't a dialogue of the deaf, but a dialogue of the dead.

The following day, when Chloé came around, I'd gone to the cinema with Juan and the policemen to see an Argentine film composed of sketches full of black humor, inspired by the most sarcastic Italian comedies: *Wild Tales (Relatos salvajes)*. It was the first time I'd gone to the cinema. It was early afternoon. The theater was almost empty. The film was so funny and so wicked that I constantly snickered into the bandage to stifle the bursts of laughter I wasn't allowed to let rip: my lip might not survive them. Going to see a comedy when you're forbidden to laugh is a strange idea, but it won't surprise people whose wounded and partly paralyzed faces have lost all expression. I wanted to live and have fun, that's all. I wanted to challenge my cicatrices' future, and perhaps defy them. And my situation added another sketch to the ones I was watching.

When I got back to the hospital, one of the interns checked the condition of the hole with the little syringe that looked like a mosquito's proboscis. The orostome had opened up again and was getting larger. Soon afterward, the intern returned to tell me: "You're going to be operated on tomorrow, no point in waiting for a catastrophe." I heard that word, *catastrophe*, vibrating in the air like a big fly. He'd uttered it with a little forced, timid smile to which I was accustomed. This intern was a bit uptight but he was very sympathetic. His compassion seemed to spring from a certain suffering, a tension that another surgeon finally managed, if not to explain, at least to clarify for me: "His parents are psychoanalysts, and his grandparents are, too. How do you expect him to cope with that?" He was carrying a burden on his shoulders, and that was what made his smile tense. In January he had told me, with the same smile that I henceforth described as sub-Freudian: "Relax! You have to stay calm, Monsieur Lançon!" Stay calm yourself, I'd thought, seeing his tension, and now I seemed to see four couches and his ancestors falling on him as he tried to explain to me, with his kind, squinting eyes: "Most of the work has been done, Monsieur Lançon, but this little area is poorly vascularized and it's resisting. We could have decided at the outset to remove all the skin burned by the bullet and pull together the remaining skin, but that would have twisted your face. We made a choice that is more aesthetic, but also more complex."

Since Chloé was not there, this time I would be operated on by her assistant, Nathalie, an efficient, silent young woman with a melancholy air, whom the department overworked. I was panicked by the word *catastrophe* and by Chloé's absence, and I mentioned this, first to the nurses, then to Christiane. The latter came to see me at the end of the day and said: "You have to understand, Monsieur Lançon. Chloé needs to take some distance. She's monitoring you very closely, but she's very involved in your case, as we all are, and she's no doubt paying the price. She has taken on herself what we call the patient's disturbance. She has to break free of it." Then she went out, leaving me with this new expression, *the patient's disturbance*, which I turned over and over in every direction until it drove out the word *catastrophe*. Was she right? I knew that I'd obtained from Chloé everything that could be expected of a surgeon, and even more. Was that the norm? The exception? Was it the norm of the exception that, because of the circumstances, my own case had become? I didn't have any idea, but I suspected that my failure to heal annoyed her. Surgeons don't like it when their patients don't justify their efforts, and Chloé had a hard time accepting failure. She had put so much energy into this face that it was not permissible to disappoint her. I had never talked to her about that.

The following day, she wrote to me:

Good evening

I stopped by, unfortunately when you were away. Nathalie told me in great detail about your little cicatricial separation. I asked her to rework the cicatrix tomorrow and redo the stitches. That will be done in the operating room but without general anesthesia, if there's a problem a little local anesthesia will suffice.

Good luck, and be assured that I'm following this closely—even from a distance!

Chloé

I went down to the operating room with a CD of the *Goldberg Variations*, performed by Wilhelm Kempff. Nathalie put it on and the operation began. I felt my lip moving toward the right, and had the impression that my whole face was being deformed. The delicacy of Kempff's interpretation, its inner clarity without tragedy, struggled against the sewing of the stitches with an efficiency that I think Glenn Gould's interpretation wouldn't have had. It applied a gauze bandage to the flesh and the spirit. The operation lasted forty minutes. Back in my room, I took up an anthology of ancient Chinese poetry that had somehow come to be there and read a poem to a nurse who was passing by. It was about snow, time, and solitude. It was short. She listened in silence, and then said: "It's sad, it doesn't make you feel great, but it's beautiful." And we laughed.

A few days later, while I was out walking, I approached, with my two policemen, the psychiatric ward. As I said above, the building in which it was located, called La Force, was one of the oldest and most beautiful parts of the hospital, and I wanted to show it to them. Unfortunately, we couldn't see the inner court where, in the past, the insane and women considered to be "lost" were chained to iron rings in the walls. A nurse was smoking, looking blankly into the distance, in front of the entrance to the kitchens. We came closer. She watched us with a wary curiosity, like the woman at the reception desk to whom my father had talked, then she asked me what had happened to me. I took out my notebook and explained it to her. I added that I was showing the building to the men who were protecting me. She threw away her half-smoked cigarette and, after having looked us over, she said: "Well, it's forbidden, but come on anyway, we'll go through the kitchen." We followed her through the smells of the cafeteria. The passage between the furniture and the stoves was narrow. The policemen walked slowly, holding their Berettas close to their bodies. Through the windows, we could see the old, forbidden courtyard. A few mentally ill people were there, some standing, others seated. The nurse showed us the marks made by the old rings on the walls. Farther on, one of her colleagues showed us the space called the "the courtyard of the massacres." Three and half centuries had passed. The women and men who had been chained up here were dead, their lives almost forgotten. There nonetheless remained traces of the suffering that had been imposed on them here, in the heart of this city devoted to the industry of health care.

The days were passing. We were waiting to see whether, after Nathalie had worked on it, the orostome was finally sealed. There was a strike at the hospital, and everything seemed disorganized. I went to see a Poussin exhibit at the Louvre, for *Libération*. The visit exhausted me. The catalogue and a monograph were delivered to my room. I put them on my bed, which I'd raised to make lectern of it, and showed the pictures to the nurses and nurse aides who passed by, asking them which ones they preferred, and why. I had an article to write and I would have liked it to mix their ways of seeing with mine, so that there might be an absolute link between the hospital and the museum. Leafing through the monograph, a nurse stopped to look more closely at *The Flight into Egypt*. She described the color of the clothing, the position of the ass, the eagle on the rock, and, after examining at length the child in his mother's arms, she suddenly told me something she hadn't mentioned in three months: how she'd lost her child, seven years earlier, to crib death.

The following night, Marion, the young nurse with cat's eyes, watched part of *Pierrot le Fou* with me. It was the second time I'd watched it there. Its Rimbaud-like despair continued to move me, but I'd never been so sensitive to its beauty. Marion didn't know the film, but its colors enchanted her. She left before the hero died, running to another room where a patient was suffocating. In my notebook, I wrote a phrase Poussin wrote in 1642 that may have summed up what I was looking for: "My nature forces me to seek and to love very well-ordered things, fleeing confusion, which is as contrary and inimical to me as light is to dark shadows."

Another night, seven broken jaws arrived. The next day I took a photo of my face and sent it to Chloé. She finally appeared and I quickly understood that even though it was still unknown whether the orostome problem was solved, my release from the hospital was on the agenda: but to go where? Was I to return to Les Invalides? My things were still over there, in the room on the Laon corridor, but the nurses' station had called my brother several times to ask him to clear out the room, though he hid this from me in order not to add to my anxiety. As a CEO, Arnaud was used to conducting negotiations. He played dead, and sensing that he wouldn't obtain anything from Chloé, he contacted the man from the Elysée, Dr. S. It was a Saturday. Dr. S told him, above all, not to reply to Les Invalides, which he would contact the following week. For my part, I felt everything but I didn't suspect anything. I was going to learn once again that in the hospital decisions often resemble the patients: they're taken in emergencies and without notice.

Four days later, Dr. S called my brother, who was still hiding the situation from me. I quote Arnaud's diary: Dr. S has spoken, on the one hand, with the surgeon, and on the other hand, with the department head at Les Invalides. Conclusion: the cicatrization is satisfactory, Philippe no longer needs to be in a medical space, he's taking root in the hospital. So he has to leave La Salpêtrière and not return to Les Invalides.

Reading this later, I nearly fell off my chair.

It has been ten days since Chloé last saw Philippe, and messages sent by the medical team suggest that "for the moment, all is going well. Let's cross our fingers." We agreed to meet with Dr. S at La Salpêtrière the day after tomorrow, at 6 P.M. I hung up, a little stunned. At the same time, I was writing to my brother that in view of the state of my cicatrization, there was no danger of La Salpêtrière releasing me in the near future.

That was when Christiane came for the first time to tell me that I had to think about leaving. It was the day for Chloé's visit: finally I saw her. I went out of my room with my drip stand and, in the hallway, with everyone looking on, planted myself in front of her, holding out my whiteboard, on which I had written: "I don't agree!" She smiled. "You don't agree with what?" I erased the board and then wrote: "With my release." She smiled again and replied: "We'll talk about it in a moment . . . I'll come back to see you." Then she entered, followed by the team, into a patient's room. I went back to mine and wrote down about ten precise questions. Chloé didn't come back.

The next day, around 8 P.M., Dr. S and my brother visited me. Gabriela, who had arrived the day before, was present at the meeting. Dr. S had finally gotten Les Invalides to take me back, "for a few weeks, no longer," even though they considered me a burden, a patient who was still too fragile, and, suddenly, he began to scold me: "You're going to have to leave the hospital, Monsieur Lançon! Or else you'll make up your mind to become an eternal patient and never leave at all, but that's another problem. If that's not your problem, and I hope it isn't, now, you have to live and think about the future." He was waving his arms and raising his eyebrows; he was the healthy bull, and I wondered if he saw the man he had under his nose and whom his injunctions were goring. He spoke to me, I couldn't respond, and I thought: is he really giving me a lesson in morality? Is he blaming me for the situation? Was I living the life of Riley at the hospital? That evening, I understood that my compassion credit with the institution was in danger of becoming a debit, and that, as we had sensed with Simon at Les Invalides, we were going to have to be cunning to obtain from Les Invalides what it did not necessarily want to give us. The fact that these institutions are devoted to helping the weakest people doesn't mean they like them. Although those who work in these establishments are full of good will, in reality they want to get rid of such people as soon as they can. Society doesn't seem to be inclined to maintain the roadsides over the long term.

The next morning I wrote Chloé my only ill-tempered e-mail:

Dear Chloé,

Dr. S spent an hour in my room yesterday evening and announced that I would be leaving for Les Invalides on Monday, explaining to me the true reasons for which they in principle no longer wanted me around: I wasn't healed (on the level of the cicatrices, the orostome). I hope that this time is the right one, because there is no "third chance": if unfortunately it's not cicatrized, I won't be able to return there.

You told me that you'd come, that you'd answer the ten or so questions that I left with you in the morning. You didn't come. That wasn't the first time, and after these two weeks of silence, not mine, but yours, I don't know what to think. I'm going off into the fog with my twisted face without knowing whether it's really cicatrized, you hardly glanced at it yesterday, didn't look inside. Now, I remember perfectly what you told me at Les Invalides when you announced my return: "This time we're not going to let you go until this is entirely fixed."

Is it entirely fixed? When you're asking for my albumin, having doubts about the cicatrization? When this morning a nurse still spotted a place that had separated? When everyone here was telling me: "Chloé will come to see you and explain to you"? I'd like to be sure about this. Telling me once again that I've got the patient-who-doesn't-want-to-leave complex seems to me inappropriate; I'm not a child, and in fact I'm now going out almost every day, I force myself to do that, I know I have to do it and I take the initiative. Believe me, it's not easy. What with the body-guards, the nutrient bags to be managed, and the fatigue, nothing is easy.

In fact, all these uncertainties and all this silence only put me in a situation of stress that's not very favorable for reconstruction, and I'm astonished that you aren't aware of that, or that you take it, perhaps, for a simple caprice. Obviously, my life is no longer at stake; but it is nonetheless. The more confidence and security there are, the better things go for the patient. At least that's how it seems to me.

With her professional eye, Gabriela, who is more or less on the same wavelength as you ("You have to get a grip on yourself"), immediately saw, after two sessions in the gymnasium, that I was still incapable of living alone in my fourth-floor apartment, and made that clear to Dr. S.

Where are we with that area right of the lip, which is open and purulent? With the little hole on the left? Can I resume mouthwashes (Nathalie advised me against them after the operation last Wednesday)? When can I begin eating again? How long will I keep the feeding tube? When will I be able to undertake reeducation? What is the condition of the jaw? When can I hope to have the rest, the teeth?

I suspect that you don't have all the answers, but I think you should listen to the questions, and take a quarter of an hour to talk to me clearly.

You will excuse this somewhat harsh e-mail, but I'm disappointed and upset; I believe in the relationship of confidence between surgeon and patient, and in any case between you and me. Neither more nor less.

Have a good day.

Philippe

This time, she replied without delay:

Dear Philippe,

I hear your many reproaches, and I find them, I must say, a little unfair. No matter.

I completely understand your anxieties and your desire for definitive answers and programs—and unfortunately, I can't respond for fear of disappointing you in the event that reality proves to differ from my prognoses. In short, and unfortunately, I know only a few things.

Nonetheless, what I observed yesterday, is that the reconstructive procedure we have been following is bearing its fruits: this morning I received the confirmation that saliva is not leaking under your lip. We'll give ourselves the weekend to confirm this result—and that's why you're not going to Les Invalides, at my express request, until Monday. The fact that there is "no third chance" leaves me quite serene: until I called in Dr. S there was not even a second chance . . .

In short, you're doing as well as possible, at least so far as what falls within my specialty.

I will see you before your departure to Les Invalides.

Have a good day

Chloé

That was—and remains—our only moment of tension. Neither she nor I, nor Dr. S, nor anyone was right or wrong. We all played our roles as best we could, from our own points of view, in an inflammatory situation. And we all acted in such a way that at the final turn, I ended up once again in a place where I couldn't crash. I purged the situation by writing a column entitled "The Guilty Party and His Cicatrices":

There comes a time when the wounded person feels guilty for his wounds: you don't have to be named Kafka for that. He no longer heals, or does so badly. Two or three months have passed. On the arms, the veins have disappeared or hardened, like twigs breaking under a mushroom gatherer's feet. They don't break, but they disappear or slip away under the pressure of the needle. The nastiest of them hold up, suggesting that they're going to cooperate, but after a few drops they say goodbye and take off for who knows where. And the patient feels guilty for this evasion as well: I have nothing more to give you, and, believe me, I regret that. How much the patient would like to participate as best he can in his healing!

But the body has given a lot, its kilos, its energy. In three months, a series of marathons, in the hospital room and on the operating table, have been run in place: the patient is a man of action, an immobile athlete. Now, with the help of nutrient bags that provide him with up to 3,000 calories a day, he's doing everything to close the wounds caused by bullets that burned his skin and those caused by surgical acts. He's attached nine to ten hours a day to his drip stand, which some people call "the girlfriend." In most hospitals, the drip stand rolls rather poorly. Its feet are dirty and it is old, its four casters have rheumatism. Walking with it exercises the arm muscles. You have to find the rolling angle—often, there's only one that works—and learn to lift it over rough patches.

That is Public Assistance: the staff is often heroic, working with worn-out equipment that seems to be related to their low salaries, the efforts demanded by their calling, their hidden pains, and the fact that here, everyone, patients and caregivers, seems to be too expensive for a society whose sole unacknowledged goal seems to be to reduce imagination, attention, and costs; because patients are not the only ones who lead hard lives. Those who take care of them have often experienced tragedies, serious illnesses, or other calamities. One learns this little by little, in the mirror of one's own condition.

I feel that I'm to blame for my cicatrices, because there always comes a time when I feel myself to be alone with them. Alone, and thus guilty, since there always comes a time when the solitary individual feels guilty of being solitary with regard to the group, to advice, to orders that are sometimes contradictory, to the institution that grinds him up and spits him out, to the burden that he represents for his family, his friends, alone facing the society that doesn't wait for him, facing everything. The patient doesn't do what he's told to do, or does it poorly, or not enough. He kneads his cicatrices too little. He doesn't put enough Vaseline on them. He forgets to buy the oil. The sun makes him guilty of exposing himself to it, even for a minute, while moving from one building to another. La Rochefoucauld was never so right: "neither the sun nor death can be looked at steadily." The patient mustn't move that lip too much, because it threatens to "separate," nor that collarbone, where the cicatrix sometimes opens a little flower of blood on the blouse. The patient goes to see his psychologist, his psychiatrist, and there his role is to speak; but isn't speaking a danger to the cicatrix? What must he do to be a good patient, an exemplary patient, that is, cured?

The surgeon tells him: "Courage and patience are the teats of cicatrization." Who would doubt that? But there are times when, like those of certain cows, these teats give nothing: neither milk nor courage nor patience, no matter whether they are milked at dawn or at dusk. Just the weight of time, of perpetual inconvenience, and the fear of "separation." What a nice word, of a deceptive gentleness! A sort of epidermic divorce, sweet and sad. A Promised Land that opens up, revealing a sinister subterranean river whose banks recede. The patient is salivating with concern, and his saliva in turn makes him guilty: it also slows cicatrization. This is the time for him, and thus for me as writer, to console himself with a remark made by Michel Foucault, whose father was a surgeon: "I've substituted for the indelibility of the scar the erasability of writing." At the same time, Gabriela's return was beginning to dissolve the suffering that I was complaining about. When she arrived from New York, she'd left her big suitcase at Eric's place, not far from the Jardin des Plantes. We'd agreed to meet in the hospital's garden, in front of the great chapel. I arrived in advance, with my mask on my face, nervous. She appeared in her big, dark overcoat, with her little dancer's bag on wheels.

The policemen moved away while I hugged her in my arms. I sensed that she was afraid of hurting me. Emotion was overwhelming me. I wept without speaking, she smiled as she spoke. We walked a short way and then sat down on a bench. There were patients out for a walk, modern sculptures, and leaves on the trees again. I took out my notebook, but she didn't want me to write: she wanted to communicate through our faces, bodies, and gestures. We were happy to see each other again.

Over the following days, we finished watching *The Taking of Power by Louis XIV*, by Roberto Rossellini. I continued to assimilate myself with this young king who was learning his new life in permanent view of the court and the servants. He wasn't allowed to make mistakes; neither was I: he to impose himself on the great nobles and the state, I to impose myself on the caregivers. Gabriela taught during the day. The policemen accompanied me several times to the small gymnasium where she worked, near the Père-Lachaise cemetery. The weather was beginning to be fine, almost warm. For an hour, in the deserted gym, she had me slowly exercise my arms and legs, working on flexibility and stretching. One policeman was waiting at the entrance, the other in the car. Next, they accompanied me back to the hospital. Gabriela wasn't authorized to ride in their vehicle, but some of the policemen allowed it. The last time, we crossed the cemetery on foot, talking about our lives that were slipping away from us. We weren't so badly off in this cemetery. The sun was caressing her face and my forehead above the mask. On a bench, a man said to a woman when he saw us: "That guy has had dental problems!" One policeman followed us. The other was waiting for us at the exit from the cemetery.

The orostome seemed to be blocked. I'd finally been permitted to begin eating liquid and shredded foods again, and, at the same time, to spend part of the weekend with Gabriela in

Eric's apartment, which was a quarter of an hour's walk away. Saturday afternoon, two policemen came to pick me up. It was the first time I'd walked alone with them through the streets without friends, without family. The one I knew best had just come back from a three-month assignment in Afghanistan, a country where danger was constant and omnipresent. I knew the neighborhood well, but I no longer recognized it. It had become a fictitious neighborhood, and the Great Mosque had become a film set that my life had abandoned, as it had almost everything. Gabriela was waiting for us in the apartment. The policemen asked us if we planned to go out, in which case they had to be informed. "It would be best," the man from Afghanistan added, "if you didn't go out before we return to the hospital." That way they would be off duty. We closed the door, I took off my mask, and for the first time in five months, I kissed Gabriela very lightly on the lips. I smelled her breath, I sniffed it. Five minutes later we were naked in bed.

Gabriela didn't know how to go about it, she remembered what Chloé had said, and she was afraid to touch my cicatrices. I was now on top of her, but between our two bodies there was still the tube and the little flower of the feeding tube that moved from right to left, from left to right, depending on our movements. I couldn't really kiss her, I was also afraid of opening the cicatrices and of smearing the Vaseline that protected them on her face. I looked at her body, her outstretched neck, her closed eyes, her long eyelashes, that peculiar grimace that seems to combine pleasure and suffering, I smelled her fragrance and my pleasure rising, and wondered if I was dreaming. Miracles are alien to me, but I had so far forgotten the possibility of desire that I wasn't far from believing in their existence. Not far, but not entirely; because, at the very moment when I rediscovered the power of the body, I also sensed its limits, in other words, to be more correct, the threat of premature ejaculation. I was fifty-one years old and I was a young virgin. Despite all my efforts, I wasn't able to control myself. It was a first time, and it wasn't one: more than thirty years of sex life had informed me regarding this situation, without allowing me to remedy it. To postpone a moment that I felt coming, I tried to make an inventory of the books lying on Eric's night table, in vain; then I looked at the little plastic flower that was caressing Gabriela's belly, imagining that in twenty-four hours it would be connected to the drip stand again. Nothing helped.

A little later, despite the policemen's instructions, we went out alone in the neighborhood. I looked at the people uneasily. They were walking fast, without looking, with an indifference that didn't exist in the hospital milieu. From a secondhand bookseller, I bought an old edition of Katherine Mansfield's *Journal*. This act brought me closer to all the people I had been in this very place since I bought my first book on the quays at the age of sixteen. We spent a quiet evening, as if the last months had never taken place. Gabriela had brought some DVDs with her. We watched Charlie Chaplin's *Modern Times*, and fell asleep on this foreign bed while Charlie and Paulette Goddard went off down the road, hand in hand. I no longer know whether it was at dawn or at dusk.

Two days later, in an ambulance and in the company of Gabriela and her big suitcase, I left the ward where I'd spent three months and returned to the little room in Les Invalides, where I was to spend six more months. Gabriela got to see the room, the gymnasium, my physiotherapists, the rabbits, and walked in the gardens and the courtyards. In the early afternoon, I watched her leave for the airport, and said to myself that nothing resembled an ambulance more than a taxi.

CHAPTER 20
RETURNS

On the afternoon of Sunday, April 19 I returned to my apartment for the first time. It was a very simple visit. I had no desire to go there. I was afraid. I had to prepare myself for it.

At dawn, I took my daily walk at Les Invalides, about an hour, that is, I made the whole tour along the moats. I was very fond of these moats, with their silent cannons: they separated us hospitalized patients from the external world, which entered mainly between 10 A.M. and 6 P.M., in the form of tourists. *The people on the other side* were figures who moved more or less quickly from point A to point B. Their itinerary had been planned to go toward the tomb, and the wind soon dispersed them, but their presence was not useless: it mixed us with the world we had left. I liked to go as far as their cafeteria, near the tomb, to watch them drink and eat, to hear them speak in every language, especially those I didn't understand. Ordinary life entered the chateau and our particular labyrinths. Thus we sensed people's mood in a form that was almost entirely forbidden to us: vacancy, frivolity, movement without pain. There is hardly any ease among patients; visitors to Les Invalides provide it for them.

In these old, beautiful buildings, patients were almost immobile silhouettes. They floated in the picture, alone or in little groups. Some of them always sat in the same places in the little garden located in front of the hospital which, with its fountain, reminded me of an Italian garden. A young architect who had suffered a stroke a year and a half earlier was sunning himself to the left of the entrance, in his wheelchair, near a bench. He read a lot, smiled often, spoke little. When I met him, he was reading a novel by Le Clézio. His face was slightly fat, slightly red. His wife had left him. Little by little, his friends had grown tired of visiting him. He was soon going to return to a furnished apartment. He didn't emphasize any of his pains. A kind smile closed the report on solitude and the uncertainties of life.

Not far away, still on the same bench, an old, crippled Harki was sitting in the shade of the trees. He lived in a home in Normandy and came here regularly for treatment. He always wore an old suit with stained trousers and an old-fashioned knitted vest. A grimace indicated that walking hurt him. His hip wound went back to the Algerian War. Once seated, he slowly drew on the ground, with his cane, geometrical figures whose meaning I never understood. I wouldn't have dared ask him about them. He, too, spoke little. His French was broken. His courtesy kept him at a distance. Like the architect, he was alone. From time to time, another Algerian, in a wheelchair, approached his bench. They began to speak in Arabic, more and more quickly, louder and louder, with big gestures, the scene was recurrent and I never found out whether they were arguing or not; then the one in the wheelchair went away, continuing to speak in a loud voice, as do sometimes two old peasants at a distance from one another, as if words were elastics that held them back and became strident when pulled upon. When he had disappeared, the Harki went back to his cane and his figures. Before leaving, he erased everything.

On a bench near the fountain, a young man of about twenty, with green eyes, was smoking in the sun. He had a delicate, nervous face, a tall, muscular body, and he was missing a leg. One evening in a northern suburb, after having taken some substance, he'd quarreled with his friend, and, as the result of a dare or his sorrow, he had positioned himself on the railway tracks when he saw a train coming. He'd gotten out of the way a little too late. In Colombia I'd seen children play this game with the mining trains. The kid who jumped back last was the winner. Many of the victors were mutilated. The fellow with the green eyes emitted a powerful, silent, threatening anger, like a perfume or smoke. He vented it in the gymnasium, pumping iron in rhythm with his groans. Such were the three main figures in the Italian garden.

I went into the main courtyard, which was deserted at that hour. On the way, I met and greeted the director of Les Invalides. He was about to leave and was pensively walking his two dogs. One of them died during my stay. At the entrance to the main courtyard, I climbed the stairway with wide, low steps, an architectural marvel that gave the impression that you were walking without effort. It led to the upper gallery, where the closed cells of the old wounded soldiers, those of the wars of Louis XIV and Napoleon, were located. Farther on, throwing weapons were affixed to the wall. Black-and-white photos of different French wars had been put on the pillars of the arcades. I stopped, as I did each morning, in front of the one that fascinated me: a soldier in the First World War, exhausted, on a road, in a devastated landscape. It wasn't clear whether he was black or white, a woman or a man. All that could be seen above a doll-like body were infinitely white eyes, their pupils pinned against the background of exhaustion and terror. His gaze reached beyond the person he was looking at and who was taking his photograph. He was a ghost.

At the end of the gallery was the main reception room. Concerts, lectures, cocktail parties, or business dinners were sometimes given there in the evening, when they were not held under a large tent erected in front of the tomb. Then at the entrance to the courtyard and the stairway, slender, blond hostesses in high heels stood smiling into the void, getting chilled by the implacable drafts as they asked guests for their invitations. I liked to go back there to have the pleasure of showing my face and embarrassing people. One evening, a guard for the company that had "privatized" the premises came up to me. "I'm a patient," I said. He looked uncomfortable, not knowing what to do. Suits and furs, rather vulgar, were passing by. It felt good to remind this deluxe poultry that there were albatrosses here.

I did my stretches and extensions in front of the main reception room, facing the base of the statue of Napoleon, which had been taken away for restoration; then I went back down the stairs and returned to the lawns with the rabbits. I went along the moats and walked on the old stone benches to exercise my leg without a fibula. My route was precise: I modified it a little only in order to accompany a patient about whom I will talk later, the disciplined Monsieur Laredo. That morning, there was a dead rabbit not very far from the main entrance. I mentioned it to the guards. The next day, the corpse hadn't been removed. I didn't mention it again. I went into the courtyard where the big cannon covered with Turkish inscriptions was, and after looking one last time at the Alexandre III bridge and the roof of the Grand Palais, I crossed the main courtyard and returned to the hospital and my room, passing in front of the nurses' cart. It was time for breakfast.

Next, I went to get some exercise on the stationary bicycle and the treadmill in the gymnasium, which the physiotherapists on duty allowed me to use every weekend in the morning. There was never anyone there. It was a moment of great relaxation. The effort fed solitude. I'd been shown how to use the gymnasium's hi-fi system. I put on some Cuban music and turned it all the way up. The African cleaning lady who smelled good and laughed loudly came in. She pushed her broom around and sang as I pedaled. When she left, she hugged me in her arms and said: "See you tomorrow!" Her perfume remained long after her departure, after the silence that followed the end of the disc. It was the Zafiros, those marvelous imitators of the Platters whose a capella quartet had enchanted the island in the 1960s. Their lives had been tragic and alcohol-soaked. Back in my room, I took a shower, shaved, and put on a protective cream. I had to be careful with the bandages, the wounds, and it took me half an hour. I had started brushing my teeth again.

My brother came in while I was talking in my room with Simon, who now had the room, some ten meters away, that had been occupied by President Bouteflika of Algeria. I recall that we were listening to a disc by Dave Brubeck, but I no longer know what we were talking about. About *Charlie*, probably, because it was a very tense time, and the articles that were appearing everywhere about the inevitable crisis being undergone by the little paper that had become symbolic and was surviving didn't help; even if they thought they understood it—no one thinks himself cleverer than a journalist, I can testify to that—the people who wrote them had no idea what we'd been through. When someone enters a field of reflection occupied by intellectuals or information-makers, a beast is awakened, and he has to wait until the most impatient and mediocre among them has cut his teeth on him. They do this with their theories, their pride, their alleged sense of a mission, their prejudices. *Charlie* had entered a field in which too many people had made up their minds not to pardon it anything.

I got into my brother's car. The policemen in plain clothes followed us in their vehicle. As usual, they'd taken over from the policemen in uniform who remained night and day in front of my room and accompanied me in Les Invalides. The city seemed to me almost deserted. Entering my street, I felt my heart beating a little faster. I wanted to run away, I was no longer at home there, but I had to go. For the first time, I was reestablishing contact with the geographical heart of my past life. The first person who saw me was Lourdes, the Basque prostitute who tricked down the street from my apartment. She hugged me and told me she'd had news from my parents and talked about my father's elegance. She was right, my father was always elegant, with his hidalgo's impeccably trimmed white beard. He could have been in the Prado, couldn't he, Lourdes? As always, we spoke in Spanish, and as always, she laughed thunderously. Her presence relieved me.

My keys were at my parents' home. I got the spare from the neighbors, friends from Mauritius whom I had known for more than twenty years and who had held it for a long time: they kept an eye on my apartment and picked up my mail when I was away. They had continued to do that after the attack. They'd been informed that I was coming by; our emotion was all the stronger because there was no surprise. We talked for a moment and they gave me a pile of mail. Another neighbor, whom I met in the stairway, hugged me. His eyes were red. I was calm, with an almost cold sensitivity. Now I had to get used to receiving these sentimental demonstrations and accept them. The hospital emergency room film, where everything is action only, was coming to an end.

The manifestations of surprise or emotion could be incongruous or even amusing. The previous evening, I'd gone, for the first time, to have dinner at Juan's place. I told the policemen that I wanted to stop at a wine shop a few meters from his apartment where I was a regular customer. The wine merchant began by looking at the lower part of my face, his eyes interested but impassive, and then his eyes rose to meet mine, and it was then that he recognized me. He said to me: "What happened to you?" I gave him a brief explanation. He almost excused himself for not having known that I'd been a victim of the attack, and told me that he'd known one of the victims well, Elsa. "You've arrived just in time," he added: the next day he was leaving the shop to go into the import-export business with Africa, without any connection to wine; and, for the first time, he gave me a reduction on the last bottle that I bought from him. "You and I," I told him, "are beginning a new life."

At Juan's place, there were friends whom I knew well, but hadn't seen for five or six months. It seemed to me that thirty years had passed. There were French people, Italians, Spanish. Their eyes were affectionate or joyous, or uneasy, or panicked. I had the impression that I was walking around in a small glass cabinet, like Degas's little dancer. All the same, I was happy to be there and, for the first time, I drank champagne. Giusi, a woman friend from Genoa who was, for Juan and me, a kind of elegant, depressed sister, took me by the arm and hung onto it a large part of the evening, murmuring, "It's going to be O.K., Philippe, O.K., O.K., O.K. . . . " There was something feline about her, but without the claws. Her words massaged me as much as her hands, which now reminded me of La Castafiore's. I would gladly have given her a saucer of milk, a kiss, or a smile, but I could neither kiss nor smile, and she preferred wine.

Eleven days earlier, she and Juan had come to see me one last time, in the evening, at La Salpêtrière. I'd just resumed eating liquid foods. Juan, a peerless cook, had brought me home-made gazpacho again. I ate it, with difficulty, in front of them, with them sitting in front of the table on wheels and I behind it, in complete silence. Night had fallen. The shutter hadn't been rolled down. It was the gazpacho of melancholy. The slow movements of the soup spoon in the bowl and of the napkin on my chin had created a void in the room and in us, a void of sadness that neither the smell of the tomato nor that of the cucumber could combat. Our old trio was reconstituted in an extreme density, at the very bottom of the bowl. Giusi and Juan ate with their eyes what I was eating, their mouths leaked along with mine. Then, we put on a disc by Bill Evans. We had no words. I pissed all night.

The two policemen, a woman and a man, didn't come into the apartment. The young policewoman had tattoos, an earring, short hair, and bright, violent eyes. Slender, determined, androgynously beautiful, she had the effect on me of a knife in the hands of an Amazon. With her, I felt secure, and as if straightened out. The man, refined and muscular, had a vague resemblance to Jack Palance, but as if the real Palance had been a caricature of the man who was protecting me, because, unlike the actor, he was handsome. He came from Bordeaux.

I went in first. The first thing that struck me was the smell—the stuffy, moldy smell of books and old carpets mentioned in the second chapter; the smell that meant to me: the person to whose home you've been invited here is the one you've become, but the visit will take place in the absence of the former; you're in the show apartment of your past life. The second thing was the big Iraqi carpet, more damaged than I'd thought. I said to myself that it was time to throw it away. The third thing was the stack of newspapers near the window. I went up to it: on top of the stack was the issue of *Libération* for January 6. Nothing had changed since the morning of the 7th. My breathing accelerated. I rooted around among the books and objects with a mechanical nervousness. After touring the apartment, searching for signs of my own presence, and not finding anything, I ran the vacuum cleaner around. My jaw was tingling. Books were piled up everywhere, any old way. I understood my parents' terror when they came in January, and moved a few of the books at random. They resisted. I was disturbing them. Approaching the stack of newspapers, I felt that if I came back soon to live here, it would be for a short time, because I would begin by jumping out the window. An hour later, we left. I returned the keys to the neighbors and took with me a book of Spanish poetry, Luis de Góngora's poems.

Warm weather had set in for months. Since the rooms at Les Invalides were on the top floor and had no air conditioning, it soon became inolerable. During the day, I thumbtacked a double thickness of cloth over my window. The policemen were suffering out in the hallway. In May, fans were given out. Some patients couldn't put up with the noise. At the hardest times, when I wasn't at the gymnasium or in a medical consultation, I went down to the basements to read or to drowse. We had access only to the first level. It was 18 degrees Celsius down there. Men and women in wheelchairs, crippled people of all kinds, and old men were coming and going in silence under its ancient vaults, sometimes helped or pushed along by nurses or nurse aides. Everyone, or almost, was silent. The lights were dim. It was like the guard room in a medieval chateau and like an old Proustian salon toward the end, in *Le Temps retrouvé* (*Time Regained*), and it was, moreover, there that I read part of the last volume of the *Recherche*; but it was not time alone that had transformed faces and bodies, it was the crimes, accidents, illnesses. In these immense stone corridors, there were a few short rows of chairs, less distant from one another than those that have been put on the platforms in the metro to prevent homeless people from stretching out on them. When I was exhausted by the heat and my jaw and by everything, I lay down on them, and despite the lack of comfort, I fell asleep for a few minutes, I dreamed. Here neither the killers nor the heat nor the outside entered. Here the past and the present were not differentiated. It was *mixed time*.

During the week, my schedule was full. At 9 A.M., I had my first reeducation session in what was called the physical therapy gymnasium. Toward 11 A.M., I went to the second gymnasium, located on the other side of Napoleon's tomb. When it was too hot or when it was raining, I went there through the basements. Sybille, a young woman volunteer with eagles tattooed on her arms, was my coach. Before long, she said to me, with a martial and amused air: "You've taken a hard knock, but I'm going to make you a warrior's body. When I'm done with you, nothing will ever be able to enter you again, except me." She demanded a lot, gave more, knew how to make me laugh about my complaints. It was a spirited alloy of overt firmness and covert tenderness. Did I tell her I'd had enough? An ironic glow and a pout appeared: "You're trying to make me cry, right? This isn't the place for that." And the exercise resumed. I pedaled and built up my muscles under her precise supervision between a great, hundred-year-old member of the Resistance and one of Mohammed Merah's victims. That was the moment when, my body working hardest, my jaw kept a low profile.

I quickly returned to my room to take a shower and eat, and then, starting in June, I hurried off to see Denise, my specialized physical therapist, for an hour and a half of efficient torture. I came back around 2:30, rested for half an hour, then went to the ergotherapy workshop, where I gradually recovered the use of my right hand, before finishing up in the first gymnasium with a second physical therapy session. Two weekly sessions had to be added, one with the psychologist, the other with the psychomotrician. They were essential, because it was in them that on several occasions what psychologists would call my "collapses" took place, and it was because of the psychologist at Les Invalides that I stayed at Les Invalides much longer than Dr. S and Chloé would have been able to imagine.

This program hardly varied for months, five days a week. In the gaps in my schedule, I read and wrote my articles for *Libération* and *Charlie*. Ultimately, they were part of the therapy. Friends came by later, around 7 or 8 P.M., after I'd eaten dinner. We drank, and then talked in the foyer, under the tomb of Napoleon. Few people were there. Sometimes, four patients, always the same ones, were playing cards: two of them were stretched out on their stomachs on rolling stretchers, because of their bedsores; one was in a wheelchair, and another had an artificial leg. One day, the latter asked me to film him for his family in Algeria, as he was walking among the trees and the flower beds. We made several takes. It had to be successful, he had to be seen moving every which way on his leg and look good. It was the only time in my life when I took myself for a film director. Friends who didn't know each other came in a dispersed order, witnessed these scenes, talked about the outside world, left together. Several of my lives were mixed up in the foyer courtyard. When my friends went away I was exhausted. Wash glove, Vaseline, toothbrush, the night nurse's visit, analgesics, sleeping pills, drool wetting the pillow, awakenings, nightmares, the view of the illuminated dome.

The physical therapy gymnasium was like a watering hole for animals in Africa: the place where all the patients met. One of the physiotherapists, Maria, a visually impaired young Bolivian, was the first to make me move the periscope that served me as a neck. Since she was going to follow her husband to Australia, Pavel, a young Pole with a shaved head who had spent time in a Buddhist monastery, took over for her. At the time I met him, he was reading a novel by Albert Camus to improve his French, though he spoke the language well. The physiotherapists at Les Invalides were excellent, attentive, and courteous, and Pavel was no exception. It was there, listening to the radio station FIP or to Cuban music, that Monsieur Tarbes drove away or put to sleep Philippe Lançon. Monsieur Tarbes was the man whose cicatrices closed. Each week, he momentarily gave way to Philippe Lançon, who returned to La Salpêtrière to check on the state of his mouth and his wounds; but Philippe Lançon was in a hurry to get back to Les Invalides, that marvelous security door, in order to become once again Monsieur Tarbes, the lover of statues.

The patients who were at the gymnasium, each with his physiotherapist, were of all kinds. The wounds some had suffered were put into perspective by the illnesses of the others: it was rare to hear a protest. We had all failed, for one reason or another, in this separate world, and in it we lived a parallel, secret life, suspended like a car in a repair shop.

There were soldiers wounded in combat, athletes injured in training. There was a very old member of the Resistance who had, for seventy years, been silently surviving his son, who had been killed in the Resistance. There was a sarcastic CEO who'd had a stroke and whose nervous sallies made the whole room laugh. There was a famous former government minister who had the same problem, and who sat in his chair, rolling his furious, desperate eyes. In our earlier lives, I had written a profile of him, but he didn't recognize me. There was an elegant, fashionable young man with an impeccable military-style haircut who was reeducating his crossed ligament. He'd been injured playing soccer. His face never twisted from effort or pain. A few months later, we saw him return for the same injury, but it wasn't him: it was his twin, to whom exactly the same thing had happened, as if he had been passed the baton. He didn't show anything, either, other than his mute chic and his good breeding. There was a handicapped man who was slowly being eaten away by diabetes, like leprosy. He'd lost a leg, and was beginning to lose the foot on his other leg. His diet was draconian, but he was regularly unable to resist eating one or two whole packages of cookies. "I know that I shouldn't," he told me one day, "but I haven't any sense of duty, even here." His passion was rock music and he found a way to get to every concert he could. There was a black boxer, Louis, who'd been shot in the back on a sidewalk after a fight in which he was trying to protect a friend. He was almost always cheery in his wheelchair, and now he teaches boxing in a seated position in a suburban gym. There was an old, bald colonel who rolled down the hallways, his chin in the air, his eyes half-closed, hardly ever responding to those who spoke to him; but when he saw a woman who pleased him, he approached her without seeming to see her, and then, planting himself in front of her, recited a classic poem for her. He knew dozens of them, his room was full of poetry collections and his memory was intact. Thus one day he planted himself in the foyer in front of Gabriela, who had come back to see me in May, and recited to her the whole of Baudelaire's *La Beauté*, without even glancing at me, even though he encountered me almost every day. There was a young soldier from Guadaloupe who had been wounded by Mohammed Merah. Quadriplegic, often depressed, he finally came out of his room when I entered Les Invalides. I pedaled a few meters from him. There was a veteran of the Algerian War with beautiful silvery hair and gray eyes, always smiling, who had been wounded in the leg over there. He had recuperated fairly quickly. Fifty years later, his wound, like a memory, had awakened, no one knew why, perhaps as a result of a dormant virus. Gangrene had appeared and the loss of his leg had definitively refreshed the memory. There was Simon, there was Fabrice, there were twenty others, and there was, finally, the disciplined Monsieur Laredo and the young woman I soon came to call little Ophelia.

The disciplined Monsieur Laredo was a gendarme of medium height, with short, gray hair and black eyebrows, broad-backed, muscular, courteous, indestructibly fragile, and entirely dressed in black, shorts, tee-shirt, and shoes. He had been sent, along with a colleague, on a mission to Erbil, in Kurdistan. The evening they arrived, when his colleague had gone out, he began to float around their little apartment. He saw the walls in motion and the couch drifting away, but this earthquake was coming from inside. He fell and, sensing that he was losing consciousness, he gathered his strength to creep as far as the telephone to make a call, murmuring the few syllables that saved him—but already he was basically unable to speak and space closed in on him. It was a stroke.

He was rushed home and since the end of May he'd been at Les Invalides, with his mute energy and his speech difficulties. He slept little. In the morning, he rose at 6 and went to walk, at a fast pace, twenty times all the way around Les Invalides. When I went out to walk, around 7:15, I saw his black silhouette passing in the gray light of dawn and sometimes I walked with him. His itinerary was still more maniacal than mine. He climbed up on the low walls bordering the moat to avoid losing a single meter of the circumference. He timed his laps as he told me about his mission, his wife, whom he called "the woman," his son, whom he called "the child." Certain phrases emerged without effort, others beat endlessly against a word. I saw him again in the gymnasium, where, between sessions with the neurologist and the speech therapist, he worked out his anxiety on the trampoline that had been installed for him in the delightful courtyard next door, which I called the Chestnut Tree Courtyard. The disciplined Monsieur Laredo jumped, and jumped, and jumped, and Pavel often told me, smiling, amused, and concerned: "If he continues on that way he's going to explode. It's worrisome." Late in the morning, I saw him again in the second gymnasium, where he was pumping iron and working on his abs without making a sound. He would probably have been capable of crossing the Sahara with a canteen and a bag of stones on his back, but unpronounceable words created obstacles more difficult to overcome than a sandstorm, and he feared like death that he would not be able to go on another mission.

The child of a noble family of soldiers, little Ophelia was a student in business school. Three days after January 7, she was locked on a balcony, at a ski resort, by practical jokers in her class. It was night. It was very cold. She was on the third floor. She tried to move over to the neighboring balcony, and up to that point it was a joke, but then she slipped or lost her balance—she no longer remembered—and fell. How, she no longer knows: the briefest violent and unexpected events take their place in our lives, because they are going to turn them upside down, but the details of their irreversible minutes seem to escape our memories—and I write with only the slender hope of being able to restitute them in part. Proust remembers everything, perhaps because almost nothing ever happened to him; but he would no doubt have forgotten, like little Ophelia, how he fell one winter evening from the Guermanteses' balcony onto the uneven pavement below—which would not have reminded him of anything in a henceforth annihilated childhood. And, instead of time lost and regained, we would have been offered what we experience: interrupted time. The book would have been shorter, and no doubt less brilliant: genius is also determined by the limits that it crosses. The time of the sudden event is obscure and infinite. It has no limits.

Little Ophelia remembered only that she had held one of her arms against her body—one day she firmly showed me the gesture, that of a bird mechanically folding a wing as it falls. I wondered as I looked at her: What hunter shot at her? After the fall, there was the coma: cranial trauma. She had ended up in Les Invalides. For months on end, we met every day in the physiotherapists' gymnasium, in the hallways, in the gardens, accompanied or not. Her mother resembled her. In her family, the women I saw all had bright eyes.

She was a tall, slender, blond young woman with a pale, angular face, and a rather long nose. All this graceful length seemed to have been reprogrammed to make of her an automaton whose sole driving force was anxiety. It was the marionette Ophelia that we met, a marionette with jerky steps, hunched shoulders, coming and going like a butterfly blinded by its fall, her nerves that no longer responded, a heroine without a crown of flowers on her head pacing up and down the vast spaces of the hospital. Her innocent and frightened gaze brushed past, almost without seeing me, who knows. It accompanied my broken jaw in spite of itself.

The world of neurology is foggy for those who undergo its traumas, just as it is for surgeons and physical therapists. It was the world of the clear and frightened gaze of little Ophelia. The person on board it was navigating the river in which the body of the true Ophelia, that of fiction, that of *Hamlet,* floated. The person in Les Invalides was so wild in her distress that I imagined without difficulty the effort she was making to recover a minimum of confidence in herself and in anyone else. At night, she sometimes wandered through the corridors, with panic in her eyes. She had a little girl's voice, which slowly dwindled. In those great deserted corridors at that hour, when visitors got lost and when ghosts themselves would have had trouble finding their way, she returned to the dependent and terrified shadows of early childhood. One day, later on, I said to her: "You couldn't find your room. Do you remember?" She smiled. "A little. I was going into other people's rooms . . . Did I come into yours?" I: "No. But once I accompanied you back to yours." That was during the time when my room was protected by policemen day and night, and little Ophelia was always lost. The caregivers no longer knew what to do to take care of her.

Maybe she was—unconsciously, or out of awkwardness—partly the cause of the attack on her own life. But here there was no difference between the patients: lives were connected through ritual with uncertain perspectives and the exercises intended to help us escape them. We were like the man transformed into a beetle in *The Metamorphosis*; but unlike Kafka's character, our entourage did not reject us, did not crush us. It helped us climb the wall, to get ourselves back on our feet as much as possible by strengthening them, but did not, however, make us forget that we had all become replicas of poor Gregor Samsa.

Why had little Ophelia fallen? Why is there so much fear?

What is the life of nerves that we don't have? We don't know much about all that. We make do. And little Ophelia was gradually learning to speak in the peculiar tone that we almost all adopted: a modest, "objective," and precise tone. She was beginning to confront her problems by reading Maupassant's *Contes de la bécasse*, the shorter tales before the longer. Two years later, we had both left Les Invalides, but not the labyrinth. One day, she went to have lunch at the Musée d'Orsay with her speech therapist. Another time, she wrote to me: "In 2015, a deviation appeared. It involved Belukha Mountain. As time goes by, the Siberian cold is diminishing. The Russians are so fascinating. It's obviously vodka that makes them that way!" She reminded me that we'd entered the world where visions prolong sensations, and that her catastrophe had made her, in her way, a writer.

Along with reeducation, the slow and gradual ceremony of returns continued.

One day, with my brother and the policemen, I returned to the place where I'd been wounded. The investigations had long since ended. Before everything was cleaned up and these accursed premises were restored to someone, I don't know to whom, survivors were invited to come pick up anything they might have left there. I'd already come back a few weeks earlier to stand in front of the building, with Gabriela. I hadn't remained there any longer than I did in the street where *Libération* is located, on the day when I went to the theater. I'd started trembling. I'd returned to a space where time repeated itself, to the point of suffocation, in a gray sky and an odor of gunpowder. The shadow of the black of the killers' legs was everywhere. Gabriela took my arm. With the policemen trailing behind us, we hastened to get back to the boulevard and the other life.

So I was feverish when I returned there. I didn't know what I'd find. I knew that my winter cap and my pea coat ripped by the bullets and the scissors of the first aid team had ended up in the purgatory of the police evidence cabinet. My telephone and also my keys had to be somewhere under lock and key. But what I wanted to get back first was the book on jazz, *Blue Note*, which I'd been showing to Cabu just before the killers burst in.

There was a new security door, policemen, and a bailiff. The offices hadn't changed, they were in their stew of violence and absence, like a forgotten stage set, but in the middle of the room where the main massacre had taken place, one essential element was missing: the big conference table. Without it, the attack became almost incomprehensible. Most of the blood had been scrubbed away: cardboard had been laid on the floor where it couldn't be removed. The impacts of the bullets were still visible. As much for those who were there as for myself, I recounted again the scene on January 7, pointed out the location of the bodies, including mine, and the entrance of the two brothers. Once again, I saw Franck, Charb's bodyguard, drawing his gun before he was killed. But I didn't find the book on jazz.

One of my female colleagues told me that the cleaners had been forced to throw it away, along with everything else that was too stained. I left with a book by Wolinski, *Mes années 70 (My 1970s)*, which he hadn't had time to sign for me, and the *Dictionnaire du jazz (Dictionary of Jazz)* that on that day I'd put in the little Colombian cloth bag, along with *Blue Note*. It was not stained. Leafing through Wolinski's book in the car that was taking me back to Les Invalides, I was able to gauge by my laughter the audacity and imagination, everything that separated us from those free years. Two hours later, I received a call. The book on jazz had been found. "But it's spattered with blood," I was told, "you should know that. Do you really want it?" I wanted it.

I described this book in the chapter on the attack. It was a magnificent collection of photos in black and white taken during the 1950s and 1960s by Francis Wolff, one of the two founders of the famous New York label Blue Note. He and Alfred Lion were German Jews who'd gone into exile before the war. From Miles Davis to John Coltrane, from Eric Dolphy to Dexter Gordon, from Horace Silver to Thelonius Monk, most of the jazz greats of that time recorded on this label musical moments almost all of which are unforgettable. In the photos, all the musicians are handsome, all are absolutely classy and chic. Almost all of them are black. What do we see in Francis Wolff's images? A world in which great artists coming from an oppressed minority, working and living at night, often traversing tunnels of drugs and alcohol, created an aristocratic music. They are the sensible forms of distinction and dignity.

The next afternoon, *Charlie*'s courier parked in front of Les Invalides just as I was going to see Denise, my specialized physical therapist. He suggested leaving the big envelope at the nurses' station, but I couldn't wait. I took it and went directly to Denise's office. In the little waiting room, I opened the envelope, took out the book, and first, examined it. Its big, dark-colored hardback cover was stained, but one hardly noticed that. All one saw was the pianist Herbie Hancock, in 1963— the year of my birth. He's wearing glasses. He's looking to the right, slightly upward, elegant and haughty, his hands on the keyboard. He's probably looking at a soloist outside the picture. The bloodstains melted into the black of the photo. I opened the book to find the photo of Elvin Jones that I'd shown to Cabu. It was then that I sensed that the pages were stuck together. I examined their edge. It was covered with an enormous stain: blood—my blood, perhaps mixed with that of my neighbors—had stuck them together as it dried. One by one, I separated them as I waited for my session with the physical therapist, going back in time to the period when, at the age of sixteen, I bought, with my first savings, my first vinyl record of John Coltrane: *My Favorite Things*. Jazz had helped me live; the book helped me not to die. The two were now marked.

For the Ascension weekend, my brother and I had planned to join our parents in the Nivernais village of our childhood, the village where our maternal grandmother's house was located. It would be my first return to the countryside. Everything was arranged with Les Invalides and with the policemen who were supposed to accompany me, but a few days before we departed, there was a little surgical incident.

One afternoon, my parents and my aunt visited me at Les Invalides. It was a warm day. We were drinking fruit juice in the shade, in my room. Suddenly, while they were talking to me, a sprinkle of little stains fell on the upper part of my shirt, a white one I'd chosen for the occasion. I thought my lip had not held in the fruit juice, until I understood that it was blood. My parents and my aunt continued to talk. They hadn't noticed anything. I was silent. I watched the words falling from the mouths and the drops of blood from my face. I finally excused myself and went into the bathroom: in the mirror, I saw a hole on my right cheek, at the top of the largest cicatrix, which was poorly covered with a thin layer of skin that looked like the film used to wrap up leftovers: a fistula had just appeared. The next day, I was at La Salpêtrière, and Chloé, with the syringe in the form of a mosquito's proboscis, confirmed that the passage between the inside and the outside had opened up again. For her, it wasn't a big deal: the hole could be stopped with the help of a "directed cicatrization"; but the procedure required the presence of a nurse capable of changing, three times a day, a dressing based on seaweed, ergosteryl. The dressing had to be carefully slipped into the hole to diminish it little by little, without forming a small recess underneath the reconstituted skin. "Bah!" Chloé said to me. "Go to the countryside and find a nurse there! After all, it's not that hard!" During the Ascension weekend, it *was* difficult, but by chance our closest neighbor in the village happened to be a retired nurse. For four days, she came to cauterize the new hole after every meal, free of charge, and to caulk another gap by making the joint, as Ernest Renan would have said, with my memories of childhood and youth.

The policemen had moved into an inn a few kilometers away. They took advantage of the situation to run around the countryside and eat well. My brother's bitch, Usoa, a Tibetan spaniel, recognized me the way Odysseus's dog recognizes him when he returns. I walked along the Yonne and the Nivernais Canal. I looked at each of the walnut trees that led to the swimming hole. I looked at the green grass around the swimming hole, the deserted campground, and the great bend in the river where I liked to swim, because it resembled the Amazon and because it was so deep. I looked at the little island covered with nettles that was across from the swimming hole, from which I had, on countless occasions, imagined it was impossible to return. I paused under the linden tree in front of the city hall where my grandfather liked to sit. I went to look for eggs at the home of Ginette, the peasant woman who talked as loudly as the Harki at Les Invalides as I was walking away from her. I tested the aggressiveness of her geese. I met peasant neighbors I'd known for half a century, with whom I had played in the silos and in the fields and hardly ever saw anymore. I smelled the odor of manure carried into the street by the north wind. I entered the enchanted garden of the parents of Toinette, my childhood friend, who had gone into my room on January 9 and who wasn't there. I visited Colette, another old neighbor who never left home, and who offered me a beer. She no longer had any hair and she was already being eaten away by the cancer that would kill her. We looked at each other for a long time, with an amused caution. She thought I'd been well repaired. I went as far as the slopes of Mont Brevois, where I used to gather blackberries, and which marked the boundary with another world, that of the next village. I walked on the hilly road that went as far as the Armance, a small river near which, at the age of seven, I'd been slightly disfigured as I was carrying my bicycle over it. I ate my dietary supplements and made alimentary compliments to my mother for the mashed dishes she'd spent time preparing. I went to visit my grandparents' grave. I looked at the old lilacs in our courtyard, under which my grandmother sat in the summertime, and I sat in the same place. On the red floor tiles of my bedroom I set a right foot that was still sensitive. I slept in my bed and had bouts of insomnia.

Back at Les Invalides, the feeding tube was found to have torn an abdominal muscle at the precise moment when I was getting out of the policemen's car. The next day, I was taken away to La Salpêtrière. I felt free and uneasy. Now I could be nourished only through my mouth. In the evening, I wrote a rather emphatic column published in *Charlie* the next week. It summarized my brief stay in the village, in a world that was neither the past nor the present, nor time regained, nor interrupted time, but in this case, suspended time. I cite it only for the information it provides regarding my condition. I omit only a passage rather hostile toward a reactionary intellectual that I prefer to forget:

Not everyone has the good fortune to have a house in the country. My family's, in Nièvre, is a small village house. Its discreet charms, which are not those of the bourgeoisie, proceed from an old stairway in stone and its stained-glass window. It was to this house that my grandparents, poor, simple people who came from the peasant world, moved after retiring in the 1960s. What would they have thought of the contemporary multiplication of humorless cretins and obsessive people? What would they have said? I can't even imagine it. They had known other horrors, to begin with, for my grandfather, the First World War.

In their house, I spent many vacations and weekends, endured childhood illnesses and periods when I was a lonely adolescent, a married man, a divorced man, a reporter returning from distant lands, a reader, a writer. I walked, ran, pedaled, drove there on every road or path within a radius of twenty kilometers. My body was partly constructed and determined in and by this well-tempered space, the valley of the Yonne. It isn't Anjou or Du Bellay, but it could be.

So it was here, after more than four months in the hospital, that I made my first long stay outside—three days. My family was waiting for me here. Neighbors and childhood friends came to see me or invited me to their homes. None of them had seen me since January 7. Their attention was calm, delicate, elegant. They were all more than horrified, made mute by the attack. On the gate of a house where I went to play as a child, there was still a sign: "Je suis Charlie."

What I saw in my village, as in the hospital ward that had brought me back toward life, was simply women and men of good will. They knew and felt—at least so it seemed to me—that they did not want a society where the sleep of reason engenders monsters like those of January 7. Do they know what they want? Let us use, in the conditional, Rousseau's expression: they would like, no doubt, an efficacious, equitable, civilized social contract. But if there is a majority of people to sign it, there is no longer anyone in France to write and execute it.

I was trying to compose it as I walked along the canal when suddenly I had a realization of my condition as a ghost. We don't know how much the places where we grew up have shaped us until we return there as if we were dead. The body and the mind recognize the familiar space, but they have changed. Like the nerves around a graft, the landscape, the light, and the air try to make their way toward them, but do not succeed. Everything takes fright, is electrified. Sometimes it's overheating, sometimes insensitivity. Everything is where it's supposed to be, as always. But the familiar place, with its hundreds of microscopic histories, its kilometers roamed countless times, no longer recognizes you. You're entirely at home and you're a foreigner. And the memories that remain your own refer you, with their flow, to the uncertain future: I was somebody, will be another, and for the moment no longer exist.

Later, I had a dream that was the negative of this visit, of this column. There is a war against the Islamists, first in Algeria, then in my village. I belong to a group, it seems, that is fighting them. But they've moved into the village (lapsus: I first wrote "the visage") and are occupying a large building in which they have gathered hostages, whom I must reach, and who are supervised by auxiliaries (their own, forced). One of them, whom I know, whispers to me that I will be the only one saved, because a few years earlier I saved the life of one of their leaders. I enter the main hall where all the hostages are kneeling. I am put with them, and the Islamists begin killing them, one by one. When they come to me, the killer says: "Stand up! This time, you can leave. We're paying our debt to you. But there won't be a second time." I'm now in my room, the door to the outside is open and a couple of friends are sunning themselves as they talk about the Islamists. These friends are military men. They no longer have any illusions. I understand that the Islamists have won, that they'll come back, and that this time they won't spare me. The village of my childhood is no longer a place of relief. No place will allow me to escape what awaits me.

Summer had settled in. I returned several times to my apartment, always with my brother and the policemen, always for an hour or two. Quite quickly, I decided to *move without moving.* I didn't have the strength either to live again in the same place or to change places. Therefore I had to redo everything from floor to ceiling. The whole apartment would be bordered by large bookshelves of birch wood, made to order by Sophia's son, who was a magnificent woodworker. These shelves would allow me to arrange the books as I wished. They were the symbol of my reconstruction. They had to be beautiful; they were. The work was done during the last three months that I spent at Les Invalides.

The following months were marked by the beginning of my work with Denise, my maxillofacial physiotherapist. She was a solid, divorced woman, as severe toward herself as she was demanding of her patients. I've seen only a few people in whom duty and pleasure seemed so much to emerge at this point, like officers, from the same regiment. She had fought hard to be free, autonomous. She practiced ballroom dancing, hiking in the mountains, and amateur theater relentlessly. She dreamed of becoming an actress; but in her youth an actress at the Comédie-Française had told her that she didn't have an appropriate voice. Idle youth, enslaved to everything . . . and first of all to the pessimistic advice of others, as soon as it's a matter of discovering and developing by art what will take, for us, the place of personality.

The therapeutic relationship goes both ways: Denise's work and her nature were well-suited only for a certain type of patient, and I was clearly one of them. How should these patients be defined—without making me look like a hero of the organized grimace and everyday life? They were good pupils, hardened against pain. They reeducated themselves in the first row, far from the dunces and the radiators. They wanted beautiful cicatrices and good grades, they obeyed the orders given by Denise, whose generosity was in no way democratic. They were, or learned to be, tough, disciplined. They knew that they were not coming here to be flattered or pampered: Denise's good will was deep, but armored. They had to leave their laziness at the door, along with their bad moods and erect cockscombs. They divined in Denise's authoritarianism and good-humored orders an additional mark of her scruples and her commitment. Chloé had warned me: "She drives patients away, and she has a tendency to believe that she's the only one who knows how to treat them, but I've never met anyone who devotes so much time, attention, and energy to them." Faithful patients quickly saw that she got results: the mouth opened, the flaccid lip got muscular, the flap took on color, the cicatrices smoothed out, the jaws relaxed. Each session, no matter how hard it was, between massages and suction cups, was a dialogue and an exchange of confessions. It ended, after the list of exercises to do better, with this repeated injunction: "And especially, especially, indulge yourself!" Denise liked galettes, ginger, and good chocolate.

Second to Chloé and before my psychologist, she rapidly became one of my therapeutic superegos. There is a great satisfaction in observing certain women: they are courageous, without vanity, and they don't tell fibs. Denise reminded me of my third grandmother, who had an ironclad will, and came and went like an old rabbit until she was eighty-five years old, her black, mushroom-shaped hat on her head, without ever complaining. Her spinal column was decalcified, and doctors couldn't understand how she could walk. But as Denise said with a smile: "Surgeons think and say certain things. We're there to surprise them."

When I wasn't doing, or doing poorly, what she told me to do, I immediately had a sensation as unpleasant as when I handed in an article that I felt was not good. I divined errors, repetitions, and commonplaces that I was too lazy to identify. I sensed the ink stains remaining on the arm of the abettor that every writer is, but unlike Lady Macbeth, I wasn't trying to get rid of them even as they were disappearing. An occasional work was always the product of an accident of the mind (or of an attack on it). The unsuccessful text is a patient who hasn't been properly operated on or reeducated. Or who would be better off dead. A battle between indolence, a guilty conscience, and oblivion begins. Indolence and oblivion often enter into alliance: for the article, tomorrow is another day that doesn't exist. For patient, it was different: his time was simultaneously interminable and limited, tomorrow depended implacably on the effort made today. I watched Denise sticking her suction cups on my cicatrices and said to myself that one should probably write only when threatened by the worst.

In the 1980s, her passion for theater and elocution had led her to imagine, with a few other people, and at a time when surgeons were little concerned with the issue, exercises to reeducate the faces, jaws, or mouths of people who had suffered accidents, had cleft lips, cancer, burns, and deformities of all kinds. I was her first patient who had been wounded by gunfire. She'd been one of those discreet but severe heroines who made the lives of *gueules cassées* easier. At this time, she was rehearsing a play by Jean Anouilh, *Les Poissons rouges*. She also talked to me about her youth at high altitude, in Chamonix. Climbing had taught her about life: "You have to prepare your body, concentrate your mind, pay attention to the slightest details. Find the best route and, while following safety rules, find the holds that are best for you. Above all, never panic. And, although you have to trust the guide, you also have to learn not to depend on him." Reeducation under Denise's guidance was a race in the mountains, on a north face that offered glimpses of possible sunshine. Some of her patients called her the wicked fairy, as she recalled with pleasure. Some surgeons said she had a sadistic side. Some of her former colleagues refused to see her again: she had the defects of her virtues, and I took advantage of the latter without having to suffer from the former. She was going to work with me, in three hour-and-a-half sessions per week, for two and half years, until she retired. The last session took place outside the office she had just left, in a dance hall where she was a regular, on a wooden floor. At the end, we folded up the massage table, put away the suction-cup apparatus, and then she took off her smock and appeared in a pretty black dress with flounces, ready to dance. Her evening was about to begin. We stood in front of the big mirror and photographed ourselves for the first time, as one bows at the end of a show. I was her last patient.

It was on the way to her office, two hundred meters from Les Invalides, that I walked in the street alone for the first time. It was late May. The preceding day, around 9 P.M., an official at the protection service called to tell me that beginning at dawn, my room would no longer be constantly guarded: the decisions seemed to have been made as abruptly as at the hospital, and at first, I felt not only abandoned but frustrated. These dozens of policemen in uniform who had taken turns guarding me night and day behind the door of my room, who had accompanied me on each of my walks inside the hospital, had become part of my life. My shadows were taken away from me without delay and without precaution. They were taken away from me and I hadn't even had time to say goodbye and to thank them, one after another. I couldn't apply one of the rituals to which I was now viscerally attached.

I would no longer see the policeman with whom we had, one morning, watched François Hollande receive the president of Ukraine in the great courtyard to the sound of a fanfare suitable for a republican ceremonial, one of those fanfares rich in brasses that had so long poured a little heroism into the hearts of citizens, and that in this place, in this light, between these arcades, theatricalized the nostalgia for the republican dream. I would no longer see the Arab policeman, a veteran of Afghanistan who had been disgusted by the war and by

American modes of behavior. I would no longer hear him telling me, in a low voice, between the statues, how in a village he'd had to fire on a child who might have been carrying a bomb and how he'd had to bring back in an armored car his best friend, whose brains were leaking out. I would no longer see the policeman who was reading Stefan Zweig and who had come back to tell me that my old bicycle was still in front of *Charlie*. I would no longer see the little policewoman who was writing a lesbian novel, or the policeman I called the Smurf with glasses, because he was forever displaying his knowledge of any subject whatever, all night long, in front of his partner, nor the policeman who improved on Jack Palance, or the one who had hurried out of my room to stop a fight he saw beginning in the street, nor the tall, steely blonde with bright eyes who had accompanied me to my parents' home one Sunday afternoon. I would no longer see them, and I wouldn't even be able to say goodbye. Instead, I wrote them a collective letter. I arranged to have it delivered to them and learned that it had been read to them.

The next morning, when I went out for a walk, there was no one in front of my room. The hallway was empty. I put on my mask and the Italian straw hat that Sophia had given me, and for the first time I went alone through the gate leading to the Boulevard des Invalides. Passing in front of the sentry box, I looked at the gendarmes and wondered whether they were going to arrest me. I had the impression that I was one of those prisoners who, in films, slip through the checkpoint in disguise. I should have called the plainclothes policemen, who were still supposed to accompany me when I left the hospital's grounds, but I hadn't done so. I was at fault, I was alone, and I was free.

Once outside, I wondered where I should go. I had the sensation that if I went too far away, I'd get lost and never return. Before going to Denise's office, I decided to walk around the outside of Les Invalides, *like the people on the other side*, keeping the buildings in view, and I was able to see Monsieur Tarbes's silhouette walking on the inside, on the other side of the moat, in the company of the disciplined Monsieur Laredo. When I got to the esplanade, I saw, this time really, a friend's ex-wife going by. She was walking along smiling vacantly, her myopic eyes in the fog. She resembled a very slim gazelle with her long, pretty snout, and wore a lightweight brown dress. It was warm. She was walking fast, and I came within a few meters from her, scared to death that she would recognize me despite my mask and my hat. I turned my head and looked at the dome of the tomb in the distance. I didn't have the strength to talk to unexpected phantoms on the sidewalk, or to have them look at me like some kind of Colonel Chabert. She passed by without seeing me, happy behind her smile that carried her forward, and I simply felt the farewell to her perfume.

After having walked all the way around, I returned, by way of the Rodin museum, to the street where Denise's office was. I looked at people's faces, not to recognize them, but to determine if they were looking at me, observing me, if there was something in me that gave them pause, for example the mask on my face that was going to protect, for more than a year, my cicatrices from the sun. Neither policemen nor brother nor friends: there were no longer any intermediaries between others and me, between the walls of the city and me, between the sky above the walls and me, between the display windows and the cars and me. I found that passersby were walking fast, that they looked preoccupied. Except for the children, who are always curious and used to the parallel world, they weren't looking at anything. That surprised me: I was coming from a world, that of the hospital, where everything was composed of precise gestures and ways of seeing—as in an artist's studio. I made my way up the narrow sidewalk on the Rue de Bourgogne, looking at the shops, very slowly, searching for old steps. A Congolese jungle wouldn't have been more foreign than that bourgeois shopping street, where everyone seemed to have rendezvous, activities, worries. I went into a superette and bought a liquid yogurt, the first since the morning of January 7. I'd taken off my mask. I saw in the cashier's eyes that she had noticed my wound. She took my money without saying anything and, on the sidewalk, after taking out a tissue, I drank the yogurt and got it all over. Each of the drops that fell on the dirty asphalt, like Little Poucet's pebbles, was showing me the way home.

On the evening of July 13, in the deserted Les Invalides, I watched, with about thirty patients, the fireworks show. The weather was mild, with a slight breeze. The wheelchairs were there. They'd made their way over the gravel to position themselves close to Napoleon's tomb. From there, the rockets launched from the Champ de Mars seemed close enough to touch. At one point, I moved away and looked at these patients, my fellows, my brothers, knowing that someday or other, soon, we would be separated. Under the multicolored lights, no one was moving. They looked like figures in a painting by Watteau. Were we embarking for Cythera, or coming back from there? I was not given the answer.

When summer came, outings became more frequent. One evening, I went to my first high society party. It was a party given by a woman friend in publishing, on the roof of the Musée de la Marine. The roof seemed abandoned, with its different levels, cracked stones, and scaling walls. A few weeds had grown on it. Rather than attend a cocktail party as a survivor in his fifties, I'd have preferred to be seven years old and play Robinson Crusoe here. I looked into every corner, imagining a hiding place, a cabin. I came upon some writers whom I hadn't seen for a long time and to whom I didn't quite know what to say. I was forbidden to eat the petits fours, so I drank champagne. My policemen had positioned themselves in a corner with those of another protected person, Michel Houellebecq. He had crouched in a corner, in the company of a smiling woman, herself a writer, who is now dead. I had never met Michel Houellebecq, the man who had been our last subject of discussion on January 7. We shook hands. He seemed a wreck, hard and compassionate. His smile stopped just short of a grimace. He put down roots wherever he was, with his ageless, sexless head, his air of a scorched fetish. I thought that any man taking on himself the world's despair with so much efficacy had to go back in time and end up in a dinosaur's skin. That was the animal that I now had before my eyes, and while we were murmuring a few barely comprehensible words about the attack and the dead, he looked at me fixedly and recited this verse from Matthew: "Men of violence take it by force." I went home a few minutes later.

W hen summer came, the last police protection ended. I now came and went alone through the city, from one hospital to another. I sometimes happened to run into those who had guarded me, for example, in uniform in front of the headquarters of an almost defunct political party, or in plain clothes in a sidewalk café, a few meters from a government minister whom they were watching. What I had lived through was superimposed on what I was experiencing in a familiar space where I would soon have to come back to life, and which belonged to fiction.

At that time, I often had a hallucination during the night. I awoke and heard, in the room where I was sleeping, a hornet flying around. Sometimes it moved away from me, sometimes it approached me. I was afraid it would sting me on my jaw or throat. Each time, I turned on the lamp, got up, grabbed a newspaper, folded it up, and set about searching everywhere for the hornet to kill it. I wasn't sleepwalking, I was wide awake. I didn't find the hornet and fairly soon, its buzzing stopped. I got back in bed, turned off the lamp, the buzzing resumed, and the hunt was on again. It wasn't the awareness that I was experiencing a hallucination that finally put an end to this: I knew that what I was experiencing was probably a hallucination, but my doubt remained stronger. Nor was it getting used to the fear: I was just as scared, if not more, the third time around as I was the first. It was, simply, fatigue.

The surgeons at La Salpêtrière had gradually laid the

foundations for a dental prosthesis. The one who was in charge of this, Jean-Pierre, had been a mathematician in his youth, and also a Maoist. He knew some of the journalists who had trained me at *Libération*. He liked sailing and Italy. He was a pioneer and a jovial ace of implant surgery. His fingers were as thick as they were muscular, as muscular as they were virtuosic. Like Denise when she was massaging me, he closed his eyes as he tested the prosthesis by screwing in the implants. I opened my eyes and watched him: an artist, perhaps a musician. I'd seen pianists of this type. They played all Liszt's nuances with a woodcutter's hands. Jean-Pierre was immediately pleased with the development of my new jawbone. Everything was going well, everything was going badly. With Jean-Pierre, I moved, little by little, toward reconstruction. But the preceding stage was in no danger of being forgotten. Chloé reminded me of it one day, during a consultation, when I complained about my absence or excess of nerve sensitivity, depending on the place, around the lip and the chin: "That's normal, you're disabled!"

In the autumn, I went home. It was no longer entirely my home, nor was it entirely someone else's home. I felt as good there as possible, in an intimate and renewed universe, my ass between two stools and my consciousness I don't know where. I placed in the bathroom the ceramic I'd been making for months with my injured hand in the ergotherapy workshop: it represented a boat pursued by a shark in a tropical sea framed by two palm trees.

Gabriela came back for a few days to help me move in. The first evening, a radiator leaked. Panicked, I wanted to go back to sleep at Les Invalides. She took this so badly that I was more afraid of her anger than of staying in the apartment. She was so furious that I slept on the sleigh bed. The apartment had been completely redone, more quickly than my face. My new bookshelves gave a second life to the thousands of books that twenty years of shambles had devoured and whose existence I had often forgotten. They reappeared like old friends encountered on the street corner, without alarming me. They were silent, patient. What I had experienced could only nourish the lives they offered me.

My life was punctuated daily by appointments at Les Invalides, La Salpêtrière, and Denise's office. I went to all these appointments on foot. The bicycle parked in front of *Charlie* had finally disappeared and I'd given up the idea of getting another one. Walking for hours had become a way of living, of feeling and breathing.

There were still and constantly first times, for anything and everything. Some of them disturbed me a lot, others less. I hadn't stopped being a virgin, but you can get used to anything—or, to be more precise, you get used to not getting used to almost anything. One first time was repeated more often than others: the worrisome encounter with the young Arab in the metro. The policemen had advised me not to take the metro, but taxis were expensive, the radio programs their drivers listened to were generally stupid, and some wanted to know what had happened to me; and then I wanted to test myself, and as Chloé would have said, "return to normal." It wasn't normal, at least for me, to fear all Arabs less than thirty years old whom I might run into.

One day in September, I got on the line 13 metro at rush hour. I stuck my flap under the passengers' noses, and quickly learned to look away while they looked at me, to be present but absent. In one station, a young Arab got on. He looked threatening, his cap pulled down on his skull. He sat on a fold-up seat. There remained only one empty seat in the car, next to him, but no one took it, and neither did I. Nonetheless, I was tired. But something in me didn't want to put my flap, my fragility, my last nine months, next to him. He shot aggressive looks to the right and left, as if to see what effect he produced:

"I'm acting in such a way as to be exactly the person you think I am, and I'm worse yet, because that's what you want." His manner, my weakness, the passengers' feigned indifference—it all made me sad beyond what I could have imagined. He got off before I did.

A few days later, it was worse. Another young Arab, this time very handsome, slender, muscular, simultaneously supple and tense, placed himself next to me. We were standing in a full car. Like the earlier Arab, he was glancing to the right and left, no longer aggressively, but with an extraordinary intensity. He seemed to be searching for something. Maybe he was simply looking in a world where most of the people don't look. And suddenly, in the middle of this crowd and the heat, he took out his cap and put it on, with an extraordinary slowness, smoothing it over the tips of his ears as if he were preparing for a race in cold weather. Then I thought of the killers at *Charlie*, the madman in the Thalys train, and the Palestinians who kill Jews with pistols and knives, and despite myself, I moved a few meters away, thinking: "If he decides to kill, he'll have to begin with the people who are between the two of us." At the very moment that I was thinking that, I was horrified by my own thought and by the amalgamation it implied. Shame, as often happens, was the Siamese twin of fear: even if it was unpleasant, it wasn't bad to remember what I'd done and confront it. I didn't take another step to move away and, although other first times of the same kind have followed, I didn't move again and I didn't get off the car.

In November, I went to New York to visit Gabriela, who had finally gotten her divorce. It was my first trip abroad since the attack. Princeton had invited me to engage in a public dialogue with the Peruvian writer Mario Vargas Llosa. For thirty years, I'd been one of his critics, and I'd interviewed him, one day, in his Paris apartment. The attack made me, for the time of a lecture, one of his interlocutors. I had hardly any ideas or information about democracy and terrorism. I imagine that my flap spoke for me. I was happy, however, to talk with a novelist I admired, an architect of narrative, whose work had succeeded in recounting the nefarious lunacies of ideology.

On the afternoon of November 13, the weather was fine and I accompanied Gabriela to Wall Street. She had an appointment with her lawyer to resolve some financial issues. I stayed in the waiting room while he received her. I opened Edith Wharton's memoir, *A Backward Glance*, and read for the second time her portrait of Henry James. "It is particularly regrettable in the case of Henry James that no one among his intimates had a recording mind, or rather that those who had did not apply it to noting down his conversation, for I have never known a case in which an author's talk and his books so enlarged and supplemented each other." I'd read James's *The Ambassadors* in the summer of 2014, in New York and at Gabriela's apartment, and I wondered what could be more nuanced, more complex, more dense than this brilliant novel. I would have liked to know Henry James and live in the civilization that had allowed such a melancholy combined with such creative delicacy. His books were first-class burials.

The light was beginning to fail. I closed Edith Wharton's book and walked to the end of the long corridor in the lawyer's office. Through the bay window, I could see the sun bronzing southern Manhattan and the sea. Everything breathed power and peace. I didn't budge until Gabriela returned. The lawyer, a New York Jew, short, stocky, and facetious, could have emerged from a Woody Allen film. Gabriela seemed satisfied. I felt happy.

Since the twilight was splendid, we decided to walk toward Broadway. We were near Trinity Church when my cell phone rang. I answered and heard the voice of Fabrice, one of my former colleagues at *Libération* who was now living in New York and who had become, by crossing the Atlantic, my friend. He had a beautiful, deep voice, quite warm, a voice that I knew well. He told me that an attack had taken place, just then, at the Bataclan night club, that there were dead and wounded, and that hostages had been taken, how many was not yet known. Fabrice added that it was clearly a terrorist attack, probably Islamist, but that no one knew for sure. "I preferred to let you know," Fabrice added, "so that you didn't find out about it just any way, on a screen, in a café, or on the street." I was on the street, and I though there was no good way to find out about such a thing, that grisly hiccup in history and in my own life. The more he talked to me, the more information came in, rectifying and darkening what he had just said and was now correcting. I thanked Fabrice, hung up, took Gabriela's arm, and said: "Let's walk."

She looked at my face, hers frowned, and she asked me: "Qué pasa?" I took a few more steps before answering her, then I asked her to look at her phone to get the latest, precise news. She told me that this news could only cause me pain and it would be better to go on walking and wait until we were at home. But could I wait? At that moment, the dark gray air smelling of gunpowder descended from the pinnacles of the skyscrapers like a leaden cloud. It enveloped me, detached by the fear of everything that surrounded me and that was called life. It was once again, as when I awoke after the attack, a *detachment of consciousness*, and I felt that it was all starting over again, or more exactly, continuing, in me and around me, in parallel with everything that was happening before my eyes. In this cloud there were the cries in the entrance to *Charlie*, Franck's tardy intervention, the bodies of my dead friends, Bernard's brain, the eyes of Sigolène and Coco, and above all the breath and the presence of the killers with black legs that surged up as if through a crack in space-time.

In a letter, Henry James wrote that he regarded "the march of history very much as a man placed astride of a locomotive, without knowledge or help, would regard the progress of that vehicle." We were no longer very far from the place where, on September 11, 2001, the locomotive had raced on again. This race had begun much earlier, specialists debate the events and the dates, but here something began whose sequel, after the milepost of January 7 when we had ended up in the boiler, was repeated as it grew. New York, a place where I thought I was sheltered from the influence of evil, didn't protect me from anything. We went into the subway and returned to Gabriela's apartment as quickly as possible, and didn't come out of it again. That night, I looked at the lights of the city and did not sleep. Around 1 A.M., I received a text message from Chloé: "I'm glad to know that you're far away. Don't come back too soon."